Applied Thematic Analysis

"There are few qualitative texts that really present a step-by-step process of how to analyze qualitative data in a systematic and rigorous way. It is very well written, students will find this text helpful. The examples are great."

—Howard K. Butcher, *The University of Iowa*

"I like that it is practice focused. The real world examples are key and the real world problems make the text more useful. The exercises are nice to pick from for in-class activities or small projects."

—Natoshia M. Askelson, *The University of Iowa*

"The use of specific research projects is very helpful for deepening the discussion. This book does a wonderful job of explaining how important thematic analysis is for producing good research and it uses rich and detailed examples to do it."

—Matthew Hartley, *University of Pennsylvania*

"The strengths of this text are the step-by-step guidance on what has traditionally been a trial and error process. Typically students collect qualitative data and then struggle to make sense of it. This book gives them guidance, and gives instructors guidance in helping students learn how to deal with messy qualitative data analysis. This book presents what all of the books I've tried to use in the past have failed to present—how to analyze qualitative data"

—Catherine C. Schifter, *Temple University*

"Many researchers who are new to qualitative methods are often overwhelmed with figuring out which software package to us. The authors provide guidance and excellent questions to help researchers figure out their study needs and understand what to look for when comparing various software programs."

—Bernadette Sanchez, *DePaul University*

Applied Thematic Analysis

Greg Guest

FHI 360, Social Research Solutions

Kathleen M. MacQueen

FHI 360

Emily E. Namey

Duke University, Social Research Solutions

Los Angeles | London | New Delhi
Singapore | Washington DC

Los Angeles | London | New Delhi
Singapore | Washington DC

FOR INFORMATION

SAGE Publications, Inc.
2455 Teller Road
Thousand Oaks, California 91320
E-mail: order@sagepub.com

SAGE Publications Ltd.
1 Oliver's Yard
55 City Road
London, EC1Y 1SP
United Kingdom

SAGE Publications India Pvt. Ltd.
B 1/I 1 Mohan Cooperative Industrial Area
Mathura Road, New Delhi 110 044
India

SAGE Publications Asia-Pacific Pte. Ltd.
33 Pekin Street #02-01
Far East Square
Singapore 048763

Acquisitions Editor: Vicki Knight
Associate Editor: Lauren Habib
Editorial Assistant: Kalie Koscielak
Production Editor: Astrid Virding
Copy Editor: Amy Rosenstein
Typesetter: Hurix Systems Pvt. Ltd.
Proofreader: Dennis W. Webb
Indexer: Will Ragsdale
Cover Designer: Gail Buschman
Marketing Manager: Helen Salmon
Permissions Editor: Adele Hutchinson

Copyright © 2012 by SAGE Publications, Inc.

Printed in the United States of America

Library of Congress Cataloging-in-Publication Data

Guest, Greg, 1963-

Applied thematic analysis / Greg Guest, Kathleen MacQueen, Emily E. Namey.
p. cm.

Includes bibliographical references and index.

ISBN 978-1-4129-7167-6 (hardback)

1. Social sciences—Research—Methodology. 2. Qualitative reasoning. I. MacQueen, Kathleen M. II. Namey, Emily E. III. Title.

H62.G828 2012

001.4'2—dc23   2011031161

This book is printed on acid-free paper.

11 12 13 14 15   10 9 8 7 6 5 4 3 2 1

BRIEF CONTENTS

DETAILED CONTENTS

PREFACE

We have been designing, doing, and managing thematic analysis for many years. The three of us have worked, at one time or another, in each of the four basic research sectors—academic, corporate, government, and nonprofit. The one consistent thread that has cut across our work in all of these research contexts is the need to teach colleagues and field teams how to analyze data generated from qualitative (and mixed methods) research projects. At first, the training we provided took the form of informal mentoring. As time passed, however, the need to formalize the knowledge and procedures we had accumulated became apparent, so we created standard operating procedures and written guidelines to enhance and maintain rigor throughout our analyses, especially in the context of team-based research. Some of this information eventually made its way into our first book, *Handbook for Team-Based Qualitative Research*. A lot of the information, though, did not find its way into publication.

As we found ourselves teaching qualitative data analysis more often and in more diverse contexts, we (and more importantly our students!) began to recognize the need to put onto paper what we knew in practice. We could not find a monograph to use as a foundational text for our courses, something that covered a good portion of the necessary material and could serve as a primary reference. Instead, for each training we compiled a binder of readings composed of two dozen or so articles and chapters from as many sources. This task got old rather quickly, so we decided to bring together what we knew about qualitative data analysis, distill the more practical elements from this corpus of knowledge, and aggregate the information in one place. The book you are holding in your hands (or viewing on your e-reader) is the end product of these efforts. It is an instruction manual of sorts that synthesizes, and expands upon, the contents of our data analysis trainings. It describes how to conduct a rigorous, inductive thematic analysis in a pragmatic and straightforward way.

HOW THIS BOOK IS ORGANIZED

Each chapter in this volume begins with one or more "learning objectives." We have found through years of teaching that introductory provision of learning objectives is beneficial for several reasons. First, they provide an audience a context within which they can place the ideas presented, thereby making the content easier to digest and process. They also provide a yardstick against which the reader can gauge mastery of the material. Finally, they keep the instructors honest by making sure they accomplish what they set out to accomplish.

Each chapter in this book is also fitted with two supplemental sections. The first is a list of additional readings. To keep the book's content as concise as possible, we cannot cover in-depth some of the theory behind the topics and issues discussed. At the same time, we feel obligated to provide readers with as much information related to qualitative data analysis as they are interested in absorbing. The additional reading sections satisfy these conflicting criteria of concision and coverage.

Each chapter, except for the introduction, is also appended with an exercises section to give readers hands-on practice working with the techniques presented, provide experiential instruction in the mechanics involved in the techniques described and further enrich understanding of the concepts discussed. Chapters also include, where appropriate, real-world examples to reinforce the ideas and procedures described.

The book is organized chronologically, generally following the same sequence of activities that a researcher might follow as he or she conducts an analysis. We make every attempt in each chapter to logically connect the concepts presented to other relevant parts of the book. To a large degree, however, each chapter in this book is intended to be able to stand on its own.

As much as possible, the chapters are written in the same sequence as the activities involved in the actual analysis process. We start, in Chapter 1, by defining terms and framing our approach to qualitative data analysis relative to other common approaches. Chapter 2 addresses one of the most important, yet overlooked (and underpublished), aspects of qualitative research—planning and preparation. This chapter gives guidelines for establishing analytic objectives, bounding the analysis, and other considerations that require attention in the early stages of the research process. The chapter culminates with specific suggestions and tools for writing up an analysis plan for qualitative data.

In Chapter 3, we cover the details of finding themes and developing codes. Topics specifically addressed are segmenting text, distinguishing types of codes, discovering and winnowing themes, developing codebooks, and linking themes to both theoretical models and real-world problems. This chapter is really the core of the book and is, by necessity, longer than other chapters. In addition to describing various procedures, we provide templates for some of the activities explained. Our hope is that the templates will enhance readers' understanding of the processes described as well as give them a starting point for their own analyses.

Although we are determined to keep discussion of theory in this book to a minimum, the concepts of validity and reliability are too important to omit in a book devoted to data analysis. Chapter 4 is dedicated to these two topics. Part of the chapter is unavoidably theoretical in nature, defining the terms and their relevance to qualitative inquiry. We have tempered this theoretical necessity with a discussion of the procedural and practical implications related to each concept and, as with other chapters, have offered examples from real research studies. Included in this discussion are suggestions for enhancing both validity and reliability during the analysis (and data collection) process. Chapter 4 also specifically addresses intercoder reliability and includes a hands-on exercise to illustrate how to measure intercoder agreement and instill a more intuitive understanding of the concept.

Although the bulk of most thematic analysis is devoted to identifying themes and developing codes, other analytic techniques can be equally important in piecing together the story the data have to tell. Chapter 5 covers some of these techniques, with corresponding illustrative examples. One of the more common of these techniques is the simple, yet highly effective, word search and associated key-word-in-context search. The chapter also discusses how to deal with unique cases or outliers (for lack of a better term) and gives the reader practical suggestions for making the most of these during the analysis. The other section in this chapter addresses special issues associated with analyzing focus group data.

Once themes have been discovered, a good codebook developed, and codes reliably applied, what happens next? How does one make sense of the data, particularly larger data sets, with hundreds or even thousands of pages of text? These questions are answered in Chapter 6. The chapter begins with a discussion of when and why quantification of qualitative data is appropriate. This is followed by a description of how to use simple frequencies to summarize data, including how to choose units and items of analysis and how to interpret frequencies in qualitative analysis. Following this, we describe how to examine co-occurrence of themes and use similarity matrices to help interpret data sets. An example of a more complex data reduction technique is provided, using a graph-theoretic approach (cluster analysis). The chapter ends with a return to the question of when quantification is appropriate, including the purpose to be served, the structure of the data collection process, and the reduction of ambiguity in the reporting of findings. As with other chapters, real-world examples and practical exercises are included.

A common goal in scientific inquiry is to compare two or more things and see how they are similar and how they differ. Qualitative inquiry is no different. It is often the case that we need to know, for example, how the experiences or perceptions of group X differ from group Y. The challenge in comparing qualitative data, however, is that they are not well suited to standard statistical comparative measures, such as ANOVA. Instead, innovative procedures and the unique qualities of qualitative data should be considered when comparing qualitative data sets. Chapter 7 provides some methods for comparative analysis and discusses some of the unique aspects of qualitative data in this regard.

Mixed methods research, that is, research that integrates qualitative and quantitative data, is increasingly common. It is important for researchers, therefore, to know how to plan for and execute data integration, the topic addressed in Chapter 8. Building on conceptual frameworks delineated in the burgeoning mixed methods literature, we describe some of the basic ways in which data can be integrated throughout a research study. The chapter covers timing and sequencing of data integration. Also discussed is the important issue of how to reconcile conflicting data, a not uncommon occurrence in mixed methods analysis (or any data analysis, for that matter).

Data analysis software is an important component of most qualitative research studies, especially those that are larger and more complex in nature. In Chapter 9 we review some of the important factors, such as study size and complexity, to consider when choosing analysis software for a given research study. We also present readers with a description of possible features and functions they might think about before selecting one or more software packages. The latter part of this chapter lays out a template for mapping analytic problems and logistical parameters against software functionality to equip researchers with a practical tool for assisting in software selection.

The final chapter brings the researcher to the endpoint of the analysis process—write-up and dissemination. The chapter begins with general guidance for writing to suit one's audience. The second part of the chapter focuses more specifically on writing up qualitative analyses and offers suggestions to help improve the quality of reporting to increase the chances of publishing your findings.

This book is the culmination of years of experience conducting and managing large, multisite qualitative and mixed methods research projects. In the chapters that follow, we do our best to impart the lessons we have learned along the way to you, the reader. No experience or knowledge, however, is exhaustive. As applied researchers ourselves, we continue to learn and evolve. In this spirit, we ask that you note how any of the procedures we outline can be improved as you read through and use this book. If you develop procedures that work better, or come across problems or issues that we do not cover in this book, note those as well. We encourage you to write about and publish what you have learned, or, at the very least, let us know directly how we can collectively improve our methods.

Greg, Kate, and Emily

Durham, North Carolina

ACKNOWLEDGMENTS

This book is a product of the many qualitative data analysis trainings the three of us have given over the years; the familiar adage that you learn by teaching is certainly true in our case. We have learned and continue to learn something from each training or workshop we conduct thanks to the thoughtful and inquisitive students we have had the pleasure of instructing. Their questions and insights have been indispensable to this book, and will, without a doubt, continue to help us evolve as qualitative researchers and instructors.

On a more personal note, Greg wishes to thank his wife, Gretel, for her unwavering support and patience during this project. She is truly his better half. Greg also thanks those colleagues who were instrumental in developing his interest in research methods many years ago and who continue to provide inspiration, particularly Jeff Johnson, Russ Bernard, and Gery Ryan.

Kate is indebted to her mentor and long-time friend, Paul Leslie, who taught her that the really interesting data are in the variance and not the mean. She has learned much of what she knows through collaborations with Greg and Emily as well as with Cynthia Woodsong. She also thanks Bobby Milstein and Eleanor McLellan-Lemal for further provocations and insights regarding large qualitative research endeavors.

Emily is extremely grateful to her husband, Jason, for making her contributions to this project possible by holding down the fort on several long afternoons and late nights. She would also like to thank Kate and Greg, Bob Trotter, Annie Lyerly, and Laura Beskow for their ongoing mentorship, collaboration, and enthusiasm for qualitative research.

Finally, we'd like to thank the wonderful folks at SAGE, particularly Vicki Knight, for their assistance and support throughout the writing and production process. SAGE is truly a first-class publisher.

SAGE Publications and the authors would also like to express their gratitude to the following reviewers for their thoughtful and constructive comments:

Natoshia Askelson, *University of Iowa*

Susan J. Bracken, *North Carolina State University*

Scott Browning, *Chestnut Hill College*

Howard K. Butcher, *University of Iowa*

Jeannine Coreil, *University of South Florida*

Karen A. Curtis, *University of Delaware*

William "Ted" Donlan, *Portland State University*

Pamela I. Erickson, *University of Connecticut*

Matthew Hartley, *University of Pennsylvania*

Greg Leichty, *University of Louisville*

Terrence E. Maltbia, *Columbia University*

Susan Prion, *University of San Francisco*

Lee Rudolph, *Clark University*

Bernadette Sanchez, *DePaul University*

Catherine C. Schifter, *Temple University*

Christina Zampitella, *California School of Professional Psychology, Alliant International University*

ABOUT THE AUTHORS

Greg Guest received an MA in anthropology from the University of Calgary and a PhD in anthropology from the University of Georgia. Over the past 15 years, he has carried out research in academia (University of Georgia, Duke University, East Carolina University), the private sector (Sapient Corporation), government (Centers for Disease Control and Prevention), and in the nonprofit sector (FHI 360). Guest has implemented and managed multidisciplinary projects in various fields of applied research, including human ecology, agricultural development, human–computer interaction, consumer experience, and international health. Greg is currently a social/behavioral scientist at FHI 360, where he manages multisite, qualitative, and mixed methods research projects related to reproductive health, HIV prevention, and other infectious diseases.

Guest's other books include two edited volumes—*Globalization, Health and the Environment: An Integrated Perspective* (AltaMira Press, 2005) and *Handbook for Team-Based Qualitative Research* (AltaMira Press, 2008)—as well as the forthcoming monograph *Collecting Qualitative Data: A Field Manual* (Sage). He has published articles in journals such as *Field Methods, American Journal of Public Health, JAIDS, AIDS Care, AIDS Education and Prevention, African Journal of AIDS Research, AIDS and Behavior, Journal of Family Planning and Reproductive Health Care, Human Ecology,* and *Culture and Agriculture.* Guest is also owner of the research consulting firm Social Research Solutions (www. socialresearchsolutions.com).

Kathleen M. MacQueen is a Senior Social Scientist and Coordinator of Interdisciplinary Research Ethics at FHI 360 in Durham, North Carolina. She is also adjunct faculty with the University of North Carolina at Chapel Hill in the Department of Social Medicine, School of Medicine and in the Health Behavior and Health Education Program, School of Public Health. She has a PhD in anthropology from Binghamton University and an MPH in health behavior from the Rollins School of Public Health at Emory University. Dr. MacQueen has been working in the area of applied research ethics and HIV prevention for 20 years, with a strong emphasis on qualitative research methods, participatory research, and mixed methods projects. Both domestically and internationally she has provided leadership on the social, behavioral, and ethical dimensions of trials of HIV vaccines, microbicides, and the prophylactic use of antiretrovirals to prevent acquisition of HIV (commonly referred to as pre-exposure prophylaxis, or PrEP). Before coming to FHI 360 in 2001, MacQueen worked 10 years at the Centers for Disease Control and Prevention as a research anthropologist and science director in the National Center for HIV, STD, and TB Prevention. She was visiting faculty in the anthropology department at the University of Georgia for 2 years, with primary responsibility for graduate seminars in research design and methods. Her scientific publications have appeared in journals as diverse as *Medical Anthropology Quarterly, Annual Review of Anthropology, American Journal of Public Health, American Journal of Preventive Medicine,* and *AIDS Care Journal.* She is currently on the editorial boards for the *Journal of Empirical Research in Human Research Ethics* and the *Journal of the International AIDS Society.*

Emily E. Namey oversees qualitative research projects at Duke University in the Institute for Genome Sciences and Policy, the Department of Obstetrics and Gynecology, and the Trent Center for Bioethics. Over the past 5 years, she has implemented qualitative research on subjects ranging from improving maternity care to vaccine trial participation during pregnancy to ethical approaches to genotype-driven research recruitment. Prior to her work at Duke, Namey spent several years coordinating international, multisite sociobehavioral studies of HIV prevention at FHI 360. She has experience in the private sector, having completed projects at Intel Corporation and Nike, Inc. She also currently serves as a qualitative research consultant for Social Research Solutions, conducting trainings on qualitative research methods, analysis, and software. Her publications include contributions to the *Handbook for Team-Based Qualitative Research* (AltaMira Press, 2008) and the forthcoming monograph *Collecting Qualitative Data: A Field Manual* (Sage) as well as articles in *Social Science & Medicine, Fertility and Sterility, AIDS Care Journal,* and the *Journal of Empirical Research on Human Research Ethics.* Namey received her MA in applied anthropology from Northern Arizona University.

If you want to understand what a science is, you should look in the first instance not at its theories or its findings, and certainly not at what its apologists say about it; you should look at what the practitioners of it do.

—Clifford Geertz (1973, p. 5)

1

INTRODUCTION TO APPLIED THEMATIC ANALYSIS

Unsatisfied with the limitations imposed by any one particular martial art, Bruce Lee developed his own composite fighting style, which he called "Jeet Kune Do" (*the way of the intercepting fist*). Jeet Kune Do is not a novel set of fighting techniques, but rather a more focused style of combat that synthesizes the most useful techniques from numerous fighting arts. For Lee, this was an emancipatory endeavor that allowed practitioners of Jeet Kune Do to choose from a wide range of techniques and employ the most appropriate ones for a given objective. In Lee's words:

> I have not invented a "new style," composite, modified or otherwise that is set within distinct form as apart from "this" method or "that" method. On the contrary, I hope to free my followers from clinging to styles, patterns, or molds. . . [A] Jeet Kune Do man who says Jeet Kune Do is exclusively Jeet Kune Do is…still hung up on his self-closing resistance, in this case anchored down to reactionary pattern, and naturally is still bound by another modified pattern and can move within its limits. He has not digested the simple fact that truth exists outside all molds; pattern and awareness [are] never exclusive. (Lee, 1971, p. 24)

Qualitative research is analogous in many ways to martial arts. Approaches to qualitative data collection and analysis are numerous, representing a diverse range of epistemological, theoretical, and disciplinary perspectives. Yet most researchers, throughout their career, cling to one style with which they are familiar and comfortable, to the exclusion (and often disparagement) of all others. In the spirit of Jeet Kune Do, we feel that good data analysis (and research design, for that matter) combines appropriate elements and techniques from across traditions and epistemological perspectives. In our view, the theoretical or philosophical foundation provides a framework for inquiry, but it is the data collection and analysis processes and the outcome of those processes that are paramount. In other words, "We need a way to argue what we know based on the process by which we came to know it" (Agar, 1996, p. 13). From such a perspective, it does not make sense to exclude a particular technique because of personal discomfort with it, or misconceptions about or prejudices regarding how and why it might be used. We are reminded here of Russ Bernard's (2005) adage that "methods belong to all of us" (p. 2). Eschewing a compartmentalized view of qualitative research and data analysis is the underlying theme of this book and the analytic process we describe. We call this process Applied Thematic Analysis (ATA). Briefly put, ATA is a type of inductive analysis of qualitative data that can involve multiple analytic techniques. Below, we situate ATA within the qualitative data analysis literature to help both frame the process and provide a rationale for the name we have given it.

Before defining our process, we first lay out the overall rationale for the book as well as provide the reader with a sense of what this book does, and does not, cover. As noted in the preface, we have written this book in response to a perceived need for a published volume that gives researchers a practical framework for carrying out an inductive thematic analysis on the most common forms of qualitative data. Although we cover some of the theoretical underpinnings of qualitative research, this book is primarily about process and providing researchers usable tools to carry out rigorous qualitative data analysis in commonly encountered research contexts. To this end, we wanted to keep the content as focused as possible and present readers with what we believe to be the most efficient, yet rigorous, analytic techniques. We begin from the point of having qualitative data in hand, and therefore do not address research design or data collection strategies.

We refer above to the "most common forms" of qualitative data. By this, we mean data generated through in-depth interviews, focus groups, or field observations (i.e., textual field notes). We recognize that qualitative data can be generated through other activities such as open-ended questions on a survey, free-listing and other semistructured elicitation tasks, or visual data collection techniques. These methods are all useful and appropriate for certain types of research objectives; however, they are not commonly used methods in the broadly defined world of qualitative research.

This book, then, is intended for the researcher, student, or other interested party who has been tasked with analyzing, and making sense of, a set of field notes or transcripts from focus groups or in-depth interviews. How does one go about thematically analyzing these types of data in a systematic way that results in credible answers to the research questions and objectives embedded within a study? Helping readers meet this challenge is the fundamental purpose of this book. Note that the process we delineate can also be used to analyze free-flowing text from secondary data sources, such as in document analysis. But to keep this book simultaneously concise and broadly appealing, the examples and exercises provided are from studies employing the more traditional qualitative data collection techniques.

DEFINING QUALITATIVE RESEARCH

Before talking about process, we should first define what we mean by *"qualitative research,"* since the definition influences how we characterize qualitative data analysis, the data items to be used in our analysis, and the types of analyses we perform on our data. Many existing definitions are constrained by a dichotomous typology that contrasts qualitative and quantitative research or assumes a particular epistemological foundation. Another common descriptive practice is to list attributes as if they are exclusive or necessary features of qualitative research. These types of characterizations exist despite the fact that the attributes listed are: (a) not always present in qualitative inquiry and (b) can also be true of quantitative research (Guest & MacQueen, 2008). A simple Google search of "qualitative research" and "definition" will bring up a host of examples, from websites and research methods course syllabi. For example, the Online Dictionary of the Social Sciences (n.d.) defines qualitative research as follows:

> Research using methods such as participant observation or case studies which result in a narrative, descriptive account of a setting or practice. Sociologists using these methods typically reject positivism and adopt a form of interpretive sociology.

Compare that to Denzin and Lincoln's definition:

> Qualitative research is a situated activity that locates the observer in the world. It consists of a set of interpretive, material practices that makes the world visible. These practices transform the world. They turn the world into a series of representations, including field notes, interviews, conversations, photographs, recordings, and memos to the self. At this level, qualitative research involves an interpretive, naturalistic approach to the world. This means that qualitative researchers study things in their natural settings, attempting to make sense of, or to interpret, phenomena in terms of the meanings people bring to them. (2005, p. 3)

Of particular note in these definitions is the joint emphasis on a philosophical stance and a particular structuring of the analytic results as interpretive. The interpretive approach is generally set in contrast to a positivist approach, and indeed, for many the two are incompatible. Quantitative research methods are generally difficult to reconcile with an interpretive approach, while qualitative methods provide considerable room for an interpretive inquiry. From this, many then conclude that qualitative research methods are difficult to reconcile with a positivist approach. This is not true. It is what you do with qualitative data, and not the methods themselves, that define whether you are engaged in a research endeavor that is interpretive, positivist, or hybrid of the two.

We prefer the simpler and more functional definition of qualitative research as offered by Nkwi, Nyamongo, and Ryan (2001): "Qualitative research involves any research that uses data that do not indicate ordinal values" (p. 1). The focus in this latter definition is on the data generated and/or used in qualitative inquiry—that is, text, images, and sounds. Essentially, the data in qualitative research are non-numeric and less structured data than those generated through quantitatively oriented inquiry, because the data collection process itself is less structured, more flexible, and inductive. An outcome-oriented definition such as that proposed by Nkwi and colleagues avoids unnecessary and inaccurate generalizations and dichotomous positioning of qualitative research with respect to its quantitative counterpart. It allows for the inclusion of many different kinds of data collection strategies and analysis techniques (which we describe later) as well as the plethora of theoretical frameworks associated with qualitative research.

Exclusion of specific data collection or analysis methods from the definition also paves the way for a more refined view of qualitative data analysis, one that distinguishes between the data themselves and the analyses performed on data. As Bernard (1996) notes, many researchers fail to make this distinction, made graphically apparent in Figure 1.1.

Figure 1.1   Qualitative and Quantitative Data Analyses (adapted from Bernard, 1996)

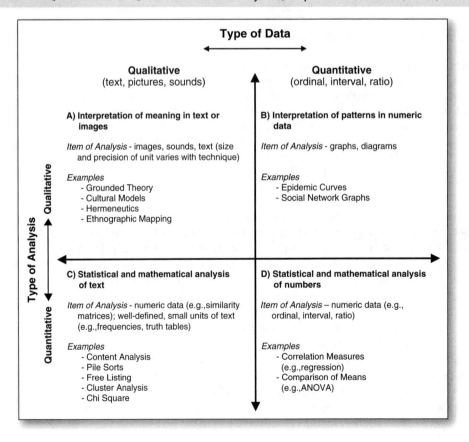

Making the simple distinction between data type and the type of procedure used to analyze data broadens the range of "qualitative research" and opens up an additional category of analytical procedures that other conceptual frameworks exclude (Guest, 2005). Most definitions of qualitative research include only the top left quadrant of the figure and miss an entire group of analytic strategies available to them—that is, those that utilize quantitative analytic procedures on qualitative data (lower left quadrant). Throughout this book, we try to emphasize the complementarity of both types of analytic procedures on the left side of Figure 1.1 and downplay any antithesis between the two.

ANALYTIC PURPOSE

The design and plan for a particular analysis depends a lot on the general approach taken and the type of outcome expected—the analytic purpose. In this book, we focus on inductive analyses, which primarily have a descriptive and exploratory orientation. Although confirmatory approaches to qualitative data analysis certainly exist, they are employed less often in social/behavioral research than inductive, exploratory analyses. We provide a summary of the differences between the two approaches in Table 1.1. Further reading on how to do confirmatory qualitative research using a thematic approach, also known as *classic content analysis*, can be found in several comprehensive works, including Krippendorf (2004), Weber (1990), and Neuendorf (2001).

Table 1.1 Summary of Differences Between Exploratory and Confirmatory Approaches to Qualitative Data Analysis

Exploratory ("content-driven")	Confirmatory ("hypothesis-driven")
• For example, asks: "What do x people think about y?"	• For example, hypothesizes: "x people think z about y"
• Specific codes/analytic categories NOT predetermined	• Specific codes/analytic categories predetermined
• Codes derived from the data	• Codes generated from hypotheses
• Data usually generated	• Typically uses existing data
• Most often uses purposive sampling	• Generally employs random sampling
• More common approach	• Less common approach

The main difference between the two approaches is that for an exploratory study, the researcher carefully reads and rereads the data, looking for key words, trends, themes, or ideas in the data that will help outline the analysis, *before* any analysis takes place. By contrast, a confirmatory, hypothesis-driven study is guided by specific ideas or hypotheses the researcher wants to assess. The researcher may still closely read the data prior to analysis, but his analysis categories have been determined, a priori, without consideration of the data. Objectives are also formulated differently: Research questions are better suited to exploratory research while hypotheses better capture objectives of a confirmatory nature. Other differences between the two approaches relate to sampling and data sources. Exploratory studies generally are based on nonprobabilistic samples of research participants and generate primary data. Conversely, confirmatory studies typically employ probabilistic sampling strategies to select text from existing sources.

The distinction between inductively exploring data versus assessing hypotheses with data are made clear above. But here we wish to emphasize that while exploratory approaches to qualitative analysis are not specifically designed to *confirm* hypotheses, this does not mean that they are atheoretical. Exploratory analyses are commonly used to *generate* hypotheses for further study. And some exploratory approaches, such as grounded theory, are used to *build* theoretical models derived from the data. Likewise, applied research initiatives, although intended to address a practical problem in the world, are based on theory. Theory, however implicit, gives direction to what we examine and how we examine it. If we had no idea at all about what the key issues for a participant might be, it would be difficult to find a starting point for questioning. We get guidance as to what's important to study from existing literature, our own knowledge about a topic, or from someone else (funder, boss, client, professor, etc.). Whatever the source, there is some reason to believe (small "t" theory, if you will) that what and who you are going to study is important.

QUALITATIVE DATA TYPES

Bernard and Ryan (1998) provide a useful typology for understanding the range of qualitative data (Figure 1.2). At the first branch of the tree, data are divided into three basic types — text, images, and sound. This book focuses exclusively on text, which is by far the most common form of qualitative data analyzed in the social and health sciences. Although many of the techniques and procedures we present can be applied to images as well, we suggest that readers seriously interested in analyzing visual data refer to other sources that deal explicitly with these topics, to ensure a more nuanced and sophisticated analysis. For analyzing video, we recommend starting with the comprehensive volume edited by Knoblauch and Schnettler (2006). For more general usage of visual data collection methods, the reader might also wish to look at Banks (2008) or Prosser (1998).

Another distinction to be made in the Bernard and Ryan typology pertains to how text is viewed vis-à-vis the object of analysis—the second level of division in the tree. We can, for example, analyze text as an object in and of itself, as shown

Figure 1.2 The Range of Qualitative Research (from Bernard & Ryan, 1998)

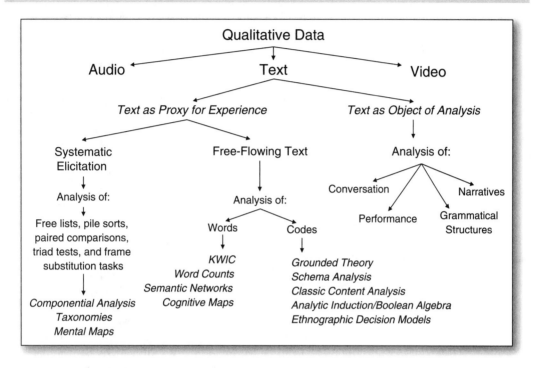

in the right branch of Figure 1.2. This strategy is most common in linguistic analyses and concerns itself with the structure and meaning within the text and words themselves. On the other side, text can be analyzed as a proxy for experience in which we are interested in individuals' perceptions, feelings, knowledge, and behavior as represented in the text, which is often generated by our interaction with research participants. This latter type of text analysis, known as the *sociological tradition* (Tesch, 1990), is the method most often employed in the social and health sciences and is the branch of qualitative analysis upon which this book focuses.

Even when utilizing text as a proxy for experience, there is substantial breadth in the ways data can be collected and analyzed. Elicitation techniques that generate data can be relatively systematic and structured, as in free listing or pile sorting, depicted in the far left of the diagram (for more details, see Weller & Romney, 1988). Data elicited with these types of techniques require a different type of analysis than does free-flowing text typically elicited in less structured data collection events such as unstructured or semistructured interviewing or document analysis. Because most qualitative data collected or available are in the form of free-flowing text (i.e., focus groups and in-depth interviews), we narrow in on this dimension and follow this branch of the tree, where we see the divide between analysis of words and analysis using themes and codes.

In quantitatively oriented word-based analyses, such as word counts or semantic network analysis, the researcher evaluates the frequency and co-occurrence of particular words or phrases in a body of textual data in order to identify key words, repeated ideas, or configuration of words with respect to other words in the text. Comparisons can then be made with respect to these metrics between groups of interest. Word-based analyses also can include associated attributes of key words and other semantic elements, such as synonyms, location in the text, and surrounding words or phrases (Dey, 1993, p. 59). The key-word-in-context (KWIC) method, for example, entails locating all occurrences of particular words or phrases in the text and identifying the context in which the word appears. Typically, one can do this by predetermining how many words (e.g., 30) before and after the key word to include in the analysis. A less formal variation of the technique simply locates the key word and includes in the analysis as many of the surrounding context words as are needed to achieve the given analytic aims (Guest et al., 2007). All of the above word-based analyses can help researchers discover themes in text (Bernard & Ryan, 1998) or to complement other analyses (see e.g., Guest et al., 2007), in addition to being analytic strategies in and of themselves.

Word-based techniques are valued for their efficiency and reliability. Specialized software can quickly scan large numbers of text files and tally key words. (IN-SPIRE software [Pacific Northwest National Laboratory, 2008], e.g., can process up to 100,000 one-page documents in under 30 minutes and produce very interesting data reduction displays). And since the original, "raw" data are used, there is minimal interpretation involved in the word counts, generally resulting in greater reliability. The main drawback to this type of analysis is that context is usually not considered or is highly constrained, limiting the richness of the summary data produced. Also, key concepts can be completely glossed over in a word-based analysis. If, for example, one was interested in seeing if in-depth interview participants talked about stigma when asked about HIV/AIDS, it is unlikely the actual word "stigma" would be used. People might talk about being shunned by their family or losing their job due to their HIV status while never using the actual term *stigma*. Word-based analyses also run into difficulties when it comes to translated text, when translator/translation variability can create problems for analytic reliability. We discuss word searches in more detail in Chapter 5.

Thematic Analysis

Thematic analyses, as in grounded theory and development of cultural models, require more involvement and interpretation from the researcher. Thematic analyses move beyond counting explicit words or phrases and focus on identifying and describing both implicit and explicit ideas within the data, that is, themes. Codes are then typically developed to represent the identified themes and applied or linked to raw data as summary markers for later analysis. Such analyses may or may not include the following: comparing code frequencies, identifying code co-occurrence, and graphically displaying relationships between codes within the data set. Generally speaking, reliability is of greater concern with thematic analysis than with word-based analyses because more interpretation goes into defining the data items (i.e., codes) as well as applying the codes to chunks of text. This issue is even more pronounced when working in teams with multiple analysts. To maintain rigor, strategies for monitoring and improving intercoder agreement, and therefore reliability, should be implemented in the analytic process (see Chapters 3 and 4). Despite these few issues related to reliability, we feel that a thematic analysis is still the most useful in capturing the complexities of meaning within a textual data set. It is also the most commonly used method of analysis in qualitative research. For these reasons, it is the primary focus in the chapters that follow.

One important dimension of qualitative analysis is not represented in Figure 1.2—the length of a datum. Text, for example, can be something as simple as a single-word response to an open-ended question on a survey (e.g., "In what city were you born?") or as complex as a corpus of text thousands of pages in length. Along this continuum, analytic strategies will likely vary, so the length of items for analysis needs to be taken into account when planning an analysis (see Chapter 2). That being said, most qualitative researchers work with transcribed data generated from in-depth interviews and focus groups that are typically 1 to 2 hours in length. Transcripts for these data collection activities may range from 10 to 40 pages per individual or group, with focus groups leaning toward the longer end of the range. Complexity of a study involving qualitative data can also vary dramatically, ranging from just a handful of focus groups to multiple data types generated from hundreds of data sources.

All of the analytic techniques described by Bernard and Ryan (1998, 2010)— are useful, and each has its place in the world of research. Usually, though, when we talk about qualitative research in the social or health sciences, we are referring to textual data generated from in-depth interviews and focus groups—which are often transcribed verbatim from audio recordings—and, to a lesser degree, participant observation notes. And, in the vast majority of cases, thematic analyses, rather than word-based approaches, are used for the reasons already indicated. This also explains the second word in the book's title. But what about the first word in the book's title—*applied*? Why was this term chosen? And where does *applied thematic analysis* fit into Bernard and Ryan's typology and in relation to common theoretical approaches to data analysis? The following section addresses these and other questions.

THEORETICAL CONSIDERATIONS

Applied Research

Let's first get the term *applied* out of the way. Most definitions of applied research refer to the common end purpose of solving practical problems. This is typically distinguished from "pure" research, oriented toward furthering existing knowledge, for the sake of curiosity and knowledge itself. The main thrust of this book has to do with understanding the world and trying to answer research problems of a more practical nature. Note that we do not make a distinction in this case between researchers in academia versus those working in nonacademic settings: The approach we outline is equally useful for researchers in either context. We also should note that one could certainly develop theory and build on knowledge using the processes we present. In fact, we include a section on building theoretical models in Chapter 3. But, here we assume that readers are interested primarily in trying to understand and explain the world in a rigorous, reliable, and valid fashion. It is our belief that theory or models (or any other assertions about the way things are) should be supported by data that have been collected and analyzed in a systematic and transparent manner. The methods we discuss, therefore, could be viewed as a necessary precursor to theory, not antonymic to it. Of course, this is predicated on the belief in the primacy of empirical observation in the generation and interpretation of knowledge. We expand on this concept in the section "Interpretivism and Positivism."

Grounded Theory

The emphasis on supporting claims with data is what links applied thematic analysis to *grounded theory*. Grounded theory is a set of inductive and iterative techniques designed to identify categories and concepts within text that are then linked into formal theoretical models (Corbin & Strauss, 2008; Glaser & Strauss 1967). Charmaz (2006) describes grounded theory as a set of methods that "consist of systematic, yet flexible guidelines for collecting and analyzing qualitative data to construct theories 'grounded' in the data themselves" (p. 2). As Bernard and Ryan (1998) note, the process is deceptively simple: (1) read verbatim transcripts, (2) identify possible themes, (3) compare and contrast themes, identifying structure among them, and (4) build theoretical models, constantly checking them against the data. Applied thematic analysis involves Steps 1 through 3 as well as a portion of Step 4. As implied by Step 4, a key attribute of the process is that the resulting theoretical models are grounded in the data. In applied research, our output may or may not be a theoretical model (which comprises a distinction with grounded theory), but as with a grounded theory approach, we are greatly concerned with ensuring that our interpretations are supported by actual data in hand.

Our approach also shares the systematic yet flexible and inductive qualities of grounded theory. As noted above, grounded theory methodology, done properly, systematically compares themes and emergent theory to data points. A consistent premise embedded throughout this book is that thematic development and subsequent interpretation of a data set should always be congruent with the raw data/text at hand. The analytic approach we present is also systematic in terms of data processing—for example, codebook development, code application, and data reduction. Although systematic, the discovery and elaboration of themes in grounded theory is inductive and constantly evolving. Likewise, the process we outline for developing a codebook, while systematic, is iterative; a codebook is never really finalized until the last of the text has been coded. We also find iteration useful vis-à-vis reanalysis of data from a different angle or using additional data reduction techniques on a data set, and revising our initial interpretations accordingly.

As mentioned earlier, our method does not preclude theoretical development. However, its primary goal is to describe and understand how people feel, think, and behave within a particular context relative to a specific research question. In this way, applied thematic analysis is similar to phenomenology, which seeks to understand the meanings that people give to their lived experiences and social reality (Schutz, 1962, p. 59).

Phenomenology

Phenomenology is based on the philosophical writings of Edmund Husserl and Maurice Merleau-Ponty. As an approach to data collection and analysis, its roots lie in humanistic psychology (Giorgi, 1970, 2009; Wertz, 2005). In phenomeno-logical research, it is the participants' perceptions, feelings, and lived experiences that are paramount and that are the object of study.

Giving voice to "the other" is a hallmark of humanism and humanistic anthro-pology, and this tradition has carried over into qualitative research in general. The notion of open-ended questions and conversational inquiry, so typical in qualitative research, is founded on this principle as it allows research partici-pants to talk about a topic in their own words, free of the constraints imposed by the kind of fixed-response questions typically seen in quantitative studies. Simultaneously, the researcher learns from the participants' talk and dynamically seeks to guide the inquiry in response to what is being learned. We feel that one of the greatest strengths of qualitative research is this ability to ask questions that are meaningful to participants and to likewise receive responses in participants' own words and native cognitive constructs. Of additional benefit in this regard is the use of inductive probing—whether in focus groups, in-depth interviews, or participant observation—which allows the researcher to clarify expressions or meaning and further permits participants to tell their story. Whether describing the technological needs of Fortune 500 customers or the lived experiences of Ecuadorian shrimp fishers, providing a voice to the research participant is part of the anthropological tradition (and qualitative research in general), and this stems from its phenomenological roots (Guest, 2002). We are not saying that quantitatively oriented research cannot have a similar populist viewpoint; only that the nature of qualitative data and the data collection process are more con-ducive to such an enterprise.

Telling a good story, as compelling as it may be, is not enough, however. Convincing other researchers and policymakers of the relevance of your data and findings in an evidence-based world will require more than presenting a few evocative or emotionally moving stories and quotes (although these can help!). Our strategy, therefore, is to use a range of analytic devices available to make our case. This includes presenting numbers and talking about how the data are structured, in addition to providing an engaging narrative. Another distinction, therefore, between the analytic method we describe and grounded theory (and phenomenology for that matter) is the use of quantification. The former typically does not include any sort of quantification. As Strauss and Corbin emphasize in their description of grounded theory, the process refers to a "**non**mathematical [bold in original] analytic procedure that results in findings derived from data gathered by a variety of means" (1990, p. 18). In contrast, applied thematic analysis uses quantitative techniques, in combination with interpretive and other techniques, to confront a research problem. This brings us to the final theoretical dimension to be discussed in this chapter—the "divide" between the interpretive and positivist approaches to qualitative research.

Interpretivism and Positivism

The controversy between interpretivism and positivism in the social sciences and humanities is no secret. Debates continue to erupt in fields of anthropology, sociology, geography, and other disciplines about the merits of either approach. Proponents of the interpretive school, popularized by scholars such as Clifford Geertz (1973), argue that the scientific method is reductionist and often misses the point of qualitative research. Instead, this approach, stemming from a hermeneutic tradition, is most interested in interpreting deeper meaning in discourse and understanding multiple realities (as opposed to one "objective" reality) that are represented in a collection of personal narratives or observed behaviors and activities. Hermenuetics was originally the practice of interpreting meaning within biblical text. Usage of the term has expanded to include interpretation of nonreligious texts in search of underlying sociopolitical meaning. To an interpretivist, the story one tells, and its effect on the intended audience, is the centerpiece of the method. This point is illustrated in the following passage from Geertz (1973):

> Cultural analysis is intrinsically incomplete. And, worse than that, the more deeply it goes the less complete it is... There are a number of ways of escaping this—turning culture into folklore and collecting it, turning it into traits and counting it, turning it into institutions and classifying it, turning it into structures and toying with it. But they *are* [italics in original] escapes. The fact is that to commit oneself to a semiotic concept of culture and an interpretive approach to the study of it is to commit oneself to a view of ethnographic assertion as . . . "essentially contestable." Anthropology, or at least interpretive anthropology, is a science whose progress is marked less by a perfection of the consensus than by a refinement of debate. What gets better is the precision with which we vex each other. (p. 29)

From a procedural standpoint, data analysis in this tradition (and phenomenology as well) tends to be less structured and typically unconcerned with measurement or quantification, highlighting instead the meaning—both personal and social—interpreted within the discourse. The analytic enterprise is strictly qualitative, falling into the upper left quadrant of Figure 1.1.

Positivism, as viewed in contemporary social science, follows a different path, one that is embedded within the scientific method. A positivist approach is based on the fundamental ideas that: (a) interpretations should be derived directly from data observed, and (b) data collection and analysis methods should, in some way, be systematic and transparent. Criticizing the interpretive school for being overly subjective and politicized, researchers from a positivist tradition attempt to ascertain as close a picture to objective reality as possible, within the limitations imposed by the study parameters. Within the field of qualitative data analysis, positivist oriented researchers devote a significant amount of energy and time to systematic analytic procedures and identification of structure within the data. The approach encourages the use of measurement and quantification and tends to fall more (though not exclusively) into the lower left quadrant of Figure 1.1.

From a procedural standpoint, Bernard and Ryan (1998) define the positivist approach to qualitative data analysis as involving "the reduction of texts to codes that represent themes or concepts and the application of quantitative methods to find patterns in the relations among the codes" (p. 596). The analytic process outlined in this book utilizes various data reduction techniques, and, admittedly is biased toward a positivist perspective. That said, the act of identifying themes within text, among other components of the data analysis process, is itself a highly interpretive endeavor. Throughout the book, we emphasize the need to always refer back to the raw data and caution against relying only on summarized forms of data. As such, the approach we advocate embraces key elements of the interpretive school of thought.

Applied Thematic Analysis

So where does *applied thematic analysis* fall relative to all the approaches and procedures described above? Applied thematic analysis as we define it comprises a bit of everything—grounded theory, positivism, interpretivism, and phenomenology—synthesized into one methodological framework. The approach borrows what we feel are the more useful techniques from each theoretical and methodological camp and adapts them to an applied research context. In such a context, we assume that ensuring the credibility of findings to an external audience is paramount, and, based on our experience, achieving this goal is facilitated by systematicity and visibility of methods and procedures.

Our intent is to keep this book as practical, focused, and concise as possible. We hope to impart a useful set of procedures that can be employed to conduct rigorous qualitative data analyses that ultimately will be persuasive to funders, policymakers, and other researchers. For this reason, with the exception of the introduction, we do not directly engage with epistemology or theory. The five additional readings at the end of this chapter will provide the interested reader with a basic guide to theory and background in the philosophy of social science.

To summarize, the ATA approach is a rigorous, yet inductive, set of procedures designed to identify and examine themes from textual data in a way that is transparent and credible. Our method draws from a broad range of several theoretical and methodological perspectives, but in the end, its primary concern is with presenting the stories and experiences voiced by study participants as accurately and comprehensively as possible. As mentioned earlier, applied thematic analysis can be used in conjunction with various forms of qualitative data; however, for the sake of concision we focus the contents of this book on analyzing text generated through in-depth interviews, focus groups, and qualitative field notes. These are by far the most common forms of textual data encountered by researchers doing qualitative research.

We need to be clear here that ATA is *not* a novel approach to qualitative data analysis. In fact, quite the contrary is true; researchers have been doing very similar types of analyses for decades. What has been lacking, at least in our view, is a practical and simple, step-by-step guide on how to do an inductive thematic analysis, particularly with an emphasis on methodological rigor. It is precisely this dearth of published instruction on the topic that prompted us to write this book.

The approach one brings to qualitative analysis will depend on a number of factors, such as

- Research objective(s)
- Researcher familiarity with a given approach
- Audience for the research
- Logistical, temporal, and funding parameters

Each approach comes with its own set of advantages and disadvantages; choices between approaches involve trade-offs. Consideration must be given to various parameters, and the outcomes for different choices weighed and prioritized. Table 1.2 summarizes some of the defining features for the aforementioned thematic analytic approaches. Note that what one researcher sees as a limitation another might see as a strength, contingent upon their epistemological bent. For example, "extrapolating beyond the data" is likely perceived by a positivist in a negative light. In contrast, a researcher with an interpretive view will probably see this additional latitude as a strength.

SUMMING UP

The ways in which qualitative data can be collected and analyzed are virtually infinite. A variety of data collection techniques can be employed to gather and/or generate data, each with its own unique properties. Data generated or collected can range from a single word to a narrative relaying an entire life history, to a photograph or video. Epistemological perspectives and theoretical frameworks also vary, which in turn influences how a researcher approaches the data when it's time for analysis. In this chapter, we have attempted to orient the reader to this diversity and position our approach—applied thematic analysis—within the existing literature.

As we acknowledged above, what we call "applied thematic analysis" is not new. It is based on commonly employed inductive thematic analyses, and shares

Table 1.2 Comparative Summary of Three Theme-Based Approaches to Analysis

	Phenomenology	*Grounded Theory*	*Applied Thematic Analysis*
Defining Features	• Focuses on subjective human experience • Analysis is typically thematic in nature • Often used in humanist psychology, but approach has been adopted in humanities and social sciences	• Uses a systematic comparative technique to find themes and create codes • Properly done, requires an exhaustive comparison of all text segments Theoretical models built on themes/codes that are "grounded" in the data	• Identifies key themes in text. Themes are transformed into codes and aggregated in a codebook. • Uses techniques in addition to theme identification, including word searches and data reduction techniques. • Can be used to build theoretical models or to find solutions to real-world problems.
Epistemological Leaning	• *Interpretive* • Subjective meaning is interpreted and extrapolated from discourse	• *Interpretive/Positivist* • Interpretive in that quantification is not included • Positivist in that it is systematic and assertions are required to be supported with evidence (text)	• *Positivist/Interpretive* • Positivist in that assertions are required to be supported with evidence (text). • Processes are also systematic and quantification can be employed. • Methods and processes in ATA (except those of a quantitative nature) can also be used in an interpretive analysis.
Strengths	• Good for smaller data sets • Has latitude to explore data more deeply and extrapolate beyond the text • Good for cognitively oriented studies	• Good for smaller data sets • Exhaustive coverage of data • Interpretation supported by data • Can be used to study topics other than individual experience (e.g., social process, cultural norms, etc.)	• Well suited to large data sets • Good for team research. • Inclusion of non-theme-based and quantitative techniques adds analytic breadth. • Interpretation supported by data • Can be used to study topics other than individual experience.
Limitations	• Focuses only on human experience • May interpret too far beyond what's in the data • Not necessarily systematic	• Does not include quantification • Time consuming ; logistically prohibitive for large data sets	• May miss some of the more nuanced data.
Key Sources	• Giorgi (1970, 2009), Moustakas (1994), Smith, Flowers, and Larkin (2009)	• Glaser and Strauss (1967), Corbin and Strauss (2008), Charmaz (2006)	• No one text. • Elements of inductive thematic analysis can be found in numerous books on qualitative data analysis.

many features with grounded theory and phenomenology. One attribute that sets ATA apart is its breadth of scope. Although grounded theory, by definition, is aimed at building theory, ATA is not restricted to this purpose. Likewise, interpretive phenomenology focuses on subjective human experience, whereas the topic of an ATA can be broader and include social and cultural phenomena as well. ATA also allows greater flexibility with regard to theoretical frameworks and, subsequently, analytic tools it can employ. Although more comfortably applied within a positivist framework, many of the principles of ATA (all really, except quantification) can be incorporated into an interpretive analytic enterprise. There is nothing about the systematicity and transparency of process within ATA that is inherently at odds with interpretivism.

In our view, the greatest strength of ATA is its pragmatic focus on using whatever tools might be appropriate to get the analytic job done in a transparent, efficient, and ethical manner. This expanded toolbox includes various forms of quantification, word searches, deviant case analyses, and other analytic tools. Our approach also takes into account the challenges of working with focus group data, comparing subgroups, and working within a mixed methods project. This is why we include a chapter on comparing thematic data and another on integrating qualitative and quantitative data, which is an increasingly used research strategy.

This book is for the practitioner of qualitative research, in both applied and nonapplied settings. Whether you conduct qualitative research to evaluate programs and interventions, as formative research within a larger study, or as a means of describing and explaining a targeted phenomenon, the procedures contained in this monograph will help instill both focus and rigor into your analysis. In the pages that follow, we provide suggestions on how to do a systematic thematic analysis using a variety of tools and approaches. The methods we describe are certainly not the only ones available. They also may not be appropriate for more specialized analyses. We have done our best to provide references in these instances. For the most part, however, we feel that the guidelines and procedures set out in the book will enhance and streamline the vast majority of thematic analyses. We have tried to take the best from the multitude of methods and techniques and blend these pieces together to comprise a comprehensive approach that we have termed *applied thematic analysis*. As much as we believe in the procedures and techniques we describe, we caution the reader against using them blindly, or thinking that the content of this book is static. It is not. In keeping with the spirit of Jeet Kune Do, we, as researchers, are constantly learning and evolving, and striving to create new techniques and improve upon existing ones. We encourage the reader to do the same.

REFERENCES

Agar, M. (1996). Schon Wieder? Science in linguistic anthropology. *Anthropology Newsletter, 37*(1), 13.

Banks, M. (2008). *Using visual data in qualitative research.* Thousand Oaks, CA: Sage.

Bernard, H. R. (1996). Qualitative data, quantitative analysis. *The Cultural Anthropology Methods Journal, 8*(1), 9–11.

Bernard, H. R. (2005). *Research methods in anthropology: Qualitative and quantitative approaches* (4th ed.). Walnut Creek, CA: AltaMira Press.

Bernard, H. R. (2010). *Analyzing qualitative data: Systematic approaches.* Thousand Oaks, CA: Sage.

Bernard, H. R., & Ryan, G. (1998). Text analysis: Qualitative and quantitative methods. In H. R. Bernard (Ed.), *Handbook of methods in cultural anthropology* (pp. 595–645). Walnut Creek, CA: AltaMira Press.

Charmaz, K. (2006). *Grounded theory: A practical guide through qualitative analysis.* Thousand Oaks, CA: Sage.

Corbin, J., & Strauss, A. (2008). *Basics of qualitative research: Techniques and procedures for developing grounded theory.* Thousand Oaks, CA: Sage.

Cowan, G., & O'Brian, M. (1990). Gender and survival vs. death in slasher films: A content analysis. *Sex Roles, 23*(3–4), 187–196.

Creswell, J. (2009). *Research design: Qualitative, quantitative, and mixed methods approaches* (3rd ed.). Thousand Oaks, CA: Sage.

Denzin, N., & Lincoln, Y. (Eds.) (2005). *Handbook of qualitative research* (3rd ed.). Thousand Oaks, CA: Sage.

Dey, I. (1993). *Qualitative data analysis: A user-friendly guide for social scientists.* New York: Routledge.

Geertz, C. (1973). *The interpretation of cultures: Selected essays.* New York: Basic Books.

Giorgi, A. (1970). *Psychology as a human science.* New York: Harper & Row.

Giorgi, A. (2009). *The descriptive phenomenological method in psychology.* Pittsburgh, PA: Duquesne University Press.

Glaser, B., & Strauss, A. (1967). *The discovery of grounded theory: Strategies for qualitative research.* New York: Aldine.

Guest, G. (2002). Anthropology in the technology industry. In A. Podolefsky & P. Brown (Eds.), *Applying anthropology: An introductory reader* (pp. 259–260). New York: McGraw-Hill.

Guest, G. (2005). The range of qualitative research. *Journal of Family Planning and Reproductive Health Care, 31*(2), 165.

Guest, G., & MacQueen, K. (2008). Reevaluating guidelines for qualitative research. In G. Guest & K. MacQueen (Eds.). *Handbook for team-based qualitative research* (pp. 205–226). Lanham, MD: AltaMira Press.

Guest, G., Johnson, L., Burke, H., Rain-Taljaard, R., Severy, L., Von Mollendorf, C., & Van Damme, L. (2007). Changes in sexual behavior during a safety and feasibility trial of a microbicide/diaphragm combination: An integrated qualitative and quantitative analysis. *AIDS Education and Prevention, 19*(4), 310–320.

Hirschman, E. C. (1987). People as products: Analysis of a complex marketing exchange. *Journal of Marketing, 51,* 98–108.

Knoblauch, H., & Schnettler, B. (Eds.). (2006). *Video analysis: Methodology and methods: Qualitative audiovisual data analysis in sociology.* New York: Peter Lang Publishing.

Krippendorf, K. (2004). *Content analysis: An introduction to its methodology* (2nd ed.). Thousand Oaks, CA: Sage.

Lee, B. (1971, September). Liberate yourself from classical karate. *Black Belt Magazine, 9*(9), 24.

Moustakas, C. (1994). *Phenomenological research methods.* Thousand Oaks, CA: Sage.

Neuendorf, K. (2001). *The content analysis guidebook.* Thousand Oaks, CA: Sage.

Nkwi, P., Nyamongo, I., & Ryan, G. (2001). *Field research into socio-cultural issues: Methodological guidelines*. Yaounde, Cameroon: International Center for Applied Social Sciences, Research, and Training/UNFPA.

Online Dictionary of the Social Science. (n.d.). *Qualitative research*. Retrieved from http://bitbucket.icaap.org/dict.pl?alpha=Q

Pacific Northwest National Laboratory (PNL). (2008). *IN-SPIRE, 4.0*. Seattle, WA: Author.

Prosser, J. (1998). *Image-based research: A sourcebook for qualitative researchers*. New York: Falmer Press.

Ryan, G., & Bernard, H. R. (2000). Data management and analysis methods. In N. Denzin & Y. Lincoln (Eds.), *Handbook of qualitative research* (pp. 769–802). Thousand Oaks, CA: Sage.

Schutz, A. (1962). *Collected papers I: The problem of social reality*. The Hague: Martinus Nijhoff.

Smith, J., Flowers, P., & Larkin, M. (2009). *Interpretative phenomenological analysis: Theory, method and research*. Thousand Oaks, CA: Sage.

Strauss, A., & Corbin, J. (1990). *Basics of qualitative research: Grounded theory procedures and techniques*. Newbury Park, CA: Sage.

Tesch, R. (1990). *Qualitative research: Analysis types and software tools*. New York: Falmer Press.

Weber, R. (1990). *Basic content analysis: Quantitative applications in the social sciences*. Thousand Oaks, CA: Sage.

Weller, S., & Romney, A. (1988). *Systematic data collection*. Newbury Park, CA: Sage.

Wertz, F. J. (2005). Phenomenological research methods for counseling psychology. *Journal of Counseling Psychology, 52*(2), 167–177.

ADDITIONAL READING

Delanty, G., & Strydom, P. (Ed.). (2003). *Philosophies of social science*. Maidenhead, UK: Open University Press.

Geertz, C. (1973). *The interpretation of cultures: Selected essays*. New York: Basic Books.

Kuznar, L. (2008). *Reclaiming a scientific anthropology* (2nd ed.). Lanham, MD: AltaMira Press.

Romney, A. K. (1989). Quantitative models, science and cumulative knowledge. *Journal of Quantitative Anthropology, 1*(1), 153–223.

Starks, H., & Trinidad, S. (2007). Choose your method: A comparison of phenomenology, discourse analysis, and grounded theory. *Qualitative Health Research, 17*(10), 1372–1380.

2

PLANNING AND PREPARING THE ANALYSIS

LEARNING OBJECTIVES

After reading this chapter, you should know how to:

- Establish an analytic objective
- Develop an analysis plan
- Choose an appropriate analytic approach
- Define appropriate boundaries for the analysis

When working with text data there is one essential, basic analytic technique: reading the text. A targeted, goal-driven analysis requires additional steps. The larger the analytic task, the greater the amount of text to be analyzed, or the more analysts whose work must be coordinated, the more important it is to develop an analysis plan before the text is read and preferably before the data are collected. A good number of books describe how to conduct a particular type of qualitative data analysis, but very little attention is given in the literature to the planning phase. How are analytic objectives established, and how do they relate to the analysis? How do you bound your data set? What is the primary purpose of the analysis? And who will be the primary audience for, and ultimate judge of, your analysis? The answers to these questions will affect your selection of an effective and efficient analysis strategy. In the pages that follow, we address these and other questions pertinent to analysis planning and provide some practical suggestions and tools for conducting an analysis that will best fit a given context.

ESTABLISHING ANALYTIC OBJECTIVES

The first step in developing an effective analysis plan is to establish clear analytic objectives. The approach taken in developing the plan will be somewhat determined by whether the data will be analyzed in real time, as they are generated, or if you are developing an analysis plan after the data have been collected, processed, and cleaned. In classic qualitative research, at least some of the data are analyzed as they are collected, and the results may be used in an iterative fashion to modify the data collection itself.

For example, if the purpose of the research is to explore a little-known or poorly understood phenomenon, the early stages of research often entail learning what questions to ask, how to ask them, and who to ask them of. This type of exploratory interview is described in detail in Schensul, Schensul, and LeCompte (1999). The approach can be fluid and dynamic, with the interviewer(s) making adjustments to the interview process in real time. Or, the approach may be purposely staggered, with interview guides being semistructured during each phase but the content of the guides being driven by what is learned from each successive phase. A more limited structured iterative approach may be used in situations where considerable knowledge exists about the research topic or phenomenon but the work is being conducted in a new context. In this case, the iterative approach may be limited to piloting of a more structured data collection strategy to ensure that the recruitment process, wording of questions, and ability to uncover new dimensions are effective for the new context. In each of these situations, on-going data analysis is crucial to the success of the endeavor.

Since our focus in this book is on data analysis, we will not get into the nuances of iterative data collection except to discuss the analytic implications of a dynamic and evolving database. In addition, our discussion assumes that more than one person is collecting the data, that is, that a data collection team or field team exists. Where appropriate, alternative strategies for one-person analysis projects are provided.

Analysis to Improve the Data Collection Process

As noted, the initial steps in the analysis process may be used to improve data collection when analysis begins before data collection is complete. To achieve this objective, an initial analysis plan should be developed with a focus on two objectives.

First, the analysis should serve to *enhance the overall quality of the data*. Are the data collectors following the protocol and asking the intended questions? Are they probing appropriately to generate richness and depth from study participants? Are descriptive notes included with an appropriate level of detail? If the data are being translated, are the appropriate nuances being captured? Is there evidence of rapport between the data collectors and the people participating in the research?

If you look closely at each of these questions, the necessary components of an analysis plan to enhance overall data quality become evident: Assess the consistency of questions asked by interviewers and evaluate the skills of the interviewers (technical and interpersonal). For example, to determine whether data collectors are asking intended questions, you could generate a report that looks something like Table 2.1 by listening to the audio from each interview or focus group and keeping a running tally of the questions asked. It can also be generated by reviewing transcripts from the interviews or focus groups. This approach works well for studies that use a more structured approach for qualitative data collection.

If data collection is less structured, or if concerns exist that data collectors are deviating too far from a semistructured guide, then a more nuanced approach is needed, that is, one that tracks the actual prompts used by the data collector. For this purpose, the report could include transcription of the exact wording used by the data collectors when asking each of the research questions or querying about each of the research domains. Since qualitative research places a premium on a conversational approach that allows for variability in the exact wording of questions and prompts, it is important to pay attention to that variability and assess its implications for the comparability of the data across data collection events. It is not just the responses to the intended questions that need to be analyzed, but rather the conversations that take place.

Table 2.1 An Example of Analyzing Data in Real Time to Determine Whether Interviewers Are Asking the Intended Questions

Data Collector	Total # Interviews Conducted to Date	Research Question	Total # Interviews Where Research Question Asked	Proportion of Interviews Where Research Question Was Asked
John	8	1A: Please describe your childhood home.	7	87%
		1B: What is your first memory about your childhood?	4	50%
Mary	5	1A: Please describe your childhood home.	5	100%
		1B: What is your first memory about your childhood?	2	40%

Effective probing is the lynchpin of the two most commonly used qualitative data collection strategies: the open-ended interview and focus groups. To determine whether data collectors are probing appropriately, you can read transcripts or listen to recorded interviews and make note of both good and bad instances of probing. Putting that information into a summary table can also be an excellent tool for retraining to improve the skills of the data collectors. Table 2.2 is an example from a series of pilot interviews for a study conducted by MacQueen in the southern African country of Lesotho. For most studies, creating a summary table like this can be done manually, for example by copying and pasting text directly from transcripts or by transcribing short illustrative sections. With a little more effort and the appropriate computer resources, it would also be possible to add audio clips from digitally recorded interviews or focus groups so that the team can hear the conversation.

If the project is large and complex, for example, with multiple data collection teams working in multiple sites, it is helpful to develop a quality-control codebook in a qualitative data-analysis software program and then code the interviews as they come in (see Chapter 3 for a detailed discussion of codebook development). Such a codebook would include a set of codes and definitions that are based on the kinds of problems described in Table 2.2. Taking this extra step would make it possible to use the reporting functions of the software program to evaluate overall quality by site, by data collector, and by research question as well as to look for improvement over time. The resulting documentation can be very useful for deciding whether a large, complex data base is adequate for secondary analyses or subanalyses in the future, when institutional and personal memory about data collection have faded.

Table 2.2 An Example of Analyzing Data in Real Time to Identify Problems With Probing and Develop Strategies to Improve Interviewer Skills

Problem	*Example*	*Potential Solutions*
Not building rapport adequately from beginning	*Interview guide question:* First, can you tell me a little about yourself? **[Let participant answer, then ask specific probes on education, etc., ONLY if not already addressed by participant.]** *Transcript:* INTERVIEWER: Ok. Eh... Well I would like to know a little bit, well, about you. You see eh mmm…tell me, where did you go to school?	The opening questions should be "soft," inviting, open-ended. Let the participant tell his or her story; encourage a story. Avoid jumping into closed-ended questions.

Table 2.2 (Continued)

Problem	Example	Potential Solutions
Failure to probe	INTERVIEWER: Mmhm, what qualities do you look for in a person to end up saying you love him? PARTICIPANT: I look at how genuine his love is. INTERVIEWER: Mmhm PARTICIPANT: Yes INTERVIEWER: Ok, …	What does the participant mean when she says "I look at how genuine his love is"?
Completing statements for the participant	PARTICIPANT: Even if I don't have money to go to the doctor ... INTERVIEWER: Yes. PARTICIPANT: She ends up giving me money so that I see to it that— INTERVIEWER: You go see the doctor. PARTICIPANT: I see the doctor. INTERVIEWER: Yes. PARTICIPANT: Yes.	Let the participant complete the statement. He might have completed the comment ("she ends up giving me money so that I see to it that—") in a different way, or offered more information.

(Continued)

Table 2.2 (Continued)

Problem	Example	Potential Solutions
Completing statements for the participant	INTERVIEWER: Do you have a wife or a sweetheart? PARTICIPANT: Well, I may say I have a— INTERVIEWER: A girlfriend. PARTICIPANT: A certain girlfriend. INTERVIEWER: Ok, so you have girlfriend? PARTICIPANT: Yes.	Let the participant complete the sentence; he might have said something other than "girlfriend."
"Pushing" for a response rather than listening and thoughtfully probing	INTERVIEWER: Can you explain for me the work your partner or sweetheart is doing? PARTICIPANT: Yes, well I don't like explaining that to you. INTERVIEWER: You can explain to me. PARTICIPANT: Mmm! INTERVIEWER: What kind of job? What kind of job is it that cannot be described? PARTICIPANT: Well, I don't think it's the kind of work that can be explained, truly speaking. INTERVIEWER: Ok, you are not able to explain it.	Interviewer could have asked why he did not like "explaining that"; for example, "Why is that?" instead of pushing directly for a response.

The second objective of analysis to improve the data collection process is to *determine whether the topical content of the research should be expanded, contracted, or refined.* The goal is to assess the effectiveness of the questions in eliciting desired information. To determine whether too many questions are being asked in one interview or focus group, a report similar to Table 2.1 could be created but sorted by question rather than data collector. It is then easy to determine whether any patterns exist with regard to missing questions. For example, if questions at the end of the interview or at the end of a section on a discrete topic tend to be missing, this may indicate fatigue on the part of either the interviewer or participant. If certain questions in the middle of an interview tend to be missing, that may indicate poor flow in the overall design of the interview guide.

This type of summary table points toward potential problems; to confirm the nature of the problem, you will need to read the transcripts and/or listen to audio of the data collection event. Are the questions too generic or so poorly specified that they fail to engage the study participants? Even if the data collectors are diligently asking the questions in the guide and making a sincere effort at probing, the resulting data may not be useful or informative. Data collectors can often identify a "problem" question within the first few interviews or focus groups and can confirm (or serve as the starting point) for this type of analysis. A quick way to track the overall quality of specific questions or topic areas is to create a report that includes the question or topic area together with the participant response from each interview. You can then look for patterns in the way the questions are asked as well as the kinds of responses that are being generated. Are the participants struggling to make sense of the question? Is the question generating information on the topic of interest? Are some of the participants interpreting the question in unexpected ways? What kind of probing is most successful at generating rich responses? In Chapter 3, we will describe a process called *structural coding* that can be implemented in most qualitative data analysis software programs that makes this kind of analysis quick and easy.

Analysis to Answer a Research Question

Answering a research question is a more challenging analysis objective than assuring the quality of the data to be analyzed. Establishing an achievable research analysis objective requires a good match between the *view* you want to generate, the *quality of the data* available to generate that view, and the *resources and time available*.

The view: The analysis objective is a short description of what you want to achieve through the lens of the data. Consider Google Earth as a metaphor: Do you want to describe the broad sweep of continents and oceans, describe major features en route from start to finish, or do you want to explore the shrubs and cracked tarmac? We will refer to this aspect of the analysis objective as the view. Defining the view is a crucial first step for applied analysis, as it will bring structure to subsequent decisions in the analysis process. For example, if you want a detailed view, then you will need a codebook that gives you the conceptual viewing power of a microscope. If you want a wider view, you need the conceptual viewing power of binoculars or a telescope, or perhaps a scope mounted on a satellite. These are very different levels of thematic identification that result in very different codebooks.

The quality of the data: There needs to be a fit between the view you want to generate (the analysis objective) and the data at hand. This requires a scan of the data. If your database is relatively small, for example, on a par with the length and richness of a good novel, you can simply read the text and make notes along the way. If the database is more like a trilogy or a library shelf of books of variable quality and form, then you probably want to do a more structured scan of the data. For this, many of the strategies outlined in the previous section for evaluating the quality of data as they are collected can be used.

If you have high-resolution, street-view data from all locations, unlimited resources, and no time constraints, you can, eventually, generate a global view by painstakingly connecting all the data points and systematically stepping back to identify larger and larger features in the landscape. The reverse is not true, however. You cannot drill down to a street-level view if you do not have comprehensive street-level data.

If you have fine-grained, rich information from some data collection events but not all, you may not be able to generate a coherent view at certain levels of specificity. For example, if qualitative data have significant gaps, you cannot make major recommendations for policy or action; the data may identify some of the key points or landmarks for more refined future investigation, but they are not sufficiently robust to support a comprehensive plan for moving forward.

The resources and time available: Equally important is an assessment of the time and resources available to conduct the analysis. If your data are sufficiently rich and detailed to permit building up a comprehensive map from street view to global, this would support a research objective centered on generating explanatory theory from empirical data, along the lines of a grounded theory approach. Conducting such an analysis, however, requires intensive effort. Many people claim to be using a grounded theory approach in their analysis, but fully developed applications of the approach are relatively rare. Grounded theory requires a painstaking, line-by-line reading of qualitative data where each statement is systematically compared and contrasted. Most people who claim to use a grounded theory approach do not analyze the data at this level of detail because they lack the time and resources or they lack data of sufficient richness to warrant such a detailed level of analysis—or both. Applied thematic analysis is an approach that explicitly takes into account the issues of resources and time as well as the quality of the data in specifying an analytic research objective. How many people will work on the analysis? What level of skill and expertise do they have? How much time will they devote to the analysis? What is the timeline for completing the analysis? What technology is available to support the analysis?

If you have rich data but limited resources and a need to generate useful results in a timely way, it can feel at times that you are throwing away valuable data. This quandary leads some qualitative researchers to attempt a detailed analysis of all the data available. Such an attempt is often counterproductive: You may end up analyzing an arbitrary subset of the data because you run out of time, resources, and energy; you may sacrifice quality checks, leading to a false sense of surety about the results; or you may spend time and money analyzing a large data set only to realize that only a small portion is relevant to the research objectives.

In applied thematic analysis, we deal with this quandary by maintaining a systematic analysis process aligned with a targeted analysis objective. You do not sacrifice quality, nor do you discard valuable data. If there are more data than you can analyze with the given resources and time frame available, it is not discarded; it is systematically cataloged so you and others can come back to it as opportunity allows. Because it is systematically cataloged, you can be strategic in your efforts to identify additional resources for analysis, whether through funding applications, internship opportunities, and so on. As with any large, complicated effort, the goal is to break it into manageable components and then systematically do the work.

You may accomplish the task in several ways. The most obvious approach is to return to the original research design that structured the data collection. If the original design included more than one research objective, then you should translate each of those objectives into an analysis objective and then outline the steps necessary to achieve that objective. You will likely find that most or all of the analysis objectives require a common set of steps. For any given objective, you may not need to go through those steps for all of the data. It may be more efficient to prioritize their completion for the full database than to repeatedly go through the same series of steps for each analysis.

For example, you generally need to catalog the type of data available, the overall quality of the data, missing components (e.g., questions that were not asked) from items in the database and other information reflective of the quality of the data. It is easier to compile that information all at once than to repeatedly go back through a large database to compile it piecemeal. For some analyses, you may be interested in knowing how frequently certain terms or phrases appear in the data. A potentially quick way to accomplish this is to run the transcribed text through an indexing program and generate a word list and frequency count. Although this sounds simple, it in fact requires some effort to refine or generate lists to omit some words (e.g., English particles such as the, a, that) and to consolidate variants (e.g., a lot, lots). Large volumes of text can take a surprisingly long time to process in this way.

If you are working with transcripts, it may also be important to process the words spoken by the study participants separately from those spoken by the data collectors. For example if one structured interview guide was used to conduct 25 interviews, then key terms embedded in the questions will automatically occur at least 25 times because the data collectors are asking the same questions in each interview. These types of considerations need to be kept in mind whenever you consider using automated procedures to scan qualitative data. We expand on word searches as an analytic technique in Chapter 5.

Another important consideration in developing an analysis plan is the way in which the results will be disseminated. Will your findings be presented as a report of recommendations to guide policy, a comprehensive dissertation to meet the requirements for an advanced academic degree, a peer-reviewed journal article to illuminate a focused topic, a book that explores multiple dimensions of a complex topic or phenomenon, a descriptive piece in the popular media, or an "in-house" report for planning purposes? A single analysis may need to meet several of these dissemination needs simultaneously. For greatest efficiency, the plan should be sufficiently fine-grained to meet the needs of the most demanding dissemination goal. This likely means that some (but not necessarily all) aspects of the analysis are rigorous enough for peer-review publication and/or development of policy recommendations.

A further consideration in the development of an analysis plan is one directly related to the objectives of the research design. Are you seeking to explore or describe something? Do want to go a step further and explain it? Is your goal one of confirming findings from other research? Do you plan to compare data between groups? Or, are you doing a bit of each of these? Each determines what you look for and how you look for it, that is, how you code the data.

The Quick and Targeted Analysis

Although we typically encourage a thorough and systematic analysis, we also recognize that this is not always warranted, or possible. In client-driven research, results are often expected almost as soon as data collection is complete. It is not uncommon, for example, for market researchers to write a summary report of focus group findings the day after focus groups have been completed. In this case, analysis is constrained by the client's timeline; an in-depth, systematic analysis, including transcription of the audio recording, is often not possible. The analysis is directed toward discovering high-level themes that have meaningful and practical implications.

Even in situations where time is not a factor, an exhaustive analysis may not be worth the time and effort. In certain mixed methods designs, for example, the primary purpose of collecting qualitative data can be simply to inform a quantitative instrument (more about mixed methods analyses in Chapter 8). In such a context, the analysis is narrowly targeted to inform specific response categories, question stems, or domains of inquiry on an instrument. A complete textual analysis in this case is not necessary. Formal codebooks, systematic coding of all that was said, and even transcription of data are overkill if the only purpose is to help in the design of a subsequent instrument or other research element, such as a sampling strategy. Instead of using more in-depth and time-consuming (albeit rigorous) analytic procedures, the analysis process can be streamlined by using a debriefing template, similar to what Miles and Huberman (1994) call a "contact summary sheet" (p. 51). Data collectors are instructed to debrief immediately after each data collection event. For in-depth interviews, this may be a solitary enterprise; for focus groups, it typically involves a discussion between the moderator and note-taker. As part of the debriefing exercise, data collectors fill in a form that has been created for the particular objectives associated with the data collection activities. Although the content of the form will vary according to the objectives of each individual project, we have found from our experience that requesting at least the following information is useful, both for designing subsequent instruments or research questions and for improving data collection quality.

- Basic data about the data collection event: date and location, participant type, name of data collector(s), number of people in group (focus groups only)
- Main themes that emerged
- Information that was confusing or contradictory
- Emergent questions or domains of inquiry that should be added to the subsequent instrument
- Response categories for questions
- Suggestions for improving the data collection event (techniques, questions, etc.)

Summing Up

As we alluded to in the opening paragraph of this chapter, qualitative data analysis should be a thoughtful enterprise, not an ad hoc process. It is true that thematic analysis should be flexible and responsive to the naturally emergent nature of the process, but many factors need to be considered beforehand to ensure that your analysis is both efficient and meaningful. In Table 2.3 below, we outline some of the questions to think about before embarking on an analysis. In fact, we strongly suggest that these be well thought out during the research design stage and incorporated into the research plan/protocol.

Table 2.3 Questions to Consider Before an Analysis

Question	Suggestions and Tips
What is the practical purpose of the analysis?	Find solutions, build theory, develop an intervention, evaluate something, inform subsequent data collection, inform ongoing data collection.
What is the analytic purpose?	To: identify, explore, explain, compare, confirm, or some combination of these purposes.
	Tip—The analytic purpose should synchronize with your research objectives.
How is the analysis connected to the research question(s)?	Your analysis should directly inform one or more of your research questions.
	Tip—Before embarking on analysis, the research team should review the study's research questions and objectives to refresh their focus and make sure the analysis is framed to inform these.
What is my timeline?	Ask yourself how fast findings from your analysis are needed. The answer can range from "tomorrow" to "no foreseeable deadline."
	Tip—If an immediate turnaround is needed, you may have to forego transcription and/or a systematic analysis. Use a debriefing template to expedite analysis.

(Continued)

Table 2.3   (Continued)

Question	Suggestions and Tips
	Tip—If you have a relatively distant timeline, prioritize which analyses are most important and execute accordingly. Identify target dates and milestones to keep the analysis on track.
What resources do I have at my disposal?	You may be the sole researcher on a project, or there may be multiple analysts. You may have access to only certain analysis software or no access at all.
	Tip—Having more analysts contributing to an analysis can speed up the process, provided they have adequate access to computers and software. However, the issue of coding reliability needs to be addressed (see Chapter 4). In general, working in teams requires more quality control checks (for a guide to doing qualitative research in teams, see Guest & MacQueen, 2008).
	Tip—Select analysis software that best facilitates your analytic needs. We provide information on software in Chapter 9.
How large is my data set?	The size of a qualitative data set can range from a few in-depth interviews or focus groups to hundreds of various types of data collection activities (observation interview, focus groups, secondary data).
	Tip—Trying to include all data from all sources in a large study is cumbersome and usually not necessary (though tempting). If you have a large data set, try to divide it up into separate analyses. An easy rule of thumb is to equate a specific analysis with a specific output, such as a list of response categories, a report for a funder, or a peer-reviewed article.
	Tip—Prioritize your analyses so that the most important and time-sensitive analyses are conducted first. Consider also how analyses can most efficiently build on each other.
How heterogeneous are my data types?	You may have data from only one type of activity, such as in-depth interviews, but in a larger study, you may have data from focus groups, observation, and secondary sources as well. You may also have quantitative data relevant to your analytic objectives.

Question	Suggestions and Tips
	Tip—Think about how you will integrate data from different types of data collection methods. Decide whether data will be pooled or analyzed separately. Will you use the same codebook for two or more types of data? Answers to these questions depend on how similar and how structured data collection instruments are, sampling methods for each data type, and your research objectives.
	Tip—Chapter 8 provides more details on how to integrate qualitative and quantitative data.
Which data should I use for a particular analysis?	The answer to the question can range from a very small section of text to an entire data set, and depends on the overall size of the data set, one's research objectives, and time constraints.
	Tip—Think about which data are essential to a specific analysis. Which sources (participant or event types) of data are needed? Are responses to all questions or topics in an interview needed? This is what we refer to as "bounding the analysis."
	Tip—Use only the data that you need. Most audiences prefer a concise, nonconvoluted story, and using only the most pertinent data keeps your story line on track.
	Tip—Be even more frugal with data selection if you have a short time frame.
Who is the audience for my analysis, and how will members judge the process and subsequent findings?	You may only be concerned with writing a report for one audience, or you may need to write for several different audiences. Think carefully about for whom a particular analysis is intended.
	Tip—Different audiences will likely require different levels of rigor. Peer-reviewed journals generally have higher standards and focus on methods. Note also that expectations vary from journal to journal and discipline to discipline. Smaller sample sizes, for example, are more acceptable in anthropology journals than in public health journals.
	Tip—If possible, choose your audience based on the type of analyses your data will support.

(Continued)

Table 2.3 (Continued)	
Question	*Suggestions and Tips*
	Tip—Ask yourself, "What type of data output will my audience want to see?" Some audiences prefer narratives with verbatim quotes interspersed throughout. Others may be more amenable to matrices or tables. Still others may have a predilection for numbers, in which case data-reduction techniques will likely be used (see Chapter 6). Whatever the output, make sure that your analysis is set up to get you there.

WRITING AN ANALYSIS PLAN

Once you have a good grasp of the desired view, the quality of the data, and the resources and time available, you are ready to develop an analysis plan. As with many writing tasks, a good place to begin is with an outline of the major decisions that need to be made.

First, specify the kind of report or manuscript the analysis is intended to support. A single study may lead to a single report, especially in the applied research context. However, many studies are sufficiently rich to generate multiple analysis projects. This may include multiple analyses for discrete sections of a report, chapters in a book, or targeted articles for specific peer-reviewed journals. If the study will require multiple analysis projects, it is good to briefly describe each of the planned analyses, though you may start by developing detailed analysis plans for only one or two. Knowing that the other analyses are in the queue can help to keep the first analysis project bounded and achievable.

Once a specific analysis objective has been identified and briefly described, you will need to decide on the basic analytic approach to be used to achieve the objective: exploratory, explanatory, or confirmatory. Each of these approaches is described in more detail below. Next you need to determine the specific data that will be used for the analysis and why. This decision, which we describe as *bounding the view*, is described in more detail below.

Once the boundaries of the analysis have been defined, you need to decide the specifics of how the text data will be coded. There are three components to this decision. First, you need to decide what tools you are going to use in the coding process. Choosing a qualitative data analysis (QDA) software program is an obvious first step. Depending on the capabilities of the QDA program and the complexity of the data, you may also need to choose programs to assist with tracking the analysis process. For example, for a large, complex study you may want to use a spreadsheet or quantitative database program to track specific analysis tasks such as coding assignments and intercoder agreement assessments. Second, you need to specify the codebook development process, especially if there will be more than one coder. Will there be specific formats used for codes (e.g., prefixes, numbering, standardized abbreviations) or will coding be done in vivo (i.e., coding for words or phrases within the text)? Will you use a structured codebook definition (e.g., with explicit instructions on when to use and when not to use the code), or will code definitions be developed along the lines of coding notes that are associated with specific text? Third, if there is more than one coder working with the data, you will need to specify the steps taken to ensure that the coders agree about the code definitions and which codes appropriately describe the meaning in the text. In Table 2.4, we provide a list of suggestions of items to include, or at least consider, in a qualitative analysis plan.

Table 2.4   Items to Consider for Inclusion in an Analysis Plan

- Specify how many separate analyses will be conducted and the timeline for each
- For each separate analysis specify:
  - Which research question(s) it will inform and how
  - Precisely which data will be used
  - How many people will be involved in the analysis and their specific roles
  - The primary analytic purpose—e.g., to identify, explore, explain, confirm, compare (note the verb used is very important so choose carefully)
  - How codes will be created and defined, including structural codes
  - Rules for applying codes to the data (e.g., will all text be coded?)
  - How coding reliability will be established, including reconciling discrepancies
  - Which data reduction techniques, if any, will be applied
  - Which between-group comparisons, if any, will be made, and how this will be done
  - How data from different data collection methods will be integrated (including quantitative data, if any)
  - What you expect as an output (e.g., in-house report, manuscript for peer-review journal, chapter in thesis)

CHOOSING AN ANALYTIC APPROACH

For analysis of primary data, the choice of analytic approach should be made in the design stages of research. There should be a clear match between the data collection and the analytic approach, with appropriate consideration of the resources that will be available once the data are in hand. Here, we briefly outline three broad approaches to analysis within qualitative research and indicate how they relate to applied thematic analysis.

Exploratory Analysis

Exploratory analysis is the classic content-driven, inductive approach that most people associate with qualitative research. It can range from a comprehensive ethnographic description of a complex social system to a focused formative assessment intended to inform the design and implementation of a formal evaluation. In exploratory analysis, the emphasis is on what emerges from the interaction between researcher and respondent. The content of that interaction drives the development of codes and the identification of themes. In this regard, the skill and sophistication of those collecting the data determine the extent to which the analysis will be successful. If the data lack richness and nuance, the analysis will similarly be lacking. Thus, in exploratory data analysis it is critically important to conduct quality checks in order to gain some sense of whether what emerges is likely to be more or less inclusive of what may have potentially emerged.

The method most commonly associated with exploratory qualitative analysis is grounded theory. As previously noted, grounded theory was specifically developed for comprehensive analysis of the richness and nuance of exploratory qualitative research. It is the most inductive of the approaches and was designed to guard against interpretive bias in the subjective analysis of textual data. The classic grounded theory approach uses all text generated from a particular data collection event such as an interview. Because of the intensity of the analytic approach, it is difficult to implement with extensive textual data. However, a modified approach can be successfully used in applied thematic analysis for subsets of textual data, if the data collection is appropriately designed.

An example will help to illustrate how applied thematic analysis can be used in a single study to provide both depth and breadth in addressing a research question. This example is drawn from qualitative interview data on the experience of "community" collected as part of a multisite study undertaken in the mid-1990s to identify effective strategies for meeting the social challenges surrounding implementation of HIV vaccine trials. An important foundational question for this research was to understand how community was conceptualized among the diverse U.S. groups with a stake in HIV vaccine trials. Qualitative interviews were conducted with 25 African Americans in Durham, North Carolina; 26 gay and bisexual men in San Francisco, California; 25 injection-drug users in Philadelphia, Pennsylvania; and 42 HIV vaccine researchers across the United States. The interviews covered a range of topics related to the way people experienced and understood community. Using an applied thematic analysis strategy, we extracted all of the responses to a single question: "What does the word community mean to you?" The extracted text was read, and a set of initial codes and definitions developed. Using the iterative codebook development process described in Chapter 3, two coders independently coded all of the text, and intercoder agreement checks were conducted, with adjustments to the codebook and recoding of text as needed. Numeric matrices were then generated to summarize which codes occurred together and then cluster analyzed to identify core elements used to define community, using the strategies described in Chapter 6. The cluster analysis helped identify similarities in the way people defined community as well as how those definitions varied across the participant groups. A key finding was the identification of a common definition of community shared by all participant groups, as *a group of people with diverse characteristics who are linked by social ties, share common perspectives, and engage in joint action in geographical locations or settings* (MacQueen et al., 2001).

The San Francisco research team simultaneously conducted a more in-depth analysis of community members' descriptions of subgroups of gay and bisexual men. They abstracted substantial sections of the text, including responses to questions on how respondents spent their time, the groups they spent time with or were a part of, the different parts or groups that made up the local gay/bisexual community, and discussions of cultural variation within the community. The analysis identified 32 discrete categories of groups cited by the study participants. They then tested whether these groups met theoretically driven criteria of perceived boundaries, evaluating whether the group was recognized by men who identified with it as well as by those who did not. The researchers identified five major subgroup categories that they labeled leather, men of color, activists, men who go to clubs, and younger men. The descriptive analysis of the responses identified important tensions between the drive to coalesce around common identities and the need to accommodate heterogeneity.

> This understanding offers a different model of community belonging . . . which we will call a multiconstitutive model. In a multiconstitutive community, subcultures and subgroups share their members with a larger community, thereby structuring the gay community as a meta-community formed from the amalgamation of groups within it. These subgroups and subcommunities may not detract from attachment to the gay community, but may be the primary way that many men connect with the diffuse and nebulous thing we call "the" gay community. (Peacock, Eyre, Quinn, & Kegeles, 2001, p. 198)

These findings from analysis at a narrower field of view enriched one of the findings from the cross-site analysis of definitions of community, which was that for gay/bisexual men in San Francisco, a strong sense of shared history and perspective was the most dominant theme, followed by a sense of identity with a specific location, the creation of strong and lasting social ties, established avenues for joint action, and the role of diversity. In contrast to the other participant groups, "Most of the San Francisco participants had thought about community, and many were struggling to reconcile their need for community with a sense of marginalization from society at large" (MacQueen et al., 2001, p. 1935). The more targeted analysis, thus, also added a comparative context to the data, illustrating differences and similarities between groups.

Explanatory Analysis

Explanatory or conceptual qualitative research uses a combination of deductive and inductive methods and is an increasingly important approach within applied qualitative research. Because such analyses are often used to inform decision making, concerns about the validity of the research are heightened. Such concerns are in fact justified if the research is premised on a philosophical rejection of objective reality and combined with an interpretation that centers on the research-er's subjective and unchallenged interpretation of the research experience. To address these concerns, we and others have focused on the identification and development of techniques that minimize the potential for what Morse and Mitcham (2002) have described as *conceptual tunnel vision,* that is, "the over-categorization of data, assigning more data to one category than actually belongs, or seeing or justifying most things as being related to, or considered examples of, the concept being investigated" (p. 30). Tunnel vision can also lead to unwarranted exclusion of relevant findings, functioning like blinders that block out data that challenge the framing of particular concepts, thereby making the data functionally invisible. To improve validity in conceptual or explanatory analysis it is critically important to explicitly note when a particular code or theme is linked to the data as well as when it is not linked to the data (see Chapter 3 for more discussion).

Morse and Mitcham (2002) outline a stepwise conceptual research process that includes deconstructing the concept to be explored from the existing literature, developing a skeletal conceptual framework for data collection that focuses inquiry but does not sharply define its limits, and using previous work as a scaffold to explore the internal structure and dynamics of the concept. This is an approach we are currently using in a series of related studies that seek to understand the contribution of concurrent sexual partnerships, or sexual concurrency, to high HIV prevalence rates in southern Africa. Concurrency is generally understood as the situation where a person has two or more sexual relationships that overlap in time. Epidemiologic and behavioral surveys in high HIV prevalence countries in south-ern Africa suggest that sexual concurrency may be sufficiently prevalent to be an important driver of the epidemic. Computer simulations incorporating empirical evidence from the surveys indicate that the reported rates of concurrency could in fact generate the observed HIV prevalence rates. From this evidence, we devel-oped a conceptual framework of sexual concurrency that served as the *skeleton* (in Morse and Mitcham's terminology) for data collection on both the cultural framing of sexual partnerships and the individual experience of such partnerships in five communities in Lesotho. The results from our Lesotho study, which included 30 focus groups and 93 in-depth interviews, were combined with results from other qualitative research on concurrency in southern Africa; this then provided a more substantial *scaffold* for designing a study of concurrency in seven communi-ties in Zambia. The Zambian study, which centers on 300 in-depth interviews, will ultimately be combined with the data from the 93 Lesotho in-depth interviews and analyzed quantitatively as well as qualitatively. In addition, the Lesotho data are being further used as a scaffold to plan a more comprehensive and largely quanti-tative sexual network study in that country.

Importantly, the sexual concurrency research in Lesotho and Zambia was initi-ated by governmental agencies in both countries with support from the Joint United Nations Programme on HIV/AIDS (UNAIDS), the U.S. Agency for International Development, and others. The data were explicitly collected to inform HIV preven-tion programming and policy. The funding and timelines were constrained, yet maintaining scientific standards was critically important given the way the resulting data would be used. The data are sufficiently rich to inform theory, but the first priority in our analysis was to explain why and how concurrency occurs, and ultimately provide timely and valid data for informed decision making by national and international policy makers confronting a persistent epidemic.

Confirmatory Analysis

In the introduction to this book, we outlined the basic differences between exploratory and confirmatory approaches. Here, we discuss considerations for planning a confirmatory analysis.

The first point to recognize is that a confirmatory analysis is testing or assessing a hypothesis; the purpose is to confirm (or reject) a predetermined idea. As such, the procedures involved are more rigorous and less flexible than in a traditional inductive analysis. In fact, there is very little induction involved. In a confirmatory analysis, the conceptual categories are determined *prior* to reviewing the text, and codes are generated from your hypotheses. Creating and defining these codes is an arduous, multistep process. For example, Hirschman (1987) wanted to test hypotheses she had related to gender and resources. In her study, she compared the expression of predetermined themes ("categories") in personal ads placed by men and by women in two large periodicals. The confirmatory nature of the study required going beyond simply creating categories and looking for them in the data. The researcher first verified that all of her 10 categories (i.e., codes) were identifiable in the ads and ensured that items were exhaustive and mutually exclusive. She did this with two other analysts to enhance reliability. Her study also employed a random sample large enough to carry out a comparative statistical analysis to test her hypotheses. In addition, strict procedures were put in place, such as blinding the data analysts to the hypotheses and conducting frequent coding agreement checks, to enhance credibility of her results. Once all of the text had been read, the data coded, and coding agreement assessed, the analysis was finished; there was no room for iteration. The bottom line is that a confirmatory analysis requires more structured procedures at all stages of the analysis process, and in some ways is more similar to quantitative analysis. We refer the reader to other books that provide more detailed instruction for a confirmatory analysis (Krippendorf, 2003; Neuendorf, 2001; Weber, 1990).

Comparative Analysis: Special Considerations

If you are planning a comparative analysis, the analysis plan should outline how that will be achieved. First, you need to identify the unit of analysis for purposes of comparison. For example, if you are coding transcripts from focus group discussions, there are several options for looking at simple frequencies. You could count the number of transcripts where a code was ever applied, in which case the unit of analysis is the focus group discussion. Alternately, you could count the number of participants in all focus groups whose comments were coded with a particular code, and the unit of analysis is then the individual participant. This approach requires data collection and transcription procedures that allow for the identification of each speaker. Or, you could count the total number of times a code was applied across all transcripts, in which case the unit of analysis is the text segment. One-on-one interviews require similar decisions. These decisions are described in more detail in Chapters 3 and 6.

The most basic comparative approach in qualitative data analysis is to note themes present in the text from each group being compared and determine which themes are the same and which are different. If the number of data collection events is sufficiently large, you can compare the frequency with which codes are applied to text derived from different populations, subgroups, or categories of people to see if the overall patterning is similar or different. If the sampling procedures for data collection are statistically robust and the number of data collection events sufficiently large, you can evaluate whether differences are statistically significant. You can use graphing or clustering techniques to compare patterns of discourse in the text from different subgroups. The analytic choices for comparing qualitative data are quite rich; Chapter 6 provides an overview of these options.

Finally, consider whether the data collection process is sufficiently similar across the groups to be compared. Here again, an initial scan of the data is important for determining whether the questions asked and the richness of the data collected will permit a meaningful comparison.

A BRIEF NOTE ON THEORY

As noted, our focus in applied thematic analysis is primarily inductive. Its strength lies in openness to theory building rather than a particular approach. If we consider the explanatory/conceptual, confirmatory, and comparative approaches described above, applied thematic analysis provides basic building blocks. First, as described in detail in Chapter 3, the code-based approach supports the development of taxonomies or classification schemes to aid in sorting and describing the data. A thoughtfully developed codebook serves as a taxonomy, a rich summary description of the range and depth of the data. Second, as described in Chapters 4 through 6, the codebook in combination with descriptive characteristics of the data sources (e.g., participants, observational settings) permits a systematic exploration of relationships in the data as well as comparative analyses of those relationships. Finally, although the analysis process is inductive, it can be incorporated into a multistage, iterative research design where theory in the form of inductive explanation generates hypotheses that can be investigated deductively.

BOUNDING THE ANALYTIC VIEW

Earlier we referred to *bounding the view* as an important decision in the development of an analysis plan. The decision involves answering three essential questions: (1) What sources of data (e.g., groups, events, individuals) should I include in my analysis? From those sources, (2) What conceptual/analytic domains should I include? And, (3) What specific questions should I include in my analysis? Remember, when we talk about your analysis we are referring to a specific analysis project that will provide you with the data needed for a given deliverable (e.g., report for funder, journal article, book chapter, conference poster, news brief, etc.). In most research studies, particularly larger ones, there are generally multiple deliverables, and therefore multiple analyses.

While establishing the boundaries of a particular analysis may seem like an important first step, it is in fact contingent on so many factors that it should be one of the last decisions made. Before you can decide what data you will use in an analysis, you need to know what data are available, how the data were collected, how rich the data are, and what gaps exist in the data. That is, you need to know what you are looking at—what is the view provided by the available data?

There is an old joke about a man standing under a streetlight, scanning the ground. A stranger asks him what he is doing and he says he lost his keys and is looking for them. The stranger asks where he lost them, and the man says "Down the street." The stranger then asks why he is not looking down the street and the man replies, "Because this is where the light is." Once you are at the point where you are ready to analyze your qualitative data, you are in the same fix as the man looking for his keys--you can only look at the ground where you let the light of your inquiry shine. This is the hard boundary within which all of your subsequent analysis decisions need to be made.

Bounding the view is essentially a question of what data to use to answer specific research questions. It is driven by the analytic objectives and is a key part of the analysis plan. In its essence, it is a process of data selection by source (e.g., individual, group, observation event), domain of inquiry, and/or question asked. Here we illustrate this process with two examples from our research.

Prioritizing Analyses From a Large Database

We conducted sociobehavioral research in parallel with a clinical trial that sought to test the safety and potential effectiveness of an antiretroviral for preventing the acquisition of HIV—a strategy generally referred to as pre-exposure prophylaxis, or PrEP. The research sought to facilitate the implementation of the trial in three West African settings and to gather information on the acceptability of PrEP and on the participants' experiences of being in the trial. The research included three phases (pretrial, trial, and post-trial) and lasted more than 3 years. A wide range of participant groups were recruited, including trial participants, clinical trial study staff, policy makers, government and nongovernment service providers, advocates, and media representatives. The research ultimately generated more than 500 in-depth interviews, 28 focus groups, and 78 participant observation events. The data available for analysis also included structured sociobehavioral data from trial participants across 13 time points. Each data collection instrument included multiple domains of inquiry. Adding to the complexity, only one site actually completed the clinical trial; the other two sites closed prematurely, one due to controversies surrounding the trial and the other due to logistical challenges. Thus, the qualitative data collected during the trial and after trial closure varied greatly from site to site. We were simultaneously confronted with a richness of data and real constraints on our ability to analyze them.

We needed to figure out where to start. First, as part of our on-going quality control, we maintained a comprehensive spreadsheet of data collection instruments and the sites where they were implemented. All transcripts were structurally coded so we were able to determine if there were significant missing data on particular questions. We could also quickly run reports on specific questions to review the richness of the data. We were thus able to identify a short list of key issues of interest and importance to the field and a parallel list of the most robust data on those issues in our database.

We chose three topics for priority analysis. First, we looked at pregnancy decision making among women enrolled in the clinical trial. A number of biomedical HIV prevention trials among women in Africa had encountered difficulties due to high pregnancy rates among participants. Because of concerns about fetal risks, women enrolled in such trials were taken off the study product if they became pregnant. This then decreased the statistical power of the trial and hence the ability of the research to definitively assess safety and effectiveness. The women enrolled in our PrEP trial had high rates of pregnancy, and to understand why, we had added questions about their use of contraception before and during the trial to one of our interview guides. Second, we looked at whether being in the trial was associated with increases or decreases in self-reported risk behavior (a phenomenon known as "risk disinhibition," "risk compensation," or "risk enhancement"). Concerns about risk disinhibition are often raised with regard to biomedical HIV prevention trials, where the actual effectiveness of the intervention is unknown and upwards of half of the participants are receiving a placebo. Third, we looked at the extent to which the trial participants found daily use of the antiretroviral pill to be acceptable. If the women in the trial found it difficult to remember to take the pill, or if they did not like the pill, or if using the pill led to stigma or other problems, there were obvious ramifications for evaluating the effectiveness of the pill for preventing HIV and also for developing viable PrEP programs if the pill were shown to be safe and effective in the clinical trial context. For each of these analysis topics, we strategically chose a combination of qualitative and quantitative data. Below, we elaborate on how we chose data sources to bound the analysis for the risk disinhibition analysis.

The primary question behind the risk disinhibition analysis was: Did the women in the trial change their sexual behavior over the course of the trial? And if so, we posed a secondary question: What accounted for any changes observed? Hence, our objective was to document and explain changes in sexual risk-taking among trial participants. To achieve this objective in an efficient manner, we needed to select only the data most relevant to our goal and underlying research questions. To address the first question, we selected quantitative data collected from all of the study participants at each monthly visit (13 time points, including baseline). We only selected data from the Ghana site because data sets for the other two sites were incomplete because of the early trial closures. Further, we decided that the quantitative measures most relevant to our analysis were (1) condom use over the past 7 days and (2) the number of different sexual partners in the past 30 days. We graphed data from these two measures and carried out a statistical Growth Curve Analysis to assess change over time and the correlates of change. In Figure 2.1, the line with circle shapes shows the trajectory for the entire study population, with respect to number of sexual partners. For a more detailed account of the analysis and our findings, we refer readers to the original article (Guest et al., 2008).

Figure 2.1 Number of Male Partners per Month During Trial

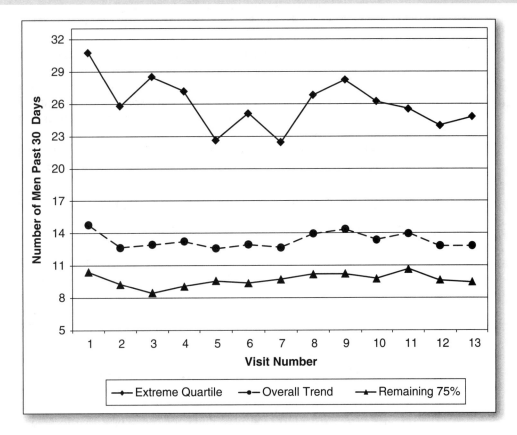

In order to address the second question, we looked to the qualitative data and chose for our analysis in-depth interviews administered to trial participants halfway through their participation in the trial. Again, we chose data only from the Ghana site. We also selected just 2 of the 20 or so open-ended questions, from one domain of the in-depth interviews to analyze (note that a targeted analysis like this is made much simpler with the use of a semistructured instrument and structural codes).

These questions, and their subquestions, below, related specifically to our analytic objective and were used to explain trends observed in the quantitative data (we elaborate further on how we integrated the two types of data in Chapter 8).

(1) Has participating in this clinical trial affected your condom use? If so, please explain.

How do you feel about these changes?

What do you think are the reasons for these changes?

(2) How has participating in this clinical trial affected the number of sexual partners you have?

How do you feel about these changes?

What do you think are the reasons for these changes?

The most important point to take away from this example is that we chose only those data that we felt were most relevant to our objectives. We could have included additional data, both qualitative and quantitative, but it would have taken more time and resources to analyze and interpret and would have provided relatively little additional information pertaining to our analytic aims. Always keep in mind the law of diminishing returns. We have often seen researchers unnecessarily bogged down in analytic complexity because they want to include as much data in their analysis as possible. We find it much more effective to break down a large study into several manageable analyses and choose only those data sources and items that will most inform each analysis, as we did in the above example.

Assessing Strengths and Weaknesses in Data

Other factors to consider when selecting data for an analysis are robustness and validity. Not only should data be relevant to the analytic objectives, they must also be of good quality. A study managed by one of the book's authors illustrates this point well. Tasked with discovering reasons for inaccurate reporting of sexual behavior (a well-documented problem in reproductive health research), Guest and colleagues designed and managed a qualitative study called the Social Desirability Bias (SDB) study (Guest et al., 2005). It was carried out in three African cities—Ibadan, Nigeria; Tema, Ghana; and Gaborone, Botswana. At each site, 30 women at high risk for HIV/AIDS were administered in-depth interviews focusing on how they talk about sexual behavior. The interview guide was composed of 17 questions spread across three conceptual domains—cultural dimensions of sexual discussion, talking about sex in a research context, and perceptions of commonly used techniques in research to enhance accuracy of self-reported behavior (e.g., audio-computer-assisted-self-interviews [ACASI], gender-matching of interviewer/interviewee, etc.). The guide was semistructured, with identical open-ended questions in the same order (but that also permitted inductive probing). The content and format, at least initially, were the same across all three sites. The overall analysis objective was comparative; the plan was to compare data across the three sites, looking for similarities and differences.

As any experienced researcher knows, the real world has a way of humbling research designs. Our SDB study proved to be no exception. The institutional review board (IRB) associated with our U.S. government collaborator for the Botswana site laid down our first bump in the road. After reviewing the protocol and in-depth interview guide, they essentially told us that we needed to ask questions about abstinence and being faithful, to provide a balance for the questions about condom use (the project was reviewed in the political environment of 2003). We had no choice but to oblige if the research were to go forward, even though we felt that adding such questions would disrupt the flow of the interview, potentially offend the participants (many of whom were sex workers), and would provide no useful information. The ethics approval process for the Botswana site also took longer than the other two sites. Because of IRB recommendations and policies, data collection in Botswana ultimately utilized a different instrument than the other two sites and data collection was significantly delayed.

We encountered another challenge when we began analyzing data. Despite pretesting the instrument and monitoring for data quality, data obtained in one of the three domains were extremely weak. The responses were thin and indicated that participants did not really understand the intent behind the questions; their validity was suspect. Faced with these challenges, we had to make some decisions regarding what data to include and how we would parse out the analyses. Our first decision was to analyze the Botswana data separately. We felt that the instrument was too different from the one used at the other two sites to effectively compare the resulting data. We also did not want to delay the analysis of the Nigeria and Ghana data while we waited for data collection in Botswana to be completed. Our second decision was not to include the weak data from the conceptual domain poorly understood by participants based on the likelihood that the views presented there were invalid. We excluded these data from all of the analyses. The result was two separate analyses and subsequent articles—one summarizing the Botswana data (Chillag et al., 2006), the other data from Nigeria and Ghana and including a comparative analysis (Guest et al., 2005) that excluded one of the three domains of questions.

As a side note, we also conducted a methodological analysis with data from the Nigeria and Ghana sites. Because the data from these sites were robust and could be meaningfully aggregated, we did our substantive analysis in a stepwise manner that documented codebook development and application of codes after the analysis of every 6 in-depth interviews, until all 60 interviews were coded. Based on this analysis and audit trail, we identified points of data saturation within and across the data sets from the two sites. The resulting article provides one of the few evidence bases for estimating nonprobablistic sample sizes (Chillag, Guest, Bunce, & Johnson, 2006).

In sum, you need to have an analysis plan, but be prepared to be flexible and responsive to exigencies that present themselves on the ground. Data may not always be of good enough quality to include in your analysis (which is *not* to say that you should not include negative cases or present contradictory evidence in your findings. We argue against such exclusions in Chapter 4). At the same time, make the most of your data. A data set may address more than your primary ana-lytic objectives, and responding to these secondary or tertiary objectives may turn out to have more impact than one might imagine. The secondary, methodological, objective of identifying points of thematic saturation in the example above proved to be an important contribution to the field of qualitative research methods, despite the challenges encountered during analysis of the primary objective.

SUMMING UP

The key to developing an effective analysis plan to answer a research question is to identify the discrete activities that need to take place in order to achieve your desired outcome. The Appendix summarizes the four key elements that are generated in the analysis of qualitative data and thus provides an overview of the process. Each element corresponds to a fundamental type of informa-tion collected in the research process. First, there are the characteristics of the sources where answers to research questions are sought. As noted previously, the sources may be individual people (including the research team) or groups of people or institutions. Second, there is the primary information collected from the sources, for example, the transcripts of interviews or focus groups. Third, there is information generated to assist in the interpretation of the pri-mary information, referred to here as secondary information to distinguish it from what is obtained directly from the sources. This secondary information includes codes, code definitions, and coding notes; the linkages between the source information and the codes, definitions, and notes; and descriptive sum-maries of the source information such as word frequencies, code frequencies, code co-occurrence matrices, and the like. Finally, there is information about the characteristics of the coders who generate the secondary information. This framework emphasizes an object-oriented definition of data where data are defined as any digital representation, including photographs, graphic displays, video, sound, text, and numeric data. All of these representations are essentially database objects or artifacts created by people. Some are created to describe or explain other objects in the database (the who, what, where, why, and how of the objects). By considering the relationships among and the content within each of these elements of a research project, qualitative researchers can systematically organize their data to make analysis and the reporting of results more efficient and reliable (MacQueen & Milstein, 1999).

Although such an overview is helpful, it is important to remember that the process is dynamic and iterative. The goal of the analysis journey is not reached by taking the shortest path between research question and answer. It is an explora-tion of little-known territory, and at the end of exploration, you should have a map that others can use to more efficiently understand and explore the same territory.

REFERENCES

Chillag, K., Guest, G., Bunce, A., Johnson, L., Kilmarx, P., & Smith, D. (2006). Talking about sex in Botswana: Social desirability bias and its possible implications for HIV prevention research. *African Journal of AIDS Research, 5*(2), 123–131.

Chillag, K., Guest, G., Bunce, A., & Johnson, L. (2006). How many interviews are enough? An experiment with data saturation and variability. *Field Methods, 18*, 59–82.

Guest, G., & MacQueen, K. (Eds.). (2008). *Handbook for team-based qualitative research.* Lanham, MD: AltaMira Press.

Guest, G., Bunce, A., Johnson, L., Akumatey, B., & Adeokun, L. (2005). Fear, hope, and social desirability bias among women at high risk for HIV in West Africa. *Journal of Family Planning and Reproductive Health Care, 31*(4), 285–287.

Guest, G., Shattuck, D., Johnson, L., Akumatey, B., Clarke, E., Chen, P., & MacQueen, K. (2008). Changes in sexual risk behavior among participants in a PrEP HIV prevention trial. *Sexually Transmitted Diseases, 35*(12), 1002–1008.

Hirschman, E. C. (1987). People as products: Analysis of a complex marketing exchange. *Journal of Marketing, 51,* 98–108.

Krippendorf, K. (2003). *Content analysis: An introduction to its methodology.* Thousand Oaks, CA: Sage.

MacQueen, K. M., McLellan, E., Metzger, D., Kegeles, S., Strauss, R., Scotti, R. Blanchard, L., & Trotter, R. (2001). What is community? An evidence-based definition for participatory public health. *American Journal of Public Health, 91*(12), 1929–1938.

MacQueen K. M., & Milstein, B. (1999). A systems approach to qualitative data analysis and management. *Field Methods, 11*(1), 27–39.

Miles, M., & Huberman, M. (1994). *Qualitative data analysis* (2nd ed). Thousand Oaks, CA: Sage.

Morse, J., & Mitcham, C. (2002). Exploring qualitatively derived concepts: Inductive-deductive methods. *International Journal of Qualitative Methods, I*(4), Article 3. Retrieved from http://ejournals.library.ualberta.ca/index.php/IJQM/article/view/4589

Neuendorf, K. (2001). *The content analysis guidebook.* Thousand Oaks, CA: Sage.

Peacock B, Eyre, S., Quinn, S., & Kegeles, S. (2001). Delineating differences: Sub-communities in the San Francisco gay community. *Culture, Health & Sexuality, 3*(2), 183–201.

Schensul, S. L., Schensul, J. J., & LeCompte, M. D. (1999). *Essential ethnographic methods: Observations, interviews, and questionnaires, ethnographer's toolkit* (Vol. 2). Lanham, MD: AltaMira Press.

Weber, R. (1990). *Basic content analysis: Quantitative applications in the social sciences.* Thousand Oaks, CA: Sage.

EXERCISES

Using the list of items to consider in an analysis plan provided in Table 2.4, write a comprehensive analysis plan for an existing or anticipated thematic analysis. Be as specific as possible. Draw a flow diagram outlining the procedures and actors involved. Review your plan and check to see if you (or we) have missed anything that might be important to note.

ADDITIONAL READING

Dey, I. (1993). Finding a focus. *Qualitative data analysis: A user-friendly guide for social scientists* (pp. 63–73). New York: Routledge.

Miles, M., & Huberman, M. (1994). Focusing and bounding the collection of data. *Qualitative data analysis* (2nd ed., pp. 40–49). Thousand Oaks, CA: Sage.

Patton, M. (2000). Qualitative analysis and interpretation. *Qualitative research and evaluation methods* (3rd ed., pp. 431–534). Thousand Oaks, CA: Sage.

3

THEMES AND CODES

LEARNING OBJECTIVES

After reading this chapter, you should be able to:

- Describe several different strategies for segmenting text for analysis
- Describe the relationship between segmenting and coding
- Outline the steps for developing a codebook
- Describe the purposes of structural and content coding
- Develop clear code definitions that can be unambiguously applied to text by multiple coders

In many books and articles that describe qualitative data analysis, there are references to "making sense of the data." This oft-used metaphor for the qualitative journey of discovery unfortunately suggests that this is what the analyst should strive for—even if the data are problematic and can "make sense" only if interpreted in highly imaginative ways. In line with our exploration and mapping metaphor, a more accurate description is that of "locating meaning in the data." In applied thematic analysis, the goal should be a skillful expedition executed with forethought, appropriate tools, and systematic planning prior to entering unexplored terrain. Contrast this approach with the potential consequences of venturing unprepared into unknown lands. Although the unprepared adventurer may gain much by way of personal experience and arrive back home with interesting stories to tell and reflect upon, the skillful expedition is much more likely to make a substantive contribution to our collective understanding of the world we live in.

In Chapter 2, we described techniques for coming up with an analytic strategy, that is, a carefully considered plan of exploration. In this chapter, we describe how to survive the journey and ensure you come home with a useful, accurate representation of the territory. In applied thematic analysis, we achieve this goal through an iterative process of identifying features (i.e., themes) and defining boundaries around those features (i.e., text segmentation). We classify themes into two major categories. Structural topics are imposed by the research design and can have both direct and indirect effects on the resulting data. In mapping terms, these are the swathes of terrain that you actually traveled and observed. Content or emergent themes describe what is observed or discussed in the context of the imposed research design. Note that in applied thematic analysis we assume that there will be a researcher effect on the data; note also that we want to be able to describe the consequences of that effect as clearly as possible.

Before we describe the process any further, we thought it would be helpful to define our terms, since qualitative analysts often use the same terms in very different ways. Over time, we are optimistic that the terminology will sort itself out and, perhaps in another generation, a consensus will emerge that ends much of the confusion. For now, the best we can offer is clarity about the way we define basic terms in textual qualitative analysis.

Data: The textual representation of a conversation, observation, or interaction.

Theme: A unit of meaning that is observed (noticed) in the data by a reader of the text.

Code: A textual description of the semantic boundaries of a theme or a component of a theme.

Codebook: A structured compendium of codes that includes a description of how the codes are related to each other.

Coding: The process by which a qualitative analyst links specific codes to specific data segments.

TEXT SEGMENTATION

Applied thematic analysis makes considerable use of text segmentation as a tool. For small data sets consisting of a few focus groups or a handful of interviews it may not be necessary to develop an explicit segmentation strategy, especially if the goal is to rapidly identify and describe a limited number of major themes. However, for moderate to large data sets, segmentation is a vital applied thematic analysis mapping tool that must be used skillfully and thoughtfully.

Segmentation is a technique for bounding text in order to (1) assess and document the overall quality of the data and (2) facilitate the exploration of thematic elements and their similarity, dissimilarity, and relationships.

Segmentation frequently gets short shrift in discussions of coding, often not even appearing in the index of qualitative research textbooks specifically addressing qualitative analysis. In part, this reflects a concern about attempting to analyze text that has been abstracted from a larger context and potentially stripped of important cues and layers of meaning. Some qualitative researchers feel so strongly about the importance of preserving the larger context of the dialog that they are reluctant to highlight text segmentation as a technique for fear that it will be misused as an analytic shortcut. As argued by Gibson and Brown (2009), "The contexts in which people speak are fundamental to the meaning which they are creating. By removing that context from the analysis, researchers remove the resources that would enable them to understand why the speakers said what they did or, perhaps more accurately, 'why they said it how they did'" (p. 189).

Yet very little qualitative analysis is done that does not rely on some form of segmentation and abstraction of text at some point in the process. The analyst is continually confronted with questions about where meaning begins and ends, and how meanings intersect and interact. Ignoring the issue of segmentation in qualitative analysis is rather like a surveyor eye-balling the locations of features rather than using a compass, transit, and other appropriate tools to systematically plot a location. Good segmentation practices facilitate the analyst's ability to identify, map, and succinctly display the context and multidimensionality of the data used to answer a particular research question and, importantly, to easily return to the full context of any feature described on the data "map."

As in map-making, the defining of boundaries in segmentation is often somewhat arbitrary, and the process can take many forms. At the most arbitrary extreme would be a "key-word-in-context," or KWIC, approach that identifies a word as the locus for a theme or concept in a body of text without predefining the textual boundaries of that locus. KWIC is essentially a tag that allows the analyst to return to the original text; it is like a pin on a map. Some software programs can retrieve variable amounts of text associated with KWIC tags, that is, the analyst can define the number of lines or characters to be retrieved before and after the tag, rather like zooming in and out on a digital satellite map. Other programs either predetermine how much text can be retrieved or allow a limited set of options for retrieval. KWIC can be used as a kind of simple segment-and-code tool, but it is best used as a way of exploring and tagging text in the early stages of analysis so you can find your way back later. It can also be used as an exploratory tool in the process of developing a detailed codebook. More details on KWIC are described in Chapter 5.

A second approach entails the use of segments that are predefined via text formatting, and as such allow for minimal flexibility. Often, a hard return at the end of each line of text or paragraph is used to define automatically the boundaries between segments. Alternatively, the segments may be defined by textual coding embedded into the electronic document before it is imported into the software. In the early days of computer-assisted qualitative data analysis, this type of approach was common, but segmenting approaches have become more flexible as software programs have become more sophisticated in their ability to work with word-wrapped rich-text formatting.

The most typical approach to segmentation used in software programs today is one where the analyst identifies a beginning point and an ending point for each segment while reading the text during the coding process. There is considerable flexibility with regard to how much text is included, and also variability in software programs as to how easily segment boundaries can be modified while maintaining coding. This approach may allow for segments that overlap and for smaller segments embedded within larger ones. There is thus great potential for a highly nuanced analysis of text—and also for total chaos.

To maximize the potential for a nuanced analysis while avoiding chaos, the boundaries of a given segment should allow the thematic features of the segment to be clearly discerned when it is lifted from the larger context. In conversational text, this usually means capturing a complete thought, often discourse between speakers, and not simply a short, evocative phrase.

THE RELATIONSHIP BETWEEN SEGMENTING AND CODING

Segmenting text, identifying themes, and content coding are not distinct processes. In fact, the act of identifying a meaningful segment of text calls for some minimal representation of that meaning as a code, a note, a query, or a tag. This is not so much a multistep process but rather a multi-part description: you identify an instance of meaning in the text, note its locus, and describe it. What meaning is conveyed or signified as you read the text? The answer to this question leads to the identification of themes. How much of the text is critical to the meaning? This guides the choice of segment boundaries. What are the specific meaningful elements in the text? This shapes the specification of codes, their definitions, and their logical relationships.

Note that we distinguish the identification of themes from the specification of codes. As explained in more detail below, codes represent a greater level of abstraction than themes, and a single theme can engender multiple codes. In applied thematic analysis, the emphasis is on empirical investigation of the way in which meaningful elements or codes are combined to generate thematic or explanatory models. The use of systematic segmenting facilitates an efficient approach that can employ frequencies, matrices, and/or clusters to identify code combinations. These combinations are then explored through a targeted review of the associated text to develop descriptive and explanatory models (see Chapters 6 and 7).

THE CENTRALITY OF THE CODEBOOK

One of the most critical components of applied thematic analysis is the codebook. Codebook development is a discrete analysis step where the observed meaning in the text is systematically sorted into categories, types, and relationships of meaning. The text is reread and analyzed via segmenting and coding into these categories, types, and relationships. We generally do this in an iterative fashion, reading text in batches and modifying the codebook as new information and new insights are gained.

We deal with the inherent messiness of the text by minimizing messiness in the code definitions and maximizing coherence among the codes in the codebook. In the early steps of theme identification, the focus is on "What does this text mean to me?" As we move toward codebook development, the emphasis shifts to, "What specific instances of meaning exist in this text?" In the final stages of analysis, the focus again shifts, this time to ask, "Are there patterns of relationship among the instances of meaning in this text?" In this way, the codebook explicitly addresses the three general sets of aims in thematic analysis as outlined by Gibson and Brown (2009, pp. 128–129): examining commonalities, differences, and relationships. An applied thematic analysis codebook provides an efficient baseline for moving beyond basic description to an explanatory analysis.

From our perspective, many qualitative researchers spend much more time than necessary negotiating the cognitive interface between themes and codes. As will be described in more detail later, the human mind has a passion for finding meaning—and for creating meaning. We love to ponder maps where the known lands fade into blank expanses described cryptically as "Here Be Dragons" or where a mysterious "X" suggests buried treasure. Such maps can spur explorations that result in revolutionary expansions of our understanding of the world. However, they have also been known to spur fabrications based on rumor, ignorance, and prejudice.

In the early steps of applied thematic analysis, we may observe things that are intriguing and unexpected. We notice, tag the text, and make a few excited notes about the potential significance of the text. But, we do not linger; we do not elaborate dragon theories; and we do not code. We keep reading. Periodically we stop and compile our tags and notes about the themes we noticed and consider the components of meaning that seem to be emerging. We label those components and begin to define what they are, what they are not, and how they relate to each other. The result is the first draft of a codebook.

Then we start reading again, and this time we code the textual data using our defined concepts. If the coding is messy in places we stop, consider the sources of the messiness, refine the codes and definitions if they are contributing to the messiness—and then go back and start coding again. When all the coding is done, we look at the overall pattern of discourse and observation to see if the analysis provides evidence to support our initial perception of the importance of that which intrigued and excited, or whether our imaginations were at work in the gaps and unexplored areas.

How much information should be included in a code definition? Over the course of many different kinds of studies in many different settings over many years, we have come to the firm conclusion that a code definition needs to include the information below (MacQueen, McLellan-Lemal, Bartholow, & Milstein, 2008). We've provided an example from one of the author's studies in the text box that follows.

Code label: This should be a short, descriptive mnemonic (4–12 characters) that helps the coder quickly distinguish codes from each other. It can be somewhat cryptic and quirky so long as the reaction of the average new coder is to say "Aha! I get it!" (rather than "Uh, why did you call it that..?") when the logic behind the code labeling is explained.

Short definition: This should be a short, descriptive phrase (20–80 characters) that captures the essence of the theme or theme component(s) that the code is intended to signify. The short definition for a particular code should not duplicate meaning in the short definitions of any other codes in a given codebook.

Full definition: This should be a short, descriptive paragraph (2–10 sentences) that highlights the key features of the theme or theme component(s) that the code is intended to signify. If there are important theoretical, conceptual, or cultural dimensions to the code, this is the place to reference them. However, keep in mind that the codebook is not meant to be a compendium of theories and concepts.

When to use: This should explicitly describe the textual cues and context that signify thematic meaning and prompt the analyst to use the code to link the text with that meaning. It is also helpful to make note of instances where the coder may want to consider the use of other codes ("double-coding") to describe the meaning of the text.

When not to use: This should explicitly describe any textual cues and context that signify thematic meaning associated with other codes but that potentially overlap with or could be confused with the code being defined. It should direct the coder to these other codes so he or she can consider whether they better capture the meaning of the text in question.

Example Code Definition

Code: MARGIN

Brief Definition: Marginalized community members

Full Definition: Community groups that are negatively perceived as socially and/or physically outside the larger community structure. In marginalized groups, boundaries are imposed by others to keep "unfavorable" groups from participating in or interacting with the mainstream community groups.

When to Use: Apply this code to all references to groups of individuals that the larger community has marginalized. These individuals or groups may be referred to as outcasts, extremists, radicals, or explicitly described as peripherals, strangers, outsiders, ostracized, bizarre, and so on.

When Not to Use: Do not use this code for reference to community groups institutionalized for health or criminal reasons (see INSTIT) or for groups that have voluntarily placed themselves on the outer boundaries of community life (see SELFMAR).

Example: "Then you got the outcasts—drug dealers, junkies, prostitutes."

These definitional boundaries between codes will be arbitrary to varying degrees; the more arbitrary they are, the more important it is to define them clearly. Doing so will not reduce ambiguity in the original text; that is not the goal. The textual data are what they are. The point is to reduce ambiguity in the coding process. Ambiguous code definitions cast shadows on the reading of the text. If two people are coding the same text differently, you want to know why and you want to resolve that difference in a way that illuminates the data. If the arbitrary boundary between two code definitions is obscuring the analysis, change the boundary until you get clarity. If clarity is unachievable, consider the possibility that you are hunting for dragons; that is, trying to impose clarity on text that is hopelessly obscure.

STRUCTURAL CODING

In Chapter 2 we touched on an approach we call structural coding, which is used to identify the structure imposed on a qualitative data set by the research questions and design. As noted, this is most clearly seen when a structured interview or focus group guide is used in a consistent way. The text can then be segmented based on the questions or prompts asked by the data collector(s) together with the responses from the research participants. As long as the data collectors follow the structured guide, there is usually a clear start and end point in the transcript for each guide-driven text segment.

A structural codebook uses the structured guide as the basis for code development. Each question in the structured guide forms the basis for a structural code, and the code definition generally includes both the main question and any probes intended to enrich the response to the question. When doing structural coding, the analyst looks for cues in the text to determine where the data collector began eliciting a response to a question set out in the structured guide—that text denotes the beginning of the text segment that will be associated with the structural code for that question. The text segment then includes the response of the participant to the question and any subsequent probes and dialogue about the question. Identifying the end of the text segment is often easy in a structured interview or focus group because the data collectors usually give linguistic cues as they move on to the next question: "Thank you, that was really interesting. Now I'd like to ask you about…." or "Hmm, what you just said leads us to another topic I wanted to talk to you about…." Of course, such cues also tell you where the next structured question begins.

The following example illustrates the structural coding process. It is excerpted from a study where Namey and colleagues used a semistructured interview guide to elicit opinions on the disposition of frozen embryos from infertility patients (Lyerly, 2006). The interview began by asking participants to reflect on a few of the positives and negatives about having frozen embryos in storage, moved on to ask about the effects of having frozen embryos on family life, and concluded with discussion of several existing options for disposition of frozen embryos. The interviews were conducted in person with women, men, and couples who had frozen embryos stored as a result of in vitro fertilization attempts. Figure 3.1 includes a few of the questions from the guide, along with the general question topic in the margin. The abbreviation FE is used for frozen embryos.

Using the interview guide as our starting point, we developed a set of structural codes for these questions, as described in Table 3.1. Note that the code definitions reflect the specific language of the interview guide. This ensured there was no confusion between the intent of the data collection process and the outcome of that process. In this example, we arranged the structural codes for the questions labeled 2, 3, and 4 within a placeholder or network code; that way we could easily pull all of the text associated with the effect of frozen embryos on families or just the text associated with the specific questions in that part of the interview. Different qualitative analysis programs provide different tools for doing this kind of grouping of related codes.

Figure 3.1   Structural Coding Example: The Interview Guide

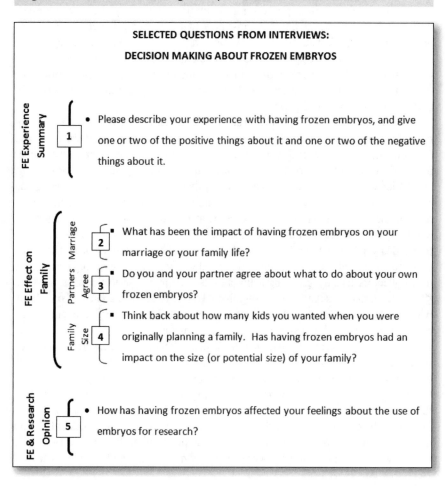

Table 3.1   Structural Coding Example—The Codebook

Interview Topic	Q#	Structural Code Name	Structural Code Definition
FE Experience Summary	**1**	**Pros/Cons**	**Brief Definition:** Pros and cons of having frozen embryos
			Full Definition: Participant opinions about the advantages and disadvantages of having frozen embryos in storage. *IDI Guide*: Please describe your experience with having frozen embryos, and give one or two of the positive things about it and one or two of the negative things about it.
			When to Use: Use this code to capture expressions of the good things and the bad things about having frozen embryos that are in direct response to Question 1 and all associated probes. May include consideration of reproductive, convenience, financial, and/or moral issues.
			When Not to Use: Do not use this code for discussion of the pros and cons of having frozen embryos that appear in responses to questions other than Question 1; use the appropriate FE Experience content code instead, along with the relevant structural code.
FE Effect on Family	**2,3,4**	**FamEffect**	**NOTE:** This is a placeholder or network code only; do not use for coding purposes. Responses to Questions 2, 3, and 4 belong to this network, but will be captured under their respective structural codes (Fam_Marriage, Fam_PartAgree, Fam_Size). Text structurally coded at any one of those three codes will automatically be associated with this placeholder code during analysis.
FE Effect on Family **---Partner Agreement**	**3**	**Fam_PartAgree**	**Brief Definition:** Discussion of partner agreement or disagreement about FEs
			Full Definition: Participant discussion of whether or not there is agreement between spouses or parental partners about what to do with or how to dispose of FEs. *IDI Guide*: Do you and your partner agree about what to do about your own frozen embryos? Probe: Tell me a little more about your position(s).

(Continued)

Table 3.1   (Continued)

Interview Topic	Q#	Structural Code Name	Structural Code Definition
			When to Use: Use this code to capture discussion of partner agreement about disposition of FEs that is in direct response to Question 3 and all associated probes. May include agreement, disagreement, and/or uncertainty.
			When Not to Use: Do not use this code for discussion of partner agreement issues that appear in responses to questions other than Question 3; use the appropriate FE Effect on Family content code instead, along with the relevant structural code.

The first column in the table provides the general topic or intent of the question or set of questions. The second column provides the question number (assigned for illustrative purposes), while the third lists the code name. The fourth column provides the code definition. For brevity, only two codes and the placeholder code are included here.

Once the codebook was established, we could systematically review transcripts to segment and assign structural codes. Figure 3.2 provides an example of an interview transcript segmented and tagged with structural codes (the corresponding question number in this example). "INT" in the transcript refers to the interviewer and "RES" to the respondent. Figure 3.3 displays the same process in qualitative data analysis software NVivo 9.

The example transcript here is relatively crisp and clean, following the question/answer, question/answer format closely. Often, however, a response to a given question involves more back and forth between interviewer and respondent, and, per the code definitions, all associated probes and responses would be captured within the segment related to a given question. Text Box 3.1 provides a few examples from other transcripts from the same study. The numbers associated with each segment refer back to the codebook in Table 3.1. Note that in the segment coded with Code 3 (Fam_PartAgree), there are responses from multiple speakers (MRES for the male partner and FRES for the female partner in the couple) in addition to a follow-up question from the interviewer included.

There are many things that can be noted in the structural coding of text. For example, how closely does the interviewer follow the structured (or in the

Figure 3.2   Structural Coding Example—The Transcript

Example

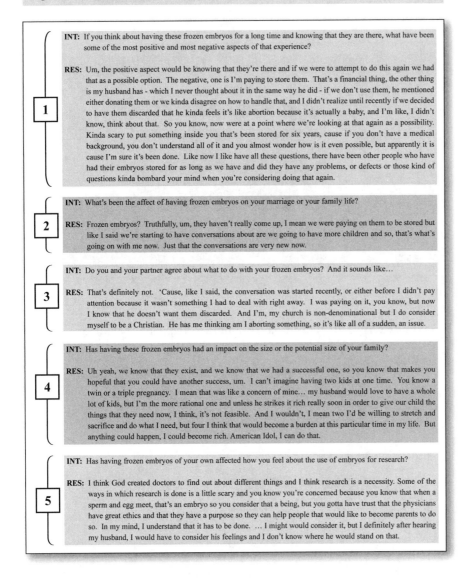

INT: If you think about having these frozen embryos for a long time and knowing that they are there, what have been some of the most positive and most negative aspects of that experience?

RES: Um, the positive aspect would be knowing that they're there and if we were to attempt to do this again we had that as a possible option. The negative, one is I'm paying to store them. That's a financial thing, the other thing is my husband has - which I never thought about it in the same way he did - if we don't use them, he mentioned either donating them or we kinda disagree on how to handle that, and I didn't realize until recently if we decided to have them discarded that he kinda feels it's like abortion because it's actually a baby, and I'm like, I didn't know, think about that. So you know, now were at a point where we're looking at that again as a possibility. Kinda scary to put something inside you that's been stored for six years, cause if you don't have a medical background, you don't understand all of it and you almost wonder how is it even possible, but apparently it is cause I'm sure it's been done. Like now I like have all these questions, there have been other people who have had their embryos stored for as long as we have and did they have any problems, or defects or those kind of questions kinda bombard your mind when you're considering doing that again.

1

INT: What's been the affect of having frozen embryos on your marriage or your family life?

RES: Frozen embryos? Truthfully, um, they haven't really come up, I mean we were paying on them to be stored but like I said we're starting to have conversations about are we going to have more children and so, that's what's going on with me now. Just that the conversations are very new now.

2

INT: Do you and your partner agree about what to do with your frozen embryos? And it sounds like…

RES: That's definitely not. 'Cause, like I said, the conversation was started recently, or either before I didn't pay attention because it wasn't something I had to deal with right away. I was paying on it, you know, but now I know that he doesn't want them discarded. And I'm, my church is non-denominational but I do consider myself to be a Christian. He has me thinking am I aborting something, so it's like all of a sudden, an issue.

3

INT: Has having these frozen embryos had an impact on the size or the potential size of your family?

RES: Uh yeah, we know that they exist, and we know that we had a successful one, so you know that makes you hopeful that you could have another success, um. I can't imagine having two kids at one time. You know a twin or a triple pregnancy. I mean that was like a concern of mine… my husband would love to have a whole lot of kids, but I'm the more rational one and unless he strikes it rich really soon in order to give our child the things that they need now, I think, it's not feasible. And I wouldn't, I mean two I'd be willing to stretch and sacrifice and do what I need, but four I think that would become a burden at this particular time in my life. But anything could happen, I could become rich. American Idol, I can do that.

4

INT: Has having frozen embryos of your own affected how you feel about the use of embryos for research?

RES: I think God created doctors to find out about different things and I think research is a necessity. Some of the ways in which research is done is a little scary and you know you're concerned because you know that when a sperm and egg meet, that's an embryo so you consider that a being, but you gotta have trust that the physicians have great ethics and that they have a purpose so they can help people that would like to become parents to do so. In my mind, I understand that it has to be done. … I might would consider it, but I definitely after hearing my husband, I would have to consider his feelings and I don't know where he would stand on that.

5

example, semistructured) guide? If there are questions that are worded differently or omitted, what are the potential implications when analyzing the complete data set? Are there places where the questions are asked differently than the way they are set out in the interview guide, yet still cover all the same topics? How effectively did the interviewer probe?

Figure 3.3   Structural Coding Example— Coding in NVivo

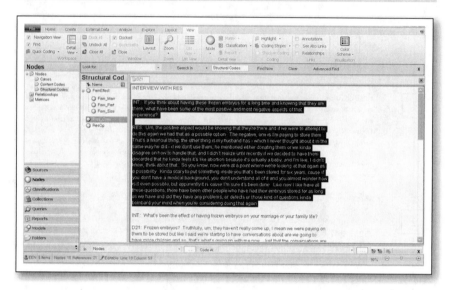

Text Box 3.1:   Structural Coding Example— Segments Including Probes or Multiple Speakers

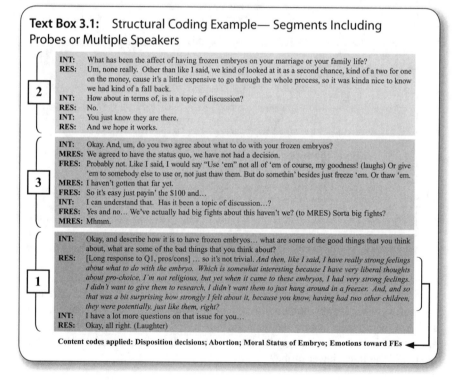

FRACTURED STRUCTURE

Even with a highly structured interview or focus group guide, the data collector is likely to stray from that structure at some point because of the dynamic and flexible interaction that is the strength of qualitative research. One common example is when a participant returns to a topic that was covered earlier in the interview, because a later set of questions brought something to mind that she or he did not think about earlier, or perhaps because the earlier topic is conceptually related to the current topic. Alternatively, a participant may spontaneously talk about a topic that is covered in later questions in the interview guide. In fact, one generally hopes for these kinds of moments in a qualitative interview or focus group as it is an indication that one is uncovering rich data (or thick descriptions). Structural coding guidelines need to accommodate such instances. There are two ways to handle these cases.

Consider a situation where you have two topics you want to explore in an interview, A and B. You then develop two structured topical questions and associated probes, QA and QB, to explore the topics with study participants. Later, you are analyzing text from an interview where the participant returns to topic A in the middle of responding to QB; let's denote this situation as A/QB, that is, "Topic A discussed in response to Topical Question B." One option is to consider A/QB as a structural component of QA and segment and code it as such. Note that this results in multiple structural segments for QA in the transcript. It also results in embedded structural segments; in this case, a segment coded as QA embedded within a larger segment coded as QB.

An alternative option is to consider A/QB solely as a structural component of QB. In order to capture the elements of Topic A embedded in the QB response, you may want to define a separate content code related to Topic A that explicitly references elements of the code definition for structural code QA or that is perhaps a "child" or "sub" code of QA. You could also choose to code A/QB solely based on its emergent content, without consideration of its relationship to QB. Figure 3.4 illustrates the difference between these two approaches.

To illustrate this with real data, we will take an excerpt from the frozen embryos interviews. Topic A here would be the general pros and cons of having frozen embryos elicited by Question 1 (QA) on the interview guide. Topic B would be discussion of disposition options for frozen embryos. In this case, the respondent jumped ahead to Topic B while answering a question about Topic A. The interviewer asked the first question (QA) and received a lengthy response, at the end of which the respondent provided the italicized quote. The italicized portion of the segment is not directly answering QA; instead, it is providing information on her opinions about disposition options (Topic B) that will be elicited later in the interview. Per the codebook definition and instruction on when not to code, this selection of text was included in the larger segment coded at Pros/Cons, and the smaller, italicized portion of it was coded using relevant content codes (see Figure 3.5).

Figure 3.4   Two Approaches to Fractured Structural Coding

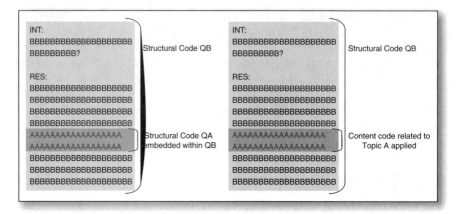

Figure 3.5   Structural Coding Example—Fractured Coding

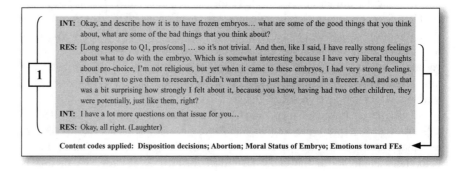

The choice between approaches for a given study will need to reflect whether you consider the response to be primarily driven by the earlier question or by the current question. This can be difficult to determine, unless the participant says something like, "Now that makes me think about something else I'd like to say about that earlier question…." Such statements are not unusual and could be used as a cue to structurally code the text as part of the earlier question. The cues would then be included in the structural code definition under the "When to Use" instructions.

If structural coding will be used mainly for quality assurance purposes (as described in Chapter 2), then it is not necessary to code A/QB as a QA segment, since the primary goal is to ensure that all questions have been asked appropriately. However, if structural coding will be used to explore the relationship between the questions asked and the elicited responses, then coding A/QB as both QA and QB may facilitate looking at the conversational flow between question and response in a more nuanced way. How these overlaps are handled has implications for later analysis, especially if quantitative comparisons of theme frequencies are planned (see Chapters 6 and 7).

In the example from the frozen embryo study, the discussion about disposition options and the participant's feelings about frozen embryos address a question that has not yet been asked. Is it important to tie those statements directly to the later questions about disposition options by coding the italicized portion as a "Topic B" segment? If you are planning a question-by-question analysis, it may be. In this case, because the structural coding was used primarily to check that all questions had been asked, we did not embed structural codes and relied heavily on the content codes created to guide our analysis.

FLAGGING POOR DATA

It is a rare interview or focus group where every statement contains useful information. Some data collection events may be rife with unenlightening tangents, misunderstandings about the questions being asked, unintelligible ramblings, or mumbled responses that can be only partially transcribed. Where significant portions of text are not fully interpretable or are meandering and of questionable value, it may be worthwhile to capture those data as distinct segments and label them with a generic code such as "Unclear_Data." As the analysis progresses and you gain a more nuanced understanding of the way that participants talk about the research topics, what appeared as poor data on an initial read may later make sense. By segmenting and labeling these segments, you can easily go back to them for a final review to ensure that all meaningful text has in fact been coded for analysis. The approach of flagging poor data can also be helpful in reviewing the quality of the data and/or the interview guide; if examples of poor data seem to repeatedly occur in a particular section or in response to a specific question, that is a good indication that something is amiss with the order, phrasing, or delivery of questions.

CODING TO IDENTIFY SPEAKERS

There may be times when you want to segment and code text associated with each speaker in an interview or focus group. As noted in Chapter 2, looking at the variability in the way that interviewers and focus group moderators ask structured questions or how they frame and probe on the research topics can contribute valuable information to an analysis. This can be done for quality-assurance purposes, especially when the research design calls for comparison of responses across populations, subgroups, or research sites. It can also be done to explore the way in which variability in the framing of the conversation by the data collector adds to the richness of the data by uncovering nuances that might not otherwise have emerged.

When more than one person is being interviewed, in a focus group or a joint interview with a married couple for example, it is important to distinguish

Figure 3.6   An Example of Segmenting by Speaker

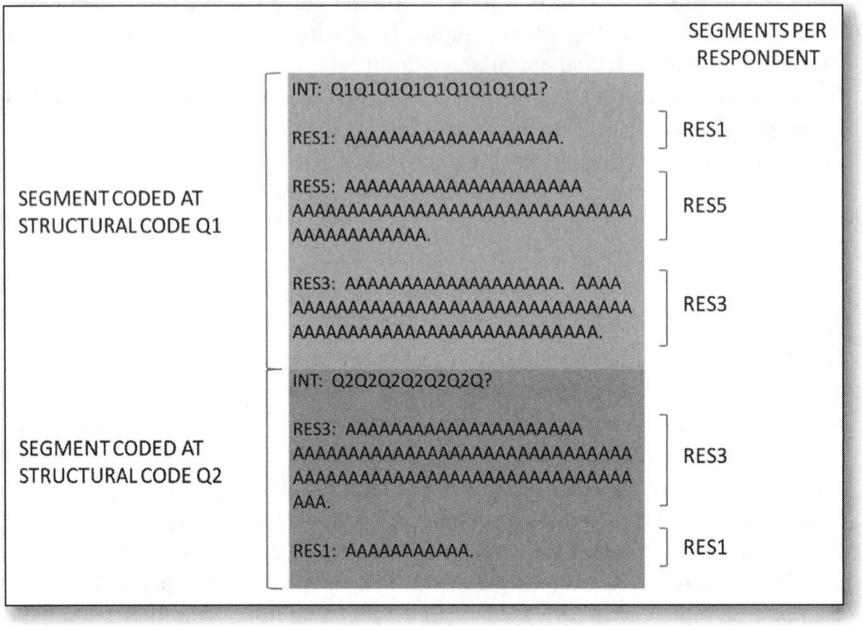

speakers (see Figure 3.6 for an example). When analyzing focus group transcripts, we want to know whether a few voices dominate the discussion or whether a given perspective is widely shared. Identification of speakers in a group can also facilitate analysis of the way in which group dynamics influence individual perspectives. Of course, planning for this level of analysis must occur during data collection so that appropriately detailed notes are made in addition to audio recording of the group discussion. This issue is addressed in more detail in Chapter 5.

CODING FOR CONTENT

In applied thematic analysis, coding for content begins by reviewing the analytic objective, reading the text to be analyzed, and indicating the kinds of meaning that the text may potentially exemplify. The basic task when coding for content in the applied context is to come up with valid and reliable approaches for grouping content at specified levels of meaning and interpretation. Content can be grouped in many different ways: responses or descriptions or explanations that are similar; things that have cause-effect relationships; things that relate hierarchically or through webs of meaning; and disparate explanations of like events. Usually, there is some content that quickly begins to seem familiar: repetition is probably the most common basis for grouping textual content. Content that includes instances of something unusual, unexpected, interesting, or emotionally compelling also stands out upon reading and can be the basis of a category or grouping.

Often, however, text is obscure, convoluted, and just plain dull. This may come as a shock to the inexperienced qualitative researcher who has only seen the hand-picked exemplary quotes that are included in publications. Transcribed conversations are full of oblique references, incomplete statements, hemming and hawing, incoherent mumblings, interruptions, and cognitive leaps from one idea to a seemingly unrelated other. Raw, transcribed text has neither plot nor editor. The qualitative analyst needs a great deal of patience to read, and reread such text.

In the sections that follow, we walk through the process of discovering themes, winnowing themes, turning themes into codes, and creating an effective code-book. As this sequence of steps suggests, thematic coding and analysis can be complex. But if it is approached in a systematic way, you will minimize the like-lihood of either creating chaos through the analysis process or fabricating order out of an inherently chaotic data set. You will also reduce the amount of time spent wandering aimlessly through text with a misplaced belief in the importance of serendipity as a coding tool.

DISCOVERING THEMES

What are themes? Some qualitative researchers suggest, essentially, that "you'll know it when you see it and until then you won't understand it." In fact, themes are not nearly as mysterious as such statements suggest.

Saldaña (2009) defines a theme as "a *phrase* or *sentence* that identifies what a unit of data is *about* and/or what it *means*" (emphasis in original, p. 139). Ryan and Bernard (2003) define themes as "abstract (and often fuzzy) constructs that link not only expressions found in texts but also expressions found in images, sounds, and objects. You know you have found a theme when you can answer the question, 'What is this expression an example of?'" (p. 87). Ryan and Bernard then go on to talk about the potential variation in scope and breadth of themes: "Themes come in all shapes and sizes. Some themes are broad and sweeping constructs that link many different kinds of expressions. Other themes are more focused and link very specific kinds of expressions" (p. 87). Indeed, themes can be developed at different levels of granularity. They can also be antithetical or complementary to other themes or subsumed within larger themes.

So how do we find themes? The first step in an applied thematic analysis strat-egy for finding themes is to refresh your understanding of the analytic objectives. They will always frame how the text is viewed and ultimately determine which themes are worth the effort of tagging, defining, and coding. Once you are famil-iar with the analytic objectives again, begin rereading the data with an eye toward addressing these objectives. One approach to assist in this task is to pay attention to thematic or linguistic cues, as described by Ryan and Bernard (2003) in their tips to identify themes:

1. *Repetition.* This is by far the most common theme-recognition technique and is based on the premise that if a concept reoccurs throughout and/or across transcripts, it is likely a theme. The number of repetitions needed to constitute a theme, however, is not set in stone and is a function of the theme's relevance to the research objectives and the analyst's judgment.

2. *Indigenous categories/typologies.* This technique looks for local terms that may sound unfamiliar to the analyst or are used in distinctly different ways than in the researcher's conceptual framework. An example of this would be a participant talking about diseases in terms of "hot" or "cold."

3. *Metaphors and analogies.* Metaphors and analogies can reveal interesting themes and insights within a data set. For example, the largely rural Basotho people allude to male promiscuity by saying, "A man is a pumpkin, he spreads into his neighbor's garden." Among the Thai, who are known for the way they blend flavors in cooking, young men describe sex with a condom as "like the sweet without the sour."

4. *Transitions.* Naturally occurring shifts in topical content by the participant may be markers for themes. Simply look for the transitions and note what is on either end of the change.

5. *Constant comparison/similarities and differences.* This method is typically used in grounded theory. As the name implies, it involves systematically comparing sections of text and noting similarities and differences between sections.

6. *Linguistic connectors.* In this approach the analyst looks for words and phrases such as "because," "if," "since," "as a result," or any other terms connoting a causal relation. These connectors can indicate places in the text where a participant's system of logic is revealed.

7. *Silence/missing data.* The absence of a theme can be quite telling. If there is good reason to expect participants to talk about something and he or she does not, this is important information and should be documented somehow. You may not develop an explicit code for such a case, but at the very least, the observation of absence should be included in any report.

(For a more detailed treatment of these techniques, refer to the original article.)

Using these more formal techniques is not always necessary, particularly in applied research that is highly focused and concerned with gaining a quick overview of the terrain rather than revealing deep cultural meaning. There is something about the phenomenological interface between the human brain (i.e., the analyst) and the textual data that facilitates common discovery of themes. The process taps into a human tendency to look for patterns, storylines, plots, causality, and relationships. By answering, "What is he saying here?" and determining how what is said relates to analytic objectives, you will be identifying potential themes. An example will likely help to clarify the process.

SEARCH FOR THEMES: AN EXAMPLE

Below is an information-rich section of text from an actual in-depth interview transcript that we often use when conducting training in thematic data analysis to bring the identification of themes from the abstract into something more concrete. As background, the study from which this was drawn had a broad analytic objective, which was to understand the experiences of people living with HIV in several different African settings. This was just one question asked during an hour-long interview. In our trainings, we project the text on a slide and ask the class to identify themes that they perceive. Take a few minutes to do the same. Jot down some themes that come to mind as you read the excerpt.

Interviewer: *How do you think you became infected with HIV?*

Participant: *No one is perfect. I love women and I have both black and white women, but I always run my [HIV] test and use condom most of the time. I believe it is not through sex alone. I want to believe that it comes through other means because I am not so loose and even though we are not married, I believe in my woman. She may be ignorant of things and this is another issue. Though, it could have come from any other source, we cannot rule out the sexual aspect, even though I doubt it.*

As noted previously, in applied thematic analysis we initially approach theme identification by asking "What are these people talking about that is relevant to the research objectives?" The first thing you are likely to notice when reading this excerpt is that the participant is talking about the topic that the data collector asked the question about—how the person believes he got infected with HIV. This is quite obvious; the question itself creates the topic! Since you already will have described that topic in your structural codebook and identified it in the text via structural coding, there is no need to make further note of it.

What else do you hear this person talking about? We have completed this exercise with qualitative research novices as well as experts, in African countries and various parts of the United States. The professional backgrounds of our students have ranged from active military personnel to physicians to PhD social scientists to economists. No matter where, or with whom, we carry out this exercise, people identify similar high-level themes, regardless of culture or personal background. Compare your themes to those commonly suggested during our trainings (provided in Appendix on page 77) and see how your theme radar compares.

WINNOWING THEMES

Often you will notice many more potential themes than you actually end up elaborating in a given analysis. Just because something is noticeable does not mean it is noteworthy. There are always ideas, phrases, or expressions that catch a coder's attention on an initial reading of the text that turn out to be oddities and distractions. If what a participant says is clearly not relevant to the analytic objectives, there is not much point in expending significant effort to code it. Analytic objectives keep you focused on the task at hand and help you prioritize which themes to develop in the analysis.

Of course, the relevance of some themes is not immediately apparent during the analysis process. A good rule of thumb, therefore, is to err on the side of caution. If you are uncertain about the importance of a potential theme as you read through a transcript, you can tag the text for later review. All qualitative analysis software programs provide options for doing this. Or, if you are working in an applied research context with collaborators of different skill levels or where there may not be sufficient funding to provide everyone with specialized software, there are simple ways to involve everyone in the identification of themes. For example, you might use word-processing software to insert footnotes in the text document to tag and record your impressions of an interesting section of text. Or you might highlight text and insert comments in a "redline" editing mode that also indicates who inserted the comments. The footnotes or comments from each person's reading of a particular document can then be merged into one master document. Though it is a little more difficult to merge comments on hard copies of the transcript(s), the pen and paper approach works just as well.

Another technique that we frequently use to tag potentially relevant information is to create a generic "unique" code to apply to any text that we think might be of some importance, but which we cannot yet evaluate for fit with the bigger analytic picture. After completing a preliminary round of theme identification, we then aggregate all of the "unique" text, look for relevance and possible patterns, and develop additional themes or revise existing ones as appropriate.

Narrowing and refinement of potential themes can take another form. Returning to the previous example about HIV transmission, there is much to *notice* in the quote described, but what is *noteworthy*? Though a single quote is not sufficient for deciding what does or does not belong in a codebook, we can use this example to further consider how richness can be focused. As illustrated, some themes may be fairly obvious and not require deep or detailed analytic probing. This does not mean that you cannot, or should not, dig a little further into the text and aim for a deeper understanding of the participant's thoughts and experiences, but analysts should be aware of the limitations imposed by a more hermeneutically oriented approach. First, the more interpretive the analysis becomes, the more tenuous are the outcomes and assertions based on the analysis. As the analysis moves closer to the realm of pure interpretation, it becomes increasingly removed from the actual data (is less "grounded"). Second, highly detailed, interpretive analyses are more time-consuming and subject to individual perception and therefore may not be conducive to larger data sets or team-based research.

Digging deeper into the text example will help to illustrate our point. If we read over the following section of the quote a few times, we can start to discern some possible, and very interesting, themes.

No one is perfect. I love women and I have both black and white women but I always run my test and use condom most of the time.

From this statement, we can infer at least a couple of things. Based on the context of the question and his response, we can assume that the participant understands that having multiple partners is a risk while HIV testing and condoms are protective practices. This is inferred by the juxtaposition of the acknowledgement that he has multiple partners and the word "but" (a linguistic connector), indicating that getting an HIV test and using condoms mitigate the risk imposed by having more than one sexual partner. Another possible theme is the participant's acknowledgment of responsibility with respect to his infection, inferred with the opening statement "no one is perfect". Or, the statement may imply that responsibility is a nonissue because this is the sort of thing a person cannot fully control in life. Is the text sufficient to support either of these themes?

The following section of text is even richer, allowing us to make more interesting inferences.

Even though we are not married, I believe in my woman. She may be ignorant of things and this is another issue. Though, it could have come from any other source, we cannot rule out the sexual aspect . . . .

From the way the participant phrases the first sentence we can assume that, at least for him, (a) wives are generally more trustworthy, and (b) his girlfriend is exceptionally trustworthy (because he trusts her even though they are not married). The following sentence (*she may be ignorant of things and this is another issue*) seems to suggest that if his girlfriend gave him HIV it was through her ignorance. And this sentence, combined with the last two, indicates that he admits that he could have gotten HIV sexually, possibly from his girlfriend.

You can see how sifting through possible meanings and logical connections that may (or may not) lie deeper within the text is an intriguing enterprise. The danger, however, is that the deeper one reads, the less the data can substantiate resulting assertions and interpretations. If, for example, someone were to ask an analyst for evidence to support the claims that the participant thinks that: (a) wives are more trustworthy than girlfriends, or (b) his girlfriend is exceptionally trustworthy, the text presented would likely not be sufficiently convincing. One way to deal with this fuzziness is to note themes of a more interpretive nature as the analysis progresses and treat them as working hypotheses. If more evidence for tentative themes is gathered throughout the analysis, as more text from different types of individuals is processed, you can upgrade their status based on supporting data. If this type of exploratory analysis is conducted while data collection is underway, it can also be used to modify questions and probes to get at the tentative themes and hypothesized relationships more directly.

As noted, themes are often readily apparent and may not require conscious use of the techniques described in the earlier section, even the most commonly used approach of searching for repetition. Note also that the salient themes in the example text were identifiable with very little information regarding the context of the interview (i.e., characteristics of the participant) or specific analytic objectives to frame a thematic search. That said, there are limitations to the analytic value of "obvious" themes. Not everyone will perceive exactly the same themes in the same way from a given snippet of data. Breadth and depth of knowledge and experience with the research setting and topic will influence what the reader perceives. Levels of abstraction may vary, as might the substantive focus of the theme searching process. This is precisely why more systematic procedures for finding, defining, and coding themes are needed.

It is common for qualitative analysts to layer text data with codes, coding notes, and coding of the coding notes so that meaning is built up via layers of textual interpretation. Done skillfully and with meticulous care, the layers should be as discernable as those of an onion and the final analysis as organically coherent. With large data sets, multiple analysts, varying levels of skill, and tight timelines, it is challenging (and at times impossible) to ensure the meticulous level of care needed to analyze text in this way. There is a risk that use of the layering approach can obscure the distinction between the original text and its interpretation. Maintaining this distinction is critical when research findings are intended for application to real-world problems.

To avoid conflation of what people say with our interpretation of what they said, we use an iterative approach that centers on the following steps:

- Read the text and propose themes.
- Refine the themes into codes with well-developed definitions.
- Have two or more analysts read a sample of the text again and identify segments that reflect specific code definitions. (If you are the only person coding the text, you can code one sample twice, e.g., with a week between codings.)
- Compare the way each analyst coded the text sample.
- If the results are the same, continue coding with periodic re-checks.
- If the results differ, identify why. Adjust the code definitions, the codes, or the analysts' use of the codes as necessary. Recode the text as necessary. Have the analysts code another sample of text and again compare the results. Repeat as necessary.

Though not explicitly mentioned in these steps, analytic memos are important in codebook development for applied thematic analysis, as they are in other approaches. The distinction is that we clearly demarcate coding memos as part of the initial theme and code generation process. In our analyses, coding memos are not source data; they are generated from our review of the original source data (note that other analysts use memos in different ways, which we briefly cover in Chapter 5). If the memos are not ultimately incorporated into the codebook (as understandings of themes in the form of definitions), then there is the risk that they will be lost and unavailable to inform the final interpretation and presentation of research results. Worse, if they are treated as data and coded, there is the risk that our interpretations and musings will be presented as original source data, cloaked as "evidence." In an applied context where research results can have direct policy or programmatic effects on the lives of people, we believe there is a moral responsibility to understand the distinction between source data and the analytic interpretation of source data.

CREATING AN EFFECTIVE CODEBOOK

Given the emphasis in this book on maintaining a systematic, replicable approach to analysis that maintains distance between source data and analyst interpretations of those data, the codebook is one of the most important analytic tools in applied thematic analysis. A well-designed codebook does not short-cut the analysis process, that is, it does not "cut out" important steps. Rather, it increases the efficiency of the process. For example, rather than creating a dense layer of codes distributed throughout the text that then need to be reviewed, consolidated, and organized, the applied thematic analysis approach incorporates elements of text directly into initial code definitions to illuminate the emerging themes. Using the rich text example from above, we could develop two initial code definitions as follows:

Suggested Code	Suggested Code Definition Elements
Imperfect	Use this code for discussions of human imperfection. This can include statements about how no one is perfect, references to imperfect behavior such as imperfect condom use, and personal shortcomings such as ignorance.
Prevention Strategies	Use this code for descriptions of how people try to prevent HIV infection. Examples can include effective strategies such as condom use, strategies that are not directly related to prevention such as HIV antibody testing, and ineffective strategies such as cleaning the genitals after sex.

As you read more text, you may refine the initial code definition elements. Consider whether the code includes too many elements and should be subdivided, or whether two or more related codes overlap to the point where they are difficult to distinguish and should in fact be collapsed into a single defined code.

As you continue to refine the list of themes/codes in your codebook, remember that an important aspect of an efficient, well-designed codebook is the organization of codes to facilitate coding. For a large or complex project, you may ultimately need dozens of codes, and the human brain is simply incapable of accurately tracking and processing that much information in real time while reading textual data. The solution is to break the codebook into logically organized sections. In applied thematic analysis, the most basic logical break is between structural and content codes. As noted previously in the section on structural coding, we often use a hierarchical approach to organize structural codes into logical groupings based on questions that center on a particular focus of inquiry. For content coding, decisions about how to group codes are often more complex, and a single code may logically fall into multiple code groups. The way codes are grouped may in turn influence the way they are applied during analysis.

Many different ways exist in which you can define the relationships between codes in a group. Hierarchical relationships are probably the most common but are not necessarily the best organizational choice for all elements in a codebook. Hierarchical code groupings work best when you are drilling down into a set of themes that can be clearly differentiated from each other at multiple levels of detail. For example:

> CODE A = Perceived ways to prevent HIV prevention
>   Code A.1 = Choose partners who look clean and healthy
>   Code A.2 = Cleansing after sexual intercourse
>   Code A.2.a = Washing of penis with soap and water
>   Code A.2.b = Washing of vagina with lemon juice
>   Code A.3 = Regular HIV testing
>   Code A.4 = Use condoms
> CODE B = Perceived sources of HIV infection
>   Code B.1 = Sex partner who has other sex partners
>   Code B.2 = Barbers reusing razors and scissors
>   Code B.3 = Mosquitoes
> Etc.

Of course, both the CODE A and CODE B groupings could be further grouped into a set of codes labeled something like "HIV transmission beliefs." This might be helpful if the text to be analyzed includes similar discussions about other diseases such as malaria and tuberculosis (TB). However, note that Code B.3 (Mosquitoes) would likely be cited as a source of infection for malaria. Should a separate "mosquito" code be defined for malaria? After all, malaria is actually transmitted by mosquitoes while HIV is not. This is a tough decision. We argue that it should be driven by the way the coded text will ultimately be analyzed and the limitations of the software that will be used for that analysis. These issues are dealt with in detail in later chapters. For now, consider the following options:

• Are you mainly interested in understanding all the ways that mosquitoes are perceived to transmit diseases? If yes, then a single "mosquito" code will be easier to compare and contrast with all coded themes at all levels of specificity. Include the same "mosquito" code under all disease categories. If you are using a software program that does not allow a single code to be included in multiple hierarchies, you may need to create a separate document that tracks the code groupings.

- Are you mainly interested in comparing and contrasting sets of beliefs about specific diseases? If yes, then disease-specific "mosquito" codes will make it easier to compare and contrast the thematic content associated with each disease. Use code names that make it clear with which disease a particular "mosquito" code is associated. Develop definitions for each code that make it clear when each should be used and not used. Consider whether a generic "mosquito" code will be needed, for example, if more than one disease is being discussed or mosquitoes are discussed outside the context of any particular disease.

- Are you uncertain how discussions about mosquitoes will play out in the analysis? Then consider using a generic "mosquito" code in combination with a generic code for each disease (e.g., "HIV-related," "Malaria-related"). These instructions for double-coding should be noted in the "When to use" section of each of the code definitions. During coding, the analyst would then double-code the relevant text with both the "mosquito" code and the disease code. Now you can easily identify all text where mosquitoes are discussed *or* find text about mosquitoes that is related to a specific disease. Or you can now create disease-specific mosquito codes and go back to the relevant text segments to recode them with the new codes if it facilitates the analysis.

- Is disease-specific text already identified via structural coding? If so, then there is no need to further code the text by disease or to include explicit instructions about double-coding text with the appropriate structural code and the mosquito code. You can keep it simple by creating a generic mosquito code. This provides the same options for pulling text by searching on the disease-specific structural code and the content mosquito code, and also for recoding the mosquito text later. One caveat: If there are multiple structural codes that would need to be referenced for each disease, this strategy will not be the most efficient for retrieving the coded data.

As these examples illustrate, an insistence on hierarchical coding structures can lead to more complexity than needed. Some codes are best grouped in a flat structure as simply "things that are similar to each other" or "things that are related to each other because…." If you are using qualitative analysis software to facilitate coding, we suggest adding a prefix to related, nonhierarchical codes so that they will appear together in an alphabetized code list. You want to organize codes in a way that will help the analyst code the text efficiently and with minimal error. The codebook is a tool for describing what is in the text.

The "Lumper-Splitter" Issue

A commonly encountered phenomenon in coding (or any group categorizing task) is the "lumper-splitter problem" (Weller & Romney, 1988). Individuals vary in the level of abstraction at which they process data. We have seen, for example, researchers generate a codebook with more than 500 codes (many with values) for a data set of moderate size. These types of coders are splitters; every detail of text is coded. On the other extreme, a lumper may only derive 6 to 10 high-level codes from, say, 50 in-depth interviews. Most people are somewhere in the middle. Even if two people come up with the same number of codes for the same text, they may conceptually lump and split the information differently if they each have detailed knowledge about different topics, for example. When working with multiple coders, you should address this natural variance. One way to help standardize levels of abstraction is to establish expectations from the outset, before any data analysis has begun. The researcher(s) leading the analysis should meet with the coding team, go through some data together, and talk about the types of codes and code levels that would be most useful for the analysis. Providing an expected range for the number of codes in the codebook, and how it should be structured (e.g., hierarchically or only single codes? With values specified?) helps immensely in this regard.

When trying to gauge the most appropriate level of abstraction for your analysis, ask yourself the following two questions: (1) At what level will extracted codes/text be manageable?, and (2) At what level would code frequencies make the most sense? Having too many codes becomes unmanageable while too few codes provides only surface-level insight into the data. We offer two rules of thumb. If you only have one instance of a code (or several codes) per 20 transcripts, you may be splitting too much. The caveat to this is if the theme that one code represents is extremely important to the analysis (e.g., a highly illustrative and/or negative/contradictory case), then you should create or keep a code. Related to this is the second rule of thumb: If in doubt, err on the splitting slide. It's always easier to aggregate than disaggregate data, especially in the context of thematic analysis and qualitative data analysis software.

Figure 3.7 Portion of Coding Tree Depicting Clinical Trial Participants' Misperceptions About Aspects of the Trial

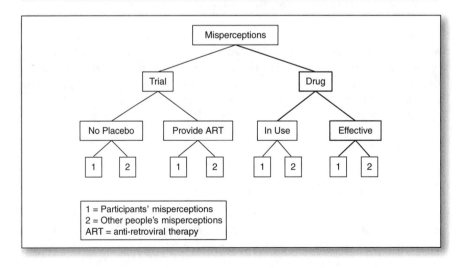

As for the second rhetorical question regarding frequencies, think about the following example below, which depicts possible levels of abstraction for an analysis documenting clinical trial participants' experiences with a clinical study.

Referring to Figure 3.7, how would it sound if we said X% of clinical trial participants had misperceptions of some kind? Would it be more informative to move down a level of abstraction and be able to state that X% of clinical trial participants had misperceptions about the drug being tested or trial procedures? We could be even more precise and calculate the number of participants who had specific types of misperceptions about the drug. Going still further, we could specify, using values, whether the misperceptions expressed were the participants' or those of others but talked about by the participants. The level you choose depends on what your analytic objectives are, how much data you have, and how rich your data set is.

LINKING THEMES TO THEORETICAL MODELS

Applied thematic analysis situates the coding process in the realm of evidence rather than ideas. In this regard, the approach is aligned with Ragin and Amoroso (2011) who argue that "ideas help social researchers make sense of evidence, and researchers use evidence to extend, revise, and test ideas" (p. 57). In this chapter, we have focused on mapping and describing qualitative evidence because in our experience this results in a better organized and more efficient analysis. This does not mean that theory is forgotten. Rather, it gives you a stronger foundation for linking ideas and evidence through the use of theories and constructs. The goal is to clearly map the path between theory and the way data were collected, between data collection and the resulting evidence, and between the evidence and theories about what it all signifies. Structural coding describes the link between data collection and the evidence generated. Content coding describes the link between the evidence and its significance. Subsequent steps in the analysis synthesize, summarize, and extend significance through the use of conceptual frameworks. We are now ready to query the data without getting lost along the way.

SUMMING UP: GOOD CODEBOOK PRACTICE

In this chapter, we provided a detailed description of what it takes to develop and use an effective qualitative codebook in applied thematic analysis. If you are working as a team, some additional guidance points need to be considered (MacQueen, et al., 2008). First, identify one person to take on the role of lead codebook manager; the manager takes charge of all changes to the codebook and documents key decisions in the code development process. This is the only way to ensure that everyone is literally working from the same page—with the same codes and the same definitions. Second, schedule regular coding review meetings with all coding team members to make sure that needed changes are made to the codebook and that everyone is using the codebook in the same way (and in the way intended). Third, develop a written plan for segmenting text to be coded. This may not eliminate variability in the exact boundaries used by each coder, but it should keep such variability within reasonable bounds and focus effort (and debate) on how to code meaning in the text.

As we have mentioned, when defining codes, do not assume that anything is obvious. Always state what the code should and should not capture, clearly and in complete sentences. Use examples. Once you stop coding, *you will not remember* anything that seemed obvious while you were deeply buried in the text. Similarly, avoid cluttering the codebook with remnants of old arguments, poorly worded explanations, and discredited suppositions. Throw out codes that do not work and rework definitions for codes that are difficult to understand or use.

Finally, accept the fact that text will need to be reread and recoded as the codebook is developed and refined. Recoding is not a sign that you have done things wrong, it is simply part of doing things well.

REFERENCES

Gibson, W. J., & Brown, A. (2009). *Working with qualitative data*. Thousand Oaks, CA: Sage.

Lyerly, A. D., Steinhauser, K., Namey, E., Tulsky, J., Cook-Deegan, R., Sugarman, J., Walmer, D., & Wallach, E. (2006). Factors that affect decision making about frozen embryo disposition: Infertility patient perspectives. *Fertility and Sterility, 85*(6), 1623–1630.

MacQueen, K. M., McLellan-Lemal, E., Bartholow, K., & Milstein, B. (2008). Team-based codebook development: Structure, process, and agreement. In G. Guest & K. MacQueen (Eds.), *Handbook for team-based qualitative research* (pp. 119–135). Lanham, MD: AltaMira.

Ragin, C. C., & Amoroso, L. M. (2011). *Constructing social research* (2nd ed.). Los Angeles, CA: Pine Forge Press/Sage.

Ryan, G., & Bernard, H. (2003). Techniques to identify themes. *Field Methods, 15*(1), 85–109.

Saldaña, J. (2009). *The coding manual for qualitative researchers*. Thousand Oaks, CA: Sage.

Weller, S., & Romney, A. (1988). *Systematic data collection*. Thousand Oaks, CA: Sage.

EXERCISES

For this set of stepwise exercises, identify an online source of interviews that you can use as a practice data set. For example, Mongabay.com has a page with links to interviews with young scientists studying wild lands and wild life (http://news.mongabay.com/news-index/interviews1.html). These exercises work best if done by groups of four to eight people.

1. At a site like Mongabay.com, take a few minutes to look at what the site is about. As a team, decide on an analytic objective that is closely related to the site's purpose. Then identify an interview posted on the site that can be used for analysis. Copy the interview file and distribute an electronic copy to each team member. As each person reads the interview, he or she should use short footnotes or redline comments to identify potential themes in the text. Designate a team leader who will collect marked-up copies of everyone's document and merge them into one document. Discuss how similar or dissimilar each person's markings are.

2. Working as a team, come up with an initial list of potential content themes that reflect the meaningful text indicated by your merged footnotes or comments. Use that list to develop an outline for a codebook that includes suggested code labels and short definitions. Divide into groups of two to three people, then divide up the suggested codes among the groups to develop full code definitions.

3. Combine the code definitions from the different groups to produce a complete codebook. Decide on a strategy for how to segment the text and include those instructions with the codebook. Assign the same or a new team leader to take charge of pulling the pieces of the codebook together.

4. Divide up into groups of two to three people as before, and have each group independently code the interview using the codebook. Have the groups come back together and compare how each group used the codebook to segment and code the interview. Ask yourselves:

- Were there places in the interview where different groups used different codes to describe the text?
- Which codes were easiest to use? Why?
- Which codes were difficult to use? Why?
- How could the codebook be improved?

APPENDIX

High-Level Themes Commonly "Discovered" in Sample Text

- **Denial of sexual route of transmission:** "I believe it is not through sex alone. I want to believe that it comes through other means....Though it could have come from any other source, we cannot rule out the sexual aspect, even though I doubt it."
- **Uses condoms**: "I always run my test and use condom most of the time."
- **Gets HIV tests**: "I always run my test."
- **Trusts his main partner**: "Even though we are not married, I believe in my woman."
- **Has multiple sexual partners**: "I love women and I have both black and white women."
- **Nonsexual source of infection:** "I believe it is not through sex alone. I want to believe that it comes through other means."
- **HIV prevention strategies:** "I always run my test and use condom most of the time."

Note that some of these themes overlap, can be hierarchically arranged, or may be combined to create other themes. How they are configured in the final analysis and codebook is part of the winnowing and codebook development process.

ADDITIONAL READING

MacQueen, K. M., McLellan-Lemal, E., Bartholow, K., & Milstein, B. (2008). Team-based codebook development: Structure, process, and agreement. In G. Guest & K. MacQueen (Eds.), *Handbook for team-based qualitative research* (pp. 119–135). Lanham, MD: AltaMira.

Ryan, G., & Bernard, H. (2003). Techniques to identify themes. *Field Methods*, *15*(1), 85–109.

Saldaña, J. (2009). *The coding manual for qualitative researchers*. Thousand Oaks, CA: Sage.

4

VALIDITY AND RELIABILITY (CREDIBILITY AND DEPENDABILITY) IN QUALITATIVE RESEARCH AND DATA ANALYSIS

LEARNING OBJECTIVES

After reading this chapter, you should be able to:

- Describe the meaning of *validity* and *reliability* as concepts in research
- Provide alternate terms for validity and reliability
- Critically apply the concepts of validity and reliability to qualitative research in general, and thematic analysis specifically
- Perform various procedures to enhance both validity and reliability during qualitative data analysis (and to a lesser degree, research design and qualitative data collection)

The terms *validity* and *reliability* are part of the research vernacular across multiple disciplines, and the connotations associated with these terms are as varied as the fields that use them. In this chapter, we examine some of the definitions of these terms that can be found in the literature, and we provide our perspective on their applicability to qualitative research, and more specifically thematic analysis. As with the rest of this book, we try to keep the theoretical discussion to a minimum and focus on the pragmatic application of the terms. We outline various procedures for improving both validity and reliability in thematic analyses to subsequently enhance the credibility of research findings and interpretations. We conclude the chapter with exercises designed to reinforce the definitions and uses of these terms in applied thematic analysis.

VALIDITY

Within the literature on research methods, there is big "V" validity and little "v" validity. The former refers to the concept as a whole while the latter refers to specific subtypes of validity. The general concept of validity (i.e., big "V") has numerous definitions:

- "An account is valid or true if it represents accurately those features of the phenomena that it is intended to describe, explain or theorize" (Hammersley, 1987, p. 69)
- "The measure that an instrument measures what it is supposed to" (Black & Champion, 1976, p. 232)
- "Accuracy" (Lehner, 1979, p. 130)
- "Degree of approximation of 'reality'" (Johnston & Pennypacker, 1980, p.190)
- "Are we measuring what we think we are?" (Kerlinger, 1964, p. 430)
- "The accuracy and trustworthiness of instruments, data and findings in research" (Bernard, 2000, p. 46)
- "The extent to which an empirical measure adequately reflects the *real meaning* of the concept under consideration" (Babbie, 1990, p. 133)
- "The meanings emerging from the data have to be *tested* for their plausibility, their sturdiness, their 'confirmability'—that is, their *validity*" (Miles & Huberman, 1994, p. 11)
- "The degree to which a test measures what it is intended to measure" (socialsciencedictionary.com, 2009)

Note that the list above is just a sample—not close to being exhaustive—but the definitions represented (and typically those not represented here as well) encompass a cross-cutting theme: the notion that one is assessing what one is intending to assess. In contrast to many of the definitions, we avoid using the term "measure" since this suggests quantification, and many qualitative analyses do not quantify data or have a quantitative outcome. We prefer Ian Dey's pragmatic, more inclusive, definition. In his words, "My dictionary defines 'valid' as 'sound,' 'defensible,' and 'well-grounded' and despite the more technical interpretations of validity in social science, this is as good a definition as any" (1993, p. 228).

Complicating the multiple meanings of the general term validity are various *types* of validity to which researchers and the research literature often refer. The types most commonly discussed are face validity, content validity, construct validity, criterion validity, and external/internal validity (although one can find many more types of validity described throughout the literature—e.g., Bernard, 2000, and Maxwell, 1992). For your reference, in the spirit of due diligence, we provide a brief definition of these common subtypes in Table 4.1. Note, however, that only "face" and "external" validity are applicable to most qualitative research. The other subtypes are more salient for quantitative data and/or experimental designs.

Table 4.1   Definitions of Specific Types of Validity

Type of Validity	Definition
Face	The degree to which an indicator for a concept (e.g., question, scale) intuitively makes sense. Determined by consensus among researchers
Content	The degree to which an instrument has the appropriate range of content for measuring a complex construct or concept
Construct	The degree to which a measure relates to other variables as expected within a system of theoretical relationships
Criterion (also called *predictive validity*)	The degree to which a measure relates to some external criterion that is known to be valid
External	The degree to which study findings are relevant to other populations and contexts (i.e., generalizability)
Internal	The degree to which one can be certain that changes in the dependent variable were actually caused by the experimental treatment

RELIABILITY

The term *reliability* is also associated with numerous definitions:

- "The agreement between two efforts to measure the same trait through maximally similar methods" (Campbell & Fisk, 1959, p. 83)
- "An ability to measure consistently" (Black & Champion, 1976, p. 232)
- "Reproducibility of the measurements . . . stability" (Lehner, 1979, p. 130)
- "Capacity to yield the same measurement . . . stability" (Johnston & Pennypacker, 1980, p. 190)
- "Whether or not you get the same answer by using an instrument to measure something more than once" (Bernard, 2000, p. 47)
- "Yielding comparable results each time. In examinations, reliability is consistency; the same result is achieved on successive trials." (socialsciencedictionary.com, 2009)

A key conceptual thread throughout the traditional definitions above is consistency when repeating or comparing assessments within a study. Note the heavy use of the word *measure* again, which stems from the provenance of the term in quantitative research and the reliance on the concept when employing highly structured instruments such as scales and standardized tests that are administered multiple times and in multiple contexts,.

The relationship between reliability and validity is often visually depicted using the target analogy in Figure 4.1, which shows four different variations of possible relationships between the two concepts.

The graphic is useful for understanding the general relationship between the two concepts, but we find it even more useful for illustrating an additional point: that it is impossible to have a situation of high validity and low reliability (Figure 4.1b). If data from a particular instrument are truly valid, then it logically follows that they will produce reliable results if applied to the same population, assuming that the properties of the population and context remain the same (and, therefore, the phenomenon that you are evaluating is not altered). This aspect of the relationship is expressed in the difficulty of visually depicting a situation in which you have high validity and low reliability in two dimensions. The relationship cannot be drawn correctly, since if you are collecting valid data each time you should be hitting the bull's-eye each time, as in Figure 4.1d. Lincoln and Guba (1985) sum this relationship up nicely: "Since there is no validity without reliability . . . a demonstration of the former is sufficient to establish the latter" (p. 316).

The bottom line is that validity is by far the more important of the two concepts. If you can be assured that your data are valid each time, they are also reliable. If data are valid but do not produce the same results on repeated occasions, you can infer that, for some reason, properties of the phenomenon which you are studying or the data collection context have changed (e.g., repeated assessment indicates that your population is less depressed over time). The same concurrence is not true of the reverse situation in which data are known to be reliable: A commonly used example is that a broken thermometer is 100% reliable but has 0% validity. As Lincoln and Guba (1985) observe, "Reliability is not prized for its own sake but as a precondition for validity" (p. 292).

Figure 4.1   Visual Relationship Between Validity and Reliability

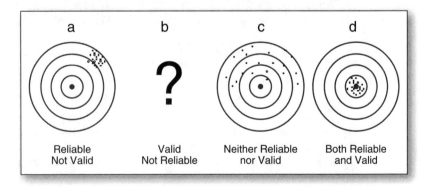

APPLYING THE CONCEPTS OF VALIDITY AND RELIABILITY IN QUALITATIVE INQUIRY

We have presented commonly used definitions of *validity* (and its various subcategories) and *reliability*. But, what do these definitions mean for the application of these ubiquitously used terms to qualitative research in general, and to thematic analysis in particular? Some researchers accurately observe that the meaning of the terms vary by discipline (Winter, 2000); this is clearly evidenced by even the abridged lists of definitions provided above. Others take this idea somewhat further and argue that the terms validity and reliability are born of the quantitative tradition and, therefore, have little or no value for qualitative inquiry and should be replaced with other terms (e.g., Auerbach & Silverstein, 2003; Corbin & Strauss, 2008; Golafshani, 2003). Because of this latter school of thought, many alternate terms have been created. Examples of these with respect to validity include *trustworthiness*, *worthy*, *relevant*, *plausible*, *confirmable*, *credible*, and *representative* (Winter, 2000). In the burgeoning field of mixed methods research, the term *legitimacy* is gaining traction (Onwuegbuzie & Johnson, 2006; Tashakkori & Teddlie, 2003, p. 354). The most commonly used terms among these, however, is still Lincoln and Guba's (1985) *credibility*—which they also call *truth value.* Credibility refers to the "confidence in the truth of the findings, including an accurate understanding of the context" (Ulin, Robinson, & Tolley, 2005, p. 25), and is commonly used in qualitative inquiry in place of the term validity.

Similarly, a parallel set of arguments and alternative terms has been proposed for reliability. Examples of the latter include words such as *stability*, *consistency*, *predictability*, and *accuracy* (see Kerlinger, 1973), but the most commonly employed surrogate term is *dependability*, made popular through Lincoln and Guba's landmark book *Naturalist Inquiry* (1985). According to Ulin and colleagues, dependability refers to "whether the research process is consistent and carried out with careful attention to the rules and conventions of qualitative methodology" (2005, p. 26).

How do we relate all of this to applied thematic analysis? For starters, we tend to agree with Bernard that "[n]othing in research is more important than validity" (2006, p. 53). If the data a researcher is collecting, analyzing, and/or interpreting do not accurately and credibly represent what a researcher intends or purports, of what use are they? In certain cases in which assessing validity is a methodological aim (and there are many such studies that look at validity issues including accuracy of self-reported behavior or the effect of the research context or instrument structure on response outcomes), invalid data can be quite informative. But for the average researcher whose goal is to understand or explain a particular phenomenon—and in the case of an applied researcher, perhaps build policy from research findings—data of any type that are not valid can be useless at best and downright dangerous at worst. So, when it comes to big "V" validity, we believe it is critical that researchers undertaking qualitative inquiry take whatever steps possible to mitigate threats to validity—and candidly report instances in the research process in which validity might have been compromised.

What about the term *validity* itself? In the big picture, when you are trying to collect the most meaningful and truthful data possible, it really does not matter what you call the concept that denotes this outcome. But for the sake of keeping things simple, we share the view of Morse, Barrett, Mayan, Olson, and Spiers (2002) that "the terms reliability and validity remain pertinent in qualitative inquiry and should be maintained" (p. 8). Morse and colleagues go on to argue that by creating special alternative terms for qualitative research, we risk marginalizing the field from mainstream science and the legitimacy with which it is associated.

The various subtypes of validity present a somewhat more complicated scenario with respect to their utility for qualitative research. For our purposes, *face* validity is probably the closest approximation of how we might determine overall validity of a study and/or the processes within and results from a qualitative study. We must rely on our own judgment and that of our peers—judgment based on the information available—to decide whether or not what we do and have done, and the findings we present, are valid. The other concept directly relevant to qualitative inquiry is *external validity*. Since this is commonly referred to in both the qualitative and social science literature as *generalizability*, we will stick with this latter term throughout the book to denote the extent to which findings can be transferred to other populations and contexts. The remaining types of validity listed in Table 4.1 relate quite specifically to quantitative data and are predicated on measurement of some kind. While in a few contexts specifying a certain type of validity might be important for a given qualitative inquiry, most of the subtypes are more useful for quantitative inquiry and corresponding structured instruments. For the remainder of this chapter and book, therefore, unless stated otherwise, when we use the term *validity* we are referring to the general concept: the credibility and accuracy of processes and outcomes associated with a research study.

As we argued above, reliability is typically less important than validity in a general research context. This is particularly true of qualitative inquiry, for two reasons. First, replication is typically not a goal in qualitative research; most studies are descriptive and are not designed to be replicated. Second, and related to the first point, is the structure of the data collection process itself. If the data collection process is unstructured, as is often the case in qualitative inquiry, one cannot expect to obtain similar results across individuals or time, since the questions that are asked may very well be different for each participant or interview context. Qualitative inquiry is by its very nature inductive, and even semistructured interviews (commonly used in multisite and/or team-based research) that ask participants identical open-ended questions in the same order, entail a great deal of inductive probing. So, although enhancing an instrument's structure facilitates comparability across participants, probing questions that follow up on participants' unique responses can lead interviews in distinctly different directions. This is a dramatically different context than being tasked with making sure that results from, say, the SATs are consistent across applications. This is not to say that reliability has no place in qualitative research. Demonstrating reliability within the data analysis process is indeed important and actually helps to enhance validity by more objectively (though by no means perfectly) connecting raw data with the conceptual analytic categories developed by researchers to represent themes within the data (i.e., codes). Below, we discuss procedures for strengthening the reliability of the analysis process, as well as other parts of the research process, to produce a thematic analysis that is rigorous, transparent, and credible.

ENHANCING VALIDITY AND RELIABILITY IN QUALITATIVE RESEARCH

In qualitative inquiry, how do we know if our data, and our summaries and interpretation of them, are valid? This is probably the most critical question a researcher can ask. The challenge to answering this question, however, is that in order to truly establish the validity of something, a researcher needs some sort of "truth yardstick" to which his representations of research findings can be compared. In quantitative inquiry, the best proxy for this type of assessment is relating variables in question to other variables, and seeing if they are associated in ways that are logical and that would be expected (Bernard, 2000). Of course, this method also assumes that the established variables and measurements being used as a standard for comparison are themselves valid—creating an inescapable tautology. This is why the concept of *face validity* is important for qualitative inquiry, as it requires only the (presumably good) judgment of researchers (and, increasingly, study participants) to establish if something is valid or not. It does not rely on measurements or variables, which are not products of qualitative research. Instead, in the words of Creswell and Plano Clark (2011), "Validity [in qualitative research] comes from the analysis procedures of the researcher, based on information gleaned while visiting with participants and from external reviewers" (p. 211). For this reason, transparency of process is critical to making a convincing case for the validity of one's findings and interpretations (Miles & Huberman, 1994, p. 278). Although explicit documentation and description of procedures does not guarantee validity, it does provide information for others (as well as the researcher/data analysts themselves) to make informed assessments regarding the credibility of the research findings and interpretations. Likewise, following the procedures described below does not automatically confer validity to research. Rather, the procedures are methods that will: (a) decrease the likelihood of making critical mistakes and unfounded leaps of logic and (b) increase the degree of transparency within a study, thereby making it easier for others to judge its merit. A tabular summary of the procedures discussed is included on page 99 (Table 4.2).

During Research Design

Validity can be enhanced through all stages of the research process, beginning with research design. A commonly advocated method for enhancing validity is triangulation of data sources and methods (Ambert, Adler, Adler, & Detzner, 1995; Byrne 2001; Fossey, Harvey, McDermott, & Davidson, 2002; Malterud, 2001; Merriam, 2009; Miles & Huberman, 1994; Russell & Gregory, 2003; Sharts-Hopko, 2002). The rationale behind combining methods and data sources (i.e., triangulation) is that by accumulating multiple points of reference, researchers can minimize the intrinsic bias that comes from single-methods, single-observer, and single-theory studies (Denzin, 1989, p. 307). The strengths of one method are assumed to compensate for the weaknesses of another (Patton, 2002).[1] During analysis, data from different methods and sources are compared and the degree to which they converge or diverge documented. If for a given study, the same trends and themes emerge within data from different participant groups and data collection methods the validity of the findings is substantially increased. Therefore, if time and budget permit, we recommend incorporating some element(s) of triangulation into your research design. Keep in mind, however, that sometimes findings are *not* congruent across groups or methods and you have to be willing to accept and report this. Incongruent data should be dealt with openly and should always be presented with the findings. We provide more guidance on this issue in the next chapter.

Procedures can be put in place during data collection as well to improve the validity of results. One obvious, though not always followed, procedure is to make sure that the data collector knows the purpose behind each question and can explicitly articulate this purpose when asked. Without a sense of purpose, inductive probing lacks both direction and relevance. This is especially true in team-based research where the person(s) designing the study may not be the one collecting the data, or there may be multiple data collectors. Training of research field team(s) is critically important to obtaining valid results. Our trainings typically consist of 1 to 2 days of instruction and practice on data collection method processes (even if we have experienced data collectors; team training ensures consistency of application) and 1 to 2 days of question-by-question review of the interview or focus group guide. In this latter part, we explain question wording (if using a semistructured instrument) as well as the type of data we expect to get from a question (i.e., its purpose). This not only puts everyone on the same page in terms of technique and purpose, but it also provides a forum for team members (who may have better knowledge about the study population than the researcher) to provide feedback on the questions. We often come out of our team trainings with substantially revised, and improved, lists and sequencing of questions.

---

[1] In the mixed methods literature, the usefulness of the term "triangulation" has been questioned, as some believe that overuse of the term has resulted in a dilution and/or misrepresentation of its meaning (Teddlie & Tashakkori, 2009, p. 33). According to John Creswell (personal communication, July 2009), the term may soon be discontinued in the mixed method literature and replaced with "concurrent design."

If the study will use a semistructured instrument, the instrument itself might benefit from standard practices established for focus group instrument development. Krueger and Casey (2009) devote an entire chapter to developing effective focus group questions. Although not all of this chapter is relevant to other qualitative data collection methods, such as individual interviews, the 7-step process they describe for creating a guide is useful.

1. *Brainstorm:* A small, and hopefully diverse, group of people familiar with the study is invited to attend a meeting and list as many ideas as they can for topics and questions.

2. *Phrase Questions:* One or two people edit the questions. They winnow out the less informative questions, and edit the remaining questions for wording and tone.

3. *Sequence Questions:* Once you have a good working draft set of questions, the next step is for one to two people to put them in order (for focus group research, questions are almost always ordered. This is not always the case with one-on-one interviews). The order must be logical and easy for participants to follow. If there are sharp topical transitions, or major changes in the type of question (e.g., going from a listing question to an explanatory question), transitional statements should be inserted at appropriate places to smooth out the flow. Often researchers use a funnel approach in which questions start out broad and move to the more specific as the interview progresses. More sensitive questions are also typically placed near the end of an interview and positive questions before negative ones.

4. *Estimate the Time for Each Question:* Estimate the time that should be spent on each question. Add the times up and combine with the time necessary for establishing rapport and administering informed consent. If the overall amount of time required is too long (we suggest a maximum of 75 minutes for an in-depth interview and 2 hours for a focus group), edit the list until it is within an acceptable range.

5. *Get Feedback From Others:* Send the end product from Step 4 back to the original brainstorming team and/or others with a stake in the research, for review.

6. *Revise the Questions:* Based on the feedback obtained in Step 5, revise the questions. If necessary, repeat Steps 5 and 6 a few times. If the comments coming back start to become nitpicky, it is time to stop soliciting feedback.

7. *Test the Questions:* With a few individuals from the target population (or as close as you can get), test the questions on two basic parameters:

    a. How does the question sound when spoken? What may look good in writing does not always sound great when vocalized.

    b. Do any of the questions confuse the participant? Do participants understand the intent of the question?

Any issues that emerge during the testing phase need to be addressed before moving on to actual data collection.

The procedures above can improve validity of research instruments. In addition, the inductive nature of qualitative data collection itself facilitates valid responses, particularly when compared to structured, fixed-choice questions one would find on a survey. How many times have you read a survey question and prepared to answer, only to realize that the response you have in mind is not presented as an option (and there is no "other" option)? This problem is avoided in most qualitative research through open-ended questioning; participants can answer in their own words and are not constrained by responses imposed by the researcher. Moreover, a good interviewer can sense when a participant does not understand the intent behind a particular question and has the flexibility to address this during the interview process through rephrasing or elaboration. No such accommodations are made in survey research, where interviewers are typically told to read (and reread if necessary) structured questions verbatim.

Reliability in qualitative inquiry is an entirely different matter. As mentioned earlier, we, along with others, feel that it is not as pressing an issue as validity, because replication is rarely the goal of qualitative research. That said, if comparison of qualitative data—between groups or periods in time—is a study goal, then reliability and consistency come to the forefront when designing a study. Valid comparative analysis requires an apples-to-apples comparison. If, for example, one wants to compare perceptions or experiences between two or more groups (e.g., between men and women) or within one or more groups over time (e.g., a pre/post design), then a certain degree of reliability is essential. Structure facilitates reliability, and therefore comparative analysis. Instruments, questions, and processes with more structure enable a more meaningful comparative analysis. With no structure, one cannot make claims that any differences observed are due to actual differences between groups, since all or most of the variability could just as easily be due to differences in the way questions were asked. Different questions will, by their very nature, elicit different responses—especially if they are presented in a different order. The trick, of course, is to moderate the use of structure to simultaneously maintain the flexibility and inductive nature of qualitative inquiry; otherwise, the research endeavor becomes shallow and negates the purpose of doing qualitative data collection in the first place (and likely does not satisfy the necessary preconditions for good comparative quantitative analysis).

Another way to ensure consistent application of a data collection protocol is to train data collectors in depth about procedures surrounding the data collection activity. Write explicit instructions in the guides—no instructions are too obvious. Monitoring data as they are collected can also help improve quality of data. For our international studies, we always review transcripts as they are sent to us. We then provide feedback (often in the form of comments within the document) on the interviewing process, pointing out examples of poor technique or exceptionally good practices. Discussing the feedback over the phone also helps. We have seen dramatic improvements in data quality as a result of these simple measures. Finally, if the field team is large and a systematic comparison is planned, it is advisable to randomly assign participants to interviewers. This helps minimize interviewer bias by ensuring that they are randomly distributed across interviews (and thus groups and time periods). Of course, random assignment needs to be balanced with efforts necessary to reduce other potential biases such as matching interviewers to participant by gender, age, and ethnicity.

During Analysis and Interpretation

Intercoder Agreement

Discussion of reliability and qualitative research almost invariably includes some mention of intercoder agreement (ICA); it is the most commonly discussed element of reliability in qualitative research (Ambert et al., 1995; Bernard & Ryan, 2010; Carey & Gelaude, 2008; Miles & Huberman, 1994). Intercoder agreement signifies the extent to which two or more data analysts code the same qualitative data set in the same way. Assessment of intercoder agreement works like this: Two analysts, using the same codebook, independently apply codes to a section of text. In most cases, this will be a few transcripts from in-depth interviews or focus groups. The analysts then compare their coding and see where they have applied codes to the same text and where their coding does not match. There are multiple variations as to how the ICA process is specifically conducted. Here we cover the ones we have seen most frequently.

The first step in an ICA check is to establish what method will be used to assess agreement. To our knowledge, the three most common methods are subjective assessment, percent agreement, and Cohen's Kappa statistic. In a subjective assessment, coders sit down (this can be done remotely via phone, if necessary) and review the double-coded text, section by section. In places where Analyst A applied a code and Analyst B did not, we say there is disagreement, which is likewise true in places where Analyst B applied a code and Analyst A did not. Each time the coders reach a point where their coding does not agree, they discuss the reasons for the discrepancy, agree on a solution, recode the master coding document, and revise code definitions if necessary. Sometimes a third party is brought in to help resolve discrepancies. In the subjective method, no metrics are generated, and, typically, all discordant coding is resolved during the ICA process.

Percent agreement is another method for assessing ICA. It builds on the subjective method, adding the step of keeping a tally of every time an agreement or disagreement in coding is observed. Percent agreement is calculated by dividing the total number of times analysts' coding is in agreement by the total number of code comparisons (i.e., the total number of agreements plus total number of disagreements). Typically, agreement of 80% or more is considered good. Exercise 1 at the end of this chapter outlines a step-by-step procedure for calculating percent agreement. As you do the exercise, you will notice how easy (though potentially time-consuming) this process can be. Note also that not all qualitative data analysis (QDA) software provides a percent agreement function, so check software features if this is something you intend to perform using software instead of pen and paper (see Chapter 9).

Another, more rigorous, method for assessing ICA is to calculate a Kappa coefficient (Cohen's Kappa) that provides a measure of intercoder reliability (or the amount of agreement, taking into account the amount of agreement that could be expected to occur simply through chance). A Cohen's Kappa of 0.8 or greater is considered a very high level of agreement; note that it is in fact higher than an 80% level of agreement. Although many researchers consider Kappas the best way to measure intercoder agreement, the downsides are that using this statistic is not always appropriate for small samples, and some qualitative data analysis software does not calculate this metric (Carey, Morgan, & Oxtoby, 1996; Lombard, Snyder-Duch, & Campanella Bracken, 2002). Generation of Kappas, as a single ICA approach, also removes the analysts from the data; instead of discussions about specific sections of text and how they relate to codes, they are discussing a statistical measurement of agreement either overall or code-by-code. Codes that show agreement of less than 80% or Kappa below 0.8 are typically reviewed and discussed, but fruitful elements of coding review can be missed by relying too heavily on Kappas to measure how similarly a pair of coders are interpreting the codebook and applying codes to text.

Previously we mentioned reviewing the text "section by section." We also use the term *segment*. In Chapter 3, we explained why it is important to carefully consider how text for analysis will be segmented. Segmenting, or how one defines an analytical "section" of text, also plays a critical role in the ICA process. If using software, any segmenting differences—even if just a one character difference—will be considered less than 100% agreement in coding. Therefore, if you plan to automate ICA, segmenting should be identical across analysts. An alternative is to broaden the unit of comparison and perform ICA at the source level (i.e., entire transcript). Although this eliminates the segmenting problem, the resulting ICA metric is less meaningful: all that it measures is whether or not analysts applied a code to a given transcript, regardless of how many times it was applied, or where in the text it was applied. When doing a more subjective ICA assessment, or calculating agreement manually (i.e., by hand), segmenting poses less of a problem. In this situation, coders can look at the text and determine roughly where the core of the theme resides and see if their code application minimally covers this part of the text.

During one of our trainings, we had a student ask us, "If you plan to resolve all of the coding discrepancies, why do you need to generate an ICA metric?" This is indeed a good question. The first reason one might generate a metric is to keep track of overall coding reliability as analysis progresses. Even if all transcripts are double-coded and all coding discrepancies resolved, it is still useful to see the overall ICA trend over time to make sure that in fact progress is being made with respect to consistency in code application. Without a metric, this is difficult to do. Another reason to use metrics is to identify particularly problematic codes. We might, for example, calculate ICA and see which codes have low agreement (i.e., a Kappa of less than 0.8 or percent agreement less than 80%). This tells us which codes —and corresponding code definitions—we need to look at more closely. A third scenario in which a metric is useful for a thematic analysis is when not all transcripts/text in an analysis are double-coded. This is often the case when dealing with large data sets and double-coding every piece of text would be prohibitively time-consuming. Here, double-coding every nth transcript—where n is determined by the overall number of transcripts/text and the amount of time a team has to code the entire data set—is an acceptable practice. Generally, the greater the percentage of transcripts/text double-coded, the better.

The convention is to double-code more data in the earlier stages of the analysis and taper this amount off as coding becomes more consistent over time. The ICA metric in this latter scenario can be used in several capacities. It can identify especially problematic codes (i.e., those that exhibit poor agreement) and allow for a more targeted recoding and codebook revision. That is, only the coding involving the identified problem codes is examined in-depth, and recoding and revisions to codebook definitions are confined to just these codes. It can also aid in situations where a data set is so large that coding of data has to be split between two or more analysts. Imagine that you have 150 in-depth interview transcripts that need to be coded in a short amount of time. You assign 50 interviews to each of three analysts. Initially, they independently code, say, five of the same transcripts and calculate an ICA metric. If the metric is acceptable, one of two procedures can follow: (1) coding discrepancies in the five transcripts are resolved and a master data set recoded based on the resolutions, or (2) one of the three sets of coding is accepted as a master and no recoding is done. Which path you take depends on how much time you have to complete the analysis. If in the same scenario the first five triple-coded transcripts result in an overall *unacceptable* level of ICA you can either (a) look at all of the coding, resolve all discrepancies, and recode all of the five transcripts in a master data set file or (b) examine only the problematic codes and reapply only those codes in the master data set. Again, the decision will ultimately depend on time constraints, but in both cases, the first option is preferable because it means that more coding discrepancies are resolved. Note that if all coding discrepancies are resolved you ultimately have perfect agreement.

Keeping with the above example, another question follows: How many ICA checks should be done after the first five transcripts? Again, this is a matter of balancing rigor with time and budget constraints. Ideally they are done frequently, but at the very least every 10th transcript. Often a graded approach is used in which the number of ICA checks decreases over time as the codebook, and presumably ICA, improves. One of the key things to consider in all of this is that greater than 95% of all coding discrepancies will likely be due to variation between analysts with respect to interpretation of code definitions, not to coding errors. Therefore, the frequency of ICA checks needs to permit enough analysis time to revise definitions. New themes will also probably emerge as the analysis progresses, and these need to be incorporated into the codebook at regular intervals. This is also why the codebook development procedures outlined in Chapter 3 are so important. The more precise the definitions, the better your ICA will be. We should note here that although quantitative measures of intercoder agreement have their place and can be useful tools, often a simple subjective assessment is all that is needed. In addition, subjective ICA processes offer several advantages. A researcher can better absorb and become more familiar with the data by reviewing text multiple times and piece by piece, even if the process takes longer. The discussions that result from ICA discussions can be incredibly helpful in crystallizing code definitions for an analysis team. Subjective assessments can also easily accommodate more than two coders, and they avoid the problem that inconsistent segmenting can create for automated measures.

Note that recoding and revising codebook definitions are not always part of the analysis plan, as might be the case in a confirmatory analysis or when time is extremely tight. In such instances, an ICA metric can simply be used as a post-coding reporting tool where the researcher documents and reports how much of the data were double-coded and the resulting ICA metric. The problem with this approach is that the credibility of your findings might be seriously questioned if you report a low level of ICA.

We must note here that some researchers have argued that having multiple coders does not necessarily enhance an analysis, particularly if neither was involved in the collection of those data (Morse, 1997). We agree that any individual who collects data brings something extra to the analysis, but this argument fails to recognize the reason for doing ICA checks in the first place—to neutralize as best one can the biases any *one* individual brings to an analysis, particularly an analysis that requires subjective categorization and interpretation of meaning. It is not surprising that in the literature pertaining to assessing quality and rigor in qualitative research, many authors, along with journal guidelines, recommend some form of coding assessments during data analysis (e.g., Ambert et al., 1995; Miles & Huberman, 1994).

A question related to the above, and one that has come up when we do trainings is, "What if there is only one data analyst staffed on the study?" This is a great question, and one that many researchers working alone on a study face. We recommend two possible courses of action. An individual can serve as both the primary and secondary coder by reviewing some, or all, of her own coding after some time has passed since the first round of coding. Taking some time to sit back and refresh one's perspective helps temper any temporary distorting effects immersion in the data can cause. An alternative to this is to provide a colleague with your codebook and ask her to look over a random selection of coded text to see if the connections between the raw text and the code definitions are intuitive and make sense. Feedback can then be used to revise definitions and recode if and where necessary. Although this method is very different from conducting formal ICA, it is still a big step toward addressing potential problems with both validity and reliability. Other suggestions can be found in the sections below that could also prove useful for the solo analyst.

External Review

Another suggested method for increasing the validity of data collected and analyzed is to have someone from outside of the research team look at the data and interpretations derived from the data. This is sometimes referred to as "external reliability" (Gibson & Brown, 2009). Miles and Huberman (1994) and Lincoln and Guba (1985), for example, suggest researchers have peers not involved with the research review the analysis process and resulting extrapolations. Peers are instructed to examine the internal consistency of the analytic process as well as probe for potential biases.

A related method—referred to as "member checking" or "respondent validation"—entails participants themselves, or members of the participants' community, reviewing the summarized data to see if they accurately reflect their intents and meanings (Byrne, 2001; Charmaz, 2006; Corbin & Strauss, 2008; Creswell & Plano Clark, 2011; Giacomini & Cook, 2000; Mays & Pope, 2000; Merriam, 2009; Saldana, 2009). Although this method typically refers to postanalysis review, it can also be used immediately after data collection (Patton, 2002, p. 383) or after an individual data collection event has been summarized (Lincoln & Guba, 1985).

Conversely, Morse and colleagues (2002) argue that participant review of analyzed and summarized data can actually detract from validity since individual responses are not easily visible within the aggregated summary. We disagree. Although it is true an individual's responses might not be explicitly visible in a data summary, surely a participant will recognize some of the themes that his voice helped create. It is also not clear how getting feedback from anyone can, in and of itself, threaten validity. External feedback should be viewed as a method to stimulate critical thinking in the author of the research, nothing more. Validity is a property of knowledge, not methods. Although using good methods, and being explicit about them, can make for better and more transparent research, ultimately it is up to a researcher's audience to determine how valid the findings from a study are.

If data collection and analysis are done by different individuals, as may occur in a team situation, data collectors can also serve as reviewers for the analysis and subsequent interpretation. We have found this method particularly useful in international research where the analysis is done in a different country and culture than data collection: local data collectors are extremely useful reviewers and can add invaluable insight into what the data mean in local terms. They can also point out where interpretations can be revised to more accurately reflect realities on the ground. Of course, an even more optimal approach is to build the capacity of the local data collection team as coders and analysts.

Using an Audit Trail and Increasing Transparency

Earlier in this chapter, we wrote about the importance of transparency. A formal technique for achieving better transparency is using what has been called an "audit trail" (Hills, 2000; Miles & Huberman, 1994; Sharts-Hopko, 2002). Audit trails involve keeping track of and documenting the entire data analysis process. At the minimum, this includes documenting: individuals involved with specific data points and analytic activities (e.g., who translated/

transcribed/coded transcript *x*), data included or not included in the analysis and rationale behind these decisions, methods used to find themes and apply codes to text, changes made to the codebook and reasons for changes, results of coding checks and actions taken, and any data reduction techniques employed.

Audit trails serve at least two important functions. First, they help researchers implement their own process checks. If, for example, there are transcription or translation problems, a researcher can easily identify the individual(s) responsible and engage in some retraining. A researcher may also want to replicate all or a portion of the analysis—what Dey (1990) calls "internal replication" (p. 221)— and having an audit trail to follow makes this task much easier. In addition, documenting the analytic process, and all of the decisions that went into it, forces researchers to think more carefully about their rationale for doing things and to be more deliberate and systematic in their approach.

An audit trail also generates readily accessible documentation that can prove useful to other audiences, particularly skeptical ones. One of the most frustrating experiences for us as readers of qualitative research is a data analysis section that reads, "We did a thematic analysis," or, "The data were inductively coded," leaving the entire analytic process a big black box. Although it may not be necessary to provide your audience with your entire audit trail (and the amount of detail you provide will vary greatly according to the audience), having one allows you to at least provide a basic description of what you did without having to recreate anything, perhaps inaccurately. Let those who are interested in your research know how you got from A to B to C.

Negative and Deviant Case Analyses

A common critique of reporting of qualitative research is that the data presented are selectively chosen to support conclusions drawn by the author or to further an agenda of some kind. And, frankly, it is tempting to engage in analytic cherry-picking when trying to present a cohesive narrative that is logical and flows well. Actively looking for, and candidly presenting, data that contradict common themes in a data set or the running narrative in a report helps combat this propensity (Dey, 1993; Elder & Miller, 1995, Mays & Pope, 2000; Seale & Silverman, 1997). This process begins at codebook development and continues through to the final report. Although contradictory data are not always easy to deal with, they reflect the messy and complex nature of the subject matter (human experience) and need to be incorporated somehow into the explanatory model or overall interpretation of findings.

Related to the above is deviant case analysis (Fossey et al., 2002; Pope & Mays, 2000). In quantitative research, deviant cases may be labeled outliers and dealt with using a variety of methods (data transformations, extraction from the data set, etc.). In qualitative inquiry, because it is inductive and relatively flexible, we use deviant cases to further inform our research question. Following the unconventional route can often lead to novel and invaluable insights. The process can be carried out while in the data collection phase, or as part of the analysis process, where deviant cases are identified and given a more in-depth examination. We provide more details surrounding this latter process in Chapter 5. Either way, searching for and reporting negative and deviant cases mitigates the tendency to highlight only those data that support a given argument and also helps ensure a more exhaustive analysis and consideration of alternate explanations.

The Importance of Quotes

As we discussed earlier, face validity is determined by one's peers and the audience to whom one reports. We have also highlighted the related importance of making data and the analytic process transparent so that others have enough information to fairly judge research findings. Nothing in qualitative research is more important to these ends than using verbatim quotes. In Chenail's (1995) words, quotes are the "stars" of qualitative research. They bring the raw data—the participants' words—to the reader and are what connect the phenomenological world of the participant to the data summary and interpretation generated by the researcher (Guest & MacQueen, 2008). The beautiful thing about quotes is that their veracity is difficult to criticize. A reviewer can critique your sampling strategy and whether or not a participant is representative of some larger group. A reviewer can also legitimately disagree with your interpretation of what a participant meant in a given section of discourse or argue that they were not accurately reporting their own views or behavior. What cannot really be refuted, however, is that the participant said what he or she said. Quotes lay bare the emergent themes for all to see. They are the foundation upon which good qualitative data analysis is based.

When presenting a thematic analysis, quotes should be a pivotal part of the narrative. We suggest using at least one exemplar quote to illustrate each theme presented in a report. Quotes presented in a report should be selected based on their ability to exemplify an intended concept (Bluff, 1997; Secker, Wimbush, Watson, & Milburn, 1995). For potentially contentious or complex themes, two quotes per theme might be necessary, but avoid going overboard. Using too many quotes defeats the purpose of a data summary and can end up reading like a string of raw text rather than a research summary. Pitchforth, Porter, van Teijlingen, and Forrest Kennan (2005) recommend that quotes be accompanied by labels identifying key demographics of the participant being quoted to give the reader a better sense of context. A quote raving about the benefits of social media, for example, may be read and interpreted differently according to the age, profession, and sex of the respondent who expressed the opinion (Was this someone born in the 1950s or 1990s? A techie or a school teacher?). Associating demographics or participant ID numbers with quotes also helps establish to a certain degree the amount of variability within the data set. If, for example, only one or two participants are repeatedly quoted throughout a report or article, the extent to which the themes cut across participants and groups is difficult to establish.

Selecting the proper length for a quote is another critical factor. Quotes should be brief but long enough to fully exemplify the intended theme or concept.

Normally, one to three sentences is a good length, but there is no fixed rule. A longer quote that brings together multiple themes can be very effective for illustrating the meaning embedded in each theme as well as relationships among themes. Often, the space limits imposed by a journal or reporting format will partially determine the length and number of quotes used. A final rule of thumb is to present quotes as transcribed from the speech. Although it is acceptable to omit the "ums" and other nonessential speech elements or to remove superfluous text (replacing it with the standard "…"), we typically strive to keep the voice of the participant intact, including grammatical idiosyncrasies.

Transcription and Translation

To do a rigorous and systematic thematic analysis, verbatim transcripts are the norm when it comes to the raw data analyzed. Although audio recording is not always possible, it is certainly recommended. If you cannot obtain a verbatim recording, make an effort to get the best representation of the data collection event as possible. That may involve having a trained person specifically assigned to the task of note-taking, allowing the interviewer to concentrate on the interview process itself while the note-taker gives all her attention to recording the event. Developing strong note-taking skills and a system of shorthand also help generate better data, as does expanding field notes as soon after the data collection event as possible. For an outline of these and other data collection procedures, we refer readers to Guest, Namey, and Mitchell (in press).

The benefits of audio recording are obvious, but just because an interview or focus group is recorded does not necessarily mean a verbatim or useful transcript will result. McLellan, MacQueen, and Niedig (2003) discuss the idea of transcription as an element of rigor in the qualitative data analysis process, and anyone who has experience dealing with transcripts can tell you that transcript quality can vary immensely from one transcriptionist to the next: It turns out that the word "verbatim" can have about as many meanings as there are transcriptionists. Probably the best way to mitigate transcription issues is to develop a transcription protocol for a given study. Guidance as to what one should consider when transcribing data is handled well by other authors (e.g., McLellan-Lemal, 2008; McLellan et al., 2003; Powers, 2005), and a good sample protocol can be found in an appendix of Guest et al., (in press). Whichever method of transcription you select, be sure that the method and style are appropriate for the analysis planned.

Translating a data collection event from one language to another adds an additional layer of complexity that can affect both the validity and reliability of the data with which a researcher works. When working in teams, there may be multiple translators, and each may have his own style. Even if only one translator is involved, verbatim translation is different from more semantic types of translation methods, where it is the meaning behind the words that is most important (which some might call "interpretation"). Based on our experience working in international settings, we have found it helpful to bring the translator into the research process as early as possible and explain to her what is expected as an end product. Provide her with guidance, for example, as to how you want culturally unique idioms translated or how she should handle words and phrases that do not have literal counterparts. We often instruct our transcriptionists to provide explanations within the text (in square brackets) if necessary, to help us better understand the meaning behind ambiguous statements. In cases where the translation of a particular word or concept is especially difficult (and potentially contentious), it is a good idea to include the vernacular with the translation, in brackets or as a footnote. This creates an additional layer of transparency for the skeptical reviewer.

If your research deals with a highly technical topic, make sure that the translator has a good working knowledge of the technical vocabulary. You can also enhance validity—that is, confirm that what the participant meant is accurately conveyed in the translated text—by having the translation reviewed by the person who collected the data and/or a third party knowledgeable about the research and subject matter. All of the strategies mentioned here improve the likelihood that the translated transcript truly reflects the meaning intended by the participant, in addition to ensuring that the data are useful for the type of analysis planned.

Addressing Biases

Recognizing and reporting potential biases that might affect the analysis or subsequent interpretation is a commonly suggested strategy for enhancing validity in qualitative research (Byrne, 2001; Dey, 1993; Horsburgh, 2003; Malterud, 2001; Mays & Pope, 2000; Pitchforth et al., 2005). Patton (2002) takes this process a step further and offers the suggestion that an analyst engage in a "mental cleansing process" (p. 553) prior to analyzing the data. Identifying possible biases can be useful in some extreme cases, but in general, we feel that the issue has been overblown in the literature surrounding qualitative research, for several reasons.

First, as we argue in an earlier publication (Guest & MacQueen, 2008), researcher bias is not a challenge that is exclusive to qualitative research. The well-known Hawthorne Effect (Parsons, 1974) and Rosenthal Effect (Rosenthal, 1966) stem from quantitative research. Likewise, an entire literature exists describing how interviewer attributes, and other contextual factors, can significantly affect an interviewee's responses on a structured survey and corresponding study results. Significance fishing—where multiple variables on a survey are repeatedly intercorrelated until an "acceptable" p-value is discovered—is also a commonly practiced approach to quantitative analysis (though disparaged among purists). The above being true, it hardly seems fair that qualitative researchers should be held to a higher standard (survey researchers are not typically asked to report their biases along with their findings). The inductive processes involved in coding qualitative data are admittedly more subjective than, say, running a chi-square or ANOVA on survey data, but this does not mean that the coding process is purely subject to the whims of an analyst. Good content coding and subsequent analysis and interpretation of codes and code configurations are always tied to the raw data, what the participants actually said. Credible thematic analysis is grounded in the data.

Even if a researcher made a valiant effort to identify and report individual biases, what would this look like? Would an analyst have to report all of his demographic characteristics (the list of which is infinite)? His mood when doing the analysis? Childhood events that might affect how he views that data? What they watched on television the night before? You can see how this becomes not only logistically infeasible but also self-defeating. If you do not report *all* of your biases, then your reporting of biases itself is biased.

However, if you have obvious inclinations that can seriously jeopardize the analysis, you should deal with them up front in an open manner. That said, we believe the word *bias* has been vexed with an unearned negative connotation. As we discussed previously, every type of research has potential for bias. When you hear someone pejoratively say, "That's a biased question," the correct response is, "Of course it is." In survey research, for example, there is no such thing as an unbiased question. Asking questions in different ways will get you different answers; survey methodologists spend careers studying the effects of question type on response direction and are quite good at predicting such biases.

And so it is with qualitative research. Any question will bias responses in one direction versus another, even the most unstructured open-ended questions. Moreover, the analytic process itself can never be bias free. Even if it were possible to completely rid yourself of all biases just before an analysis, the attention and direction of the analysis will be guided by the research objectives. If it is not, your codebook will be unmanageably long, not to mention meaningless in terms of addressing the study goals. Bias exists, but we do not believe that it is as big of a problem as others do. Employing some or all of the procedures described above—external review, coding checks, triangulation, supporting assertions with quotes, and seeking out negative cases and disconfirming evidence—will provide ample checks and balances to enhance the validity and reliability of your data analysis and interpretation.

SUMMING UP

The discussion surrounding the concepts of validity and reliability is extensive and goes much deeper than what we have presented here. We have, however, attempted to provide the reader with a basic understanding of the terms and how they have been applied (or not applied) to qualitative research. Although some good arguments have been made in favor of abandoning these terms for qualitative inquiry, we argue that employing them, while simultaneously understanding their limitations, is the lesser of two evils. Should the interested reader choose to dig deeper into the discussion, we have provided key references as a jumping off point.

We conclude this chapter with some practical recommendations for enhancing the quality of output from a thematic analysis. A good place to start is with Charmaz's (2006) set of questions a researcher should consider when assessing credibility:

- Has your research achieved intimate familiarity with the setting or topic?
- Are the data sufficient to merit your claims? (Consider the range, number, and depth of observations contained in the data.)
- Have you made systematic comparisons between observations and between categories?
- Do the categories cover a wide range of empirical observations?
- Are there strong logical links between the gathered data and your argument and analysis?
- Has your research provided enough evidence for your claims to allow the reader to form an independent assessment—and *agree* with your claims? (p.182)

The six criteria above are useful at a conceptual level. In Table 4.2, we provide some guidance on how to address these criteria from a procedural and practical standpoint.

Table 4.2 Techniques for Enhancing Validity and Reliability

Technique	What It Does
Research Design Stage	
Use multiple methods and/or data sources	• Collecting data via multiple methods or from a variety of sources provides the opportunity to compare findings in analysis for convergence or divergence (triangulation).
Team-based instrument development (if using a guide) and pretest	• Involving the whole research team in steps of the instrument development process increases reliability by familiarizing the team with the connection between research objectives and questions on the guide at an early stage. • Brainstorming specific questions to include may increase validity of the questions, since multiple perspectives will be considered (reduces bias from any one person). • Pretesting facilitates validity by ensuring questions make sense to participants.
Data Collection Stage	
Train field team in collection techniques	• Training data collectors on the purpose behind the questions and on probing techniques improves data relevance and contributes to better reliability between data collectors.
Adjust structure of instruments to fit goals and structure of study	• Increasing structure of a data collection instrument also increases the ability to compare data across data collectors, and across time and geography. • Less structured instruments are good for exploratory research that does not entail comparisons or multiple data collectors.

(Continued)

Table 4.2   (Continued)

Technique	What It Does
Monitor data as they come in	• Providing data collectors with immediate feedback improves data quality and consistency.
Elicit feedback from participants after summarizing their interview	• Having participants review what they said improves validity and provides the researcher an opportunity to clarify anything that was unclear or ambiguous

Data Analysis Stage	
Transcribe data using transcription protocol	• Transcription provides verbatim account of data collection event, thereby enhancing validity. • Using a transcription protocol ensures that transcription is done consistently and is of the appropriate type for the analytic aims.
Establish translation expectations at beginning	• Translation techniques and styles vary greatly. Establishing your translation approach up front increases the likelihood that your data will be useful for the analysis planned.
Develop and use a precise codebook	• The vast majority of coding reliability problems are due to differing interpretations of code meanings. The more descriptive and precise a codebook, the better intercoder reliability will result. • Good codebooks also facilitate data comparison if using the same codes in a different study. • Codebooks serve as documentation of the themes relevant to a given analysis and provide easy access to code meanings for internal reviews.
Use multiple coders and intercoder agreement checks	• Use of multiple coders facilitates coding reliability by providing checks on individual biases and variance in interpretation of code definitions. • Iterative revision of the codebook as a result of coding checks improves the precision of codebook. • ICA checks can provide metrics for assessing progress in consistency of code application (if using percent agreement or Kappa statistic).
External and/or peer review of coding and summaries	• Outside review facilitates coding reliability by providing checks on individual biases and variance in interpretation of code definitions.
Create an audit trail	• Documentation of analysis steps and codebook revisions makes the analysis process more transparent for other researchers to review. • An audit trail facilitates internal review of processes and the ability to accurately replicate procedures if desired.

Technique	What It Does
Triangulate data sources	• If analyzed properly, convergent data from different methods/sources validate findings. • Divergence of data indicates a need to adapt explanatory models and provide potential reasons for the discordance.
Negative case analysis	• Consciously including negative cases in an analysis mitigates analyst biases by forcing analysts to look for and report any evidence contrary to prevailing patterns identified in the data.
Support themes and interpretations with quotes	• Using verbatim quotes increases the validity of findings by directly connecting the researcher's interpretations with what participants actually said.

This chapter has outlined various tools and procedures for enhancing validity (or credibility) and reliability (or dependability) of qualitative research and data analysis. Employing the methods and suggestions offered in this chapter should enhance the credibility of a qualitative research study (and data analysis in particular) for almost any audience. They serve to increase systematicity, rigor, and transparency, all of which lead to better research outcomes. This said, a word of caution is in order. Procedures alone can never replace sound research or compensate for inadequate understanding of basic research principles. A study that meets all of the criteria outlined in Table 4.2 but that is poorly conceived, or not adequately described, will never attain credibility. The procedures presented are suggestions for enhancing rigor and transparency, but in and of themselves, are not sufficient to guarantee excellence in qualitative research or analysis (see Barbour, 2001; Eakin & Mykhalovskiy, 2003). As Lambert and McKevitt (2002) warn, uncritical application of methods and procedures can "legitimise substandard research" (p. 210). In our view, guidelines are intended to provide direction for research practitioners and help make the analysis and reporting processes more systematic and exhaustive. They are not designed to be substitutes for professional training, good judgment, and critical thinking.

REFERENCES

Ambert, A., Adler, P., Adler, P., & Detzner, D. (1995). Understanding and evaluating qualitative research. *Journal of Marriage and the Family, 57,* 879–893.

Auerbach, C., & Silverstein, L. (2003). *Qualitative data: An introduction to coding and analysis.* New York: New York University Press.

Babbie, E. (1990). *Survey research methods* (2nd ed.). Belmont, CA: Wadsworth Publishing Company.

Barbour, R. S. (2001). Checklists for improving rigour in qualitative research: A case of the tail wagging the dog? *BMJ, 322,* 1115–1117.

Bernard, H. R. (2000). *Social research methods: Qualitative and quantitative approaches.* Thousand Oaks, CA: Sage.

Bernard, H. R. (2006). *Research methods in anthropology: Qualitative and quantitative approaches* (4th ed.). Walnut Creek, CA: AltaMira Press.

Bernard, H., & Ryan, G. (2010). *Analyzing qualitative data: Systematic approaches.* Thousand Oaks, CA: Sage.

Black, J., & Champion, D. (1976). *Methods and issues in social research.* New York: Wiley.

Bluff, R. (1997). Evaluating qualitative research. *British Journal of Midwifery, 5*(4), 232–235.

Byrne, M. (2001). Evaluating the findings of qualitative research. *Association of Operating Room Nurses Journal, 73*(3), 703–706.

Campbell, D., & Fiske, D. (1959). Convergent and discriminant validation by the multi-train-multimethod matrix. *Psychological Bulletin, 56*(2), 81–105.

Carey, J., & Gelaude, D. (2008). Systematic methods for collecting and analyzing multi-disciplinary team-based qualitative data. In G. Guest & K. MacQueen (Eds.), *Handbook for team-based qualitative research* (pp. 227–274). Lanham, MD: AltaMira Press.

Carey, J., Morgan, M., & Oxtoby, M. (1996). Intercoder agreement in analysis of responses to open-ended interview questions: Examples from tuberculosis research. *Cultural Anthropology Methods Journal, 8,* 1–5.

Charmaz, K. (2006). *Constructing grounded theory: A practical guide through qualitative analysis.* Thousand Oaks, CA: Sage.

Chenail, R. (1995). Presenting qualitative data. *The Qualitative Report, 2*(3). Retrieved from http://www.nova.edu/ssss/QR/QR2-3/presenting.html

Corbin, J., & Strauss, A. (2008). *Basics of qualitative research* (3rd ed.). Thousand Oaks, CA: Sage.

Creswell, J., & Plano Clark, V. (2011). *Designing and conducting mixed methods research* (2nd ed.). Thousand Oaks, CA: Sage.

Denzin, N. (1989). *The research act: A theoretical introduction to sociological methods* (3rd ed.). Englewood Cliffs, NJ: Prentice Hall.

Dey, I. (1993). *Qualitative data analysis: A user-friendly guide for social scientists.* New York: Routledge.

Eakin, J., & Mykhalovskiy, E. (2003). Reframing the evaluation of qualitative health research: Reflections on a review of appraisal guidelines in the health sciences. *Journal of Evaluation in Clinical Practice, 9*(2), 187–194.

Elder, N. C., & Miller, W. L. (1995). Reading and evaluating qualitative research studies. *Journal of Family Practice, 41*(3), 279–285.

Fossey, E., Harvey, C., McDermott, F., & Davidson, L. (2002). Understanding and evaluating qualitative research. *Australian and New Zealand Journal of Psychiatry, 36,* 717–732.

Giacomini, M., & Cook, D. (2000). Users' guide to the medical literature XXII: Qualitative research in health care. Are the results of the study valid? *JAMA, 284,* 357–362.

Gibson, W., & Brown, A. (2009). *Working with qualitative data.* Thousand Oaks, CA: Sage.

Golafshani, N. (2003). Understanding reliability and validity in qualitative research. *The Qualitative Report, 8*(4), 597–560.

Guest, G., & MacQueen, K. M. (2008). Re-evaluating guidelines for qualitative research. In G. Guest & K. M. MacQueen (Eds.), *Handbook for team-based qualitative research* (pp. 205–226). Lanham, MD: AltaMira Press.

Guest, G., Namey, E., & Mitchell, M. (In press). *Collecting qualitative data: A field manual.* Thousand Oaks, CA: Sage.

Hammersley, M. (1987). Some notes on the terms 'validity' and 'reliability.' *British Educational Research Journal, 13*(1), 73–81.

Hills, M. (2000). Human science research in public health: The contribution and assessment of a qualitative approach. *Canadian Journal of Public Health, 91*(6), 4–7.

Horsburgh, D. (2003). Evaluation of qualitative research. *Journal of Clinical Nursing, 12,* 307–312.

Johnston, J., & Pennypacker, H. (1980). *Strategies and tactics of human behavioral research.* Hillsdale, NJ: Erlbaum.

Kerlinger, F. (1964). *Foundations of behavioral research.* New York: Holt, Rinehart & Winston.

Kerlinger, F. (1973). *Foundations of behavioral research* (2nd ed.): New York: Holt, Rinehart & Winston.

Krueger, R., & Casey, M. (2009). *Focus groups: A practical guide for applied research* (4th ed.). Thousand Oaks, CA: Sage.

Lambert, H., & McKevitt, C. (2002). Anthropology in health research: From qualitative methods to multidisciplinary. *BMJ, 325,* 7357, 210–213.

Lehner, P. (1979). *Handbook of ethological methods.* New York: Garland STPM Press.

Lincoln, Y., & Guba, E. (1985). *Naturalistic inquiry.* Beverly Hills, CA: Sage.

Lombard, M., Snyder-Duch, J., & Campanella Bracken, C. (2002). Content analysis in mass communication: Assessment and reporting of intercoder reliability. *Human Communication Research, 28,* 587–604.

Malterud, K. (2001). Qualitative research: Standards, challenges, and guidelines. *The Lancet, 358,* 483–488.

Maxwell, J. (1992). Understanding and validity in qualitative research. *Harvard Educational Review, 62*(3), 279–300.

Mays, N., & Pope, C. (2000). Assessing quality in qualitative research. *BMJ, 320,* 50–52.

McLellan-Lemal, E. (2008). Transcribing data for team-based research. In G. Guest & K. MacQueen (Eds.), *Handbook for team-based qualitative research* (pp. 101–118). Lanham, MD: AltaMira Press.

McLellan, E., MacQueen, K. M., & Niedig, J. (2003). Beyond the qualitative interview: Data preparation and transcription. *Field Methods, 15*(1), 63–84.

Merriam, S. (2009). *Qualitative research: A guide to design and implementation.* San Francisco, CA: Jossey-Bass.

Miles, M., & Huberman, A. (1994). *Qualitative data analysis* (2nd ed.). Thousand Oaks, CA: Sage.

Morse, J. (1997). "Perfectly healthy, but dead": The myth of inter-rater reliability. *Qualitative Health Research, 7,* 445–447.

Morse, J., Barrett, M., Mayan, M., Olson, K., & Spiers, J. (2002). Verification strategies for establishing reliability and validity in qualitative research. *International Journal of Qualitative Methods, 1*(2), 1–19.

Onwuegbuzie, A., & Johnson, R. (2006). The validity issue in mixed research. *Research in the Schools, 13,* 48–63.

Parsons, H. (1974). What happened at Hawthorne? *Science, 183,* 922–932.

Patton, M. (2002). *Qualitative research and evaluation methods* (3rd ed.). Thousand Oaks, CA: Sage.

Pitchforth, E., Porter, M., van Teijlingen, E., & Forrest Keenan, K. (2005). Writing up and presenting qualitative research in family planning and reproductive health care. *Journal of Family Planning and Reproductive Health Care, 31*(2), 132–135.

Pope, C., & Mays, N. (2000). *Qualitative research in health care.* London: BMJ Books.

Powers, R. (2005). *Transcription techniques for the spoken word.* Lanham, MD: AltaMira Press.

Rosenthal, R. (1966). *Experimenter effects in behavioral research.* New York: Appleton-Century-Crofts.

Russell, C. K., & Gregory, D. M. (2003). Evaluation of qualitative research studies. *Evidence Based Nursing, 6,* 36–40.

Saldana, J. (2009). *The coding manual for qualitative researchers.* Thousand Oaks, CA: Sage.

Seale, C., & Silverman, D. (1997). Ensuring rigour in qualitative research. *European Journal of Public Health, 7,* 379–384.

Secker, J., Wimbush, E., Watson, J., & Milburn, K. (1995). Qualitative methods in health promotion research: Some criteria for quality. *Health Education Journal, 54,* 74–87.

Sharts-Hopko, N. C. (2002). Assessing rigor in qualitative research. *Journal of the Association of Nurses in AIDS Care, 13,* 84–86.

Social Science Dictionary.com. (2009). *Validity.* Retrieved from http://www.socialscience-dictionary.com/validity

Tashakkori, A., & Teddlie, C. (Eds.). (2003). *Handbook of mixed methods in social and behavioral research.* Thousand Oaks, CA: Sage.

Teddlie, C., & Tashakkori, A. (2009). *Foundations of mixed methods research: Integrating quantitative and qualitative approaches in the social and behavioral sciences.* Thousand Oaks, CA: Sage.

Ulin, P., Robinson, E., & Tolley, E. (2005). *Qualitative methods in public health: A field guide for applied research.* San Francisco, CA: Jossey-Bass.

Winter, G. (2000). A comparative discussion of the notion of 'validity' in qualitative and quantitative research. *The Qualitative Report, 4*(3&4). Retrieved from www.nova.edu/ssss/QR/QR4-3/winter.html

EXERCISES

INTERCODER-AGREEMENT

Required:

- Two "analysts"
- Two copies (one for each analyst) of three different transcripts, two to three pages each in length
- Coding template (provided below)

Procedure:

- Both analysts work together to develop a working codebook for the transcripts (refer to tips on creating a codebook in Chapter 3 if necessary).
- Independently, each analyst codes the transcripts using the team codebook, using brackets in the margin to roughly delineate segments.
- After coding is completed, decide who will have the "master" set of transcripts and who will have the "secondary" set. Note that for the most part this is an arbitrary decision.
- In the left column on the template, marked "Code," write down the names of each of the codes in your codebook (Tip: Enter the codes alphabetically so they will be easier to find.) Use as many sheets as necessary and number the pages.

- Look at the first coded segment on the master set of transcripts, and find the applied code in the first column on the coding agreement template. Was this same code applied to similar text on the other analyst's transcript? If yes, make a tick mark in the column labelled "Agree" next to the code. If no, make a tick mark in the column labelled "Disagree."
- Still looking at the same text segment, check to see if the secondary set of transcripts contains an applied code that is not on the master. If yes, find that code on the coding agreement template and make a tick mark in the column labelled "Disagree."
- Now move on to the second coded segment on the master set of transcripts, and find the applied code on the coding agreement template. Once again, compare the master with the same segment of text in the secondary set of transcripts and vice versa, making a tick mark for each code that agrees or disagrees, as appropriate.
- Continue the comparison process until all of the applied codes from both analysts have been compared.
- On the coding agreement template, count the number of ticks in each "Agree" and "Disagree" cell for each code and write the total in the cell. Add the number of "Agree" and "Disagree" totals; this is the total number of times the code was applied by both the master and secondary coder. Write this total in the column marked "Code Total."
- For each code, divide the "Agree" number by the "Code Total" number. This is the percent agreement for that code. Write that number in the column marked "Agreement."
- Now total all of the numbers in the column marked "Agree"; write this total in the appropriate space at the top of the first page of the coding agreement template. Do the same for the numbers in the column marked "Disagree"; again, write this number at the top of the first page. Add the total number for "Agree" and the total number for "Disagree"; this is the total number of codes applied to both the master and secondary sets of transcripts. Write this number in the appropriate space at the top of the first page.
- Divide the Total Number Agree by the Total Number of Codes Applied; this is the Overall Percent Agreement. Write this number in the appropriate space at the top of the first page.

Total Agree: _____

+ Total Disagree: _____

Total # Codes: _____

Overall % Agreement: _____

Code	Agree	Disagree	Code Total	Agreement
....n				
(i.e., have one row for every code in your codebook)	Total:	Total:		

REFLECTIVE PROBLEM-SOLVING

For a past, present, or future (could be hypothetical) research project, map out the research process in detail from design, through data collection and analysis to interpretation and write up. Include all of the individuals, data, and procedures involved, including communication between individuals. Note all possible areas where problems might have occurred, are occurring, or could occur with respect to validity, reliability, and overall integrity of the analysis and interpretation. For each problem area identified, try to create a feasible solution.

EXTERNAL REVIEW

After collecting data from a few sources (e.g., five interviews or two focus groups), develop some preliminary codes and a summary of the data. Have a peer or two review your work, looking for consistency of logic, connectedness to the data, and overall credibility. At the same time, ask several participants from whom the data were collected to look over your findings.

Compare feedback from your peers and participants. Are they telling you similar things? If their feedback suggests problems with your analysis, what are they, and how will you address them?

ADDITIONAL READING

Carey, J., & Gelaude, D. (2007). Systematic methods for collecting and analyzing multi-disciplinary team-based qualitative data. In G. Guest & K. MacQueen (Eds.), *Handbook for team-based qualitative research* (pp. 227–274). Lanham, MD: AltaMira Press.

Guest, G., & MacQueen, K. M. (2007). Re-evaluating guidelines for qualitative research. In G. Guest & K. M. MacQueen (Eds.), *Handbook for team-based qualitative research* (pp. 205–226). Lanham, MD: AltaMira Press.

McLellan, E., MacQueen, K. M., & Niedig, J. (2003). Beyond the qualitative interview: Data preparation and transcription. *Field Methods, 15,* 63–84.

5

SUPPLEMENTAL ANALYTIC TECHNIQUES

LEARNING OBJECTIVES

After reading this chapter, you should be able to:

- Perform word searches and key-word-in-context analyses to inform thematic analyses
- Make an informed decision about if and how a deviant/negative case analysis can inform a larger thematic analysis
- Explain the unique analytic characteristics of focus group data

---

This book focuses on the most common form of qualitative data analysis—inductive generation and interpretation of themes. The preceding chapters address the core aspects of applied thematic analysis—planning, coding data, and enhancing reliability of procedures and credibility of findings. However, as we emphasized in the first chapter, our approach to data analysis utilizes whatever analytic tools help achieve a given analytic objective. In this chapter we describe some of the more common techniques used to enhance, or supplement, thematic analyses: word searches and negative case analyses. We also cover the unique aspects of focus group data and how to highlight these in a thematic analysis.

WORD SEARCHES

Word searches and key-word-in-context (KWIC) techniques are simple yet highly effective analytic methods. The former involves searching for, and in some cases counting, specific words in a body of text. KWIC techniques are methodological cousins to word searches. The main difference is that KWIC searches also take into account the text surrounding words of interest (i.e., the context) and may also document relationships between pieces of text such as word co-occurrences (also known as *co-location*). As supplemental techniques in a thematic analysis, word searches and KWIC reports are employed differently than in their traditional methodological home—classic content analysis. One difference is that the primary unit of observation in an inductive thematic analysis is a text segment that exemplifies an instance of a concept or theme. In contrast, the unit of measurement in a classic content analysis is an individual word or verbatim phrase. Classic content analysis is therefore more quantitatively oriented, and the objective typically confirmatory in nature. Word searches and KWIC analyses play a different role in an inductive thematic analysis. Rather than being the primary analytic method, they are used in a complementary fashion. Both techniques can enhance an inductive thematic analysis in at least three fundamental ways—assisting in codebook development, checking for and filling in analytic gaps, and generating more detail about existing themes.

Codebook Development

In Chapter 3, we briefly discussed the potential role of word searches in developing a thematic codebook. The basic thinking behind this process is that frequently expressed key words are potential markers for themes. A few simple steps comprise the process:

- Generate a list of all unique words in the text. Exclude common words with limited semantic value, such as articles, prepositions, and so on.
- Count the number of times each of the words occurs in the text (more accurately, have the computer do the counting!).
- Collapse the list as much as possible by combining synonyms into single categories. Sum the initial word frequencies to get frequencies for the newly formed words/categories.
- Single out categories that occur relatively frequently and that are conceptually related to your research objectives. Use this list as the starting point for building your codebook.

A good example of this type of theme identification process is found in Ryan and Weisner's work (1996). In their study, they asked fathers and mothers of adolescents to describe their children in their own words. From the verbatim transcripts of responses, the authors created of list of all the unique words in the text. They then counted the number of times particular words were used by mothers and fathers. Not surprisingly, mothers and fathers tended to use different words to describe their children. Mothers used words like "friends," "creative," "time," and "honest," whereas fathers more often used words such as "school," "good," "lack," "student," "enjoys," "independent," and "extremely." Ryan and Weisner used these word lists as a starting point for identifying and describing themes in their subsequent analysis. Researchers need to be careful, however, to not become overly reliant on word searches for theme identification. In many cases, important themes are (a) not identifiable by a single word and (b) not expressed frequently. Also remember to segment the text to be analyzed so that it excludes prompts from the interviewer(s) that may artificially inflate word counts. When developing a thematic codebook, word searching—if used at all—is just the beginning of a more comprehensive process.

Gap Analysis

KWIC techniques are also helpful for double-checking a thematic analysis to ensure that all corners of the text have been explored to inform an analysis to the fullest. This is often done when an analyst has already developed a working codebook and has at least carried out an initial thematic analysis on a data set. A KWIC analysis may then be performed if the analyst suspects that the codebook may still be missing a key element or feels, for some reason, that she needs to probe a potential theme more directly.

A research study published by Guest and colleagues (2007) illustrates this technique. The researchers were tasked with measuring risk disinhibition among female participants in a clinical trial testing the safety and feasibility of a vaginal gel in combination with a diaphragm for HIV prevention. Risk disinhibition is the phenomenon of individuals increasing certain sexual risk behaviors based on the (unfounded) perception that they are protected by a new technology. In the particular study, the authors quantitatively documented participants' frequency of sexual intercourse and rate of condom use with their partners (self-reported) over the course of the trial to assess whether or not risk disinhibition was occurring because of gel/diaphragm use. The study was conducted among 120 South African women in monogamous relationships. Combined qualitative/quantitative interviews were administered at enrollment and months 1, 3, 5, and 6 of the trial. Based on repeated measures ANOVA of the survey data, the authors found that condom use increased significantly between enrollment and months 3, 5, and 6 ($p = .0001, .0012,$ and $.0033$, respectively), and between months 1 and 3 ($p = .0168$), visually depicted in Figure 5.1.

The quantitative data in the above study indeed showed us the "what," but could not answer the "why." The authors leveraged the qualitative data to fill this knowledge gap. Analysis of thematic structure in the qualitative data collected over time suggested no development of significant new themes/codes that could directly explain the observed changes in condom use. The authors, therefore, employed a KWIC search of "condom," across 120 in-depth interviews, to look at all of the instances of the word. They then reviewed the output of this search in the context of condom use change. Based on this analysis, they posited an explanation for the increase in condom use. Data from the KWIC analysis indicated that enhanced use of condoms was attributable to increased partner involvement in the decision to use condoms, participants' commitment

Figure 5.1   Male Condom Use Over Time Among Women Who Had Sex in the Past 7 Days (from Guest et al., 2007)

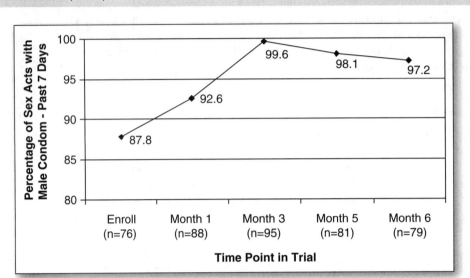

to the trial instructions (one of which was to use condoms in every intercourse event), increased negotiating power for women that was afforded by their study participation, and study provision of condoms that were free and perceived to be of high quality.

Namey and Lyerly (2010) provide another illustration of how KWIC techniques are used in supplemental capacity. In their initial thematic analysis of women's childbirth experiences, the authors identified five primary themes related to a "good" birth experience: self-determination, respect, personal security, attachment, and knowledge. However, they felt that something might be missing. In the authors' own words:

> The term and concept of control was present and coded in the text, but did not strike us as a stand-alone domain of the same explanatory value as the others; control seemed to fit into both none and many of the primary domains. To explore how control might feature in women's schema of a "good" birth, we . . . performed a key word concept analysis of the complete set of narratives. We searched our data and thematically coded any discussion of control that had not been previously coded as part of the larger coding process. We also applied codes signifying whether the woman had used the term spontaneously or had been asked a question about control. (Namey & Lyerly, 2010, p. 771)

From this supplemental analysis, Namey and Lyerly were able to carry out a more complete and targeted analysis of one of the key concepts in their study.

To summarize, the primary reason for using KWIC searches in the above examples was to make sure that nothing was missed. A targeted, secondary analysis allowed the authors the opportunity to generate better insight into their research problem. An anecdote told by Naomi Quinn (2005, p. 71) exemplifies rather nicely the rationale behind using KWIC techniques in this way. For several years, Quinn had been using text from in-depth interviews to develop a cultural model of the American concept of "marriage." Familiar with her work, one of Quinn's colleagues asked her why the concept of "love" was nowhere to be found in her analysis of marriage. The question prompted Quinn to re-examine her textual data and carry out a KWIC analysis on the word "love." Quinn (2005) describes the beneficial outcome of this targeted analysis:

> I did take a systematic look at interviewee's usages of the word "love". I discovered a cultural schema for love, and it was one that did have important and interesting implications for marriage. (p. 72)

The result of Quinn's re-examination, similar to the two aforementioned examples, was a more refined and complete understanding of the research question. This is always a good thing.

Providing More Detail on a Theme

Using KWIC techniques to flesh out details pertaining to themes is simpler and less involved than the two processes described previously. In this analytic capacity, the analyst simply asks one question: "Did participants mention word/phrase X in the context of theme Y?" A simple example entails an analysis one of the authors performed on in-depth interview data from HIV-positive individuals in West Africa. Interviewers asked participants how they believed they became infected with HIV. One of the most frequent themes to emerge was what the analysis team termed "Sharps." Sharps is a medical term for objects having corners, edges, or projections capable of cutting or piercing the skin, and it was used in a similar, though broader sense, by interview participants. After coding the data, and as the authors were writing up a report, they wondered whether or not the theme "Sharps" included scissors. To quickly answer this, an analyst simply did a word search for "scissors" across the data set to see if it was used in the context of HIV transmission: The word "scissors" did indeed appear in the context of discussion of HIV transmission, and so it was added to the report as an object classified as a "sharp." Note that had the analytic question been broader, that is, "What are all of the things that comprise 'Sharps'?"—a word search would not have been the best technique to use. Instead, it would have been more appropriate to extract all of the segments coded "Sharps" and then manually create a list of all the objects mentioned as possible vehicles of infection transmission. To reiterate, word searches and KWIC analyses are best suited for precisely targeted analytic questions.

Strengths and Limitations of Word Searches and KWIC

As supplemental techniques, word searches and KWIC analyses hold several advantages. First, they are simple and quick relative to other data analysis techniques. Many software programs perform them, and the resulting reports are straightforward and easy to understand. Word-based methods are also flexible and can be used at virtually any point in the analysis process, serving as a handy backup tool if and when needed. They can help find analytic gaps and generate more complete analyses than an inductive thematic analysis alone.

These same techniques are limited, however, in what they can accomplish. For one thing, searching for a single word will not capture any other terms used to describe something. In the condom example discussed above, we knew that "condom" was the only word used by participants to denote a latex sheath designed to fit over the penis and used to (presumably) prevent pregnancy and sexually transmitted infections. We knew this was the case because the transcripts analyzed were translated into English from Zulu, and only the English word "condom" was used in the translation. Had the study been done in an English-speaking country, we would have had to search for all of the other words and slang known to denote condoms. The take-home message here is to make sure that all known words and synonyms for a particular item or concept are searched.

Another disadvantage of word searches is that they cannot always capture more complex constructs. To give an example, in our thematic analysis of interview transcripts with HIV-positive individuals, we found a common theme of "Stigma." But a word search for "stigma" would have been futile, for the simple reason that interviewees never used the word "stigma." They talked at length about being ostracized, shunned from their families/villages, and fired from jobs because of their HIV status. These are all poignant instances of stigma and important to our analysis, but a single word could not capture the concept in this particular analytic context.

Word searches may also generate a lot of noise, such as words with little semantic salience—that is, articles, prepositions, modifiers, and so on. Similarly, if an interviewer's questions are included in the transcript, key words from the questions themselves will likely appear high on the word frequency list but will not accurately represent participants' responses. In either of these cases, analysts must decide how they are going to deal with extraneous words. The best time to do so is before executing the word search. In the case of key words within the instrument questions, it means removing the questions from the transcripts. For common words with little meaning, a dictionary, or some method of search exclusion, must be incorporated into the search query before running the analysis.

Finally, analysts must take care when doing any sort of literal search in translated documents. In some cases translation may actually simplify things, as in the above-referenced case of the KWIC search of the word "condom." But this will not always be the case. Different translators may use different translated words for the same referent word, thereby negating any sort of aggregate or comparative analysis based on words. Moreover, not all words in other languages have a direct equivalent in the language to which they are being translated. Again, this was not the case with the condom example, and often is not with terms denoting concrete things. However, the more complex and abstract the concept, the smaller the chance of finding word-to-word equivalents between languages.

ANALYZING DEVIANT/NEGATIVE CASES

In Chapter 4 we discussed the use of negative and deviant cases as a means to enhance validity. In Chapter 10 we talk about using negative cases to ensure an accurate and balanced report. Indeed, the process provides a hard check on cherry-picking data, thereby producing a more objective account of the data. Another benefit is that hypotheses and theoretical models can be substantially strengthened through the process, rendering a fuller and more sophisticated description of the phenomenon under study (Corbin & Strauss, 2008). Many important scientific discoveries and theories have resulted from following up on what appear at first to be anomalous cases. Keeping an open mind and being willing to let go of preconceived notions in the face of contradictory data are hallmarks of a good scientist, and these qualities are especially critical for qualitative researchers. In this section, we describe the various ways in which deviant and negative cases can enhance a study, and we provide concrete steps for incorporating them into a thematic analysis. Before doing so, however, we must first define what we mean by the terms "deviant" and "negative" case.

Across the qualitative methodological literature, authors use the terms "negative case" and "deviant case" (and occasionally "disconfirming case") synonymously. In our view, there is a subtle, yet important, distinction. Negative and deviant cases are similar in that both terms refer to cases that "do not fit within the pattern" of a data set (Patton, 2002, p. 554). But it is *how* they differ from the pattern that determines whether or not they are deviant or negative. Negative cases are a *type of* deviant case that contradicts, as opposed to just deviates from, the general pattern. Deviant cases diverge from the pattern, and may represent the extreme end of a dimension, but do not necessarily contradict a trend in the data (an analogy in mixed methods research would be "divergent" and "contradictory" data).

One of our recent studies provides an illustrative example of a negative case. Beskow and colleagues (submitted) conducted in-depth interviews with participants in genetic research to understand how they felt about being recontacted by researchers who wanted to recruit them into new studies. Of the 74 interviewees who answered the question "Generally speaking, if you're in one study do you think it's all right for researchers to contact you about being in another study?", only one person expressed concern about being recontacted (excerpts taken from the entirety of the interview):

> *I mean, it don't tickle my fancy if anybody calls me to contact me for another study or anything since I've already done this one. . . . So, that's all the blood they're going*

to get out of me. . . . I don't want five different doctors calling me to go do some study like I'm a pig or something. . . . I don't want to be bugged a whole lot, you know. . . . Don't bug 'em to death. That's my only thing. Because if I start getting bugged to death, I back out.

This person not only disagreed with the idea of recontact, but continued to elaborate on the importance of protecting participants' privacy throughout the interview, creating a stark contrast to the overwhelming majority of participants who had no problem with, and even welcomed, recontact from researchers.

Similarly, negative cases comprised a key component in a study by Guest and colleagues (2005). The researchers conducted in-depth interviews with 35 HIV vaccine clinical trial participants across multiple sites in the United States. One of the research objectives was to understand if and how disinhibition occurred as a result of trial participation. In other words, did participants feel a false sense of protection from having received an injection, despite its unknown efficacy (particularly since half of the participants received a placebo)? The authors reported that the overall trend in the interview data was a decrease in sexual risk behavior, due largely to the process of participants talking about their sexual encounters since the last HIV counseling session. However, there were exceptions to this trend that the authors sought to explain (Guest et al., 2005, pp. 53–54):

In only two cases was an explicit connection made between potentially having received the vaccine and engaging in risky sex, yet in both cases other contributing factors were also present. In one case alcohol use was mentioned as an influence:

Interviewer: What differences, if any, have you noticed in your sexual practices since you enrolled in the trial?

Respondent: At the beginning, I was still doing the things . . . having sex without condoms, unprotected sex. Later on, little by little, I just started . . . but you still think "Oh, boy, you know, I have the vaccine, I don't care." And after the alcohol . . . with drugs, you just don't care. You just want to party. You want to lead the life. You want to live every single moment of life in that way, and just have sex. What am I gonna use condoms for [laughs]?

In the other case, the nature of the relationship and current social norms were ascribed influences:

Respondent: I remember an incident where my ex . . . came down, and I've known him for many, many years. To the point where I feel like I can trust him to a certain extent and I know his sexual behaviour. I'm aware that the activities that we engaged in when he came down and I felt comfortable, and I mean there were things that we might have done that might be considered high-risk and, I think one of the reasons why I decided to continue with it was that yeah part of the vaccine study. I mean maybe this sends red lights for the researchers, but it's a reality and I think that it did give me a sense of false security. But I wouldn't say that was the main reason why I engaged in that activity. I think it's a combination of things . . . the fact that I knew him and we were both pretty down in our situations. And we knew

exactly what our sexual behaviour was like because we were having ongoing con-
versation over the phone and all that so. But again, I think being part of the study
made me think, "Oh, maybe it's not a big deal."

The overall trend in the interview data was for participants to talk about being sexually safer since trial enrollment, and many attributed this change to the interactions they had with staff counselors. Quotes from the two participants above contradict this trend and indicate that risk disinhibition had occurred to a certain extent. Since understanding risk disinhibition was one of the primary objectives of the research, the authors explicitly presented these cases in the report. The minimal degree of risk disinhibition was later confirmed with quantitative data (Bartholow et al., 2005).

Deviant cases simply differ or diverge from the majority, without necessarily contradicting larger patterns observed. In another study led by one of the authors (Guest), interviewers asked Ugandan long-distance truck drivers to identify their reasons for having multiple sexual partners. These men cited two primary factors—desire for sexual variety and long absences from home (as demanded by their occupation). Conversely, only 1 out of the 20 truck drivers in the sample expressed an idea that the analysis team termed "weak heart," the notion that it is simply in an individual's nature to be unfaithful and to seek out many sexual partners. (A manuscript highlighting the study results is currently under review.) "Weak heart" is a deviant case in that it is different in substance than other identified themes but yet does not contradict them.

Most qualitative data analysis texts discuss negative case analysis as a means to validate or test a researcher's interpretations of, or hypotheses generated from, a data set (e.g., Berg, 2009; Warren & Karner, 2010). The idea is to deliberately look for data that disconfirm the theories/hypotheses/interpretations researchers postulate based on an initial analysis of the data (Stake, 2010). Berg (2009, p. 360) outlines a four-step process to this end. We have taken the liberty of adding substeps to Step 3 of Berg's process to help readers decide which of the three options to choose (discard the interpretation, revise the interpretation, or discard the case).

1. Develop initial hypotheses and/or interpretations based on a first round of analysis. These could be represented in statements, flow chart, or other graphical form.

2. For each hypothesis or interpretation, conduct an exhaustive search through the data set to locate cases that do not fit the relationship postulated.

3. If a negative case is found, (1) discard the hypothesis/interpretation, (2) reformulate the hypothesis/interpretation, or (3) discard the negative case. Refer to Steps 3a through 3e for guidance as to which of these three paths to take.

3a. First, ask yourself: Is the unique case related to the study objectives? If not, ignore or discard the case. For example, in one of our studies (Guest et al., 2005), researchers asked HIV vaccine clinical trial participants about their experience with the study's risk reduction counseling. One participant (out of 35) talked effusively—for nearly two pages of text!—about the glorious properties of banana-flavored lubricant. Though interesting to read, this section of text had little to do with the research objectives and was not coded for inclusion in the analysis.

3b. If the answer to 3a is "Yes, the concept is relevant," next ask yourself if the case is representative of an underlying process or phenomenon or if it is idiosyncratic. As a rule, the more deviant cases you find, the less likely the difference is due to idiosyncrasy. If after careful consideration you determine that the case is idiosyncratic (and this is often a judgment call), discarding the case is a viable option. Note that this process takes time and requires a relatively broad view of the data. And, as we note in some detail later, not all idiosyncratic cases should be discarded.

3c. If after 3b you're still in doubt, start looking for things to explain the deviant case. Examining the characteristics of the source of the deviant case is a good starting point. Perhaps something about the respondent's demographics (e.g., age, religion, occupation) sets him apart from the rest, giving a different perspective. Maybe a deeper search through the data reveals unique contextual or experiential parameters associated with the source that can explain a differing view. For example, in a market research context, a participant may be talking about a test product in the context of a gift for a child, while the other adult participants are talking about it as something they would buy for themselves. Or, perhaps the one participant that expresses dissatisfaction with a program was one of the first to be enrolled before all of the wrinkles had been ironed out. Like a detective, it's the researcher's job to investigate further to explain what she observes. If answers are not found within the data set under analysis, proceed to Step 3d.

3d. If available, bring data from other sources into the analysis. External data may take the form of traditional secondary data or be composed of another data source within the same study. Consulting local experts, such as individuals from the study population, can often significantly illuminate your data.

3e. If after Steps 3c and 3d a reasonable explanation emerges, you will likely be able to modify your theory or hypotheses to include a new pathway or qualifying condition. If, however, an answer still eludes you, it's time to consider abandoning at least the portion of the theoretical model in question. Sometimes explanations for deviant cases are simply not evident—and they may not be necessary. For your audience it may be perfectly fine to say that the majority of respondents had a positive experience with the program, but that a few did not. Not everyone is going to agree all the time, nor will data sets show complete internal harmony. Getting the story 80% right can sometimes be enough, particularly in exploratory research.

4. Examine all cases from the sample until you are confident that your resulting model adequately accounts for the variation observed in the data. Once this variability is determined, the next step is to decide whether or not to incorporate deviant cases into subsequent data collection and analysis procedures (if any) and how to include them in a study report (if at all). Below, we address these two questions.

Much qualitative research is descriptive in purpose and not concerned with generating explanatory models or evaluating hypotheses. Further, deviant/negative cases are not always explicitly sought but often simply emerge from the data. Regardless of the context, the question of what to do with unique cases remains. The degree of flexibility in the analytic process and the point in the analysis at which a deviant case is discovered are primary considerations here. If the analytic process is iterative and unexpected cases/themes are identified early on in the process, follow-up inquiry can be initiated. A study by Lyerly and colleagues (2006) exemplifies this analytic route. The authors aimed to describe factors that affect infertility patients' decision making regarding their cryopreserved embryos. The initial in-depth interview guide was relatively narrow in scope, designed to capture opinions about each of the four disposition options currently available for cryopreserved embryos (thaw and discard, use for future pregnancy, donate to research, or donate for adoption). Within the first few interviews an unexpected theme emerged within one transcript—the desire to have some sort of ceremony for unused embryos. Feeling this was an important avenue to explore further, the researchers added a specific question to the interview guide to capture this theme more directly. Participants in subsequent interviews largely agreed that this option would be welcome. No doubt this was partially a result of the added question on the subject, but the trend did show that, in the end, this was an important view to be considered. In fact, the question was added to a subsequent nationwide survey, and 18% of the respondents indicated that a ceremony for thawing of frozen embryos was a choice they would somewhat or very likely choose for their own embryos (Lyerly et al., 2010). Whether or not the desire for a ceremony would have been a true deviant case within the study sample above (i.e., only mentioned once or twice) had the researchers not added the more direct question is impossible to know. The take-home point is that unexpected findings can prove extremely useful during the data collection and analysis process and lead researchers in unanticipated, yet important, directions.

Not all qualitative research designs afford such flexibility. Often researchers conduct qualitative data collection and analysis sequentially, thereby obviating the ability to inductively alter study instruments or data collection processes. How are deviant cases to be handled then? This, as with much in research, is a judgment call in which at least two factors should be considered. One factor is related to Step 3a—the relevance of the deviant theme to the study objectives. In the previous example, banana-flavored lubricant was clearly of negligible importance to the study; discarding the case from the analysis and study report in a situation like this is a fairly straightforward decision. At the other extreme, imagine a study in which only 1 out of 100 nursing home residents mentions staff abuse. In this instance, even one case would warrant inclusion into a report (as well as involve other legal and ethical obligations).

But not all cases are so clear-cut. The aforementioned study about genetic research subjects' willingness to be recontacted for additional research is a case in point. Should the researchers include in their study report the sole case (out of 74) who was opposed to being recontacted? Consideration must be given to both the intensity of the case and its relevance to policy. In this particular situation, the participant's negative view of recontact is vehemently expressed *and* the protection of human research subjects' privacy is a high priority for ethics committees. So from a policy or decision-making perspective (from which this study was born), an *n* of 1 is likely worth inclusion in a report. Conversely, in the Ugandan truck driver example described earlier, the researchers decided not to include the "weak heart" theme in their published findings. It comprised a minority view; but more importantly, the finding is not actionable in terms of policy or intervention.

In applied research the salience of deviant cases and their import with respect to policy and intervention are key determinants in the decision to include them in the analysis and write-up of findings. It would be reckless to discard unique cases that represent extreme yet informative situations or views. Even if not extreme, deviant cases can contain valuable insights into the phenomenon being studied that, for some reason, others in the sample failed to experience or express. Perhaps, for example, the deviant cases in a program evaluation are individuals in positions or roles that give them a more comprehensive view of the program. Or maybe they comprise a small subgroup who, by virtue of their station, experience the program differently than the majority. Further inquiry is warranted (see Step 3c).

On a summary note, we should point out that while the above four-step process dictates searching for negative cases after the initial coding has been completed, steps can be taken during coding to expedite the process. In Chapter 3 we talk about using the "unique" code for chunks of data that do not seem to fit with observed patterns or whose relevance to the study objectives is uncertain at the time of coding. This same type of coding can be used to tag potentially deviant or negative cases, and hypotheses and interpretations can be revised, either partially or completely, during the coding process.

OPTIMIZING FOCUS GROUP DATA

Several good sources on analyzing focus group data are available (e.g., Henderson, 1995; Krueger, 1998; Krueger & Casey, 2009). Much of the content in these works, and others like them, however, cover just the basic process of inductive thematic analysis. What is covered much less often in these texts, and in less detail, is the unique nature of focus group data and the implications they have for analyses. Certainly, one could analyze a set of focus group transcripts the same way one would in-depth interview transcripts (and this is often done), but this strategy does not capitalize on the unique nature of focus group data, and it may also lead to poor analytic practices, as we will discuss.

Focus groups are defined by interaction among group participants. This dynamic structure has numerous ramifications for analysis, limiting some types of analyses and expanding the opportunity for others. In this section, we synthesize and present the best practices published to date that pertain specifically to analysis of focus groups. Note that the body of literature on the subject is rather limited (Duggleby, 2005): Much more research is needed to further existing knowledge and practice on the topic.

Response Interdependence

As Bernard and Ryan (2010) and others observe, individual responses in a focus group setting are neither equally distributed among the group nor independent of each other. Most moderators do not ask every individual in a group to respond to a particular question, and even with a skilled moderator, stronger personalities can dominate a discussion, rendering less vocal participants silent or spurring them into a state of complacent acquiescence. The outcome can be a "me too" effect in which individuals follow the line of thinking expressed by more assertive and compelling personalities or by normative obligation. The narrative in "The 'Me Too' Effect" text box from the movie *The Three Amigos*, provides a humorous example of this phenomenon.

Implications of the interdependent nature of responses are several. First, unlike one-on-one interviews, calculating frequencies at the individual level in focus groups is not a valid analytic technique (Carey, 1995). When we report frequencies for focus group data, we report the number of *groups* in which a particular theme was expressed. However, this technique is not always appropriate or meaningful either, since most studies contain only a few focus groups and do not

---

The "Me Too" Effect

Dusty: *Lucky. What are you gonna do with your share of the money?*

Lucky: *A car . . . a big, shiny, silver car. I'll drive all over Hollywood . . . What about you?*

Dusty: *New York. Maybe Paris. A lot of champagne. Parties. Be a big shot for a while. How 'bout you, Ned?*

Ned: *I'm gonna start a foundation to help homeless children.*

Dusty: *That occurred to me to do that at one point, too.*

Lucky: *I meant I would do that first, and then I would get a big, shiny car.*

Source: *The Three Amigos,* Orion Pictures.

comprise a large enough sample for truly meaningful frequencies. If you are convinced that you need frequencies at the individual level within focus groups, one strategy is to create response independence for part of the data collection process. This can be done by administering short surveys to individuals prior to the discussion or through more sophisticated techniques such as electronic "voting devices," hand-held controls that immediately capture responses of each participant.

Although one must be extremely cautious using frequencies in focus group contexts, information pertaining to prevalence of themes should not be ignored or discounted. There must surely be a difference, say, between a theme that only one person in a group of 10 expresses (and with whom no one else concurs) and one in which all 10 individuals in a group agree is important. To be able to make note of this, audio/video recording and/or transcripts must be set up in a way that facilitates this type of observation. It must be clear on the tape and transcript who within the group is speaking and if there is general agreement or disagreement among the ranks. This type of detail can be generated only through good note-taking and transcription practices (see Guest, Namey, & Mitchell, in press). If the data are collected and set up properly, general trends (not individual frequencies) within groups can be analyzed and documented descriptively. One can state, for example, that most of the group "agreed" or "nodded in assent" with respect to a given idea, or that one person expressed an opinion that several others opposed. Capturing this variability is a useful endeavor and can be highly informative, as long as it is interpreted within context and without individual frequencies.

Capturing Interaction

One of the defining features of focus groups is the interaction between participants. Carey and Smith (1994) suggest that to fully understand focus group data an analyst needs to consider three levels of analysis: individual, group, and the relationship between the group and its constituent individuals. Documenting several types of basic interactions aid in achieving this aim.

Social Norms and Shared Understandings

Focus groups are great at eliciting social norms, since individuals are speaking in a social setting with others who share similar cultural or experiential traits. Esoteric or (sub)culturally specific language and idioms are often markers for shared norms and can be used to tag certain text segments. Another clue to shared social norms and understandings is participants' ability to read between the lines, exhibiting an implicit understanding of intended meaning in the absence of explicit expression Take, for example, the brief hypothetical exchange below between two friends at a bar who share the same culture (American). Readers from the United States will pick up on the norms easily, but imagine if the context were injection drug users talking about drugs or prison inmates talking about prison life—understanding the implicit social norms in such unfamiliar contexts (at least for many) would require more analysis and insight.

What Was Said	Implicit Understanding
Buddy #1: *Hey, check out the woman at that table. She's giving you the eye. Go talk to her.*	In the context of a bar, a woman looking at a man indicates social interest It's acceptable for a man to approach a woman in a bar if she's looking at him
Buddy #2: *I can't flirt with her, I'm married.*	Marriage entails fidelity Flirting is a breach of fidelity

Divergent and Convergent Viewpoints

As any experienced moderator can tell you, people don't always agree in focus groups. This is in fact one of the reasons for conducting focus groups. Whether evaluating a product or program, or brainstorming solutions for a community-wide problem, disagreement can be very informative. Identifying points of contention and disagreement is a first step to developing more acceptable solutions. If total agreement can't be achieved, at least a researcher will know what problems to expect and can prepare clients or stakeholders for the impending situation. Likewise, noting areas of agreement can tell policy makers where discordance is unlikely so they can target their resources and energies accordingly. If a moderator has done a good job in probing areas of convergence and divergence, reasons behind agreement/disagreement can be revealed, providing rich data to inform the research objective and subsequent applied problem.

Interpersonal Influences

One of the key dynamics that can be observed in focus groups is what Krueger (1998) calls "internal consistency" (pp. 34–35), the stability of responses throughout the focus group. Focus group members often change their minds during the course of the data collection event ("internal *in*consistency"). Group members can influence the thinking process or opinion of others. Sometimes individuals change even their own minds while in the process of thinking and talking. Whatever the reason for the change of heart, it is critical to document it. If, as a researcher, you can understand how people within your study population are influenced to think one way or another, you can effectively inform your clients, collaborators, policy makers, and so on. This is precisely the type of information for which marketing companies pay a lot of money: you've just found out how to persuade their target market to buy their product!

Nonverbal Data

Above we discussed techniques for analyzing what people actually say. Krueger (1998) suggests taking the analysis a step further and examining nonverbal cues, such as body language/gestures, intensity of expression, and tone of voice. For example, if someone flips the bird to a group member, it's probably worthwhile to document. Likewise, if someone is yelling her point in anger, you should take note. Inflection of voice can also be informative (and is constantly used and implicitly recognized in everyday communication). The following example from Krueger (1998, p. 33) illustrates the importance of inflection in imparting meaning.

Comment	Translation
"This was GOOD!"	It was good
"This was GOOD?"	It was supposed to be good, but it wasn't
"THIS was good!"	This one was good, but the others were not
"This WAS good."	It used to be good, but not anymore

Another element worth noting in focus group data (and in-depth interview data as well) is whether certain discourse emerged spontaneously or was in response to a specific question or probe. Typically, spontaneous expressions are given more weight than prompted responses, as they are inferred to hold more cognitive salience for the speaker. In a similar manner, Krueger suggests taking note of whether or not something an individual says is specific and based on personal experience or is vague and impersonal. The former context provides more robust and convincing data.

Implications for Analysis

So far, we've presented concepts to observe and document in focus group data. But what does it all mean in terms of actually doing analysis? We suggest creating a method for tagging any or all of the elements discussed above. Whether or not you choose to use a formal code, a coding memo, or some other type of notation depends on how you want to incorporate any of the elements discussed into the coding structure. Do you want to run a co-occurrence report between, say, a thematic code and whether or not it was spontaneously expressed, or do you simply want to be able to refer back to the text and see what was spontaneously generated? You need to figure out how you will integrate the verbal (i.e., thematic codes) with the nonverbal and set up your analytic framework accordingly. A lot also depends on the depth of analysis you can afford, the size of your data set, the availability of good notes and audio (or video) recording, and the nature of your study objectives. Also keep in mind that any nonverbal analysis you do should be carried out in a systematic way, which can prove to be rather labor intensive, especially for larger data sets. The following schematic (Figure 5.2) gives general guidance in this regard.

To help readers start thinking about some of the nonthematic elements for which they might wish to create codes or memos, we present a list below, based

Figure 5.2 Appropriateness of Analyzing Nonverbal Behavior

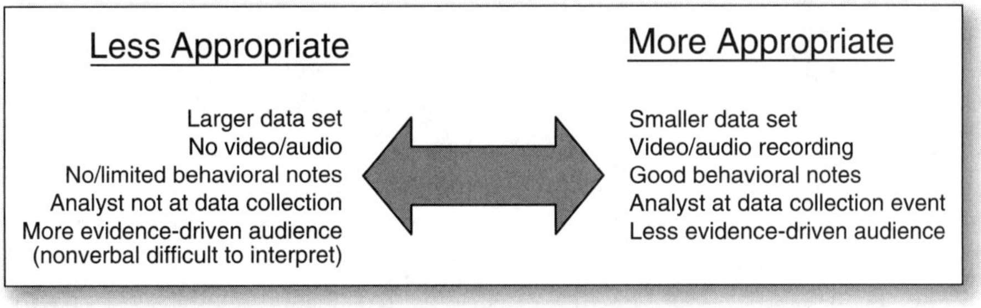

Less Appropriate | More Appropriate

Less Appropriate	More Appropriate
Larger data set	Smaller data set
No video/audio	Video/audio recording
No/limited behavioral notes	Good behavioral notes
Analyst not at data collection	Analyst at data collection event
More evidence-driven audience (nonverbal difficult to interpret)	Less evidence-driven audience

on the contents of this chapter. Note that this list is not exhaustive. We encourage researchers to think about, use, and write about other elements that might be useful to tag during a thematic analysis. Which elements one chooses or develops will depend on the factors listed in Figure 5.3 as well as resources and research objectives.

Figure 5.3 Possible Elements for Metacoding and Memoing

- Group-level dynamics
  - Convergence/agreement
  - Divergence/disagreement
- Interpersonal influence
  - persuade to the affirmative
  - persuade to the negative
  - self-induced change
- Intensity of response (can create categories of degree)
- Spontaneous vs. prompted or in response to a question/probe
- Meaningful inflection
- Meaningful body language/gesture
- Personal/specific vs. impersonal/vague

A Note About Memoing

In this chapter and Chapter 3, we give examples of how memos can be used in the analytic process. Our examples depict memos as short narratives (i.e., no more than a few sentences) that are appended to raw data and that typically

(Continued)

(Continued)

contain an analyst's thoughts about a certain section of data. We need to note, however, that for some authors memoing can take on a more involved and prominent role in the analytic process. Grounded theorists often employ memos as the primary analytic process (e.g., Charmaz 2006; Corbin & Strauss, 2008, pp. 119–141). And they may do so in various forms of media—for example, hard copy transcripts, note cards, QDA software. Memos of varying lengths are attached to the raw data throughout all stages of analysis and are incrementally interwoven to generate a rich and thorough understanding of a data set.

Other authors use the term "memo" more broadly, and, in addition to the analytic usage described above (i.e., memos as metadata) also use memos to hyperlink different units and types of raw data together. In the words of di Gregorio and Davidson (2008), "Memos were part of the manual tradition of qualitative research, and, as they enter the electronic world of QDAS, their possibilities (through hyperlinking) are expanded exponentially" (p. 39). Indeed, with qualitative data now typically being in, or transformed into, some form of electronic medium prior to analysis, an analyst can insert hyperlinks that connect text segments to other text segments, to photos, Internet sources, or any other electronic unit of data. Such a technique allows an analyst to simultaneously view multiple data sources and forms related to a particular source, idea, concept, theme, or code.

SUMMING UP

Qualitative data analysis is both an art and a science. The artistic part is reflected in the range of options from which one can choose, in terms of analytic tools and approaches. As we stress throughout this book—be creative. Our suggestions and examples are intended to be useful in many research contexts, but they are not exhaustive, or the only way to go about a thematic analysis. Your own research context should encourage you to build on what we've presented above or to develop entirely new techniques.

The scientific nature of data analysis, in our opinion, is reflected in the systematic manner in which data are approached and analyzed as well as in the use of procedures to establish validity wherever and whenever possible. The techniques presented in this chapter represent both the scientific and creative sides of data analysis. If done properly and in the appropriate context, they will add richness to, and enhance the credibility of, your analysis. They are intended to aid and inspire some of the processes more indigenous to thematic analysis as well as help create a fuller overall understanding of a particular research topic. This is, after all, the ultimate goal of any research endeavor.

Thematic analysis is about seeing patterns in the data. But, as we point out in this chapter, if we ignore cases that initially seem incongruent with what we observe, a serious injustice is done to the data, the research participants, and the study's audience. Patterns can be more complex than we initially think, or interpretations falsified by a few contradicting cases. Conducting a thorough analysis requires taking into account disconfirming evidence and presenting it in an honest and fair manner when reporting findings from the study.

REFERENCES

Bartholow B., Buchbinder, S. Celum, C., Goli, V., Koblin, B., Para, M., Marmor, M. R. . . . Mastro, T. for the VISION/VAX004 Study Team. (2005). HIV sexual risk behavior over 36 months of follow-up in the world's first HIV vaccine efficacy trial. *Journal of Acquired Immune Deficiency Syndrome, 39*, 90–101.

Berg, B. (2009). *Qualitative research methods for the social sciences* (7th ed.). Boston, MA: Allyn and Bacon.

Bernard, H., & Ryan, G. (2010). *Analyzing qualitative data: Systematic approaches.* Thousand Oaks, CA: Sage.

Beskow, L. M., Namey, E. E., Cadigan, R. J., Brazg, T., Crouch, J., Henderson, G. E., et al. (submitted). *Research participants' perspectives on genotype-driven research recruitment.*

Carey, M. (1995). Comment: Concerns in the analysis of focus group data. *Qualitative Health Research, 5,* 487–495.

Carey, M., & Smith, M. (1994). Capturing the group effect in focus groups: A special concern in analysis. *Qualitative Health Research, 4,* 123–127.

Charmaz, K. (2006). *Constructing grounded theory: A practical guide through qualitative analysis.* Thousand Oaks, CA: Sage.

Corbin, J., & Strauss, A. (2008). *Basics of qualitative research: Techniques and procedures for developing grounded theory* (3rd ed.). Thousand Oaks, CA: Sage.

di Gregorio, S., & Davidson J. (2008). *Qualitative research design for software users.* New York: Open University Press.

Duggleby, W. (2005). What about focus group interaction data? *Qualitative Health Research, 15,* 832–840.

Guest, G., Namey, E., & Mitchell, M. (In press). *Qualitative data collection: A field manual.* Thousand Oaks, CA: Sage.

Guest, G., Johnson, L., Burke, H., Rain-Taljaard, R., Severy, L., Von Mollendorf, C., & Van Damme, L. (2007). Changes in sexual behavior during a safety and feasibility trial of a microbicide/diaphragm combination: An integrated qualitative and quantitative analysis. *AIDS Education and Prevention, 19*(4), 310–320.

Guest, G., McLellan-Lemal, E., Matia, D., Pickard, R., Fuchs, J., McKirnan, D., & Neidig, J. (2005). HIV vaccine efficacy trial participation: Men-who-have-sex-with-men's experience of risk reduction counseling and perceptions of behavior change. *AIDS Care, 17,* 46–57.

Henderson, N. (1995). A practical approach to analyzing and reporting focus groups studies: Lessons from qualitative market research. *Qualitative Health Research, 5,* 463–477.

Krueger, R. (1998). *Analyzing and reporting focus group results.* Thousand Oaks, CA: Sage.

Krueger, R., & Casey, M. (2009). *Focus groups: A practical guide for applied research* (4th ed.). Thousand Oaks, CA: Sage.

Lyerly, A. D., Steinhauser, K., Namey, E., Tulsky, J., Cook-Deegan, R., Sugarman, J., Walmer, D., & Wallach, E. (2006). Factors that affect infertility patients' decisions about disposition of frozen embryos, *Fertility and Sterility, 85*(6), 1623–1630.

Lyerly, A. D., Steinhauser, K., Voils, C., Namey, E., Alexander, C., Bankowski, B., Cook-Degan, R., & Wallach, E. (2010). Fertility patients' views about frozen embryo disposition: Results of a multi-institutional U.S. survey. *Fertility and Sterility, 93*(2), 499–509.

Namey, E., & Lyerly, A. (2010). The meaning of "control" for childbearing women in the US. *Social Science and Medicine, 71*, 769–776.

Patton, M. (2002). *Qualitative research & evaluation methods* (3rd ed.). Thousand Oaks, CA: Sage.

Quinn, N. (2005). How to construct schemas people share, from what they say. In N. Quinn (Ed.), *Finding culture in talk* (pp. 35–82). New York: Palgrave MacMillan.

Ryan, G., & Weisner, T. (1996). Analyzing words in brief descriptions: Fathers and mothers describe their children. *Cultural Anthropology Methods Journal, 8*, 13–16.

Stake, R. (2010). *Qualitative research: Studying how things work.* New York: The Guilford Press.

Warren, C., & Karner, T. (2010). *Discovering qualitative methods: Field research, interviews, and analysis.* New York: Oxford University Press.

EXERCISES

1. Find a body of text you wish to analyze. It might be a transcript from your research project, a political speech, or some other text of interest. Using an online text analysis tool, do a word frequency analysis to calculate frequencies for each unique word in the text chosen. Think about (a) how you might filter the search and (b) how you might begin creating codes from the list.

Software and Internet URLs change all the time, so we suggest doing a Web search for "text analysis" or "word counts" to find a free tool. At the time of writing, the following sites were active:

> http://textalyser.net
> http://neon.niederlandistik.fu-berlin.de/en/textstat
> http://www.provalisresearch.com/wordstat/Wordstat.html (free trial)
> http://www.wordle.net (this site generates visual representations, based on word frequencies, but not frequencies themselves)

Note also that QDA software packages are becoming increasingly sophisticated, and many now have word frequency functions and corresponding visual displays.

2a. Locate two or three research articles that include focus group data analysis. Review the "Methods" and "Results" sections of the articles. Make notes documenting any techniques the authors used to capitalize on the group nature of the data. If the authors don't describe any specific methods (and this may often be the case), think about what you would have done differently to optimize the focus group data for these studies.

2b. Describe some of the advantages and limitations associated with including nonverbal behavior in a thematic analysis.

3a. Locate two or three qualitative research articles in your field. Assess if and how they deal with negative or deviant cases. What could they have done better?

3b. Briefly explain two reasons for employing a negative case analysis.

ADDITIONAL READING

Bernard, H., & Ryan, G. (2010). KWIC analysis, word counts, and semantic network analysis. *Analyzing qualitative data: Systematic approaches* (pp. 191–220). Thousand Oaks, CA: Sage.

Duggleby, W. (1996). What about focus group interaction data? *Qualitative Health Research, 15,* 832–840.

Kidd, P., & Parshall, M. (2000). Getting the focus and the group: Enhancing analytical rigor in focus group research. *Qualitative Health Research, 10,* 293–308.

Krueger R., & Casey, M. (2009). *Focus groups: A practical guide for applied research* (4th ed.). Thousand Oaks, CA: Sage.

6

DATA REDUCTION TECHNIQUES

LEARNING OBJECTIVES

After reading this chapter, you should be able to:

- Summarize qualitative data using code summary tables and matrices
- Identify when, how, and why quantification of qualitative data is appropriate
- Appropriately summarize qualitative samples and coded data using simple frequencies
- Use simple Boolean searches and matrices to explore the co-occurrence of themes and source characteristics
- Identify research questions where the use of matrix algebra for cluster analysis is appropriate

Data reduction in the context of applied thematic analysis can take many forms, from simply limiting the data set to those items relevant to a particular analysis, to preparation of qualitative code summaries and matrices, to advanced cluster analysis or graphing techniques based on code frequencies. Like coding, data reduction is an integral part of the iterative qualitative data analysis process. As Miles and Huberman explain:

> Data reduction is not something separate from analysis. It is part of analysis. The researcher's decisions—which data chunks to code and which to pull out, which evolving story to tell—are all analytic choices. Data reduction is a form of analysis that sharpens, sorts, focuses, discards, and organizes data in such a way that "final" conclusions can be drawn and verified. (1994, p. 11)

There may be instances where a particular analysis requires only the data collected from a certain subgroup of the sample population. If you have interviewed both physicians and patients, for example, but plan to analyze and write up their views separately, you may "reduce" your data to include only the physician interview transcripts for your first analysis. Similarly, if your interview guide contains questions on three or four related but separate domains, you may wish to focus on only one or two domains in a given analysis. If you have used structural coding to tag specific question/response couplings in your data, you can easily create a smaller data set for analysis that includes only the domains of interest. This process of data reduction, sometimes referred to as framing the analysis, can be incorporated into an analysis plan during the research design phase.

Another way to manage or limit the tremendous amount of data generated by qualitative research is to focus on specific themes identified in the data for a particular analysis. You can extract all of the data coded at specified codes of interest and create a qualitative matrix that includes the coded text alongside any demographic or personal characteristics of the respondents that may be interesting. You might organize separate matrices for men and women and compare (and possibly recode) the content, looking for similarities or differences in trends or patterns. Lyerly and colleagues used this method to sort data about how people thought about their frozen embryos (Lyerly et al., 2006). Responses to questions about disposition options for frozen embryos were arranged in a matrix and sorted by the length of time a person had had frozen embryos stored (see Table 6.1).

Qualitative data summaries or matrices can be very helpful for giving an overview of coded data while also keeping the researcher "close" to the raw data and quotes from which they were drawn. In the sample table, it is very easy to identify the source of the quoted material so that an analyst could refer back to the larger text for context. Qualitative data analysis software makes this even easier by providing a direct link to the source document and/or line numbers to easily locate a given segment of text. For smaller qualitative data sets with very narrow or limited research objectives, these types of tables may be sufficient to advance the analysis and describe findings, though additional coding and analysis are often required to further synthesize the data into a coherent whole. For larger data sets, qualitative data analysis software can again help facilitate development of coded text summaries and matrices (see Chapter 9); however, there is a limit to how much information you can fit into a single table and to how much qualitative information a human brain can process.

To organize and examine larger qualitative data sets, it is often helpful to add some kind of quantification to your data reduction techniques. The practice of "reducing" qualitative data to numbers often sparks debate, and therefore must be done with deliberation and understanding of when and why quantification of qualitative data is appropriate. Throughout the rest of this chapter, we will identify ways to use quantification in your qualitative analysis, define the types of quantification possible, illustrate the most common uses of quantitative analytic techniques for qualitative data, and attempt to outline parameters for determining when quantification of qualitative data might be most useful and appropriate.

Table 6.1 Sample Data Reduction Matrix, Codes, and Text Arranged by Participant Category (Length of Time Embryos Frozen, Category One Indicates < 1 Year, Category Four Indicates >5 Years)

Category	Study ID	Disposition Codes	Quote
One	IDI 1	Undecided	No, um, it's not there yet (laughs). We don't have any frozen embryos, but we, but we still, I don't know what we would do.
One	IDI 2	Store for another attempt	[And your decision has always been …?] To, well, use 'em if I need them, yeah…I think I always thought, I think I was always afraid that I would need them.
Two	IDI 3	Store for another attempt Research—negative Discard—negative Adoption—positive	To put them all back in me. . .I would say that I don't think that there should be any research done on these embryos, there shouldn't even be an option that they can be destroyed. Regarding adoption, I would say to allow them to be adopted; I would want them to be adopted.
Two	IDI 4	Store for another attempt	We knew that 12 eggs does not equal 12 embryos, and we knew of the diminishing stats with this. . . .we would be really fortunate in having anything transferred from that. . . .So we knew that we would either attempt to use them in one or two transfers or as long as it took to have a pregnancy that would work for us.
Three	IDI 5	Store for another attempt	Oh yeah, well we just discussed we were trying to hurry up and get to 'em and that's all we ever discussed just implanting them. . . .
Three	IDI 6	Undecided	Not sure what we'll do, I mean, along with adoption, we've put it all on hold. It just depends on what happens in the next couple of years whether I get pregnant naturally or if we decide to go back to try those frozen embryos or whether we decide to not do that.
Four	IDI 7	Undecided	[On original intention for frozen embryos. . . .] I didn't really think about it. I just was trying to get my baby. Like I said, you don't think about that kind of thing at that particular time, not like you would later. Now. . . .it's really hitting me that it's time to do something or not. Pass it on, try again or whatever, so, I'm just really thinking about it. I'm not trying to not answer but. . . .
Four	IDI 8	Discard Research Adoption—negative	I told him, he can throw them away or do whatever you gonna do, just don't give 'em to no one. I don't care. . . .I can tell you now, I wouldn't donate them [for adoption], you could use them for research.

WHAT COUNTS?

As mentioned, counting is a controversial topic in qualitative data analysis. There are some researchers, particularly those who subscribe to an interpretivist approach to qualitative research, who feel strongly that quantification of qualitative data is a violation of the fundamental goals and assumptions of qualitative research (Suddaby, 2006), and therefore detracts from or invalidates the data. Others, likely of a more positivist perspective, believe that counting and quantification of qualitative data can serve to enhance the validity and persuasiveness of qualitative data (Miles & Huberman, 1994; Silverman, 2000), by providing evidence that "the findings were derived by means of a rigorous, objective analysis of the qualitative data" (Hannah & Lautsch, 2010). Our view is that both qualitative and quantitative analytic techniques can be brought to bear on qualitative data so long as the data collection strategy, sampling design, and research question are aligned with the analytic technique.

How Do We Count?

One of the reasons some people believe that qualitative data cannot be analyzed quantitatively is because they assume that all quantitative analyses are statistical. In general, if you did not design all aspects of a qualitative study with a statistical analysis in mind, then the data are unlikely to be suitable for such an analysis. But that does not mean that you cannot do an arithmetical or numerical analysis of the data.

A basic arithmetical analysis describes qualitative data in terms of quantities (addition), differences (subtraction), proportions (division), and scale (multiplication). You can add up the number of times a theme appears in the data to describe the frequency of the theme. You can use subtraction to look at the difference in the frequencies of two themes. You can look at the proportion of men who talk about a given theme and compare that to the proportion of women who talk about it. You can see if the difference in the proportion of men versus women is bigger or smaller than the difference in the proportion of old people versus young people who talk about a theme. None of these operations can tell you what the data mean. But they can help you summarize and describe the patterning in the data in an unambiguous way. Consider the following two statements:

- Most of the men said they never used condoms with their main partners.
- Nine of the 12 men interviewed said they never used condoms with their main partners.

Which is less ambiguous? It should be rather obvious. More important, the lack of specificity in the first statement actually makes it more likely that the reader will inappropriately think that the finding about "most men" is generalizable to "most men everywhere." When you specify "nine of the 12 men interviewed," you are reminding yourself and the reader about the specificity and limited generalizability of the findings.

A numerical analysis also looks at different mathematical properties than a parametric statistical analysis. Parametric statistics assume that the data are representative of an underlying distribution of themes and characteristics in the population being studied. This means that the population needs to be sampled in ways that reflect the underlying distribution and account for the influence of chance and bias. Sampling in qualitative research is generally purposive with small sample sizes and the goal of describing the range of variability but not its distribution across a general population. When purposive sampling is used, the basic task of qualitative analysis is one of categorizing (coding) and describing relationships (between codes). As such, much of qualitative analysis is amenable to approaches developed in the field of discrete mathematics, including set theory, Boolean algebra, matrix algebra, and graph theory. It is also amenable to the class of nonparametric statistics, that is, statistics that do not assume that the variables being analyzed are parametric. We will discuss some of these uses in further detail in this chapter.

There is always a danger that others will misinterpret qualitative findings that are summarized and presented in numeric form. That does not mean we should abandon the use of numbers. It does mean you need to be clear about what you are doing with numbers, why you are doing it, and how to appropriately interpret the findings.

Uses for Quantifying Qualitative Data

Although much of the debate about quantifying qualitative data focuses on the presentation of "numbers" in a qualitative analysis report or publication, most of the uses for quantifying qualitative data relate to the analysis rather than dissemination portion of the research process. Table 6.2 summarizes various uses for quantifying qualitative data and the associated research phase.

Table 6.2   Reasons for Quantifying Qualitative Data

Purpose	Phase in Research Process
a. Quality control and assurance	Structural coding, prior to content coding
b. Codebook revision	Anytime after initial round of thematic coding
c. Identify and explore patterns in data	
d. Identify and explore relationships in data	Anytime during the coding/analysis process
e. Provide a check on analyst bias	
f. Generate hypotheses	Anytime during analysis
g. Refine analysis strategy	
h. Report findings	At conclusion of a particular analysis

One of the most practical and straightforward ways of using code frequencies to quantify qualitative data is for quality control and assurance purposes. If you are using a structured or semistructured interview guide and structural codes (see Chapters 2 and 3), structural code frequencies are helpful for identifying whether all questions (N) were asked of all participants and/or were coded (n). If $n<N$, you can go back to identify whether there is a problem in the interviewing or coding. For example, if you have an "informed consent" code, you can easily check to make sure that verbal consent was obtained for each participant by checking that n (number of data items coded at informed consent) equals N (number of data collection events).

Once you have developed content or thematic codes, it can be helpful to run code frequencies and identify codes at the extreme ends of application (either never used or nearly universally used) to help refine a codebook. Codes that have not been used may be deleted or combined with a similar code; codes that are used "excessively" are likely too broad and should be narrowed.

During the analysis process, code frequencies can help to highlight patterns in the data that may be difficult to discern otherwise. Do two subgroups mention the same themes in relation to a particular set of questions? Are men talking about a particular theme more often than women? Numerical summaries of code applications provide an easy way to look across the data set for similarities and differences in responses: code frequency may be read as a proxy of salience or relevance of a given theme to a particular analysis (Guest & McLellan, 2003). Taking this a step farther, code co-occurrence frequencies help to identify relationships within the data, illustrating not just which codes appear together but how often, providing a means of assessing the prominence of the combination. (Code co-occurrence frequencies may also indicate areas for codebook development if two co-occurring codes are very similar and could be combined.)

Another purpose for preparing code frequency reports, related both to identifying patterns and quality control, is to check analyst bias. When collecting or reviewing data, analysts often come up with preliminary "findings" that strike them as interesting or noteworthy. If codes exist to capture these ideas, a code frequency report can be a useful tool for getting a better idea of whether the trends noted by the analyst are borne out in the coded data. For example, an analyst may recognize that younger women seem to provide a certain explanation more often than older women. A code frequency report stratified by age of respondent can help to confirm or refute this observation, which will in turn help direct further coding and analysis.

Building on the pattern identification processes above (c–e in Table 6.2), a researcher might use quantification of qualitative data to generate hypotheses—either about what the main points or trends in the data are or to ask new questions. These hypotheses can be "tested" by returning to the qualitative data, rereading, (re-)coding, and possibly filtering or combining the data in new ways. Any of the "findings" from quantitative data reduction techniques during the coding and analysis process can be incorporated into the analysis strategy, pointing to new or expanded areas of inquiry or to areas that need more careful qualitative attention.

The main controversy arises when code frequencies or other numerical summaries of qualitative data are presented in a final report or publication, but even here there are several modes and purposes for presenting quantified qualitative data (Hannah & Lautsch, 2010). The appropriateness of these strategies depends on many factors, which are described in more detail in the sections below.

FREQUENCIES: HOW AND WHAT TO COUNT

Describing Participants

Numbers help us describe qualitative data and findings in a variety of ways. The most basic, and least controversial, use of numbers is to describe the sources of qualitative data. How many people participated in the research? How many focus groups were conducted? How many of the participants were men and how many were women? What are the relevant age groups and how many participants fell into each of those groups? Such counts provide a quick overview of the diversity of viewpoints that the data are likely to encompass.

If the total number of participants is reasonably small and easily characterized for the purposes of the analysis, it may be acceptable to provide a qualitative descriptive summary. The summary should include a clear statement about the number of people who participated in the research and contributed data to the analysis. Here is an example from a study looking at stigma and HIV/AIDS management among young people in a South African community:

> This case study took the form of 3-hour interviews conducted in 2003 with 44 people, 11 focus groups involving a total of 55 people, and fieldworker diaries. Informants included young people and peer educators both in and out of school, teachers, a school principal, community health workers, community leaders (traditional leaders, the local ward councilor, youth leaders, and members of the local development committee), CYA [Christian Youth Alliance] staff, a traditional healer, clinic nurses, parents, people with AIDS, church ministers, a government official, and representatives of a multinational company that employs local people. (Campbell, Foulis, Maimane, & Sibiya, 2005, p. 809)

For more complex qualitative research designs, the easiest way to describe and characterize participants is to include a descriptive table with frequencies and percentages, using much the same format as used in quantitative studies. However, the table will not look exactly like the kind used to describe the distribution of diversity for a statistical analysis. Tables 6.3, 6.4, and 6.5 illustrate this distinction, using tuberculosis (TB) treatment research as an example.

Moonan and colleagues (2011) used statistical techniques to look at the relationship between TB transmission rates and policies on how a strategy called directly observed therapy (DOT) was implemented in two counties in the State of Texas. Specifically, they compared evidence of recent TB transmission within and between communities implementing programs that differed only in their DOT practices. One county used criteria to selectively enroll patients into DOT versus self-administered therapy while the other county universally enrolled all patients into DOT.

Table 6.3 provides basic demographic information on TB patients in each county, how the demographic characteristics of TB patients in each county differed from those for the general population in each county, and how the two counties differed with regard to racial composition. If you are not familiar with basic statistical concepts such as *p*-values, this table is likely to be difficult to interpret. But for those with such familiarity, it contains a considerable amount of nuanced information that is important for interpreting the study findings. For example, although the two counties are not fully comparable with regard to racial composition (e.g., the Universal DOT county has a predominately white population while the Selective DOT county has a clear plurality of races/ethnicities), they both exhibit racial/ethnic disparities in the distribution of TB.

Table 6.3 Demographic Characteristics by County

		Selective DOT County			Universal DOT County		
Demographic		TB Patients (*n*=1,194)	General Population	*p*-value	TB Patients (*n*=512)	General Population	*p*-value
Age (years)	<5	2%	8%	<0.0001	1%	8%	<0.0001
	5–17	3%	20%		2%	20%	
	18–64	85%	64%		84%	64%	
	>64	10%	85		12%	8%	
Sex	Male	66%	50%	<0.0001	67%	49%	<0.0001
	Female	34%	50%		33%	51%	
Race/Ethnicity	Black	42%	20%	<0.0001	29%	13%	<0.0001
	Hispanic	29%	30%		24%	20%	
	White	17%	44%		31%	62%	
	Asian	11%	4%		15%	4%	
	Other	0%	2%		1%	1%	

Source: Moonan et al., 2011.

Tables 6.4 and 6.5 are taken from a qualitative study centered on adapting and evaluating a "deskguide" for TB DOT in China. Wei and colleagues (2008) conducted the research in two provinces that were selected because they were dissimilar; within each province, they then selected one prefecture for piloting the deskguide and a second control prefecture with similar population, socioeconomic development, and TB rates. In the pilot sites, the deskguide was used along with the existing national policy guide for routine in-service training and supervisory trips; in the control sites, only the national policy guide was used. For the evaluation, the researchers conducted in-depth interviews and focus groups with participants as described in Tables 6.4 and 6.5.

Table 6.4　Number of Interviewees in Guangxi and Shandong Provinces in the Qualitative Study

	Guangxi Province		Shandong Province		
	Pilot prefecture	Control prefecture	Pilot prefecture	Control prefecture	Subtotal
Interviews					
County TB doctors	4	4	5	3	16
Township public health doctors	4	4	4	4	16
Village doctors	4	5	4	4	17
Focus group discussions					
TB patients (2 focus groups in each prefecture)	14	15	18	16	63
Family members (2 focus groups in each prefecture)	12	11	18	16	57
Sub total	38	39	49	43	169

Source:　Wei et al., 2008.

As with Table 6.3, the two tables from the China study provide considerable nuanced information about the study population. Although the total number of participants is large for a qualitative study ($n=169$) they were not selected to be statistically representative. Rather, the diversity of the research participants is intentional and reflective of the purposive sampling incorporated into the study design. It would be inappropriate (and meaningless) to calculate p-values as was done for the Texas study. Because of the superficial similarity between the tables from the China study and the one from the Texas study, some quantitatively oriented scientists may be prone to misinterpreting the presentation of qualitative research in a format such as Tables 6.4 and 6.5. However, as publication of the China study demonstrates, there is growing understanding and acceptance of qualitative research designs that warrant inclusion of quantitative data summaries.

Describing Thematic Content

Although quantitative presentation of sampling strategies and participant characteristics may be increasingly common, there continues to be some resistance to quantification of thematic content. However, we feel strongly that code frequencies provide an important overview of the data landscape, whether or not you choose to report the findings numerically. Frequency alone cannot tell you the importance of a given theme for answering a particular research question, but it gives a rough outline of the way participants in this sample responded [to given questions] and how coders interpreted the responses.

Table 6.5 Basic Demographics of the Interviewees in the Pilot and Control Sites

		Pilot site interviewees	Control site interviewees	Total
County TB doctors	Average age (yrs)	40.5	38.3	39.6
	Number	9	7	16
	Male (%)	7 (77.8%)	6 (85.7%)	13 (81.3%)
Township public health doctors	Average age (yrs)	36.1	31.9	34.0
	Number	8	8	16
	Male (%)	6 (75%)	6 (75%)	12 (75%)
Village doctors	Average age (yrs)	38.2	44.8	41.7
	Number	8	9	17
	Male (%)	7 (87.5%)	7 (77.8%)	14 (82.4%)
TB patients	Average age (yrs)	50.3	50.0	50.1
	Number	32	31	63
	Male (%)	23 (71.9%)	18 (58.1%)	41 (65.1%)
Family members of TB patients	Average age (yrs)	44.9	41.2	43.1
	Number	30	27	57
	Male (%)	14 (46.7%)	16 (59.3%)	30 (52.6%)

Source: Wei et al., 2008.

Understanding Code Frequencies

Perhaps the most common method of quantifying thematic content is to count the number of times a specific code was applied to a particular item or unit of analysis, often called a code frequency. Code frequencies can be extremely useful for a variety of analysis purposes (see Table 6.2) and are often the foundation of more advanced quantitatively oriented qualitative data reduction techniques (Namey, Guest, Thairu, & Johnson, 2008). It is therefore important to have a clear idea of what code frequencies are and how they are derived.

Remember that codes are not data themselves, they are metadata: formal renderings of themes that exist at the interface of the raw data and the analyst's mind that are codified, and then applied to text (see Figure 6.1A).

Code frequencies, then, are several steps removed from the raw qualitative data, which is one of the reasons cited by detractors of quantitatively oriented data reduction techniques. However, direct references back to the qualitative data always exist and must be consulted to interpret code frequencies (and identify new themes, thus starting the cycle over again). When reviewing code frequencies, it is therefore imperative to review examples of text associated with the codes to maintain a feel for how people talk about particular themes.

Figure 6.1A Relationship of Data and Metadata Items in Qualitative Analysis

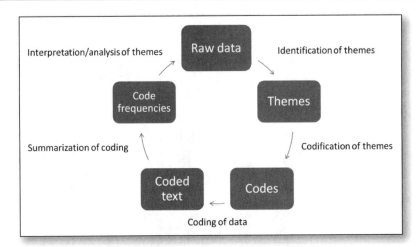

The usefulness and validity of counting code applications is highly dependent on the study design, research objectives, the quality and process of data collection and coding, and on protocols established to maximize reliability of these processes (see Figure 6.1B). Elements of rigor and systematicity added to these individual steps of the research process increase the confidence with which you can tabulate, interpret, and perhaps report code frequencies. For example, if your study objectives support asking the same questions of all participants, this provides a structure for later counting code applications per question (or set of questions) with confidence that participants were responding to the same issues. In the case of codebook development, the more thorough and detailed the code definitions and descriptions, the more likely multiple coders will apply them the same way, enhancing reliability. Similarly, having discrete rules or protocols on code application (how to segment, when not/to apply) will minimize variability in coding practices, which maximizes confidence in any resulting quantifications. Therefore, quantification of qualitative data—including code frequencies—is not something to think about during analysis, but rather during design.

Generating and Interpreting Code Frequencies

When generating code frequencies, you will need to decide how to define the text boundaries within which a code is determined to be present or absent. The boundaries can be very wide (e.g., all text associated with a particular participant, including multiple interviews), wide (e.g., all text included in each transcript), narrow (e.g., text associated with a particular subset of questions in each transcript), or very narrow (e.g., text included in each defined segment of text in each transcript). Next you need to decide whether it is important to know

Figure 6.1B   Flow Diagram of Study Factors Affecting the Validity of Code Frequencies

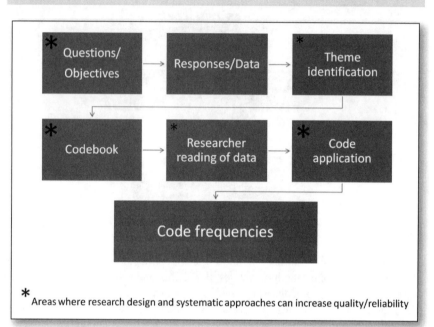

how many times the code was applied within the text boundaries or if it is sufficient to know that the code is present or absent.

In making this decision you will need to consider whether there are any important differences in the way the data were coded (part of the "Code Application" process in Figure 6.1B). For example, consider a situation where the text was coded by two people. Coder A tended to use large segments and coder B tended to use lots of shorter segments. They may agree that two pages of text should be coded for theme X, but coder A defined two segments with theme X while coder B defined six such segments. In this situation it will be very difficult to interpret the meaning of a sum of all occurrences of a particular code in the data set.

Figure 6.2 summarizes the kinds of decisions that need to be made when quantitatively summarizing thematic information. The top half of the figure looks at the intersection of different dimensions of the data, including data items (e.g., interview transcripts, observational field notes), participants, research questions (or structural codes), and thematic codes. The lower half of the figure considers the frequency count of a particular code based on how the frequency question is framed. The framing determines which data will be sampled and also how wide the textual boundaries will be as a result of that sampling strategy.

Figure 6.2 Dimensions to Be Considered When Quantitatively Summarizing Thematic Information

Data item	Item01	Item02	Item03	Number of items = 3	
Participants	ID001	ID001	ID002	Number of participants = 2	
Question X ___ Code A				Question X text segments = 2 ID001 = 1, ID002 = 1 Item01 = 1, Item02 = 0, Item03 = 1 Code A text segments = 5 ID001 = 5, ID002 = 0 Item01 = 2, Item02 = 3, Item03 = 0	
Code A frequency of occurrence by data sampling strategy					
How many people talked about A?	ID001 = Yes		ID002 = No	Participant sampling (n = 1)	Very wide text boundaries
In how many data items was A talked about?	Item 1 = Yes	Item 2 = Yes	Item 3 = No	Item sampling (n = 2)	Wide text boundaries
In how many responses to Question X was A talked about?	QX = Yes		QX = No	Question sampling (n = 1)	Narrow text boundaries
How many times was A talked about?	Segments = 2	Segments = 3	Segments = 0	Segment sampling (n = 5)	Very narrow text boundaries

In general, *relative* code frequencies, those determined based on the number of individual participants who mention a particular theme, are used more commonly than *absolute* code frequencies, the total number of times a theme appears in the data set. This may be based on the assumption that the number of individuals independently expressing the same idea is a better indicator of overall thematic importance than the absolute number of times a theme is expressed and coded. One talkative participant, for example, could express the same idea in many of his/her responses and thus significantly increase the overall frequency of a code application (Namey, Guest, Thairu, & Johnson, 2008).

This possibility—and many other ramifications of choice of data items and levels in code frequency construction—is illustrated in Figure 6.2. Ultimately, the structure and scope of a given code frequency report will depend on research and analysis objectives. In some cases absolute frequency of code application will be the better indicator of a pattern in or across your data set. If you are planning to report code frequencies as part of your report or publication, explain which elements you included in your frequencies, why you have used them, and how they affected, supplemented, or changed your view of the data and the analysis.

In an applied setting, and especially in situations where the main goal is to generate a rapid scan of a concise set of topics, quantitative analysis of qualitative data may go no further than generating these types of frequency summaries. Reports of focus group findings that are intended solely for formative research, for example, often limit the analysis to a simple description of the coded themes and their relative frequencies. However, frequencies can and generally should be used to refine the analysis strategy and explore patterning in the data. In other words, simply running code frequencies does not constitute qualitative data analysis; frequencies are, again, a data reduction technique intended to facilitate a more comprehensive qualitative analysis.

CO-OCCURRENCES

An important part of qualitative analysis is the exploration of relationships between and among themes and characteristics. Do men and women talk about family relationships in the same way? Do people talk about economic responsibilities in the same breath as family relationships or do they tend to discuss them as separate topics? Does the emotional content of conversations about family relationships differ for legal and illegal migrants? Which themes resonate with multiple other themes in discourse and which tend to stand alone?

A good first step in exploring relationships is to identify the frequency at which pairs of codes and/or characteristics occur together. If you have a relatively small number of codes and characteristics, it may be helpful to create a single table that includes all of them. Table 6.6 is an example from a study that looked at attitudes toward HIV vaccine trials in three U.S.-based populations (African Americans in Durham, North Carolina; injection drug users in Philadelphia, Pennsylvania; and gay/bisexual men in San Francisco, California). Note in particular the footnote to the table, which indicates that the text sampling frame centered on responses to a specific question about "Information" desired. The numbers in each cell indicate how often items (codes and characteristics) occurred together with this issue of "Information" in the data.

This table is useful first to provide a quick view of which themes were expressed most frequently and may be said to have the most salience relative to "Information" and one another. Presenting the data in this format further provides an opportunity to look for patterns across the different sites of data collection so that an analyst might learn which areas of the data set could be productively examined in greater qualitative depth to identify *why* these patterns might exist.

Though helpful, such tables quickly become unwieldy and uninterpretable with even a moderate number of codes and characteristics to be explored. This is where having an analysis plan is important. With the analysis plan as guide, you can revisit the research question in tandem with the raw frequencies and the codebook to consider the sets of relationships that warrant further exploration. It is helpful to frame each relationship as a subquestion to explore. In the HIV vaccine trial

Table 6.6 Freelist Responses: Desired Information About Preventive HIV Vaccine Trials. Co-occurrence of Themes and Location

Themes	Durham ($n = 18$)[a] n (%)	Philadelphia ($n = 30$) n (%)	San Francisco ($n = 40$) n (%)
1. Trust and confidentiality	5 (27.8)	—	12 (30.0)
2. Assistance with complications	2 (11.1)	2 (6.7)	14 (35.0)
3. Incentives	2 (11.1)	3 (10.0)	8 (20.0)
4. Effectiveness of vaccine	5 (27.8)	9 (30.0)	15 (37.5)
5. Future availability of vaccine	2 (11.1)	1 (3.3)	5 (12.5)
6. Risk of getting HIV/AIDS	1 (5.6)	10 (33.3)	13 (32.5)
7. Potential side effects	11 (61.1)	18 (60.0)	34 (85.0)
8. Methodology			
a. Duration of trial	3 (16.7)	7 (23.3)	24 (60.0)
b. Previous research	4 (22.2)	4 (13.3)	18 (45.0)
c. Sample makeup	4 (22.2)	7 (23.3)	16 (40.0)
d. Researchers/funding	6 (33.3)	—	12 (30.0)
e. How vaccine works	—	6 (20.0)	11 (27.5)
f. Vaccine contents	2 (11.1)	4 (13.3)	10 (25.0)
g. Placebo versus test groups	2 (11.1)	3 (10.0)	8 (20.0)
h. Participation affecting day-to-day life	2 (11.1)	—	16 (40.0)
i. Purposes and uses of trial information	4 (22.2)	1 (3.3)	9 (22.5)
j. HIV-positive test result	1 (5.6)	1 (3.3)	10 (25.0)

Source: Strauss et al., 2001.

[a]$n = 2$ were missing data.

Note: Percentage indicates the number of participants who gave response(s) for each theme divided by the number of respondents who gave a freelist response to the specific question about "Information desired."

attitudes analysis by Strauss and colleagues (2001), the authors generated similar tables to summarize the themes that emerged in response to questions about perceived benefits and risks of trial participation. In this example, note the continuity between the questions asked during data collection, the thematic coding, and the data reduction via the summary table.

Beware that you can quickly generate many tables using this analytic strategy if the analysis is not highly focused. Rather than generate a listing of every conceivable group of relationships, strive to build a systematic approach for identifying broad patterns in the data. For example, develop a stepwise plan for comparing thematically related groups of codes by major participant characteristics such as gender, age, and socioeconomic status (if your research design and sample are conducive; you may not be able to make substantive comparisons if the sample size of any given category is extremely small). After each step in the plan, summarize the main patterns that emerge and note any puzzling, contradictory, or interesting aspects. Keep in mind that this is an exploratory step in the analysis. For relatively straightforward questions such as the freelisting approach used in the HIV vaccine trial acceptability analysis, the aim of which was to preliminarily identify all of the types of information, risks, and benefits that participants might consider important, it may prove sufficient to generate findings. But for more complex qualitative data it may generate questions and hypotheses about relationships that require further exploration. If so, a systematic approach will help you drill down into the descriptive text detail without losing sight of where you have been and where you still need to go.

At the end of this exploration you should have a detailed description of the emergent themes (the codebook), how common those themes are in the data (the code frequencies), the general patterning of themes in the data (the code co-occurrences), and, possibly, a set of questions or hypotheses for more detailed exploration. At this point, you may wish to put aside further numeric analysis and focus on the richness of the text data. In that case, you can use the questions or hypotheses as a framework for querying the data. Such a framework can take the form of an evolving diagram that shows the relationships identified through the numeric analysis as well as those identified through in-depth reading of the text itself. Many software programs include functions that allow for the creation of diagrams that let you drill down from the code labels to the text itself (see Chapter 9 for review of qualitative data analysis software programs and features). Again, the quantification here is part of a larger, iterative process: The frequency and co-occurrence tables can be used to generate Boolean search statements to pull text for review and in-depth analysis.

A Word of Caution

When you begin to drill down into the text, you are once again in danger of following digressions and straying from specific research objectives. The larger the text data set, the greater the risk that this will happen. Remember, the whole point of developing a systematic codebook was to provide a comprehensive map of the textual terrain. If you find yourself going in circles or stuck in one small corner of the text, stop. Skim through the codebook, look at the frequency tables, review the summary co-occurrence tables, and re-read the questions you identified for more in-depth exploration. Get back to the big picture. Make note of where you are getting lost and describe exactly what is pulling you in that direction. Then, consider the analytic options. Do you need to add new codes, redefine old ones, rethink the code groupings, or explore co-occurrences that previously seemed unimportant? If so, take the time to refine the coding. Is there an unusual but meaningful aggregation of themes that the quantitative summary does not capture? If so, describe it and consider the implications for the rest of the analysis, modifying the analysis plan as appropriate. Or are you possibly reading more into the text than is, in fact, there? If so, make a note of what you thought you were seeing, why it looked that way, and what evidence you would need to see in further readings of the text to warrant taking any additional detours in pursuit of your analysis objectives. Though it may sometimes feel like a step backward, this type of reflection and revision of codes, coding, or analysis plans is a critical step forward in the iterative analysis process.

SIMILARITY MATRICES

One of the reasons people get lost in large text data sets is because they are attempting to process multidimensional relationships among large numbers of conceptual items. The brain is labeling these conceptual items and then subjectively calculating the similarities and differences among them. It is like walking through a forest and attempting to describe in words the three-dimensional positioning of leaves, branches, trunks and roots, the flight of birds and scurrying of squirrels, and the play of sunlight and shadow—and doing so for an audience who may never have been inside a forest.

If you can't see the forest for the trees, you might consider using matrix algebra as a descriptive tool. A matrix is a special kind of table that lets you record the multidimensional positioning of items relative to each other. If you are thoughtful and systematic with regard to how you generate the values in a concurrency table (refer to Figure 6.2), you can use matrix algebra to efficiently analyze the relationships in an otherwise large and unwieldy table. Matrix algebra can be used to visualize the structure of the relationships among items in ways that make intuitive sense to the human brain. These visualizations may resemble some of the diagrams that qualitative researchers create as they mentally read, code, and process the text. But there is a critical difference. Matrix algebra processes all of the data included in the table using a predetermined algorithm with clearly stated assumptions. Every time that algorithm is run on the same data matrix, it generates the same visualization of the relationships. Matrix algebra shows us exactly how the data were coded. In contrast, a mental model developed from close reading of the text shows us how a particular researcher or research team selects and interprets the coded relationships in the data.

If the research team continues to code the text in an iterative fashion with the development of the mental model, the end result may be highly subjective and interpretive. There is considerable debate among researchers as to whether such indeterminate subjectivity is good or bad. In applied thematic analysis we feel quite strongly that indeterminate subjectivity should be minimized. Otherwise, when presenting your findings to skeptical decision makers, your main defense of the data will be, "Trust me, I know what I'm doing." This is because in order to replicate the analysis and generate the same representation of the data, another researcher would need detailed documentation on which relationships were explored and how this exploration was done. That is the point of the extensive annotation called for by many qualitative analysis strategies. "I think X and Y are related because person A and person B both referenced X and Y when asked about Z. To explore this relationship I did a Boolean search on X and Y and Z. But then I realized that only women talked about X and Y and Z so I did separate Boolean searches on X or Y and Z by gender. It turns out that men either talk about X or talk about Y in relationship to Z but never about both X and Y...."

You can do the same kind of exploration much more systematically and efficiently using matrix algebra in combination with graph theoretic techniques. What is a matrix? At its most basic, a matrix is simply a set of numbers arranged into rows and columns. This arrangement is called the matrix dimension or order. The dimension of a matrix with 3 rows and 4 columns of numbers is 3×4. The dimension of a matrix with 12 rows and 6 columns is 12×6. The intersection of each row and column (i.e., each cell in the table) is called an element. A square matrix has the same number of rows and columns. A symmetric matrix is a special kind of square matrix, where the diagonal splits the matrix into two triangular halves that are mirror images of each other.

Say you have a set of codes and you want to compare pairs of codes to see how often each item in the set gets applied to the same bounded text with each other item in the set. You can create a matrix where the code labels for each item form the rows and the columns and the elements indicate the number of times that code combination was applied to the same text (Table 6.7). You can also quickly see which codes do not occur together—those would be the elements or cells that equal zero.

Table 6.7 Example of Symmetric Matrix Comparing Frequencies for Five Codes

	Code A	Code B	Code C	Code D	Code E
Code A	—	12	0	24	5
Code B	12	—	15	4	9
Code C	0	15	—	2	0
Code D	24	4	2	—	15
Code E	5	9	0	15	—

Note: In this example the diagonal cells are left blank; however, they could also note the frequency for each of the five codes, on the assumption that each instance of a code occurrence is an instance of its co-occurrence with itself. Note that the values in the cells above the diagonal mirror those in the cells below the diagonal.

Does this sound familiar? It should, because every co-occurrence table is a kind of matrix. Consider an example comparing the thematic co-occurrence patterns for men and women. In matrix algebra terms, we would create two matrices with the same dimensions (one for code co-occurrences for women, one for code co-occurrences for men) and compare the elements in those two matrices to each other. When matrices have the same dimensions, they can be added to (or subtracted from) each other. This is done by adding (or subtracting) each element in one matrix to (or from) the corresponding element in the other matrix. This creates a new matrix with the same dimensions but different elements that summarize how similar or dissimilar the two original matrices were. This simple arithmetic calculation can be extended to make more complex comparisons and generate a new matrix that succinctly summarizes those comparisons. That's basically what matrix algebra is about.

Now consider an example where we have x interviews, y codes, and z participant characteristics. You could review frequencies and co-occurrences, then methodically use Boolean logic to search for and look at groups of comparisons. Or, you could use a computer program to create a cross-tabulation of every comparison. Which would be most efficient? Which would be least prone to human error?

The complex relationships summarized in a similarity matrix are less obvious when just eye-balling the values in the matrix. In Table 6.7 for example, code A may co-occur a lot with both code B and code C but codes B and C may rarely co-occur with each other. Codes A and B may have been used with high frequency while code C is used with low frequency. Should we consider the three codes as an important group, given C's low frequency? Or, should we consider A and B to be a separate group from C? These are extremely difficult relationships to parse within the context of a large, complex data set. But it is exactly the kind of parsing that can be done efficiently with graph theoretic techniques.

GRAPH THEORETIC TECHNIQUES: THE EXAMPLE OF CLUSTER ANALYSIS

Hierarchical cluster analysis is a method for grouping "like" observations with each other and distinguishing those groups from other "like" groupings (Aldenderfer & Blashfield, 1984; Anderberg, 1973). Cluster analysis uses the information generated from similarity matrices to identify the groupings of like observations. The similarity matrices used for cluster analysis can be binary (using zeros and ones to indicate whether two items co-occur), or they can be valued (using a range of values to indicate the degree or strength of similarity). For a reader-friendly explanation of how hierarchical cluster analysis works, refer to Borgatti (1994) in the Additional Reading section.

For an example of how cluster analysis can be used to drill down into coded text, we will look at an article describing how people who participated in an HIV vaccine acceptability study defined community (MacQueen et al., 2001).

The analysis included in-depth interviews with participants from the same three populations described in the paper by Strauss and colleagues (2001) plus interviews with HIV vaccine researchers from multiple locations in the United States. In total, 113 interviews generated responses to the questions about how people defined and thought about community, and 17 distinct themes were identified that appeared in the definitions of at least two participants. To deal with the large number of themes generated by four distinct participant groups, cluster analysis was used to identify similarities in the way people defined community and the extent to which those similarities cut across the participant groups.

Hierarchical cluster analysis identified four clusters among the themes. A core cluster contained five elements: locus, sharing, joint action, social ties, and diversity. Each core element reflected some aspect of face-to-face interaction. A second cluster centered on group-based elements of community: divisiveness, leverage, pluralism, and responsibility. These elements reflected social cohesion and community involvement and often acted as boundary-setting or -maintaining mechanisms. Each element of these two clusters was cited by at least four members of each participant group. The third and fourth clusters centered on elements that reflected stresses experienced by communities or their members. The first stress cluster included the elements of criminality and drug use. The second centered on the elements of AIDS and unity (MacQueen et al., 2001, p. 1930).

The core cluster was then looked at in considerable detail in order to identify and understand similarities and differences across the four participant groups. This included looking at the co-occurrence of each of the five themes and the frequency of each of those themes by participant group. Richly detailed quotes were presented to illustrate how participants not only talked about particular themes but how they were woven together in discourse. It is worth noting that this particular analysis involved quite a bit of wheel-spinning until the analysis team decided to try using graph theoretic techniques to explore the thematic relationships. The hierarchical cluster plots succinctly summarized the multiple dimensions of meaning and context. Readers who desire more methodological detail about this particular technique should refer to Guest and McLellan (2003).

Another example of how cluster analysis can be used to parse complex data is seen in an analysis of pregnancy prevention practices among women participating in an HIV prevention trial in three African countries. Pregnancy was an issue for the trial because little human data existed with regard to the safety of the study drug in pregnancy. As a result, women who became pregnant had to be taken off the drug. High pregnancy rates among the women in the trial undermined the ability of researchers to retain participants long enough to accomplish their objectives.

To explore why pregnancy rates were higher than anticipated in the trial, we added questions about pregnancy prevention to qualitative interviews with a subsample of women. The interviews were conducted 7 months after women enrolled into the trial. Table 6.8 summarizes the themes identified from responses to these questions.

Table 6.8 Code Frequencies for Participant Responses at Month 7 Follow-Up Visit (*n* = 67)

Code	Brief Definition	No. Participants With Code Applied (%)
Change	Reports a change in pregnancy prevention since enrollment in the study	44 (65)
No change	Explicitly states that she has made no changes in pregnancy prevention since enrollment in the study	23 (34)
Pre-condom, post-condom	Reports using condoms for pregnancy prevention before enrollment (pre-condom) or since enrollment (post-condom) in the study	Pre-condom: 27 (40) Post-condom: 56 (84)
Pre-hormonals, post-hormonals	Reports using hormonal methods (oral contraceptives or injectables) for pregnancy prevention before enrollment (pre-hormonals) or since enrollment (post-hormonals) in the study	Pre-hormonals: 9 (13) Post-hormonals: 4 (6)
Pre-drugs, post-drugs	Reports using drugs (including antibiotics) for pregnancy prevention before enrollment (pre-drugs) or since enrollment (post-drugs) in the study; does not explicitly refer to oral contraceptives	Pre-drugs: 7 (10) Post-drugs: 3 (4)
Pre-folk remedy, post-folk remedy	Reports using a folk remedy for pregnancy prevention or emergency contraception before enrollment (pre-folk remedy) or since enrollment (post-folk remedy) in the study; could include salt, water, douching, or whiskey	Pre-folk remedy: 5 (7) Post-folk remedy: 4 (6)
Pre-natural, post-natural	Reports tracking her cycle or use of withdrawal for pregnancy prevention before enrollment (pre-natural) or since enrollment (post-natural) in the study	Pre-natural: 11 (16) Post-natural: 3 (4)
Pre-nothing, post-nothing	Reports using nothing for pregnancy prevention before enrollment (pre-nothing) or since enrollment (post-nothing) in the study	Pre-nothing: 7 (10) Post-nothing: 0
Pre-abortion, post-abortion	Reports having induced abortion for pregnancy prevention before enrollment (pre-abortion) or since enrollment (post-abortion) in the study	Pre-abortion: 4 (6) Post-abortion: 0
Change counsel	Explicitly attributes change in pregnancy prevention since enrollment in the study to the counseling received during the study	20 (30)
Dual protection	Any discussion of experience using condoms for dual protection to prevent HIV/AIDS and pregnancy	14 (21)

(Continued)

Table 6.8 (Continued)

Code	Brief Definition	No. Participants With Code Applied (%)
Partner	Any discussion concerning partner-related family planning issues; for example, using a condom is up to a partner, using condoms depends on the type of partner, or partner may not approve of family planning use	10 (15)
Change-access	Attributes change in pregnancy prevention since enrollment in the study to access to condoms or family planning methods during the study	5 (7)
Change-KnowHowCondom	Reports improved skills or knowledge of condom use since enrollment in the study, credited to counseling received during the study	5 (7.5)
Preg-fate	Any discussion of the lack of intentionality for pregnancy; respondent may state that she has no control over whether or not she gets pregnant (e.g., it is a matter of fate, it is up to God) or that pregnancy is a state of being (e.g., you are pregnant or you are not pregnant)	6 (9)
Preg-intention	Any discussion of intentionality for pregnancy; a respondent may state that she has control over whether or not she gets pregnant (with or without making reference to pregnancy prevention methods)	7 (10)

Source: MacQueen et al., 2007.

Figure 6.3 shows the results of two cluster analyses of the thematic data, one including a code for the participant's site of location (6.3B) and one excluding that code (6.3A). The column labels represent the codes described in Table 6.8, and the levels refer to the unit of analysis (in this case, the participants). The levels indicate the largest number of participants associated with a given cluster. Codes grouped at higher levels indicate co-occurrence of the themes and higher frequency of the themes in the responses. For example, a level 5 cluster with 3 codes indicates that the responses of 5 participants were coded with all 3 of the codes linked at that level in the cluster. Each code, however, may have been applied to the text of other participants as well. That is, the code frequency may be greater than the level of the same code within a cluster.

In Figure 6.3A, cluster A is clearly the dominant pattern and can be summarized as women who changed their pregnancy prevention practices to the use of condoms for dual protection as a result of the counseling provided during the trial. Cluster B centered on women who had been using condoms for dual protection before enrolling in the trial and continued this practice after enrollment. Cluster C centered on women who used hormonal contraceptives before and after trial enrollment. Women using natural methods (e.g., calendars, withdrawal) formed a separate group (cluster D) that was also linked with a minor cluster of women using folk remedies for pregnancy prevention. When the site code was included (Figure 6.3B), the importance of population-specific factors became evident. Cluster B emerged as a largely Nigerian pattern, and cluster D was largely Cameroonian. The codes associated with the previously dominant cluster A split into two clusters. Cluster H was associated with Ghanaian participants and centered on a switch in pregnancy prevention practices from hormonals to condom use. Cluster I centered on a change to condoms for dual protection and was not associated with a specific site. To bring these patterns to life, descriptive vignettes were drawn from the in-depth interviews showing how the patterns were enacted in the trial context.

As illustrated in both examples here, cluster analysis data reduction techniques offer an efficient and relatively objective method for identifying patterns or clusters in qualitative data, but it is up to the researcher to interpret those clusters, give them a name, and figure out an explanation (based on the data) of why the codes group together this way. Though the output is quantitative, it is based on careful qualitative coding and analysis, preceding and following the cluster analysis, respectively.

WHEN IS QUANTIFICATION APPROPRIATE?

Having reviewed all of the information in this chapter, that question remains. As we alluded to in the introduction, one of the reasons it is difficult to know when quantification of qualitative data is appropriate is that there are very different views on the subject. Hannah and Lautsch label this the "multiple audience" problem:

Figure 6.3 Complete-Link Hierarchic Cluster Analysis of Codes Applied to Participant Responses (A) and With Participant Site Codes Added (B).

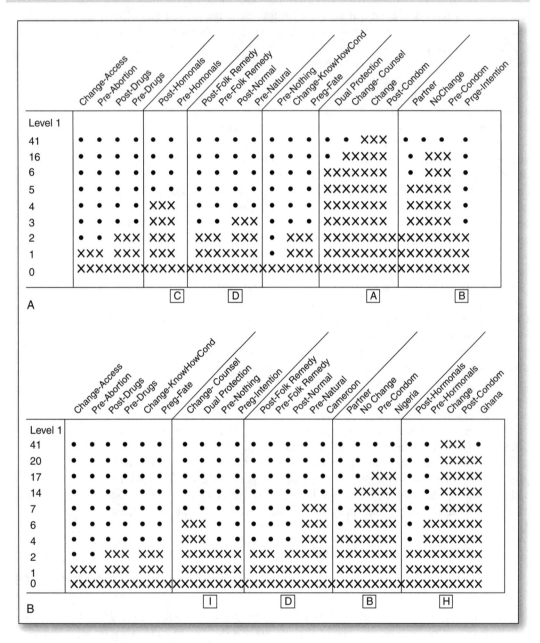

Source: MacQueen et al. 2007.
Note: Major clusters are designated with uppercase letters.

> Different audiences for qualitative research may have different beliefs about what
> constitutes good qualitative research. On occasion, those beliefs will contradict one
> another. Therefore, if qualitative researchers try to satisfy the preferences of one
> audience, they risk not meeting the preferences of another audience. (2010, p. 2)

The "multiple audience" problem can arise during any phase of the research, from design to publication, and often involves thoughtful, reasonable people who simply view qualitative research and methods differently. When considering the factors below with regard to quantifying qualitative data, we keep in mind the *primary* audience for the given issues, recognizing that there will likely still be some disagreement. Our aim is to guide decision making in a rational and defensible way so that useful and efficient techniques for qualitative data reduction are not dismissed simply because they are quantitatively oriented.

Purpose

As described in Table 6.2, there are many different purposes for quantifying qualitative data. For those that fall outside the realm of dissemination, quantification is always a possibility. It is part of the analysis and understanding-your-data process and is done in close contact with the raw qualitative data. Since the analysis process (and subsequent findings) may be described without reference to the quantification techniques used, there is not much controversy here. These techniques may be described as "closeted" counting (Hannah & Lautsch, 2010) that assist the researcher in discovering the "story" of her qualitative data. Purpose is vitally important for considering whether quantification of qualitative data is appropriate for dissemination of findings as well. The nature and intent of the publication or final report you will write, as well as the audience for that publication, help to determine whether or not to present theme frequencies, co-occurrence matrices, or any of the other "results" of quantification activities.

Generally speaking, on one end of the purpose continuum are "reports" of findings, articles or summaries with an applied focus where the intent is that the reader can or should be able to *do* something with the information from your research. If your research design includes objectives related to policy development or evaluation of a concept, intervention, or product, you will more likely want to include some kind of frequency summaries, for two reasons. First, it is very difficult to assess how much weight to give to a policy recommendation or how strongly a group of people liked or disliked a given program based solely on a qualitative description of the range of themes evident in a data set. If we find that "most" people hold a positive impression of Action X, does that mean 51% of my sample or 89%? When I move from this general level of summary to more nuanced qualitative description of the range of "positive" findings, what subset of participants am I including here? Second, the audiences to which these findings will be addressed are more likely to expect a positivist approach and/or understand quantified results. Qualitative quotes and data can deliver a strong emotional connection; quantitative summaries help translate these emotions into potential actions.

By contrast, if your research objective is very exploratory, aims to generate theory or build conceptual models, or follows an ethnographic or life-history approach, there is likely very little need for frequencies or quantification in the dissemination of your findings. Indeed, if you have taken an interpretive approach from the beginning of your research, it may well be impossible to meaningfully quantify your findings—and rightly so. These differences should be reflected in the research design and data collection guides long before questions about quantifying findings arise.

Structure

Related to the point about research design, the structure of data collection will also help determine how appropriate quantification of results may be. Two kinds of structure are important here: the structure of individual questions and the structure of the interview guide. If we look first at the level of individual questions, we are interested to know what types of questions are asked and the responses those questions generate. Some questions are truly open-ended and will elicit responses that are not immediately codeable. The answers to "How did you decide to be a firefighter?" will likely vary along themes that will be recognizable only after we have asked the question of many firefighters. Other questions are still open-ended but elicit responses that fall into easily recognizable dichotomous or trichotomous categories. For example, "How did you feel about the school redistricting plan?" will likely generate some answers that are positive, some negative, and some ambivalent or neutral. Code frequencies are particularly useful and appropriate in the latter case, common in policy and evaluation work, for providing a high-level summary of opinions. The overarching summary of the distribution of these responses *within your sample* gives readers a quick frame of reference for the more nuanced, qualitative findings that you will present to characterize the positive and negative responses. This does not mean that you are asking closed-ended yes/no questions or trying to replicate survey methodology, but that the intent and framing of your questions leads to responses that can be relatively easily categorized as positive or negative or neutral (and there will likely always be an "other" category in qualitative data of this nature). It also is not meant to imply that "analysis" stops with the simple categorization of responses; the thematic analysis of each subset of responses is where the qualitative data are more thoroughly examined and presented.

The second part of the data collection structure that affects whether qualitative data can be quantified is the nature of the interview process. Quantification, in some respects, is dependent on asking the same or similar questions of everyone. If only some participants are asked a particular question, there is less validity in presenting code frequencies because a participant may not have had a chance to mention a particular theme if not asked directly. Conversely, there is more justification for providing thematic frequencies when all participants have been asked the same questions.

Following from this, and as discussed in conjunction with Figure 6.1B, coding must be replicable (reliable) and codes clearly defined to have confidence in code quantifications. Since many frequencies compare code applications, often across demographic characteristics or domains, you (and your reader) have to be able to trust your coding as a valid representation of the themes in the data. The more systematic you are in the coding process, the more confident you can be presenting thematic frequencies. Procedures for comparing and maintaining intercoder reliability should be outlined in the research design, adhered to during coding, and clearly articulated in any publications.

If you are contemplating comparing frequencies between subgroups in your sample, consider whether the subgroup sample sizes are comparable or at least of a standard minimum size. Again, this goes back to the research design process: if you are interested in comparing sample heterogeneity or subpopulation similarities and differences, design and sample accordingly. Comparing what was said by half of 30 respondents to half of 6 is tenuous. That said, if the sample was chosen based on important features shared among those in the sample (people who are key informants of some kind, regardless of their demographic or other characteristic differences), you might use frequencies for the whole of the sample, but provide only qualitative descriptors for the parts (subthemes or subsamples).

Ambiguity

Finally, also consider the ambiguity that may result from *not* providing some quantification of qualitative data. Some researchers advocate using quantitative descriptors only (all, many, most, some, few), and it is possible that you might even define what these terms mean at the outset of your paper (see Guest et al., 2005, for an example). However, to be able to say even these terms, you must have performed some kind of "closeted" quantification during your analysis. If after reviewing the other determining factors it is still a possibility, consider providing frequencies (in the form of "n of N" or percentages) to readers to let them decide how they would describe the prevalence of given views. For applied thematic analysis in particular, where the salience of a given theme is important information for a reader to be able to assess with regard to a particular policy, program, or evaluation event, the less ambiguous your presentation of findings, the clearer the implications. Qualitatively describing the range of themes, related meanings, or conceptual findings with the qualitative data and metadata as your reference points is possible and perfectly appropriate for some types of qualitative inquiry, detailed above, that are highly exploratory, interpretive, and/or designed to generate theory. Audience and purpose are again considerations in thinking about the level (and definition) of ambiguity acceptable in qualitative research findings.

Even if reporting code or theme frequencies, code co-occurrence tables, or cluster analysis plots is appropriate, always remember that quantification of qualitative data is a tool, an organizing reference to help identify interesting patterns and meanings, not *the* finding in and of itself. When used in dissemination activities, the quantifications serve to orient the reader to larger patterns in the data before the richer qualitative findings from which the numbers were drawn are reported.

SUMMING UP

Qualitative data reduction seeks to highlight and preserve the meaning, structure, and relationships inherent in the data relative to the research question being asked. It is often helpful to focus an analysis simply by refining the data set in accordance with a particular analysis objective. Once the relevant data have been extracted, code summaries or code-by-characteristics matrices can be developed to facilitate focused reading of the relevant data to look for trends or patterns. Strategic and thoughtful use of quantitative summaries can also facilitate qualitative data reduction. This cannot be done simply by applying the kind of parametric statistical analyses that are most commonly used in quantitative social science research. Rather, the data reduction methods need to be selected with the nature of qualitative data research in mind, including sampling strategies and units of analysis. The presentation of quantitative summaries of qualitative data needs to be done in such a way that the reader is not misled with regard to statistical representativeness or generalizability. With those caveats in mind, quantitative data reduction can be effectively used to increase the efficiency of qualitative data analysis, the reliability of the findings, and the clarity of the presentation.

REFERENCES

Aldenderfer, M. S., & Blashfield, R. K. (1984). *Cluster analysis.* Beverly Hills, CA: Sage.

Anderberg, M. R. (1973). *Cluster analysis for applications.* New York: Academic.

Campbell, C., Foulis, C. A., Maimane, S., & Sibiya, Z. (2005). "I have an evil child at my house": Stigma and HIV/AIDS management in a South African Community. *American Journal of Public Health, 95*(5), 808–815.

Guest, G., & McLellan, E. (2003). Distinguishing the trees from the forest: Applying cluster analysis to thematic qualitative data. *Field Methods, 15,* 186–201.

Guest, G., McLellan-Lemal, E., Matia, D. M., Pickard, R., Fuchs, J., McKirnan, D., & Neidig, J. L. (2005). HIV vaccine efficacy trial participation: Men who have sex with men's experiences of risk reduction counseling and perceptions of risk behavior change. *AIDS Care, 17*(1), 46–57.

Hannah, D., & Lautsch, B. (2010). Counting in qualitative research: Why to conduct it, when to avoid it, and when to closet it. *Journal of Management Inquiry, 20,* 14–22.

Lyerly, A. D., Steinhauser, K., Namey, E., Tulsky, J., Cook-Deegan, R., Sugarman, J., Walmer, D., & Wallach, E. (2006). Factors that affect decision making about frozen embryo disposition: Infertility patient perspectives. *Fertility and Sterility, 85*(6), 1623–1630.

MacQueen, K. M., Johnson, L., Alleman, P., Akumatey, B., Lawoyin, T., & Nyiama, T. (2007). Pregnancy prevention practices among women with multiple partners in an HIV prevention trial. *JAIDS, 46*(1), 32–38.

MacQueen, K. M., McLellan, E., Metzger, D. S., Kegeles, S., Strauss, R.P., Scotti, R., Blanchard, L., & Trotter, R. T. (2001). What is community? An evidence-based definition for participatory public health. *AJPH, 91,*1929–1938.

Miles, M. B., & Huberman, M. A . (1994). *Qualitative data analysis: An expanded sourcebook* (2nd ed.). Thousand Oaks, CA: Sage.

Moonan, P. K., Quitugua, T. N., Pogoda, J. M., Woo, G., Drewyer, G., Sahbazian, B., Dunbar, D., . . . Weis, S. E. (2011). Does directly observed therapy (DOT) reduce drug resistant tuberculosis? *BMC Public Health, 11*, 19. doi:10.1186/1471-2458-11-19

Namey, E., Guest, G., Thairu, L., & Johnson, L. (2007). Data reduction techniques for large qualitative data sets. In G. Guest & K. MacQueen (Eds.), *Handbook for team-based qualitative research* (pp. 137–161). Lanham, MD: AltaMira Press.

Silverman, D. (2000). *Doing qualitative research: A practical handbook.* Thousand Oaks, CA: Sage.

Strauss, R. P., Sengupta, S., Kegeles, S., McLellan, E., Metzger, D., Eyre, S., Khanani, F., Emrick, C.B., MacQueen, K. M. (2001). Willingness to volunteer in future preventive HIV vaccine trials: Issues and perspectives from three U.S. communities. *JAIDS, 26,* 63–71.

Suddaby, R. (2006). What grounded theory is not. *Academy of Management Journal, 49,* 633–642.

Wei, X., Walley, J. D., Liang, X., Liu, F., Zhang, X., & Li, R. (2008). Adapting a generic tuberculosis control operational guideline and scaling it up in China: A qualitative case study. *BMC Public Health, 8,* 260. doi:10.1186/1471-2458-8-260

EXERCISES

1. Select six business websites in the same general sector, three for-profit and three nonprofit, and find the companies' mission statements. Using the template below, construct a data matrix using the mission statement as your quoted text data. You may include statements of values or visions in the "data" column if you wish. Complete as many cells as possible based on the information available on the website. Once the matrix is complete, review it for patterns or trends, comparing based on company type. Sort the matrix on a column other than "type of company" and see if you notice anything different.

Company name	Company type	Business sector	Date est'd	Company mission statement (data)	Codes applied*
Example A	Nonprofit	Health/ Development	1975	"To bring sustainable health and sanitation systems to the world's poor."	Sustainability Health Altruism
Example B	For-profit	Health care	1989	"To help Americans get and stay well while providing individual attention and care."	Health Health maintenance Personal attention

*Per mission statement, list qualities that you might have coded if this were drawn from a larger data set.

2. Select three articles on a similar topic that used similar qualitative methods for data collection. Compare how the authors describe their findings and answer the following questions:

- What do you think is effective about the style of the presentation? What might be improved?
- How are tables used to help explain the data?
- Are any code or theme frequencies provided? Are any advanced quantitative data reduction techniques used?
- How confident are you in the style of presentation, given the information in the methods section and what was discussed about appropriateness of quantification of data here?

Here's a sample of qualitative articles based on women's birth experiences:

Fowles, E. (1998). Labor concerns of women two months after delivery. *BIRTH, 25*(4), 235–240.

Gibbins, J., & Thomson, A. M. (2001). Women's expectations and experiences of childbirth. *Midwifery, 17*, 302–313.

Kabakian-Khasholian, T., Campbell, O., Shediac-Rizkallah, M., & Ghorayeb, F. (2000). Women's experiences of maternity care: Satisfaction or passivity? *Social Science & Medicine, 51*, 103–113.

Melender, H. (2006). What constitutes a good childbirth? A qualitative study of pregnant Finnish women. *Journal of Midwifery and Women's Health, 51*(5), 331–339.

Walker, J. M., Hall, S., & Thomas, M. (1995). The experience of labour: A perspective from those receiving care in a midwife-led unit. *Midwifery, 11*, 120–129.

3. Suppose you asked the question, "What advice would you give to a woman preparing to give birth for the first time?" and coded the responses using codes from your larger data set. You are now interested to know which themes (codes) co-occur in expressions of advice offered. Using Table Ex. 3, which indicates whether five particular codes appeared within 10 participants' responses to the advice question, create a two-sided co-occurrence data matrix following the template below. Which codes co-occur most frequently? Do you have any hypotheses about why? Based on this matrix, formulate two questions that would guide you in revisiting the qualitative data. (Also note how the small sample size affects the results.)

Table Ex. 3: Presence (1) or Absence (0) of Five Codes in Participants' Responses to "What Advice Would You Give to a Woman Preparing to Give Birth for the First Time?"

			Code Names		
Study ID	Pain relief	Information	Control	Relax	Location
P01	1	0	1	0	1
P02	0	1	0	1	1
P03	1	0	1	0	1
P04	0	0	1	1	1
P05	0	1	1	0	0
P06	1	0	0	1	0
P07	1	0	0	1	1
P08	0	1	0	1	1
P09	1	1	1	0	0
P10	0	0	1	1	1

Aggregated Code Co-occurrence Summary Template

	Pain relief	Information	Control	Relax	Location
Pain relief	X				
Information		X			
Control			X		
Relax				X	
Location					X

ADDITIONAL READING

Borgatti, S. (1994). How to explain hierarchical clustering. *Connections, 17*(2), 78–80.

Hannah, D., & Lautsch, B. (2010). Counting in qualitative research: Why to conduct it, when to avoid it, and when to closet it. *Journal of Management Inquiry, 20,* 14–22.

Namey, E., Guest, G., Thairu, L., & Johnson, L. (2007). Data reduction techniques for large qualitative data sets. In G. Guest & K. MacQueen (Eds.), *Handbook for team-based qualitative research* (pp. 137–161). Lanham, MD: AltaMira Press.

7

COMPARING THEMATIC DATA

LEARNING OBJECTIVES

Upon finishing this chapter, readers should be able to:

- Describe qualitative methods of comparing thematic data
- Describe quantitative methods of comparing thematic data
- Use several graphical techniques for visualizing comparisons

Comparison is a cornerstone of much social and behavioral research as well as qualitative inquiry (Mills, 2008). Whether attempting to discern similarities and differences across groups of individuals, within groups over two or more data collection time points, or across different data types, comparisons are fundamental to the data analysis process and presentation of findings. In experimental or quasi-experimental research, comparison is factored into the study design. In quantitative observational studies, comparison of groups along key demographic and other variables of interest is standard practice. In qualitative research, especially that in which inductive thematic analysis is undertaken, comparison is often much less explicit and transparent, yet comparison can deepen understanding and explanation of a particular phenomenon (Miles & Huberman, 1994).

As Corbin and Strauss (2008) astutely note, "Doing comparative analysis is another one of those staple features of social science research" (p. 73). The primacy and value of comparison is also acknowledged explicitly for analysis of focus groups. In the words of Krueger (1998), "Perhaps the most useful strategy in qualitative analysis is finding patterns, making comparisons, and contrasting one set of data with another" (p. 17). Although qualitative researchers acknowledge the usefulness of performing across-group or within-group comparisons over time, descriptions of procedures for doing so are limited. Corbin and Strauss (2008), for example, delve into great detail as to how comparisons are used to develop codes and coding trees but do not explicitly address comparing codes and coding trees across groups after all of the data have been coded. For systematic qualitative data collection methods aimed at understanding cultural semantic domains, such as componential analysis, freelisting, and pile sorts, some good examples of comparative analyses exist (Bernard & Ryan, 2010; Leech & Onwuegbuzie, 2007; Weller & Romney, 1988). Yet, instruction for such procedures in an inductive thematic analysis, at least in the qualitative and mixed methods literatures, is difficult to find.

The reality is that many researchers who plan a thematic analysis are faced with research questions of a comparative nature: How do women's experiences with program X differ from men's experiences? How do perceptions of disease Y differ between highly educated versus less educated participants? We hope this chapter provides readers with some ideas about how such comparisons might be done to address research questions such as these as well as highlight some of the limitations associated with certain comparative methods. We further hope that this chapter stimulates much needed discussion on the topic of comparing thematic data within an inductive analysis.

This chapter provides readers with some techniques for systematically comparing thematic data across groups after data have been inductively coded. We also discuss the appropriateness of using probability-based statistics on nonprobability samples as well as some of the limitations associated with quantifying qualitative data for comparative purposes. Before moving further, however, we must first distinguish between across-group comparisons as part of an inductive thematic analysis—after codes have been developed and applied to data—with other uses of the comparative method in qualitative research. We do not discuss, for example, the "constant comparison" method employed in Grounded Theory and used to develop codes and coding trees (Corbin & Strauss 2008; Glaser & Strauss, 1967). Nor do we cover the use of Boolean algebra to compare macrolevel data, as in Qualitative Comparative Analysis (Ragin, 1987, 2008), or comparing themes in the context of hypothesis-driven Content Analysis (e.g., Krippendorf, 2008). We would also remind the reader of our working definition of qualitative research outlined in Chapter 1 that focuses on the data generated and/or used in qualitative inquiry—that is, text, images, and sounds (Nkwi, Nyamongo, & Ryan, 2001, p. 1). As discussed in Chapter 6, this outcome-oriented definition conceptually permits the transformation and quantitative analysis of qualitative data (see also Guest, 2005), which comprises a portion of the techniques described below.

QUALITATIVE COMPARISONS

Conducting a purely qualitative (interpretivist) thematic comparison infers that themes are not counted. Instead one qualitatively compares the content of narratives and highlights similarities and differences between two or more data sets (groups). At the most basic level, an analyst simply examines the differential expression of themes across groups and notes which themes/concepts are similar across groups and which are different. This type of comparison is driven by two overarching questions: "Are some themes present in one data set but not another?"

and, "If a theme is present in data sets from both groups in an analysis, is the expression of that theme different between groups?" Results from this type of comparative analysis of qualitative data are most commonly presented in narrative form within the results and discussion sections of a report. The two excerpts below—one from an ethnographic study and the other from an inductive thematic analysis—are indicative of this commonly used comparative technique. The first example, based on ethnographic research of Luber (2005) compares the healing strategies for "Second Hair" illness used by two different ethnic groups in Mexico—the Tzeltal Maya and the Mixe. Luber observes that both groups are similar in the disease's diagnosis, prognosis, and course of illness, but that they exhibit distinctly different healing strategies:

> One of the most striking differences between the Tzeltal and the Mixe explanatory models is in the treatment strategy. Both cultures agree that the second hairs are the pathological agent in these illnesses, and both treatments target the new type of hair growing on the scalp. While the Tzeltal treat the hairs and scalp by applying medicinal plants, the Mixe attempt to cure this illness by removing the offending hairs by shaving them off. (Luber, 2005, p. 141)

The second example is from a vasectomy acceptability study conducted in Tanzania among potential and actual vasectomy clients and their female partners (Bunce et al., 2007, p. 17). The data presented are from a combination of focus groups and in-depth interview transcripts. The excerpt below is included in a subsection devoted to one of the study's main themes—Spousal Influence—in the context of vasectomy acceptability.

The issue of faithfulness and trust in one's spouse was common in the transcripts. Male respondents worried that their wives might be unfaithful or leave if they wanted more children or if the husband's sexual performance suffered. Some pointed out that the physical evidence of infidelity (e.g., if the wife of a vasectomized man became pregnant) would lead to the end of the marriage. One man explained his initial hesitation:

> Another thing that I had in mind initially . . . was the fear that once you undergo vasectomy operation, your wife might lose faithfulness and bear a child with other men. And this is still a big problem to many men, especially those who are not yet to understand well. But I trust my wife very much; that is why I decided to undergo the vasectomy operation.—Vasectomy client, Kibondo

For women, lack of trust in their husbands' fidelity was both a reason for and a barrier to vasectomy. Some female respondents argued that vasectomy would ensure that they were not burdened with children resulting from their husbands' extramarital relations. One woman explained why she insisted on vasectomy instead of tubal ligation:

> The man can tell you, go and have tubal ligation. You go and have it done. Then your husband goes outside and gets a child; he will continue making you unhappy. But when you tell him to go and get vasectomy, and if he agrees and gets a vasectomy, you women will live in harmony.—Wife of vasectomy client, Kigoma

Comparison of the above two excerpts illustrates that, in the context of vasectomy, trust and fidelity are key issues for both men and women. The qualitative nature of the comparison further allows us to see how the expression of these concepts differs between the two participants (and, as it turns out, between men and women in the larger sample). From the woman's perspective, vasectomy prevents a husband from fathering children with other women, thereby enhancing harmony within the marriage. The man had similar concerns about infidelity, but trust in his wife facilitated the decision to undergo vasectomy.

Comparison can also be done by extracting text associated with a particular code for each of the groups of interest, reviewing it for more detailed content, and then comparing. This method can be facilitated with software and entails using a matrix approach to organize data (e.g., Bazeley 2003, p. 399). In this approach, coded text is organized by the concept of interest and displayed in a concept-by-text matrix, like

Ethnographic Authority

Note the style of presentation and tone of voice used by Luber (2005) and Bunce and colleagues (2007) in the excerpts from their studies. They are illustrative of a common (though not by any means exclusive) distinction between ethnographic and shorter term applied research. Traditional ethnographers travel alone to an exotic and remote place and live with the local people for a year or more (although this process is changing and becoming more varied). With the luxury of time, proximity to the field site, and ability to coordinate data collection in an integrated and inductive manner, research findings are often based on data from a number of data collection types and events, some of which may be implicit. Often results are presented with what Clifford calls "ethnographic authority" (Clifford, 1983); that is, credibility of the findings presented are based on a researcher's intimate, in situ, knowledge of the study community. Moreover, the research topic of interest is often at the cultural level, focusing on shared practices and norms.

In shorter term, more applied research contexts, qualitative inquiry is typically more targeted and based on set procedures outlined in a study protocol. And the subject of inquiry can range from sociocultural phenomena to individual experiences and perceptions. Procedures are also executed in a pre-established manner and research findings are often the result of one or two explicit data collection techniques. In this latter context, it is difficult to claim ethnographic authority, so data collection events and data themselves (i.e., codes and raw text) need to be made explicit, and tied to one's findings, to establish credibility. Related to this is the intended audience and/or journal for a research report. Some audiences will find the use of ethnographic authority perfectly acceptable while others will want detailed substantiation of every result presented in a report. In most journals outside of anthropology, the latter is the norm, which is one of the reasons why throughout this book we emphasize substantiating claims and being transparent in your research and analytic processes.

the one described in Chapter 6, Table 6.1. Data fields in the matrix can take the form of text/code summaries or verbatim text. If the latter, text may be extracted from qualitative data analysis (QDA) software and entered into a spreadsheet, or a spreadsheet can be created within the QDA software itself, using a cross-tab functionality (refer to Chapter 9). Whichever form a matrix takes, the next step is for the analyst to qualitatively look for and identify patterns within and across groups (variables).

Let's imagine, for example, that one wanted to determine if young people and older people in a study experience prejudice differently while job seeking. One way to approach this is to have a code for "prejudice" that is applied to both data sets. By pulling out the text associated with the code for individuals in each group, one can look for specific instances and examples of prejudice. One might find, for example, that when young people talk about prejudice, they give examples of being rejected for a job because of lack of perceived experience or knowledge while older folks talk about prejudice in terms of employers asking questions about their physical health and stamina. Depending on how the data are coded, one could achieve a similar comparison by looking at co-occurrences of codes. If in the example above we had coded at a level of granularity such that "lack knowledge" and "health/stamina" were codes applied to the data, we could run two co-occurrence reports in our software ("prejudice" + "lack knowledge" and "prejudice" + "health/stamina") and see how these codes are co-configured across our two groups of interest. A study by Gibbs (2002, p. 191) that looked comparatively at job-searching strategies between men and women provides a clear example of this simple technique (Table 7.1).

Table 7.1 Job-Searching Strategies by Gender

Theme	*Female*	*Male*
Routine	My routine's determined by child-care requirements (Pauline). I get the paper every day, without fail (June). I used to go down Racetrain a lot, . . . I also joined Job Club . . . I kept a file and a record of all the letters I received (Sharon).	I used to spend mornings going through the papers or go down to the library. Afternoons writing off places for information or filling application forms in, and then evenings, papers again (Jim).
Haphazard	Not really, I just do it. It happens because my husband works shift work (Mary).	No routine, but I keep meself busy, like—keep meself occupied—I've plenty of gardening to do (Dave). No, not really. I usually go down and have a look Monday, Wednesday, Friday, something like that (Andy).
Entrepreneurial	Personal approaches to firms and through friends (June)	I . . . spend . . . a couple of days every week with a company. I make sure that they know that I'm there (John).

Visual presentation of qualitative data is especially useful for making comparisons and conveying relationships (although it is an underutilized technique in social science research). An example of this is creating an aggregated conceptual model for each of the groups to be compared. Themes (i.e., coding trees) are configured into some form of model depicting conceptual relationships (as borne out by the data) between themes. Figure 7.1 illustrates such a model from a study exploring changes in women's sexual behavior during a clinical trial that tested the safety and efficacy of a daily pill for HIV prevention. Note that the women were primarily sex workers from a large West African city (see Guest et al., 2008)

Figure 7.1   Model of Sexual Risk Behavior Among Trial Participants, With Supporting Quotes

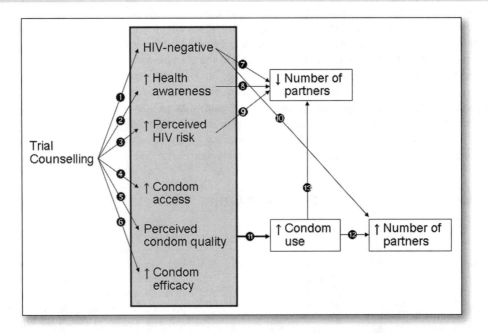

1. Testing HIV-negative was an eligibility criterion for enrolling in and continuing the trial. Status was revealed to participants during counseling.

2. When I enrolled, they exposed a lot of things to me: the effects of the disease [HIV] on the affected person and his family . . . hence my decision to use condoms. — *P#15*

3. Because even though there was news about HIV everywhere, I didn't really pay attention to it; but since I enrolled, I listen carefully . . . and because of the way you people do the counseling, I have now realized that the disease is real. — *P#23*

4. When I go out I don't think of how to get condoms because I always have some . . . I just fill my bag with it. . . . It is good I joined this study of which I get as much condoms as I want for my outing. — *P#16*

5. If the condoms were not made available to us, we would be purchasing them from the drug store and those ones are of poor quality, unlike the ones we collect from this place, which are of a better quality. — *P#7*

6. I used condoms . . . but there were occasions when I slept with people who did not want to use condoms because I couldn't talk . . . but now . . . after joining the study . . . I insist. — *P#17*

   Before I joined the study, I was reluctant to use condoms . . . because any time I used it, it burst, but I was taught how to wear it and ever since I have not had the problem of bursting again. — *P#5*

7. Whenever he [a client] asked me to have sex without a condom, I did it because of money, but after I enrolled, I told him "No," I was not going to do it without a condom . . . because I had done the test and I knew I was okay, so he left me for a long time. — *P#4*

8. Because of the education we receive here, the number [of partners] has decreased a little. — *P#7*

9. **Int**: What do you attribute the reduction in the number of partners?

   P: I am scared of the disease that's why there are fewer of them now. — *P#10*

10. Whenever a man visited me . . . I gave them the books they [study staff] gave to me . . . so that made them love me the more because they themselves were afraid of their status . . . so when they got to know that I have done the test, and had passed, automatically they felt secure. There are some who just come to visit me, but after they read the books and know that I am clean, they decide to do business with me. — *P#4*

11. Oh, I would say my condom usage is better now . . . because initially, whenever I used a condom, within the shortest period of time it got torn . . . I didn't know how to fit a condom . . . but when I came here, they taught me how to fit a condom. — *P#4*

12. Talking about the increase . . . formerly I couldn't have sex for a long time, but now that I use condoms . . . I am able to get about three clients a day . . . so it has increased. — *P#14*

13. I used to have a lot of sexual partners but ever since I joined the study and started using condoms the number of my sexual partners has reduced because most of them don't want to use condoms. — *P#18*

The model indicates relationships expressed by at least 1 of the 24 women interviewed and provides a supporting quote for all relationships presented, thereby grounding the model in the data. So, for example, conceptual relationship #13 indicates that, for at least one individual, increasing condom use led to a decrease in the number of sexual partners she had. The quote then elucidates the causal mechanism behind this connection: demanding condom use among clients led to the decrease in partners because men did not want to use condoms and likely took their business elsewhere. To use this model comparatively, one would have to create another model from a different data set and then identify places where the models differ or converge. Note that comparative data sets need to be available. In the above example we could not compare the model with data from two other sites participating in the clinical trial because the trial at the other sites experienced various problems and closed prematurely. We did not have similar data to compare.

Path analysis models can also be used to compare concepts across time, as in the following diagram showing the hypothesized factors that influence smoking behavior across three different points during one's life course (International Development Research Center, 2011).

Figure 7.2 shows how influences on smoking behavior, and their relative importance, change with age. At a younger age, for example, people rebel against

Figure 7.2   Influences on Smoking Behavior Over the Life Course

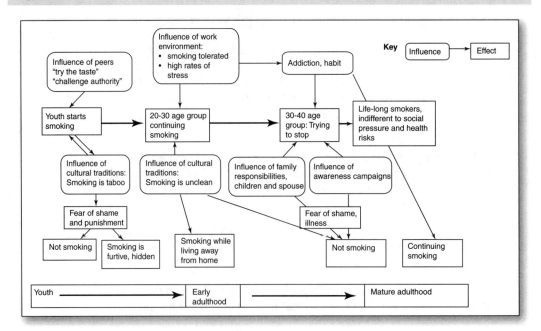

Source: International Development Reasearch Center, 2011.

traditional taboos—a peer influence plays a major role in youth smoking. As the smoker gets older, he or she is more responsive to cultural norms such as "smoking is unclean." Later in life, when family responsibilities become more apparent, appeals to health or financial considerations are likely more effective.

Visualizations don't have to be complex to be informative. The depiction in Figure 7.3 is based on Marshall Sahlins's ethnographic research in Melanesia and Polynesia. Side by side, the two pictures show very clearly the sociopolitical differences between the roles of a "big man" and a "chief."

Figure 7.3 Qualitative Comparison of a Melanesian "Big Man" and a Polynesian "Chief"

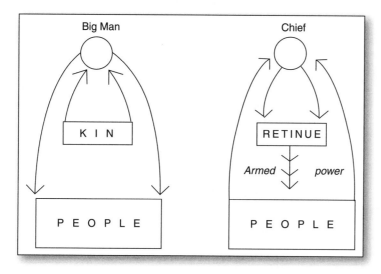

Source: Nielsen, 1989.

In similar fashion, Lieblich, Tuval-Mashiach, and Zilber (1998, pp. 94–96) use simple diagrams to represent prototypical life-course trajectories that were created from narrative analyses of life histories. The diagrams in Figures 7.4a through 7.4e show different types of life-course experiences (i.e., subgroups) that were identified within individual narratives and synthesized into composite groups.

Each of these line graphs depicts a prototypical life-story structure:

a) Moratorium: Nothing of consequence happens in this trajectory, as if the person's life has been on hold
b) Trial and Error: Life is a series of ups and downs characterized by trying new things, sometimes failing and sometimes succeeding
c) Slowly Ascending: Life has gradually gotten better over time
d) Risk and Gain: A big risk was taken and paid off with a substantial gain

Figure 7.4   Prototypical Life-Course Structures

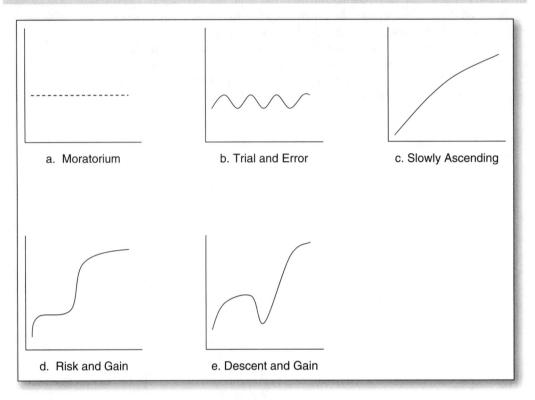

a. Moratorium   b. Trial and Error   c. Slowly Ascending

d. Risk and Gain   e. Descent and Gain

Source: Lieblich, Tuval-Mashiach, and Zilber (1998, pp. 94–96).

e) Descent and Gain: Some sort of adversity or low point was experienced but was endured and followed by a period of prosperity

Comparability typically requires a certain degree of structure in the qualitative data collection process (e.g., a semistructured interview guide containing the same questions) to keep conditions as similar as possible across data collection events (interviews, focus groups, time, etc.). Some structure is also required in data analysis procedures so that meaningful comparisons can be made. One exception to this need for similarity in data collection and analysis procedures is within concurrent mixed methods designs in which independent qualitative and quantitative data sets are compared. In these types of analyses, data collection procedures, by definition, are different, as is the degree of structure of instruments. Nonetheless, comparative analyses can be done. Kawamura Ivankova, Kohler, and Perumean-Chaney (2009), for example, employed a concurrent design and compared outputs from their qualitative (grounded theory) and quantitative (structural equation modeling) data sets. The purpose of their study was to develop a model to help understand the degree to which parasocial

Figure 7.5 Working Integration Model

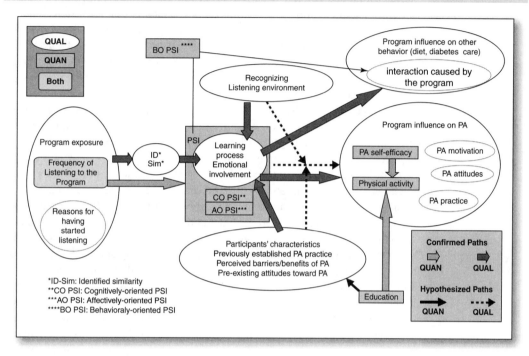

Source: Kawamura et al., 2009.
Note: PA = physical activity; PSI = parasocial interaction.

interaction affected entertainment-education radio drama listeners' levels of self-efficacy and practices pertaining to physical exercise. In their article, they present a path analytic diagram depicting both qualitative and quantitative paths, and indicate the paths shared by both models (Figure 7.5). We discuss mixed method analyses in more detail in Chapter 8.

QUANTITATIVE COMPARISONS

As discussed in Chapter 6, there are often reasons to quantify qualitative data. One such reason is to facilitate a systematic comparison across groups. Whether this is appropriate is primarily a function of the size of the data set and the research objectives. Larger data sets are more conducive to quantification, and research designed with an explicit comparative objective will require a more systematic approach to comparison. The bottom line, as Sandelowski, Voils, and Knafl (2009) remind us, is that a researcher needs to decide whether or not data transformation is necessary and worth the effort. And, as we describe below, whether data are transformed or not will determine how data can and cannot be compared.

All forms of quantitative thematic comparison first require the fundamental step of establishing theme frequencies. At the most basic level, themes can be categorized as either absent or present (a truth table). Dichotomized information, although very basic, can be highly informative. If, for example, the theme of "Poor Access to Health Services" is observed in patient focus groups but not in focus groups among the health practitioners who serve those patients, there would appear to be an important difference in perception of health care access between the two groups.

The prevalence of themes, often depicted in the form of theme or code frequencies (Chapter 6), can also be quite telling. Once frequency counts have been generated, the central question becomes how to compare the resulting numbers across groups in a meaningful and informative way. One method that builds on the path model method described above is to annotate the lines or arrows (paths) between concepts and themes in the model with frequencies, to provide a rough indication of relationship strength. Paths can be ascribed an actual number, or alternatively, the size or shade of a path can be adjusted according to its strength. You can measure this strength by the number or percentage of participants expressing the given relationship at least once (i.e., a dichotomous measure, with the unit of analysis being the individual participant) Or alternatively, you can measure theme frequency by summing all occurrences of each theme across your entire sample, or theme "intensity" (see Boyatzis, 1998, p. 133). The former measure reflects the breadth of theme expression *across* one's sample. The latter measure is a better indication of overall thematic intensity. (Note that there are variations of similar visualization approaches available online—e.g., http://www-958.ibm.com/software/data/cognos/manyeyes/; http://www.wordle.net.)

Another useful visual method is a line graph technique that has been used in some public health publications (e.g., Guest, Bunce, Johnson, Akumatey, & Adeokun, 2005; MacQueen et al., 2001). Theme frequencies are simply plotted for two or more comparison groups (e.g., using the Chart Wizard in Excel), as in the example below (adapted from Guest et al., 2005), which compares frequencies of the five most commonly expressed themes observed in transcripts from women aged 30 years or older and those aged younger than 30. Comparing themes in this way allows for the visualization of theme frequencies relative to other themes. In Figure 7.6, the importance of the themes, relative to one another, appears to be consistent across groups, as indicated by the similar line patterns. In terms of overall frequency, however, more women in the younger group mentioned each of the themes. These are two interesting patterns that can be further investigated and/or explained.

You may also use bar charts to visually examine relative frequencies of specific codes. Figure 7.7 provides an example of a three-dimensional bar chart produced in NVivo 9 to display the relative frequency of opinions about a specific question (whether genetic results should be returned in a certain situation) across six different substudy populations. Though the sample sizes for each substudy varied, this bar chart provided a means of comparing the relative frequency of each of three opinions, to help direct the researchers' qualitative analysis.

Note that in all of the examples cited previously, only frequencies from the most frequent or theoretically important themes are plotted. Although it is possible to

Figure 7.6   Line Graph Comparing Theme Frequencies

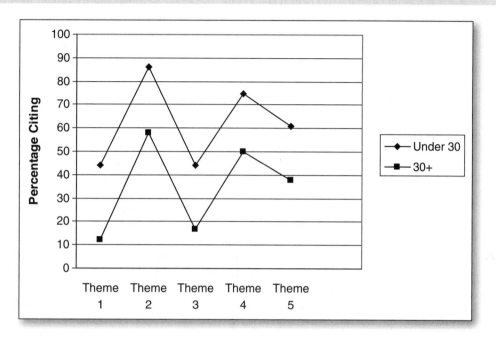

Figure 7.7   Example of a Three-Dimensional Bar Chart

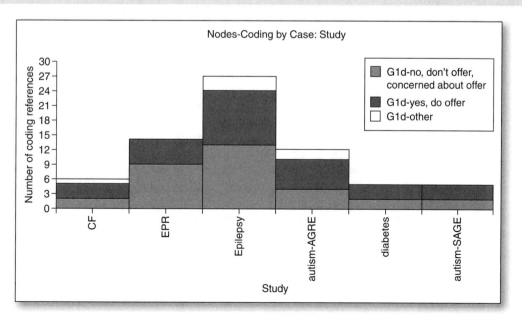

simultaneously present all themes in an analysis, such an inclusive approach is often impractical, with typical codebooks containing 30 to 60 codes. Criteria are needed to establish which themes are presented and which are not. Deciding how many themes to display is a subjective enterprise, but a common method is to create a scree plot (or just eyeball the frequencies) and look for natural break points. For the study represented by the line graph, the researchers used the frequency metric to determine the cut-off. Or, as in the bar chart example, you might use a more qualitative approach based on other factors, such as the perceived relevance of a theme to one's research objectives, to determine inclusion.

Matrices are another useful method for quantitatively comparing data. They have been used to compare more macro-level qualitative data, and combined with Boolean minimization techniques, can reveal causal relationships (Ragin, 1987, 2008). Much of Miles and Huberman's qualitative data analysis tome (1994) is devoted to matrices. Although informative, and useful for certain types of data, none of these works deals directly with comparing themes that have been identified within free-flowing text and systematically coded. In a recent study that examined reasons for discontinuing injectable contraception, Burke and Ambasa-Shisanya (n.d.) conducted an inductive thematic analysis of data from 14 focus groups, representing six different injectable contraceptive stakeholder groups. The analysis resulted in a total of 65 thematic codes. The authors then created a cross tabulated matrix using the "matrix coding" function in NVivo 8 software. For the sake of brevity and pedagogical purposes, Table 7.2 shows only a portion of their matrix. Thematic codes are represented in rows, stakeholder groups in columns, and cells are filled with binary data (i.e., "1" or "0," indicating presence or absence of a code for a specific focus group).

From this simple matrix the authors could systematically identify which themes were: (a) common across all most/groups (Infertility, Sickness/Poor health), (b) differentially expressed by certain groups (Lack of cash, Like weight gain), and (c) those which were possibly idiosyncratic (Reddish eyes). The authors subsequently combined this pattern analysis with a deeper text analysis to generate recommendations for decreasing discontinuation rates of injectables. Given the nature of the data, and how they were analyzed, these recommendations could be group-specific and therefore more salient and effective.

A variation of the typical quadrangular matrix is The Spectrum method of data visualization (Slone, 2009). This is essentially a standard group-by-theme matrix, but in which the two vertical ends of the matrix have been bent around to form a circle or semicircle. Data fields are filled with solid circles that can represent either dichotomous data (circle/no circle) or degrees of thematic expression (shades of gray, with the darker indicating more frequent or salient expression). The center of the circle typically contains information about the study sample, sample size for the overall study and each of the groups being compared. The example in Figure 7.7 is from a study comparing two types of companies across six qualitative categories (Collins & Porras, 2002).

A logical analytic extension of a respondent type by frequency matrix is to think of it as a cross-tab. Some authors (e.g., Carey & Gelaude, 2008)

Table 7.2 Code by Stakeholder Group Matrix

CODE	Village Leaders		Current Users				Husbands		Long-Term Users		Mothers-in-Law		Service Providers	
	Group 1	Group 2	Group 1	Group 2	Group 3	Group 4	Group 1	Group 2	Group 1	Group 2	Group 1	Group 2	Group 1	Group 2
Infertility	1	1	1	1	1	1	1	1	1	0	1	1	1	1
Sickness/Poor health	1	1	1	1	1	1	1	1	1	1	1	1	1	1
Lack of cash	0	1	0	0	0	0	1	1	1	1	0	0	1	1
Like weight gain	0	0	0	0	0	0	0	0	1	1	1	1	0	1
Reddish eyes	0	1	0	0	0	0	0	0	0	0	0	0	0	0

Figure 7.7 Spectrum Display of Data Comparing Two Types of Companies Across Six Qualitative Categories

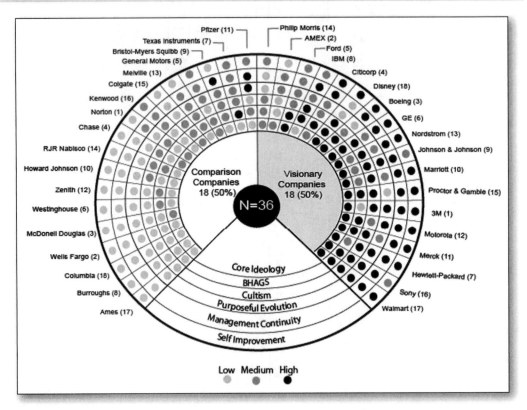

Source: Collins & Porras, 2002.

subsequently run a chi-square statistic on code frequencies by group on qualitative data generated through a large survey. Indeed, if comparative groups have been generated via a probability-based random process (i.e., either through random sampling or randomization), then standard inferential methods such as chi-square tests can validly be applied to compare frequencies across groups. In this context, the chi-square *P*-value can be interpreted as an indicator for whether a difference as large or larger than the one observed would have been expected simply by chance. However, in more typical cases in which groups represent nonrandomized samples, conventional inferential statistics (i.e., *P*-values and confidence intervals) should no longer be given such probabilistic interpretations (Greenland, 1990). If authors insist on reporting these statistics, it is imperative to clearly state that they are presented for descriptive purposes only and are not intended to be inferential toward any larger population. Of course, interpretation is in the eyes of the reader, so there is always the danger that readers will supply their own inferential interpretation to these statistics, despite any warnings provided by the authors. Another, theoretical, problem with using chi-square (or similar statistical techniques) on thematic data is that thematic data are generated from open-ended questions and are, therefore, not true dichotomous data. Because the response options are theoretically infinite, we cannot assume that the expression of a theme is to the exclusion of its absence, and vice versa. In other words, A ≠ not-B, which is the true form of dichotomous data.

For these reasons, we recommend that these statistics should not generally be used to compare data from nonrandomized samples. Instead, we encourage authors to use the purely descriptive methods of comparison outlined here and described in more detail in the cited references. If you do decide to use statistical comparisons, we suggest at least acknowledging their limitations. And, be sure that conditions associated with the statistics, such as cell frequencies for chi-square, are met.

Themes can also be compared over time within a data set and be compared both qualitatively and quantitatively in a given analysis. In a study documenting the degree of data saturation over the course of a thematic analysis, Guest, Bunce, and Johnson (2006) compared the codebook configuration and code application to the data set as their analysis progressed. The data set included 30 in-depth interview transcripts from women living in Accra, Ghana, and another 30 from Ibadan, Nigeria ($N = 60$). The semistructured interview guide covered the topic of norms pertaining to sexual communication and was identical for both sites.

The authors wanted to find out how many interviews were needed to get a reliable sense of thematic saturation and variability within their data set. They therefore documented the progression of theme identification—that is, the codebook structure—after each successive set of six interviews, for a total of 10 analysis rounds (totaling all 60 transcripts). They monitored changes in the code network and noted any newly created codes and changes to existing code definitions. The results were represented quantitatively (Figure 7.8 and Table 7.3) as well as qualitatively (Table 7.4).

The authors also documented the frequency of code application after each set of six interviews. The reasoning behind this latter measure was to see if the relative prevalence of thematic expression across participants changed over time. The driving question was at what point did relative frequency of code application stabilize (if at all)? To assess this, the authors used Cronbach's alpha to measure the reliability of code frequency distribution as the analysis progressed. They presented alpha values between each successive round of analysis, with each round containinInternal Consistency of Code Frequencies. They also indicated the data transition point from one country to the next (Table 7.5).

The methods described so far can reveal interesting patterns and bivariate associations, but they are limited in the degree to which they can represent the complexity of overall thematic configuration within a large data set, and subsequently between groups. As demonstrated in Chapter 6, graph-theoretic techniques, such as cluster analysis, can be useful in this regard. The resulting output—a dendrogram—provides a bird's-eye view of how codes are applied to the data, vis-à-vis each other (refer to Figure 6.3).

Figure 7.8   Code Creation Over the Course of Data Analysis

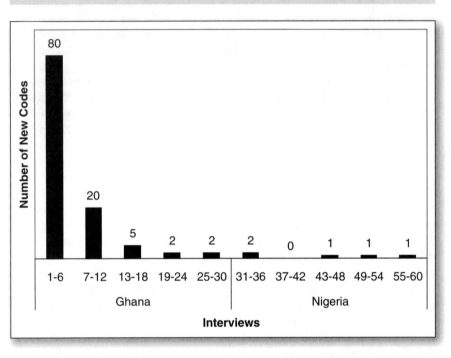

Table 7.3   Code Definition Changes by Round of Analysis

	Analysis Round	Interviews Analyzed	Definition Changes in Round	Percentage	Cumulative Frequency	Cumulative Percentage
Ghana Data	1	6	4	11	4	11
	2	12	17	47	21	58
	3	18	7	20	28	78
	4	24	3	8	31	86
	5	30	2	6	33	92
Nigeria Data	6	36	3	8	36	100
	7	42	0	0	36	100
	8	48	0	0	36	100
	9	54	0	0	36	100
	10	60	0	0	36	100

Table 7.4 Sample Code Definition Revisions

	Original	*Revision 1*	*Revision 2*
Trust Necessary (52%)	Full definition: Discussion of the necessity of trust before will discuss sexual matters with another woman; if there is no trust, will not talk about it When to use: Have to know somebody's "character" before can talk personally; can't trust just anybody, and often don't know most of the women well (R1)	Full definition: Discussion of the necessity of trust before will discuss sexual matters with another woman; if there is no trust, will not talk about it When to use: Have to know somebody's "character" before can talk personally; can't trust just anybody, and often don't know most of the women well; includes statements on confidences coming back to haunt you (R2)	Full definition: Discussion of the necessity of trust before will discuss sexual matters with another woman; if there is no trust, will not talk about it When to use: Have to know somebody's "character" before can talk personally; can't trust just anybody, and often don't know most of the women well; includes statements on confidences coming back to haunt you; includes setting the right atmosphere (sharing own personal information, creating a safe space, etc.) before asking personal questions (R6)
Talk with SW friends (73%)	Full definition: Talk among the participant and a close friend who is a SW When to use: Often occurs as: can only share very personal matters with 1–2 close friends (concept of space—can go to their rooms, but nobody else's) (R1)	Full definition: Talk among the participant and a close friend who is a SW When to use: If use the word "friend" in this discussion, use this code; often occurs as: can only share very personal matters with 1–2 close friends (concept of space—can go to their rooms, but nobody else's) (R1)	Full definition: Talk among the participant and a close friend who is a SW When to use: If use the word "friend" in this discussion, use this code; often occurs as: can only share very personal matters with 1–2 close friends (concept of space—can go to their rooms, but nobody else's); use if obvious/implied that the friend is a SW, even if not specifically stated (R2)

DIRECT COMPARISON

So far, we have presented techniques for comparing data among groups of individuals. But what if your study calls for comparing responses across individuals? Such a scenario is commonly found when doing research with intimate couples or other types of dyads. By directly comparing each half of a married dyad, for

Table 7.5   Sample Code Definition Revisions

	Rounds	Interviews	Cronbach's Alpha
Ghana Data	1–2	1–12	.7048
	1–3	1–18	.7906
	1–4	1–24	.8458
	1–5	1–30	.8766
Ghana and Nigeria	1–6	1–36	.8774
	1–7	1–42	.8935
	1–8	1–48	.9018
	1–9	1–54	.9137
	1–10	1–60	.9260
	μGhana, μNigeria	1–30, 31–60	.8267
	10	60	0

example, we can say a lot more about how specific couples may or may not differ regarding the research topic, as opposed to men and women in general.

In order to do such a comparison, the data need to be collected so that data from individuals are linked to each other, using some sort of connecting ID numbers. Once data are collected and put into a data management/analysis program, you'll have to decide how to compare data between individuals. Done properly, a direct comparison requires reading through a transcript from one half of the dyad and then reading through the other transcript. This can be done sequentially—one complete transcript analyzed then the next transcript in the dyad. Using this process, the analyst then compares the code summary for each half of the dyad and interprets the similarities and differences accordingly. A more granular technique is to use a staggered approach, in which only a portion of one transcript is analyzed and then a corresponding portion in the second transcript is analyzed and the two segments compared. The transcripts are analyzed segment by segment, until finished. The critical element here is to determine the appropriate manner in which to create segments for comparison. The most logical way is to analyze and compare data by each question asked of participants (note here the importance of structural coding). It provides a context for the comparative analysis: that is, it allows the participants to be compared by each specific question. Keep in mind, though, that this is not the only way to divide up text for a comparative analysis; your research objectives should ultimately guide your decision.

An efficient way to set up a direct comparative analysis (assuming you have used a semistructured instrument) is to use a matrix approach. For each individual, key themes by question are documented. Halves of each dyad are presented together and a separate column(s) can be used to note and characterize the relationship between responses within a dyad. In the case of married couples, an analysis matrix for a particular question might look something like that presented in Table 7.6. Note that the matrix should be viewed primarily as an analytic tool, not as an output to be included in a report in its entirety. Rather the matrix provides a foundation from which an interpretive summary can be generated.

SUMMING UP

Comparison is a central tenet of social and behavioral research, and the scientific method in general. Above we have described a selective set of techniques that have been used to compare data generated from applied thematic analyses. Although we have attempted to provide a useful list, we do not claim to have found every comparative method used in such a context. Many innovative analyses are not published or are hidden within substantive articles in journals spanning a range of academic disciplines. Our hope is that this chapter serves as a starting point for discussion and inspires other

Table 7.6 Comparison of Responses Between Husbands and Wives—Question 1

Participant	Key Theme(s)	Key Quote(s)	Comparative Relationship	Comments/Notes
Husband #1	Themes a, b, d	*bISeH'eghlaH'be'chugh latlh Dara'laH'be'*	Contradictory and divergent themes	Different views may be due to x and y, as expressed in the following quotes:
Wife #1	Theme b-, c, e	*Heghlu'DI' mobbe'lu'chugh QaQpu' Hegh wanI'*		
Husband #2	Themes a, f	*Elen sila lumenn omentilmo Nae saian luume' Cormamin lindua ele lle Saesa omentien lle Mae govannen*	Complete convergence	Factor z might account for similarity
Wife #2	Theme a, f	*Aa' lasser en lle coia orn n' omenta gurtha Aa' i'sul nora lanne'lle Aa' menle nauva calen ar' ta hwesta e' ale'quenle Aa' menealle nauva calen ar' malta*		
Husband *n*	Theme a, f		Partial convergence	In a different context (Q3), wife expresses Theme a
Wife *n*	Themes b, f			

researchers to develop and write about additional methods for carrying out comparisons within thematic analyses.

We also discussed the application of statistical techniques to qualitative data and nonprobabilistic samples and some of the limitations associated with such applications. All statistical techniques are founded on assumptions pertaining to research design and sampling, and therefore require the fulfillment of certain conditions in order to be used with any validity. The use of chi-square and other comparative statistics is no exception. We urge caution and consideration before applying any statistical method to qualitative data and encourage researchers to ensure that any conditions associated with a particular technique be fulfilled if you do go this route.

On a final note, we wish to emphasize that certain types of data collection techniques and forms lend themselves to comparative analysis better than others. Figure 7.9, adapted from Bernard and Ryan (2010, p. 47), provides a nice visualization of the relationship between structure of the data collection event, the medium of record, and the appropriateness of comparison.

Succinctly put, the more structure involved in the questioning process, the more feasible and appropriate a meaningful comparative analysis is. Likewise, the more complete and accurate the record of a data collection event is, the more conducive the data are to comparison.

Figure 7.9   Data Structure, Medium, and Comparability

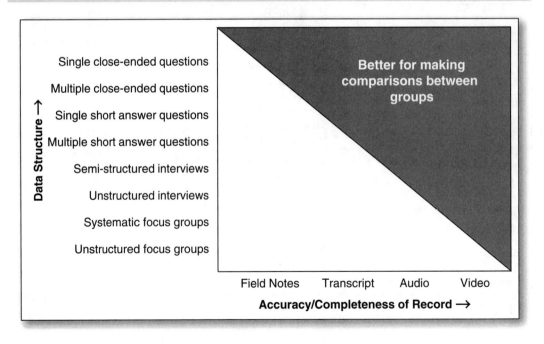

REFERENCES

Bazeley, P. (2003). Computerized data analysis for mixed methods research. In A. Tashakkori & C. Teddlie (Eds.), *Handbook of mixed methods in social and behavioral research* (pp. 385–422). Thousand Oaks, CA: Sage.

Bernard, H., & Ryan, G. (2010). *Analyzing qualitative data: Systematic approaches.* Thousand Oaks, CA: Sage.

Boyatzis, R. (1998). *Transforming qualitative information: Thematic analysis and development.* Thousand Oaks, CA: Sage.

Bunce A., Guest, G., Searing, H., Riwa, P., Kanama, J., & Achwal, I. (2007). Factors affecting vasectomy acceptability in Tanzania. *International Family Planning Perspectives, 33*(1), 13–21.

Burke, H., & Ambasa-Shisanya, C. (n.d.). *Reasons women discontinue using contraceptive injectables in Nyando District Kenya* [Unpublished manuscript]. Research Triangle Park, NC: Family Health International.

Carey, J., & Gelaude, D. (2008). Systematic methods for collecting and analyzing multidisciplinary team–based qualitative data. In G. Guest & K. M. MacQueen (Eds.), *Handbook for team-based qualitative research* (227–274). Lanham, MD: AltaMira Press.

Clifford, J. (1983). On ethnographic authority. *Representations, 2,* 118–146.

Collins, J., & Porras, J. (2002). *Built to last: Successful habits of visionary companies.* New York, NY: HarperCollins.

Corbin, J., & Strauss, A. (2008). *Basics of qualitative research* (3rd ed.). Thousand Oaks, CA: Sage.

Denzin, N., & Lincoln, Y. (2000). *Handbook of qualitative research* (2nd ed.). Thousand Oaks, CA: Sage.

Gibbs, G. (2002). *Qualitative data analysis: Explorations with NVivo.* Buckingham: Open University Press.

Glaser, B., & Strauss, A. (1967). *The discovery of grounded theory.* Chicago, IL: Aldine.

Greenland, S. (1990). Randomization, statistics, and causal inference. *Epidemiology, 1*(6), 421–429.

Guest, G. (2005). The range of qualitative research. *Journal of Family Planning and Reproductive Health Care, 31*(2), 165.

Guest, G., Bunce, A., Johnson, L., Akumatey, B., & Adeokun, L. (2005). Fear, hope, and social desirability bias among women at high risk for HIV in West Africa. *Journal of Family Planning and Reproductive Health Care, 31*(4), 285–287.

Guest, G., Bunce, A., & Johnson, L. (2006). How many interviews are enough? An experiment with data saturation and variability. *Field Methods, 18,* 59–82.

Guest, G., Shattuck, D., Johnson, L., Akumatey, B., Clarke, E., Chen, P., & MacQueen, K. (2008). Changes in sexual risk behavior among participants in a PrEP HIV prevention trial. *Sexually Transmitted Diseases, 35*(12), 1002–1008.

International Development Research Center. (2011). *Module 6: Qualitative data analysis.* Retrieved from http://web.idrc.ca/es/ev-106563-201-1-DO_TOPIC.html

Kawamura, Y., Ivankova, N., Kohler, C., & Perumean-Chaney, S. (2009). Utilizing mixed methods to assess parasocial interaction of an entertainment-education program audience. *International Journal of Multiple Research Approaches, 3*(1), 88–104.

Krippendorff, K. (2008). *Content analysis: An introduction to its methodology* (2nd ed.). Thousand Oaks, CA: Sage.

Krueger, R. (1998). *Analyzing and reporting focus group results.* Thousand Oaks, CA: Sage.

Leech, N., & Onwuegbuzie, A. (2007). An array of qualitative data analysis tools: A call for data analysis triangulation. *School Psychology Quarterly, 22*(4), 557–584.

Lieblich, A., Tuval-Mashiach, R., & Zilber, T. (1998). *Narrative research: Reading, analysis, and interpretation.* Thousand Oaks, CA: Sage.

Luber, G. (2005). Globalization, dietary change and "Second Hair" illness in two Meso-American cultures. In G. Guest (Ed.), *Globalization, health, and the environment: An integrated perspective* (pp. 133–156). Lanham, MD: AltaMira Press.

MacQueen, K., McLellan, E., Metzger, D., Kegeles, S., Strauss, R., Scotti, R., Blanchard, L., & Trotter, R. (2001). What is community? An evidence-based definition for participatory public health, *American Journal of Public Health, 91*(12), 1929–1938.

MacQueen, K., Johnson, L., Alleman, P., Akumatey, B., Lawoyin, T., & Nyiama, T. (2007). Pregnancy prevention practices among women with multiple partners in an HIV prevention trial. *Journal of Acquired Immune Deficiency Syndromes, 46*(1), 32–38.

Miles, M., & Huberman, A. (1994). *Qualitative data analysis: An expanded sourcebook* (2nd ed.). Thousand Oaks, CA: Sage.

Mills, M. (2008). Comparative analysis. In L. M. Given (Ed.), *The SAGE encyclopedia of qualitative research methods* (p. 100). Thousand Oaks, CA: Sage.

Nielson, F. (1989). The dual and the real: Thoughts on an essay by Claude Lévi-Strauss. Online document. http://www.fsnielson.com/txt/mir/mirrors-ch2.htm

Nkwi, P., Nyamongo, I., & Ryan, G. (2001). *Field research into socio-cultural issues: Methodological guidelines.* Yaounde, Cameroon: International Center for Applied Social Sciences, Research, and Training/UNFPA.

Ragin, C. (1987). The comparative method: Moving beyond qualitative and quantitative strategies. Berkeley, CA: University of California Press.

Ragin, C. (2008). Redesigning social inquiry: Fuzzy sets and beyond. Chicago, IL: University of Chicago Press.

Sandelowski, M., Voils, C., & Knafl, G. (2009). On quantitizing. *Journal of Mixed Methods Research, 3*(3), 208–222.

Slone, D. (2009). Visualizing qualitative information. *The Qualitative Report,* 14(3), 489–497.

Weller, S., & Romney, A. (1988). *Systematic data collection.* Thousand Oaks, CA: Sage.

EXERCISES

Conceptual Questions ("answers" in the Appendix)

1. When deciding whether or not to use chi-square to compare theme frequencies across groups, what are the two most important questions to ask yourself?

2. You are interested in comparing how men and women think about sports cars and have coded data from 60 in-depth interviews, 30 with women and 30 with men. When comparing theme frequencies, how should you count themes (i.e., what should be your unit of observation)? Explain why.

3. What are some of the challenges associated with comparing a qualitative data set with a quantitative data set?

4. When designing a qualitative study with a comparative component, should you tend toward less structure or more structure in terms of processes and instruments? Why?

   a. Think about specific examples of how you would achieve your answer above.

5. Try to find thematic comparative techniques in the literature, or from your own work, that are not covered in this chapter. Please send them to the authors and we will try to incorporate them in subsequent publications (with appropriate credit given, of course).

APPENDIX

"Answers" to Exercise Questions

1. The two most important questions to ask are:
   a. Was the sample probability-based or groups randomly allocated?
   b. Are all of the other requirements associated with chi-square met, such as cell frequencies?

If the answer to both of these questions is "yes," it is appropriate to use chi-square. If the answer is "no" to only b, consider using Fisher's exact test. Note, however, that this also comes with its own assumptions and requirements.

2. Your unit of observation should be the individual participant. That is, you note whether or not a theme is present or absent for each interview. Since you are interested in seeing how themes are differentially configured across participants, this is the most informative means of counting. Counting the total number of times a theme was coded across interviews would render an "intensity" score and be less informative in this case since individual proclivities and talkativeness could significantly skew results.

3. The main complication is the fact that one is comparing apples and oranges. Even if the questions asked are similar in content, the structure and process through which they are asked are quite different. Although a concurrent mixed method design can be highly informative, the question always remains, "Do the differences observed between the QT and QL data sets reflect actual differences in participants' experiences, or are they a methodological artifact?"

4. No matter the type of inquiry, more structure lends itself better to comparison than less structure. The simple reason is that as structure increases, so too does the ability to standardize processes and instruments. The more standardized these are across data collection events, the more confident you can be that any differences observed are a result of participants' experiences and not due to inconsistency or disparity of process.

4a. In qualitative inquiry we look for the balance between the need for structure for comparison and the need to maintain an open-ended and inductive process of data collection and analysis. Some ways to achieve this include:
   - Using semistructured data collection instruments, with verbatim (but open-ended) questions. Inductive probing is still crucial here, because it is probing that provides the richness of qualitative inquiry. At the very least, make sure that interviewers are covering the same topics within their questions.
   - If more than one person is conducting the data collection, conduct training to ensure consistency of process. Training should include in-depth discussion of the study's purpose and the purpose behind each question to be asked. Doing so helps keep probing relevant and focused.
   - If transcribing data, use a transcription protocol to ensure that the output is consistent and done in the way that is most useful for your analysis.
   - Standardize the analysis process as much as possible. Have two or more analysts involved in the codebook development if possible and conduct intercoder

agreement checks. If using more than one coder, try to randomly allocate transcripts to coders so as to minimize coder effects on the results. Avoid having one coder work exclusively on one data set and another coder exclusively on a second data set, because this will increase the likelihood that any differences observed between the two groups is a result of coding style.

ADDITIONAL READING

Bazeley, P. (2003). Computerized data analysis for mixed methods research. In A. Tashakkori & C. Teddlie (Eds.), *Handbook of mixed methods in social and behavioral research* (pp. 385–422). Thousand Oaks, CA: Sage.

di Gregorio, S., & Davidson, J. (2008). Microbicides development programme case study. *Qualitative research design for software users* (pp. 196–209). New York, NY. Open University Press.

Miles, M., & Huberman, A. (1994). *Qualitative data analysis: An expanded sourcebook* (2nd ed.). Thousand Oaks, CA: Sage.

8

INTEGRATING QUALITATIVE AND QUANTITATIVE DATA

LEARNING OBJECTIVES

Upon finishing this chapter, readers should be able to:

- Define "mixed methods research"
- Describe the major mixed methods designs
- Understand and reproduce basic mixed methods notation
- Effectively plan and execute a mixed methods analysis that includes thematic data

---

MIXED METHODS RESEARCH

The practice of mixing data collection methods and data types has been around for centuries. In the social sciences, a mixed method approach has been used in field research, particularly anthropology, for more than 100 years. Mixed methods as a formal subfield, however, has only been around since the late 1980s when researchers began to operationalize data integration and develop mixed methods design typologies (e.g., Greene, Caracelli, & Graham, 1989; Morse, 1991). In the two decades that have ensued, mixed methods research has become increasingly common and continues to expand, both theoretically and in practice. It is because of this growing popularity that we have included a chapter on the subject here. In addition, we felt that this chapter was best placed after all of the technical analytic sections, but before we discuss choosing software and disseminating results.

Numerous definitions of "mixed methods research" have been posited (for a useful summary of some of these, see Tashakorri & Teddlie, 2003, p. 711). These definitions vary in scope and detail, but virtually all refer to some form of integration of qualitative and quantitative research methods (for an exception, see Morse & Niehaus, 2009). Perhaps the most concise definition comes from Bergman, who writes that mixed methods research is "the combination of at least one qualitative and at least one quantitative component in a single research project or program" (2008, p. 1).

The basic premise behind using a mixed methods research design is that the combination of both approaches provides a better understanding of a research problem than either approach could alone. Creswell and Plano Clark (2007, p. 9) identify at least six potential advantages to integrating methodological approaches:

- The strengths of one approach offset the weaknesses of the other
- Can provide more comprehensive and convincing evidence
- Can answer certain research questions that a monomethod approach cannot
- Can encourage interdisciplinary collaboration
- Encourages the use of multiple worldviews/paradigms
- Is "practical," in that it permits the usage of multiple techniques and approaches

The same authors also make the case that there are general types of research problems that benefit from integrating methodological approaches (Creswell & Plano Clark, 2011, p. 7–11), specifically, when a researcher is seeking to

- supplement insufficient data from one source
- explain initial results
- generalize exploratory findings
- enhance a study with a second method
- best employ a theoretical stance
- understand a research objective through multiple research phases

From our perspective these are all potential benefits of, and reasons for, using a mixed methods design. The overarching thread is that the integration of the two approaches should provide some benefit in answering the research problem and to the research study overall; if there is no clear benefit to using more than one method, then there is probably no point in employing a mixed methods design. Many research questions can be answered sufficiently with a monomethod approach, and in such cases, creating a larger and more complicated design is not justified. Based on our experience, however, we believe the majority of research questions can benefit from some degree of methodological integration. Below we discuss the most common mixed methods typologies and how, in a more pragmatic sense, qualitative and quantitative data can be used in a complementary and synergistic manner.

Diffusing the Dichotomy

Are qualitative and quantitative approaches dichotomous, opposing, and mutually exclusive in their characteristics? Most presentations of information on the two approaches would lead you to believe so. In most descriptions of qualitative and quantitative research, the two are presented in the following either/or fashion:

Qualitative		Quantitative
Hypothesis generating		Hypothesis testing
Explanatory/contextual		Predictive/contextually void
Holistic	VS	Specific
Subjective		Objective
Has researcher bias		
Is from participant's perspective		
Non-quantifiable		Amenable to statistical analyses
Non-probabilistic samples		Probabilistic samples
Case-specific		Generalizable

This is a *false dichotomy*. Although it is true that each approach has its own strengths and weaknesses and would therefore be more suitable for certain types of uses relative to the other, the division is by no means absolute or mutually exclusive. Regarding the relationship to hypotheses, for example, it is true that qualitative research is often employed in a hypothesis-generating capacity. However, much qualitative research does not have this as on objective, aiming instead to collect stand-alone data. And, as demonstrated in Chapter 1, qualitative data can indeed be used to **test** hypotheses. Moreover, countless hypotheses over the decades have been generated from quantitative data.

The same relationship can be applied to the second point—purpose of the research and the ability to capture context. Both approaches can be used to explain and/or discern reasons behind phenomena (although the inductive nature of qualitative inquiry does a better job of it in many situations). Both can also address (or not) context in a study. Not all qualitative inquiry takes broad context into account, for example. Sometimes qualitative interviews can be very targeted and examine a phenomenon that is not contextually variable (e.g., habitual behavior), and thus not delve into contextual factors. And, quantitative methods (especially direct observation) can indeed include context as a domain of inquiry. On many of our structured HIV risk surveys, for example, we ask participants many closed-ended, quantitatively-oriented questions about the context surrounding a sexual event.

(Continued)

(Continued)

Third on the list is degree of specificity. Suffice it to say that a small, focused mono-method qualitative study can certainly be specific in scope whereas complex statistical analyses, such as structural equation modeling, can be quite holistic in nature.

Moving on to the degree of subjectivity, you'll notice two subpoints. The first deals with researcher bias. Admittedly, the inductive, less-structured nature of qualitative inquiry permits more input from those who implement and analyze the research. We recognize this. But, as we point out in Chapter 4, there is an entire literature surrounding social desirability bias in quantitative research and how a researcher's characteristics and the research context can bias the results of surveys or observational studies. As for the second subpoint under "subjective," you'll often hear people say that qualitative research is unique in that it elicits data that are "from the participants' perspective." If a structured survey asks a participant how they feel or think about something, is that not also "from the participants' perspective"? We would argue that it is, as long as the questions are clearly worded, have good validity, and offer response options that incorporate the participant's own understanding of the range of choices. With regard to how qualitative data is analyzed, Chapter 6 is probably the best counterargument to the notion that qualitative data cannot be quantified; it can be, and often is (whether and how it *should be* is altogether separate issue). Similarly, as shown in the top right quadrant of Figure 1.1, we can also analyze the output of quantitative analyses in a qualitative manner.

The last two points in the comparison relate to sampling. Certainly, qualitative research most often uses nonprobability sampling for a number of methodological and logistical reasons. Notwithstanding, random sampling methods can be, and sometimes are, utilized for qualitative research (for a more in-depth discussion of this, see Guest, Namey, & Mitchell, in press). Furthermore, a lot of quantitative studies do not have a probabilistic sample as a foundation (much to the chagrin of statisticians and the delight of mean-spirited reviewers). Sample design, of course, relates to the degree (or not) of the generalizability of a study's findings. Some larger qualitative studies— particularly those which involve content analyses—that use random sampling and rigorous analytic procedures could certainly not be classified as "case specific." Even in most thematic analyses it is the patterns *across* individuals that are the most salient and oft reported. Conversely, findings generated from the most structured and rigorously implemented instrument cannot be generalized if the sample is small and haphazardly drawn.

What we hope to illustrate is that qualitative and quantitative approaches are not opposites, nor are they mutually exclusive. Which approach will be best for a study, or certain component of a study, depends on many factors, including the research objective, availability of data, and how data will be analyzed, integrated, and interpreted.

A Summary of Mixed Methods Typologies

Over the past two decades, researchers have developed typologies of mixed methods research designs (Creswell & Plano Clark, 2007, 2011; Greene, 2007; Greene, Caracelli, & Graham 1989; Johnson & Onwuegbuzie, 2004; Morgan, 1998; Morse, 1991; Morse & Niehaus, 2009; Teddlie & Tashakorri, 2009). It is beyond the scope of this chapter to describe each of these typologies in detail. Moreover, typologies are constantly being revised; Creswell and Plano Clark's volume on the topic changed typologies between editions, in the 3 years between editions. Instead we have extracted three dimensions from the existing typologies that we feel cover the range of most mixed methods research designs and that are most useful in helping investigators think about, and plan for, method integration. These three dimensions—timing, weighting, and purpose—all refer to the integration of qualitative and quantitative data sets. We describe these below and follow with examples to better explain their meaning and to illustrate their practical application. (For more mixed methods examples, see Plano Clark & Creswell, 2008. Part 2 of their reader contains nine exemplar studies.) As will be evident from the examples, these dimensions are all interrelated to a certain degree.

Timing

Timing of integration refers to how data sets are used chronologically and analytically with respect to each other. The two most commonly used terms in this regard are *sequential* and *concurrent* designs (Creswell & Plano Clark, 2011; Morgan, 1998; Morse, 1991). Sequential designs are those in which integration occurs across chronological phases of a study and where data analysis of one data set type informs another type of data set. In other words, the latter data collection and analysis procedures are dependent, in some way, on the previously existing data set. In contrast, in a concurrent design data sets are not dependent on each other and are integrated at the same time within an analysis.

Here we need to add a point of clarification regarding the research activity to which timing refers, since multiple phases and activities occur over the course of a standard research study (e.g., planning, data collection, data analysis, interpretation, and write up). So, when we talk about integration occurring across chronological phases, or integrated at the same time, what do we mean? For the vast majority of mixed methods designs, timing of integration refers to the *use* of a data set type relative to another. In a sequential design, for example, findings from one data set are used either to inform a subsequent data set or data collection procedure (exploratory), or to explain and provide further insight to findings previously generated from another data set (explanatory). Note that in the case of exploratory sequential designs, timing of a data set's use coincides with data collection timing, since in order for a data set to inform the other it must precede it chronologically. The same cannot be said of an explanatory sequential or concurrent design. If study instruments are well thought out, with their explicit purpose in mind, data collection in either of the two designs can occur simultaneously or sequentially. It is how they are *used* relative to each other that is key.

Weighting

Known also as *dominance*, weighting refers to the priority given to each methodological orientation (qualitative or quantitative) in a mixed method study. It does not mean that the less-dominant approach is not important to the study objectives, but rather it is not the central data set in the study and will likely not get top billing in the write up of study findings. Note that weighting refers to relative dominance as anticipated and planned for in the initial research design. As we discuss in Chapter 10, how research findings are ultimately presented will depend on a number of factors and may not adhere to the original plan.

Purpose

There can be multiple purposes behind collecting and integrating data sets. However, the three most common include: (1) providing information for subsequent data collection and analysis procedures (exploratory/formative design), (2) explaining the results of a previously analyzed data set (explanatory design), and (3) comparing two data sets (concurrent/triangulation design) and interpreting whether data converge, diverge, or are contradictory.

Tables 8.1 and 8.2 illustrate the interconnection of these three dimensions. Table 8.1 describes the more common typologies and includes generic examples of the various permutations of mixed methods designs. Table 8.2 delineates the general process entailed in each design. The specific examples that follow the tables will help to illustrate how these designs are put into practice.

TYPOLOGIES AND REAL-WORLD COMPLEXITY

Typologies are created by imposing conceptual demarcations between items subsumed within. Categorization is a way of reducing and summarizing the complexity of phenomena, with the goal of generating a simpler, more manageable view. The result of this reduction in complexity is that some categories within a typology may not be exhaustive or mutually exclusive. Moreover, altogether different dimensions may be used when creating a typology for a given domain, resulting in equally valid, yet divergent, views. The case with mixed methods typologies is no different. The dimensions described above are those that cross-cut the majority of mixed methods categorization schemes, but they are certainly not exhaustive. In the spirit of due diligence, we feel obligated to at least describe three other types of designs that have been described in the literature—conversion (Teddlie & Tashakkori, 2009), multilevel (Teddlie & Tashakkori, 2009), and embedded (Caracelli & Greene, 1997; Creswell & Plano Clark, 2011). In our view, these designs conceptually span the three dimensions presented and so are not treated in this book as designs in and of themselves.

Conversion—In this design family, one type of data is transformed and then analyzed both qualitatively and quantitatively. The bottom left and upper right

Table 8.1   Mixed Method Designs and Examples

Timing	*Weighting*	*Description*	*Generic Example*
Exploratory Sequential	QUAL dominant	Smaller quantitative study helps data collection in a principally qualitative study	Using data from a survey to sample individuals for in-depth interviews (i.e., extreme case sampling)
	QUAN dominant	Smaller qualitative study helps guide data collection in a principally quantitative study	Focus groups used to help develop survey topics and instruments
Explanatory Sequential	QUAL dominant	Smaller quantitative study helps evaluate and interpret results from a principally qualitative study	Survey used to assess prevalence and variability of themes—at the population level—derived from qualitative case studies
	QUAN dominant	Smaller qualitative study helps evaluate and interpret results from a principally quantitative study	In-depth interview results used to explain statistical patterns (e.g., correlations) generated from survey analysis
Concurrent	Varies	Combine/compare Quan and Qual data sets	Results from in-depth interviews are compared with survey results to validate (convergence), broaden explanatory model (divergence, contradiction), or explain (explanatory)

Source: Adapted from Creswell & Plano Clark, 2011, p. 215.

Table 8.2   Basic Mixed Methods Procedures

Concurrent Design *QUAN + QUAL*	*Explanatory Sequential Design* *QUAN → QUAL*	*Exploratory Sequential Design* *qual → QUAN*
1. Concurrently collect QT and QL data as two independent databases	1. Collect and analyze QT data in Phase 1	1. Collect and analyze QL data in Phase 1
2. Separately analyze each database	2. Examine QT results for follow-up ideas (what aspect and with whom)	2. Examine QL results to identify or develop variables and instruments
3. Merge the two databases	3. Collect and analyze QL data in Phase 2	3. Collect and analyze QT data in Phase 2
4. Employ integrative purpose (triangulation, explanation, etc.)		

Source: Adapted from Creswell & Plano Clark, 2011, p. 215.

quadrants in Figure 1.1 in Chapter 1 are illustrative of these types of designs. To provide one example, text from in-depth interviews can be analyzed thematically (qualitative) and then the prevalence of thematic expression across the sample can be summarized by simply calculating theme frequencies (quantitative). Going a step further, theme co-occurrence measures can be entered into a hierarchical cluster analysis algorithm (quantitative) and a resulting dendrogram generated (qualitative). The outcome of these different types of analyses can then be combined and interpreted. Conversion techniques are discussed in detail, without that label, in Chapter 6. (We should point out also that traditionally-qualitative data collection techniques can be used to generate quantitative data, such as in the Delphi Method [Linstone & Turoff, 1975]).

Multilevel—Multilevel designs analyze, and then combine, different data types that are collected at different levels of analysis. In other words, integration occurs across multiple levels of sampling. So if, for example, you were interested in student achievement, you might collect quantitative data, such as test scores, at the student level (individual) as well as do in-depth interviews with students' families (household). The range of possibilities is infinite. Bernard and Ryan (2010, p. 129) provide a useful graphic for thinking about the various, interconnected levels of

Figure 8.1 Levels of Analysis

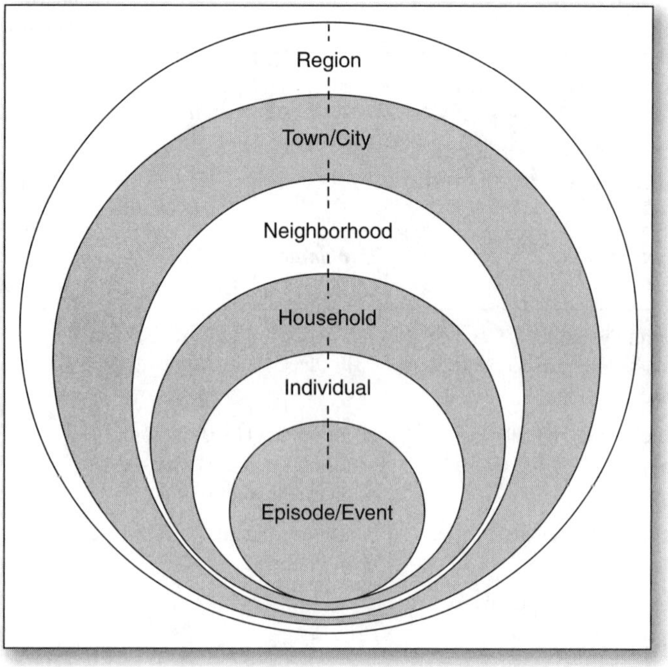

Source: Adapted from Bernard & Ryan, 2010.

analysis that, together, create the "context" surrounding a behavior or event (Figure 8.1). Note that a multilevel design can be either sequential or concurrent.

Embedded—Creswell and Plano Clark (2011) define the embedded, or nested, design as a "mixed methods design in which the researcher collects and analyzes both quantitative and qualitative data within a traditional quantitative or qualitative design to enhance the overall design in some way" (p. 411). Such a design is often used when a researcher needs to embed, for example, a small qualitative component within a large quantitative study, such as an experimental design. Note that this design is not clearly distinguished conceptually from a concurrent design in which, for example, the QUAN component is dominant. One argument used to justify this difference is that the degree of dominance of the primary method in an embedded study is much greater than in other designs. The less-dominant component truly plays a supportive role, and results from this secondary method alone would not be publishable on their own. Whichever the criteria used, the distinction between types is gray and a matter of interpretation, as with many classification schemes.

The Distinction Between Theory and Practice

While attending a workshop at a mixed methods conference, one of the authors was struck by the disconnect between the typologies presented by the instructors and the real-world examples that attendees brought to the seminar. A common sentiment expressed by attendees was something to the effect of, "But my study is more complicated than depicted in any of these typologies." Indeed, much of the mixed method research conducted (including ours) is more complicated than can be accounted for in the typologies delineated in the literature. Figure 8.2 outlines the interconnections between research components in one of the author's National Institutes of Health (NIH) 3-year study that describes the sexual networks of men at high risk for HIV in two African cities.

For illustrative purposes, we have divided the study into two conceptual components—research process and data analysis. As depicted, the process component utilizes an exploratory sequential design. Each step provides information for the next so that sampling strategies and data collection instruments are incrementally developed and refined. The chronological sequence is represented from left to right, with the in-depth interviews and surveys being conducted at the same time in the research schedule. From an analytic perspective, however, the design is concurrent, with enhanced explanation being the purpose of data integration (i.e., participant observation and in-depth interviews help explain the survey findings). Because we chose to emphasize the survey results in our analysis, the design can be designated with the notation QUAN + qual. Note that analytically this is not a sequential design because the questions asked in the in-depth interviews were developed at the same time as the survey questions; question structure and content for one data collection method was therefore not dependent on the other. This cross-sectional study with three methodological components illustrates how quickly the relationship among and integration between methods can get

Figure 8.2 Multistrand Design Example

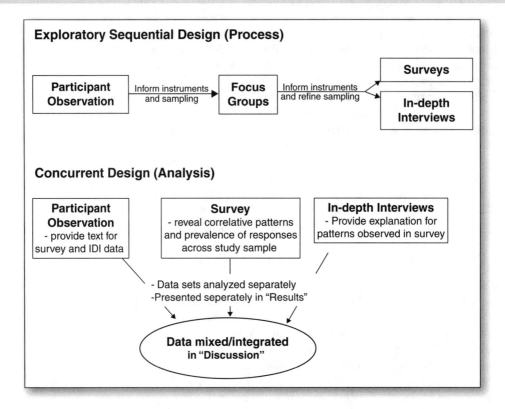

complicated. Many studies are longitudinal in nature and have a greater number of components and integration points, thus exponentially increasing the level of complexity. An example of such complexity is what Teddlie and Tashakkori (2009) call a "fully integrated" design, in which mixing occurs at all stages of a study and each component is linked in an interactive and dynamic manner to other components. Another type of complexity involves employing more than one type of design in one study, as in the example below (Figure 8.3).

As a final note, complexity can be added at the most basic level of instrumentation. In the study shown in Figure 8.2, for example, the focus-group guide had three explicit purposes—to inform sampling procedures, to inform subsequent data collection instruments, and to provide preliminary data for another research proposal (the latter purpose is not represented in Figure 8.2 because it is not directly relevant to the objectives of the study depicted).

We present these examples to illustrate that large research projects are usually complex and cannot always be adequately captured in a typology. Avoid getting hung up on systems of classification or what you should call your study. Typologies are useful guides, but they don't always simplify things. Focus instead on what types of data and data integration techniques will best inform your research questions within given time and resource constraints.

Figure 8.3   Cross-Comparative Case Study With a Hybrid Concurrent/Sequential Design

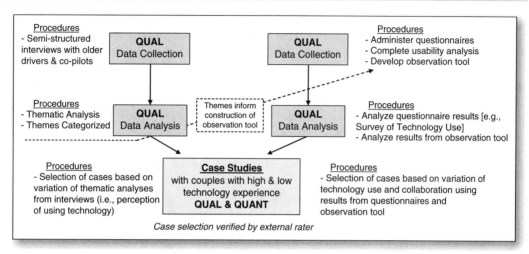

Source: Vrkljan, 2009.

Mixed Methods Notation

Qual	Qualitative
Quan	Quantitative
UPPERCASE	Indicates that method is dominant in the study design and purpose (e.g., QUAL)
lowercase	Indicates the less-dominant method in study (e.g., qual)
QUAL, QUANT	Comma indicates both methods equal in dominance
QUAL + QUAN	Plus sign indicates methods occur at the same time (i.e., concurrent design)
QUAL → quan	Arrow indicates methods occur in a sequence (i.e., sequential design) with the first noted method occurring chronologically before the latter
QUAN(qual)	The method in brackets is embedded within a larger design, with the nonbracketed method being dominant (i.e., embedded design)
QUAL→←QUAN	Methods are implemented in a recursive process (e.g., qual→quan→qual→quan)
QUAL→QUAN→ **[QUAN +qual]**	Mixed methods (QUAN + qual) is used within a single study/project within a series of studies
QUAN + QUAL =	Equals sign denotes purpose of integration in a concurrent design (e.g., = convergence, divergence, explanation)

Source: Adapted from Creswell & Plano Clark, 2011.

MECHANICS OF DATA INTEGRATION

Probably the least developed area of mixed method research is the process of data integration, or mixing. This is particularly true for concurrent designs in which two very different types of data are compared (for a summary of logistical and political barriers to integration, see Bryman [2007]). In the sections that follow, we discuss the practical aspects of data integration within some of the more common mixed methods designs, as they apply to thematic analysis. Table 8.3 provides a very general framework for the integration process within sequential and concurrent designs, and indicates where integration typically happens. We elaborate on the table's content and discuss how integration can occur within more specific designs, providing examples along the way, and then outline, in Table 8.4, the implications each design type has specifically for a thematic analysis.

Exploratory Sequential

One of the most common mixed methods designs is the exploratory sequential approach, in which data collection from a prior phase informs a subsequent phase of a research study. Within this design, the qual→QUAN variation is by far the most widely used. In fact, using qualitative data to inform quantitative instruments and procedures is so common that Morse and Niehaus (2009, p. 18) argue the procedure is not a true mixed methods design. For them it is a standard part of instrument development and should be regarded as such. Nevertheless, given the widespread use of the design, we, along with others, feel it is important to cover this as a type of mixed method design. We begin with the most common of these designs, the qual→QUAN, where the qualitative component feeds into the quantitative.

Table 8.3   Integrating Qualitative and Quantitative Data

Type of Integration	Type of Design	Method of Integration	Point of Interface
Connecting	Sequential	One phase builds on the other	Between data analysis (phase 1) and data collection (phase 2)
Merging	Concurrent	Bring results together	After analysis of both Quan and Qual. Often mixed in the Discussion. Can also be mixed in matrices or transformed and integrated in both the Results and Discussion sections.

Source: Adapted from Creswell & Plano Clark, 2011, p. 215.

Two important considerations in a qual QUAN design to be considered are: (1) the *degree* to which the QUAN component is informed by the qual and (2) the degree of rigor that is warranted, and feasible, for a given study. With respect to the former, a researcher, for example, may already have a solid survey instrument developed and just wish to qualitatively test it for comprehensibility and cultural appropriateness for the study population, and then revise it based on the qualitative findings. On the other end of the spectrum, an investigator may not even know the most relevant topics to ask survey respondents about and so might use qualitative research to come up with survey domains and questions. These are two very different enterprises, and where a particular study falls on the continuum depends on what is already known about both the topic and the study population.

The second dimension—the degree of rigor/formality—can also be viewed on a continuum. On the less rigorous end, one may only have time and/or resources for what we call the "taxi driver test." This simple technique entails administering the instrument to easily accessible individuals from the larger population (e.g., taxi drivers), and identifying any major problems with question content and wording. Conversely, more sophisticated and involved instrument development and pretesting techniques, such as cognitive interviewing (Willis, 2004), might be warranted to test and revise a survey instrument. Which end of the spectrum one chooses largely depends on study objectives and resources/time available. For a more detailed discussion on developing QUAN tools from qual data, refer to Onwuegbuzie, Bustamante, and Nelson (2010) in addition to the plethora of survey development textbooks available.

In the quan Qual variation of the exploratory sequential design, the most typical application is using quantitative data to select participants for follow-up qualitative inquiry. Quantitative data in this case can be generated (through surveys, structured observation, or other quantitative techniques) or garnered from secondary sources. An example of the former is choosing the nth percentile of survey respondents on a variable of interest. The size of n in this case is predetermined by estimating how many individuals are necessary for follow-up study. These participants are recruited for in-depth interviews, or participate in focus groups, on the topic (variable) of interest. This type of design is often used in what are sometimes called "exemplar" or "deviant" studies. For example, if we want to know, *qualitatively*, what distinguishes the most frequent TV viewers from individuals who don't watch any TV, we can use a survey measure of TV viewing and then choose the most frequent viewers (e.g., top fifth percentile) and the least frequent views (lowest fifth percentile) for follow-up qualitative inquiry. Namey and colleagues used this approach to select institutional officials who scored very high or very low on an index of five survey questions to better understand the underlying knowledge and beliefs of officials who presented strong views on either side of the response spectrum.

Sometimes an investigator may only be interested in one group—defined by a key variable of interest—for follow-up. A study carried out by Steiner and colleagues (2007) exemplifies this approach. In a study documenting condom failure (breakage and slippage) among 314 Jamaican men, they discovered that a relatively large number of men reported condom failure. From the quantitative data they identified 22 individuals with the highest reported failure rates (i.e., higher than 20%) and conducted in-depth interviews to understand the reasons for such high failure rates. Qualitative data revealed that improper storage/exposure to heat, improper handling while putting on condoms, and use of lubricants/improper lubricants all contributed to failure.

Secondary data can also be effectively used to sample individuals or other types of sampling units for a follow-up study. Using tax records, an investigator can identify, for example, the busiest (at least in terms of revenue) bars or restaurants in a community and subsequently choose certain locations for participant observation activities. The possibilities are almost infinite, limited only by the availability of data and the ability to identify individual sampling units within a quantitative data set.

Explanatory Sequential

Explanatory sequential designs are less common than their exploratory counterparts, but are being used more and more frequently, and for good reason. The basic idea behind this design is that a subsequent data set explains, at least to a certain degree, findings from another data set previously analyzed within a study. In our view, it is these types of designs where the complementary nature of quantitative and qualitative data truly shines. How many times, for example, have we read purely quantitative articles that masterfully show how two or more variables are correlated in the results section and then the authors spend the entire discussion section *speculating* on what this correlation means—that is, the how and why behind the association. Conversely, the status quo for qualitative research is to provide thick description of a phenomenon without indicating the variability of the findings (e.g., themes) within the larger study population. Sequential explanatory designs combine the strengths of each of the two method types to address their inherent shortcomings.

An example of an explanatory sequential analysis, in which qualitative data are used to explain patterns observed in a quantitative data set, can be found in Guest and colleagues (2007) as described in Chapter 5. In this mixed methods analysis, the authors first analyzed the quantitative data and discerned changes in condom use over time (Figure 5.1). Their next task was to try to find the reasons behind the changes observed. Using a key-word-in-context technique, they identified all of the instances in which the word "condom" was used, and looked for explanations in each of the text segments. The qualitative data from this subsequent analysis documented four possible explanations for the patterns observed in the quantitative data.

A study by Abildso, Zizzi, Gilleland, Thomas, and Bonner (2010) provides another example of an explanatory sequential study. The authors set out to evaluate the physical and psychosocial impact of a 12-week cognitive-behavioral weight-management program and identify factors associated with weight loss. Quantitative data in the form of a survey were used to establish program completion rates and weight loss among participants ($n = 55$). Phone-based in-depth interviews were subsequently administered to 11 participants—spread across three dimensions of weight loss/completion rates, based on the survey results—to identify potential mechanisms behind weight loss. A subsequent thematic analysis of the in-depth interview data identified four major themes associated with degrees of program success: (a) fostering accountability, (b) balancing perceived effort and success, (c) redefining "success," and (d) developing cognitive flexibility.

Note that not all examples of explanatory (or any mixed methods) designs need to be published in the same report. In another risk disinhibition study conducted among participants in an HIV vaccine efficacy trial, quantitative and complementary qualitative results were published separately (Bartholow et al., 2005; Guest et al., 2005, respectively). The quantitative study documented the degree to which sexual behavior changed over the course of the 3-year trial while the qualitative component helped explain the trajectories observed in the quantitative data. Although the explanatory intent of the qualitative component was embedded in the original research design, and data were collected for this purpose, logistical issues (independent analysis teams and different analysis schedules) prevented integration at the manuscript level.

Another, less common, form of the explanatory sequential design entails using quantitative data to further explain qualitative findings. Probably the most common variation of this design is to follow up a qualitative analysis with a probabilistically sampled survey (Morgan, 1998). Here the goal is to ascertain the prevalence, and associated variability, of thematic expression among individuals within a population. An example of this design can be found in the consumer marketing literature (Hausman, 2000). Using semistructured interviews, the researchers examined the reasoning behind impulse purchases. They employed a grounded theory approach to analyze 60 qualitative interviews, the outcome of which was a series of hypotheses that was subsequently tested with a structured survey among 272 consumers.

Testing hypotheses is only one possible objective of an explanatory sequential design. In many cases a researcher may simply want to know, descriptively, how pervasive a particular perception, belief, or behavior is within a population. Themes derived from a qualitative inquiry with a small nonprobabilistic sample can be transformed into structured questions and administered to a larger probabilistic sample to assess the degree of variability within the larger population. In such a situation, description, not hypothesis testing, is the primary objective of the quantitative component.

Note that in some ways the explanatory sequential examples above could also be considered exploratory sequential, whereby the qualitative data directly informs, almost completely, the survey instrument. A distinction can be made, however, with respect to the intended use of the two data sets. The primary intent of the survey in these examples is to provide further explanation for the qualitative data; the survey is not the ultimate goal of the research. For a more in-depth discussion of the theory behind, and practice of, sequential explanatory designs, see Ivankova, Creswell, and Stick (2006).

Concurrent

The defining feature of the concurrent design is the relative independence of the data sets prior to mixing. All concurrent designs share the practice of conducting data analysis for each data set separately and then integrating/mixing *after* analysis of each is completed. Neither data set is dependent upon the other.

Reasons for data integration in a concurrent design can differ. One common purpose can be generally classified as *triangulation*. As with all concurrent studies, in the triangulation design, qualitative and quantitative data sets are analyzed separately and integrated during the interpretation phase of the analysis, often in the Discussion section. During data mixing, the analyst looks for evidence of convergence, divergence, or contradiction between the two data sets (recall the "=" notation in the textbox above: this is the symbol that is used, at least by certain authors, to denote purpose of integration). Although it is certainly possible to actively, and exclusively, look for areas of divergence or contradiction in a triangulation approach, more often analysts conduct an inductive comparative analysis between data sets and let the data guide the outcome. An excellent example of this approach is Kawamura, Lvankova, Kohler, and Perumean-Chaney (2009) study that looked at the relationship between parasocial interaction and self-efficacy, in the context of physical exercise, among radio listeners. The investigators administered structured surveys to 105 listeners of a particular radio program (a drama intended to motivate individuals to exercise) and generated a path analytic model based on structural equation modeling of the quantitative data. Eighteen participants were selected from the larger sample for in-depth interviews, which were subsequently analyzed using a grounded-theory approach. Resulting explanatory models from each data set were then compared (refer to Figure 7.5 in the preceding chapter). According to the authors, "The major finding in this study is that there is a divergence in the findings based on the interpretation of the results of the path analysis and the grounded theory" (Kawamura et al., 2009, p. 99).

A Word About Triangulation

Researchers of all types and from the entire range of field research disciplines have used, and continue to use, the term *triangulation* rather liberally and with multiple intended meanings (Hammersly, 2008). Some posit that the term is overused and now has such a broad meaning that it has become virtually meaningless (A. Bryman, personal communication, July, 2010; Sandelowski, 2003, p. 328). The term itself, for example, at least as used in social and behavioral science, does not indicate what is triangulated (one can triangulate data types, sources, paradigms, etc.), how and when things are combined, and for what purpose. Nor is it synonymous with mixed methods research, as some authors infer. Another problem is that the traditional denotation of the term—coming from geometry and subsequently

> (Continued)
>
> sailing—refers specifically to the use of three data points. Much mixed methods research involves only two data sources or approaches, some more than three, thus adding to the confusion. Because of these issues, some mixed methodologists have begun to question the appropriateness of the term in the research context and suggest that we abandon the term altogether (Creswell & Plano Clark, personal communication, July, 2009; Teddlie & Tashakkori, 2009, p. 32), preferring instead to use terms such as *integration* or *concurrent design* and then specifying the what, why and how of method combination.

The divergent outcome of the Kawamura and colleagues study is not an uncommon occurrence and presents one of the major challenges in a triangulated design. Convergent findings are clean and easy to explain (i.e., findings are corroborated and have increased validity), but what do you do with divergent or contradictory results? They need to be explained. One possible, generic, explanation is that the observed disparity is a methodological artifact—for example, the difference in question wording and/or process of inquiry are responsible. A more thoughtful approach is to broaden or adjust one's theoretical perspective. As with the case of outliers (see Chapter 5), conflicting data can be the foundation for developing more sophisticated (and presumably more accurate) explanatory theories. In fact, Greene and colleagues (1989) point out that seeking divergence is an appropriate, and often informative, explicit purpose for a concurrent design. The bottom line is that, whether intentionally sought or not, divergent findings need to be accounted for; researchers must be prepared for this possibility when planning and executing a triangulated concurrent design.

The concurrent design example above uses the most common type of data mixing in concurrent designs—analyzing qualitative and quantitative data sets separately, presenting them as independent data sets in the Results section and integrating/mixing them in the Discussion. Two alternate mixing strategies are described by Plano Clark, Garrett, and Leslie-Pelecky (2010). One technique is to merge results in a matrix. As shown in Table 8.4, key findings can be merged in such a way as to connect and present both sets of findings in one place. In this table the two left columns contain quantitative data in the form of respondent category (professional discipline) and comparative measures on a key variable (skill improvement) that was part of an evaluation of a nontraditional graduate education program. Qualitative data are presented in the two columns to the right, with one column showing key themes and their frequencies, and the other illustrative quotes. With this integrative method, the reader can see the qualitative and quantitative data alongside each other and look for convergence and/or divergence between groups and data collection methods. Note that the number of possible permutations of how data are presented in matrix form is virtually endless

Table 8.4 Example of Matrix Form of Mixing

Discipline	QUAN Comparisons "Improved Skills" $M(SD)$[a]	Most Prominent Qualitative Themes about Benefits (% of statements)	Sample Quote
Biological Sciences ($n=6$)	40.17 (3.06)[b,c]	Improved Communication Skills (30%)	It also let me translate very complicated concepts to children and it helped me work on my communication skills.
		Improved Teaching Skills (23%)	If I choose to go into academia I feel that my teaching skills have improved. My evaluations have been significantly more positive since working with [the program].
		Improved Marketability (23%)	[The program] has made me a more marketable scientist. I believe it has enhanced my CV.
Physical Sciences and Engineering (n quan $= 15$; n qual $= 13$)	36.07 (4.11)b	Improved Communication Skills (37%)	Mostly, I learned a lot about communication. And it wasn't just about communicating with [teaching] students. I learned a lot about communicating with professionals.
		Camaraderie and Friendship (22%)	I found the support of the other fellows to be very helpful on poor research days or weeks, since it often feels that the atmosphere is somewhat competitive within my own department.
		Improved Confidence (14%)	By gaining the ability to talk science with everyone, I am a more confident, coherent scientist in public and at work.
Mathematics (n quan $= 14$; n qual $= 13$)	34.79 (2.67)c	Improved Teaching Skills (39%)	One of the main goals of a Ph.D. in Mathematics is the betterment of one's teaching ability. I simply cannot say enough about the positive effect [of the program] with respect to my teaching.
		Improved Marketability (23%)	Participating in [the program] has made me a more desirable candidate for a teaching position. I have heard that a credential such as this is highly desirable in the tenure track job market.
		Working with People Outside Field (16%)	I was able to teach material and work with individuals outside my subject area. This will help me be more effective in interdepartmental collaboration in the future.

Source: Plano Clark, Garrett, & Leslie-Pelecky, 2010.

[a]ANOVA test found a significant difference for the improved skills variable ($P=.011$).

[b]Univariate post hoc comparisons found significant differences between Biological Sciences and Physical Sciences and Engineering ($P=.048$).

[c]Univariate post hoc comparisons found significant differences between Biological Sciences and Mathematics ($P=.008$).

and what a researcher ultimately chooses depends on the types of data available, the robustness of findings, and the intended purpose of the matrix and report.

Bryman also advocates a matrix technique, arguing that presenting QUAL and QUAN data separately in the results section is not an optimal form of mixing and that the subsequent integration that does occur in the discussion is often shallow in nature (A. Bryman, personal communication, July, 2010). Building on the work of Ritchie, Spencer, and O'Connor (2003), Bryman suggests using a matrix in which themes, instrument domains, or theoretical constructs (whichever best unifies the qualitative and quantitative data sets) constitute the rows, and qualitative and quantitative data points or summaries are listed in two separate columns and cross-referenced with each theme/construct. Fields in the qualitative or quantitative data columns can be either summaries (e.g., correlation coefficients, P-values, means, theme definitions, or frequencies) or raw data points (e.g., quotes, ratios). Note that more columns can be added that further summarize various aspects of integration. Table 8.5 provides a generic example of this type of mixing matrix.

Another integrative method involves data transformation. Some examples include transforming qualitative data into quantitative data, in the form of frequencies or other measure, and comparing them with the (original) quantitative data. Similarly, qualitative findings can be used to inform the transformation of quantitative data—for example, creating new variables—to be subsequently used in analysis. For a more detailed description of this method refer to Plano Clark et al. (2010).

MIXED METHODS DESIGNS AND THEMATIC ANALYSES

In the previous sections, we have described mixed method typologies and data integration procedures at a relatively generic level. In this section, we target the discussion more specifically on the implications a particular type of mixed method design has for how a thematic analysis might be done. We present these in the form of an annotated table (Table 8.6)

Table 8.5 Matrixed Data Integration

Theme/Construct/ Domain	Method 1 (QUAN)	Method 2 (QUAL)	Method n	Relationship (e.g., convergence, divergence, explanation)	Interpretation/ Comments
Theme 1	Data	Data	Data		
Theme 2	Data	Data	Data		
Theme 3	Data	Data	Data		
Theme n	Data	Data	Data		

Table 8.6   Data Integration and Implications for Thematic Analysis

Basic Design Type	Implications for Thematic Analysis
Exploratory Sequential qual→QUAN	**Analytic Approach** • Determine the *degree* to which the quan data collection instruments/processes need to be informed. If building an instrument from scratch, a thorough thematic analysis is justified. If pretesting an existing instrument, a thematic analysis not typically warranted; instead, analysts can review specific feedback, at face value, for each question and revise accordingly. • Determine the degree of analytic rigor possible within the study parameters. If time/resources are constrained, only a cursory thematic analysis may be possible: analyst(s)—usually the interviewers/moderators—briefly review their notes and write a report based on the most prominent themes. The more time/resources available, the more elements of rigor, described in this book, can be added to the analysis (e.g., formal codebook, reliability checks, data reduction techniques). **Data Integration** • Qualitative data are analyzed first. The results of this analysis are then directly used to inform the subsequent quantitative phase(s). **Potential Challenges** • Data from the earlier phase(s) turn out to be weak or invalid. • Data from the earlier phase(s) reveal completely unexpected information.
Exploratory Sequential quan→QUAL	**Analytic Approach** • Overall approach to qualitative *analysis* is not typically affected by the quantitative analysis in this design. If, however, quan data are used to sample two or more groups for follow-up qualitative inquiry (e.g., positive and negative deviants), a comparative approach to thematic analysis is likely (see Chapter 7). **Data Integration** • Quantitative data are analyzed first. The results of this analysis are then directly used to inform the subsequent qualitative phase(s), usually sampling parameters. • Key decision required is the demarcation point to use for inclusion into second phase. Scree plots (data driven) or existing relevant metrics within other or larger populations (theory driven) are helpful. **Potential Challenges** • Not enough variability in quantitative data to create evenly numbered or meaningful groupings. • Data from the earlier phase(s) reveal completely unexpected information.

Explanatory Sequential qual→quan	**Analytic Approach** • The primary goal of the qualitative analysis in this design is to identify key themes during the first phase. A standard inductive thematic analysis is appropriate; however, analysts must decide on the degree of systematicity and rigor of the analysis. If the desired end product is qualitative (e.g., QUAL quan), then a more more rigorous and lengthy thematic analysis is best. If the quantitative data will be primary, then less rigor can be tolerated. • Other important decisions that need to be made are (a) how many themes to follow up on, and (b) how to transform themes into meaningful structured questions. **Data Integration** • Qualitative data are analyzed first. Key themes, or other summative representations of the qualitative data, are generated. Findings are then transformed into structured questions and administered to a larger (usually probabilistic) sample. Quantitative analysis is conducted on responses to the structured questions. Results of the quantitative analysis are used to describe (explain) the variability of key themes/findings (derived from the qual) among a larger population. Generalizability is thereby significantly enhanced. • Need to decide which data set to highlight in write-up (see Chapter 10). **Potential Challenges** • Data from the qualitative and quantitative data sets are divergent or contradictory. This needs to be explained, or at least addressed, somehow.
Explanatory Sequential quan→qual	**Analytic Approach** • In this context, the optimal general approach to thematic analysis is probably hypothesis/theory-driven (see Chapter 1). Because analysts are looking to explain specific quantitative findings, thematic analysis is guided to a certain degree by a (theoretical) framework. Analysis is targeted since it is focused on explaining certain relationships, trends, and so on. • Key-word-in-context or other word-based techniques are useful tools in this context since they often pinpoint key pieces of text for analysis. **Data Integration** • Quantitative data are analyzed first. Key findings are summarized—usually in the form of descriptive or correlational statistics—and qualitative data are then used to explain, and/or provide context for, the quantitative findings. Causal understanding of the topic is increased, as is face validity. • Need to decide timing of collection of data sets, vis-à-vis each other. For example, qualitative and quantitative data can be collected simultaneously, requiring well-planned and systematic coordination of instruments and procedures. A more targeted approach can be used, where quantitative results are collected and analyzed first and qualitative instruments/procedures are informed by the quantitative results. Logistics and time available are two of the key factors that determine relative timing of data collection.

(Continued)

Table 8.6 (Continued)

Basic Design Type	*Implications for Thematic Analysis*
	Potential Challenges • Data from the earlier phase(s) turn out to be weak, invalid, or problematic in some way. • Data from the qualitative and quantitative data sets are divergent or contradictory. In the process of explaining the quantitative data, it may turn out that some of the qual findings contradict elements of the quantitative findings. Such a situation needs to be addressed. Refer to section on "concurrent" designs.
Concurrent	Analytic Approach • Analysis is guided by the stated purpose of the concurrent design. An analyst needs to determine which type of data to actively look for—instances of convergence, divergence, contradiction, explanation, or a combination of them. • The next step in the decision process is to establish rules and procedures for analyzing/documenting instances outside of the purpose. If looking for convergence, for example, how should instances of divergence in the data be analyzed, documented, and presented? (see Chapter 10 for some suggestions) • Because this design requires the direct comparison of qualitative and quantitative data, it is important that the thematic analysis be as systematic as possible, to reduce analytic bias. Although this is generally a good idea in all thematic analyses, the comparative nature of the design increases the need for systematicity. Data Integration • Both data sets are analyzed separately. • The most common method of combining data sets is to present findings from each data set separately in the "Results" section and then integrate them in the "Discussion" narrative. • Other methods include using matrices and transforming data. • An alternative is to carry out the primary integration in the Results section, followed with additional, more interpretive, integration in the Discussion. Chapter 10 provides some more guidance on this matter. Potential Challenges • Most researchers who use a concurrent design are looking (and hoping) for convergence. Be prepared for the possibility of divergent or contradictory data. Such a scenario must be explicitly acknowledged and addressed. Refer to section above on "concurrent" designs. • Some audiences may use the "apples and oranges" argument to critique your study, claiming that they cannot meaningfully be compared. Be prepared to explain and justify comparison of these two very different types of data (and possibly sampling procedures).

Table 8.6 presents suggestions on how to integrate thematic and quantitative data in some of the more common mixed methods designs. We do not have the scope in this chapter (or book) to cover all of the possible permutations and combinations of data integration. We feel that the basic concepts covered are transferable to the majority of multimethod designs and can be used as a methodological muse for the creative minds of other researchers. Remember that in reality, most mixed methods designs are much more complex and variable than the typologies presented here. More important, there is no "right" or fixed way of integrating data. The field of mixed methods is still young, so researchers should be free (perhaps even obligated) to be creative and develop new and interesting ways of mixing research methods. There are at least two journals whose explicit focus is mixed methods research (*Journal of Mixed Methods Research* and *International Journal of Multiple Research Approaches*) and various methodological journals that regularly publish mixed methods articles (e.g., *Field Methods, Quality and Quantity,* and *Qualitative Health Research*). Also, topic-focused research journals in many fields are increasingly receiving, and accepting, manuscripts based on mixed methods designs. Publish your findings! The key is to do the best you can to generate valid data and meaningful findings and be transparent about your processes.

One element not typically covered in existing typologies is the potential multi-purpose of research methods and instruments. Earlier in this chapter we provided the example of a 3-year NIH study to illustrate the point that data sets can serve more than one purpose for a given study. This multiplicity can be built into a data collection instrument itself, where specific sections are explicitly designated for different purposes within the study (and possibly external to it). One section of a focus group guide, for example, may be designed to inform a survey instrument while another section may be intended to generate information that is directly informative, in and of itself, to the research question.

Timing of data collection is another element to consider and has indirect implications for thematic analysis. In a QUAN qual explanatory sequential design, for example, the sequential timing refers to the *use* of data sets, not necessarily data collection. Data sets in this case can be collected either simultaneously or sequentially (QUAN preceding the qual). The decision often comes down to logistics and resources. It is often easier and faster to collect data simultaneously. Concurrent data collection also permits an integrated sampling approach, thereby ensuring participants sampled for both data sets are from the same theoretical population. The disadvantage of collecting data sets simultaneously in this type of design is that qualitative data collection instruments cannot be tailored *directly* to explain the quantitative findings. This results in a more diffuse qualitative data set, at least with respect to specific quantitative results. Searching for themes that directly inform the quantitative data, therefore, is less directed and efficient, and ultimately, less informative. Research is all about trade-offs. In one situation (simultaneous data collection), expediency is gained but precision is sacrificed, in the other situation (sequential data collection) the reverse is true. Ultimately, the researcher must make a decision as to which attribute is more important.

An entire data set can also be analyzed in multiple ways, at different points in time, for different purposes (refer to Chapter 2). One data set, or components within it, might be used as a foundation for multiple manuscripts, being analyzed slightly differently for each. Or, time may be critical factor, driving analysts to complete analysis on only one portion of a data set, or analyzing an entire data set in a relatively cursory manner. The important thing to remember is that data don't usually disappear. Most researchers have the ability to revisit and analyze data at subsequent points in time (funding permitting). There is no rule that states all data must be analyzed with the same approach and within the same time period. We talk more about strategizing write-up and dissemination in Chapter 10.

One last caveat is in order. The methodological scope for most mixed methods studies (and social science research in general) is confined to the three most common data collection methods—surveys, in-depth interviews, and focus groups. For this reason, our examples and suggestions overwhelmingly emphasize these methods. We wish to emphasize , however, that the majority of principles discussed in this chapter, and the book as a whole, also apply to other forms of data collection. Data sets can be comprised of diary entries—both qualitative and quantitative (see Alaszewski, 2006)—and analyzed accordingly. One could just as easily conduct a thematic analysis on a set of qualitative diaries to explain survey findings as one could using in-depth interviews. Conversely, data from quantitative diaries can be used to provide a baseline measure for a particular behavior and then mixed with qualitative data to explain patterns observed. Illustrative of this approach is the research of Guest (2003), whose goal was to understand the factors associated with fishing effort in a small coastal town of Ecuador. Guest had a group of local fisherman keep daily diaries and document hours fished, gas used, and pounds of shrimp caught. The data were plotted over time and correlated with other variables (e.g., gas prices, shrimp prices, weather). Qualitative data, from semistructured and unstructured interviews, were used to provide context for, and understand the reasoning behind, fishing activity.

Observational techniques—direct observation (quantitative) and participant observation (qualitative)—are commonly employed in sociobehavioral field research. Not surprisingly, data sets from these activities can easily and effectively be used in mixed methods studies. Participant observation, for example, is often used to generate topics for subsequent data collection instruments and processes (both qual and quan). Likewise, quantitative observation can be combined with qualitative techniques. An example of the latter can be found in the same research study with Ecuadorian fishermen discussed previously (Guest, 2003). For more than 6 months, Guest counted the number of artisanal, inshore, fishing boats that left the village estuary each morning. He plotted the observed daily number of active boats over time and then correlated these data with other quantitative measures (similar to the diary analysis above). Qualitative data from participant observation and ethnographic interviews once again provided a more in-depth understanding of the processes and reasoning involved in the decisions of small-scale fisherman, as well as a context in which to place the quantitative data.

SUMMING UP

Mixed methods as a formal discipline is a young, but growing, field of methodological interest. And although not every research topic warrants the use of multiple methods, the thoughtful integration of qualitative and quantitative approaches can enhance validity, increase explanatory power, and generate a more thorough picture of a research topic.

In this chapter, we have described some of the more common mixed methods design typologies. These certainly do not comprise the entire range of typologies, nor do all mixed methodologists agree on the importance of the three primary dimensions that we covered—timing, purpose, and weighting. We presented readers with what we believe to be the most widely accepted and most practical aspects of the mixed methods design literature. That said, we want to once again remind readers not to be overly concerned with typologies. Much of what is done in the research world is more complex than is depicted in the typologies, and given the recent emergence of the mixed methods field, typologies are constantly changing. We suggest that readers view this chapter as a basic theoretical framework that they can use to design their own studies and execute their own unique mixed methods analyses. Incorporate what is useful; disregard or improve upon what is not. The underlying theme of this chapter, and the entire book, is pragmatism. We therefore conclude this chapter with a few practical suggestions regarding planning a thematic analysis in a mixed methods study:

- Be able to explicitly justify why you're using a mixed methods design and why each component is necessary. The point in using multiple methods is to enhance the study in some way, beyond simply using two completely independent approaches.
- Thoughtfully plan timing of both data collection and data integration at the onset. These are two different processes, and how they are timed has implications for how a thematic analysis can be conducted.
- For each methodological component of the study, think about how, specifically, each data set will be analyzed, and subsequently linked, to other data sets. Draw a schematic of your study, depicting how and when each component is related the others.

REFERENCES

Abildso, C., Zizzi, S., Gilleland, D., Thomas, J., & Bonner, D. (2010). A mixed methods evaluation of a 12-week insurance-sponsored weight management program incorporating cognitive-behavioral counseling. *Journal of Mixed Methods Research, 4*, 278–294.

Alaszewski, A. (2006). *Using diaries for social research.* Thousand Oaks, CA: Sage.

Bartholow B., Buchbinder, S., Celum, C., Goli, V., Koblin, B., Para, M., Marmor, M., . . . Mastro, T. for the VISION/VAX004 Study Team. (2005). HIV sexual risk behavior over 36 months of follow-up in the world's first HIV vaccine efficacy trial. *Journal of Acquired Immune Deficiency Syndrome, 39*, 90–101.

Bergman, M. (Ed.). (2008). *Advances in mixed methods research.* Thousand Oaks, CA: Sage.

Bergman, M. (2008). Introduction: Whither mixed methods? In M. Bergman (Ed.), *Advances in mixed methods research* (pp. 1–7). Thousand Oaks, CA: Sage.

Bernard, H., & Ryan, G. (2010). *Analyzing qualitative data: Systematic approaches.* Thousand Oaks, CA: Sage.

Bryman, A. (2007). Barriers to integrating quantitative and qualitative research. *Journal of Mixed Methods Research, 1*, 8–22.

Caracelli, V., & Greene, J. (1997). Crafting mixed-method evaluation designs. In J. Greene & V. Caracelli (Eds.), *Advances in mixed-method evaluation: The challenges and benefits of integrating diverse paradigms* (pp. 19–32). San Francisco, CA: Jossey-Bass.

Creswell, J., & Plano Clark, V. (2007). *Designing and conducting mixed methods research.* Thousand Oaks, CA: Sage.

Creswell, J., & Plano Clark, V. (2011). *Designing and conducting mixed methods research* (2nd ed.). Thousand Oaks, CA: Sage.

Greene, J. (2007). *Mixed methods in social inquiry.* San Francisco, CA: Jossey-Bass.

Greene, J. C., Caracelli, V. J., & Graham, W. F. (1989). Toward a conceptual framework for mixed-method evaluation design. *Educational Evaluation and Policy Analysis, 11*(3), 255–274.

Guest, G. (2003). Fishing behavior and decision-making in an Ecuadorian community: A scaled approach. *Human Ecology 31*, 611–644.

Guest, G., Johnson, L., Burke, H., Rain-Taljaard, R., Severy, L., Von Mollendorf, C., & Van Damme, L. (2007). Changes in sexual behavior during a safety and feasibility trial of a microbicide/diaphragm combination: An integrated qualitative and quantitative analysis. *AIDS Education and Prevention, 19*(4), 310–320.

Hammersly, M. (2008). Troubles with triangulation. M. Bergman (Ed.), *Advances in mixed methods research* (pp. 22–36). Thousand Oaks, CA: Sage.

Hausman, A. (2000). A multi-method investigation of consumer motivations in impulse buying behavior. *Journal of Consumer Marketing, 17*(5), 403–417.

Ivankova, N., Creswell, J., & Stick, S. (2006). Using mixed-methods sequential explanatory design: From theory to practice. *Field Methods, 18*, 3–20.

Johnson, R., & Onwuegbuzie, A. (2004). Mixed method research: A research paradigm whose time has come. *Educational Researcher, 33*, 14–26.

Linstone, H., & Turoff, M. (1975). *The Delphi method: Techniques and applications.* Reading, MA: Addison-Wesley Publishing Company.

Kawamura, Y., Ivankova, N., Kohler, C., & Perumean-Chaney, S. (2009). Utilizing mixed methods to assess parasocial interaction of an entertainment-education program audience. *International Journal of Multiple Research Approaches, 3*(1), 88–104.

Morgan, D. (1998). Practical strategies for combining qualitative and quantitative methods: Applications to health research. *Qualitative Health Research, 8,* 362–376.

Morse, J. (1991). Approaches to qualitative-quantitative methodological triangulation. *Nursing Research, 40,* 120–123.

Morse, J. (2003). Principles of mixed methods and multimethod research design. In A. Tashakkori & C. Teddlie (Eds.), *Handbook of mixed methods in social and behavioral research* (pp. 189–208). Thousand Oaks, CA: Sage.

Morse, J., & Niehaus, L. (2009). *Mixed method design: Principles and procedures.* Walnut Creek, CA: Left Coast Press.

Onwuegbuzie, A., & Leech, N. (2005). Taking the "Q" out of research: Teaching research methodology courses without the divide between quantitative and qualitative paradigms. *Quality and Quantity, 39,* 267–296.

Onwuegbuzie, A., Bustamante, R., & Nelson, J. (2010). Mixed research as a tool for developing quantitative instruments. *Journal of Mixed Methods Research, 4,* 56–78.

Plano Clark, V., Garrett, A., & Leslie-Pelecky, D. (2010). Applying three strategies for integrating quantitative and qualitative databases in a mixed methods study of a nontraditional graduate education program. *Field Methods, 22,* 154–174.

Plano Clark, V., & Creswell, J. (2008). *The mixed methods reader.* Thousand Oaks, CA: Sage.

Ritchie, J., Spencer, L., & O'Connor, W. (2003). Carrying out qualitative analysis. In J. Ritchie & J. Lewis (Eds.), *Qualitative research practice: A guide for social science students and researchers* (pp. 219–262). London: Sage.

Sandelowski, M. (2003). Tables or tableaux? The challenges of writing and reading mixed methods studies. In A. Tashakorri & C. Teddlie (Eds.), *Handbook of mixed methods in social and behavioral research* (pp. 321–350). Thousand Oaks, CA: Sage.

Steiner, M., Taylor, D., Hylton-Kong, T., Mehta, N., Figueroa, J., Bourne, D., Hobbs, M., & Behets, F. (2007). Decreased condom breakage and slippage rates after counseling men at a sexually transmitted infection clinic in Jamaica. *Contraception, 75,* 289–293.

Tashakkori, A., & Teddlie, C. (1998). *Mixed methodology: Combining qualitative and quantitative approaches.* Thousand Oaks, CA: Sage.

Tashakkori, A., & Teddlie, C. (Eds.). (2003). *Handbook of mixed methods in social and behavioral research.* Thousand Oaks, CA: Sage.

Tashakkori, A., & Teddlie, C. (Eds.). (2010). *Handbook of mixed methods in social and behavioral research* (2nd ed.). Thousand Oaks, CA: Sage.

Teddlie, C., & Tashakkori, A. (2009). *Foundations of mixed methods research: Integrating quantitative and qualitative approaches in the social and behavioral sciences.* Thousand Oaks, CA: Sage.

Vrkljan, B. (2009). Constructing a mixed methods design to explore the older driver-copilot relationship. *Journal of Mixed Methods Research, 3,* 371–385.

Willis, G. (2004). *Cognitive interviewing: A tool for improving questionnaire design.* Thousand Oaks, CA: Sage.

EXERCISES

1. Find mixed methods articles in your field of research (if none are available choose an alternative, related field). Review the articles and describe the studies' designs using the notation presented in this chapter. Use the guidelines below (from Creswell & Plano Clark, 2010, and Ivankova et al., 2006). Keep your diagram as simple as possible and limit it to one page. For illustrative examples of graphic depictions of mixed methods studies, refer to Creswell and Plano Clark (2011) and Plano Clark and Creswell (2008).

---

1. Give a title to the diagram

2. Choose either a horizontal or vertical layout for the design

3. Draw boxes for the quantitative and qualitative stages of data collection, analysis, and interpretation

4. Use uppercase and lowercase letters to designate relative priority of methods

5. Use single-headed arrows to represent the flow of procedures

6. Specify procedures for each stage of qual and quan data collection and analysis

7. Using concise language, specify expected products or outcomes of each procedure

---

2. Answer the following questions:

   a. What is the primary distinction between a concurrent and a sequential design?
   b. What are some of the major challenges in implementing a concurrent research study?
   c. How might you approach qualitative data collection and analysis differently (if at all) for the following two scenarios? (1) Pretesting the draft form of a survey instrument that you created. (2) Creating survey content from scratch for a population about which you know relatively little.

ADDITIONAL READING

Creswell, J. (1998). Mixed-method research: Introduction and application. In G. Cizek (Ed.), *Handbook of educational policy* (pp. 455–472). San Diego, CA: Academic Press.

Creswell, J., & Plano Clark, V. (2011). *Designing and conducting mixed methods research* (2nd ed.). Thousand Oaks, CA: Sage.

Creswell, J. W., Goodchild, L., & Turner, P. (1996). Integrated qualitative and quantitative research: Epistemology, history, and designs. In J. Smart (Ed.), *Higher education: Handbook of theory and research* (Vol. XI., pp. 90–136). New York: Agathon Press.

Guest, G., McLellan-Lemal, E., Matia, D., Pickard, R., Fuchs, J., McKirnan, D., Neidig, J. (2005). HIV vaccine efficacy trial participation: Men-who-have-sex-with-men's experience of risk reduction counseling and perceptions of behavior change. *AIDS Care, 17,* 46–57.

Guest, G., Namey, E., & Mitchell, M. (In press). *Collecting qualitative data: A field manual*. Thousand Oaks, CA: Sage.

Morgan, D. (1998). Practical strategies for combining qualitative and quantitative methods: Applications to health research. *Qualitative Health Research, 8,* 362–376.

Teddlie, C., & Tashakkori, A. (2009). *Foundations of mixed methods research: Integrating quantitative and qualitative approaches in the social and behavioral sciences.* Thousand Oaks, CA: Sage.

9

CHOOSING QUALITATIVE DATA ANALYSIS SOFTWARE

LEARNING OBJECTIVES

After reading this chapter, you should be able to:

- Summarize a brief history of qualitative data analysis software
- Identify some of the leading qualitative data analysis software packages
- Describe the different functions that qualitative data analysis software performs
- Identify factors to consider when choosing a qualitative data analysis software program

---

The number of researcher-designed (and -tested) software programs for qualitative data analysis continues to grow, offering a variety of choices with a dizzying array of accompanying features. In this chapter, we will review some of the general considerations that affect the decision to use and select software, and then review some of the common features of qualitative data analysis software (QDAS) as they relate to tackling particular analytic problems in thematic analyses. As Lewins and Silver (2009) note, "'Which is the "best" [QDAS] package?' is perhaps the most frequently asked question we receive; however, it is impossible to answer!" (p. 3) We concur with this statement, based on the varying advantages and disadvantages of each software package available, and on the fact that the field of QDAS is always changing. For these reasons, we do not detail specific software programs. Rather, we provide a brief history of QDAS, introduce some of the current software options, and devote most of the chapter to presenting a range of considerations that can be applied to any QDAS package to assist in the selection process.

A BRIEF HISTORY

The procedures we have outlined for applied thematic analysis are certainly possible without the help of QDAS. Prior to the widespread availability and use of the personal computer, the tools of qualitative data analysis were easily accessible: paper, highlighters, note cards, scissors, and tape. A researcher, most likely an anthropologist or sociologist, would gather all of the typed or handwritten interview transcripts, field notes, and supplementary material collected for a particular project and begin reading. The researcher would highlight interesting passages, write notes in margins or on separate note cards, and photocopy and cut out segments of text to tape next to similar sections of text elsewhere. Several readings of the data set were completed and notes and passages were rearranged, until a coherent analysis of the data was reached (Weitzman, 1999). This process worked for most of the history of the social sciences.

Then, in the mid-1980s, as personal computers became more widely available, the first DOS-based QDAS programs were written (The Ethnograph and Nud*ist). A decade later, there were at least 10 such programs (Weitzman and Miles reviewed 24 programs in five major categories in 1995). As Friese (n.d.) relates:

> The program developers or designers were often researchers who needed a software-based solution for a specific project. As a consequence, the requirements posed by the data at hand, the respective research topics and the chosen methodological approach often had an impact on the software development and design. . . . Thus, these computer programs are ultimately the product of specific events and, to a certain extent, they each have own story to tell. (Assessing a Quarter Century of Qualitative Computing, section 1)

In fact, many of the QDAS companies that have been in the field since its inception relate the history of their QDAS product(s) on their websites, providing an idea of both the necessity and philosophy that drove the creation of a particular program.

Over the past 25 years, the field of QDAS offerings has simultaneously expanded and converged. Take for instance the five types of software categorized by Weitzman and Miles in 1995 (see Table 1).

Although the authors acknowledged that QDAS programs likely had functions in overlapping categories, they felt it was possible to "focus on the 'heart-and-soul' of a program: what it mainly is intended for" (Weitzman, 1999, p. 1246). Today, nearly all of the main QDAS packages offer all of the capabilities listed in Table 9.1; they have converged to the point of being superb textbase managers with text- and code-retrieve functions that facilitate theory and conceptual network building—and much more. QDAS packages also routinely support

Table 9.1 Types of QDAS	
Text Retrievers	Specialize in finding all instances of words and phrases in text, in one or several files. May include word co-occurrences, counting, key words in context, concordances.
Textbase Managers	Database programs specialized for storing text in an organized fashion by linking files to information about those files. Allow sort and retrieve according to selected criteria.
Code-and-Retrieve Programs	Specialize in allowing the researcher to apply category tags (codes) to passages of text and later retrieve and display the text according to the researcher's coding. May include search and memo capacities.
Code-Based Theory Builders	Based on a code-and-retrieve model, but with special features to support theory-building efforts, such as representing relationships among codes, classifying categories, or formulating theoretical propositions about the data. May include more sophisticated search-and-retrieve programs and memoing functions.
Conceptual Network Builders	Emphasize the creation and analysis of network displays or graphic representations of the relationships among concepts.

Source: Adapted from Weitzman and Miles, 1995.

multiple forms of qualitative data (beyond text), the integration of quantitative data, and advanced features for visual displays and representations of data. Some QDAS programs, new and old, are experimenting with Web-based platforms that facilitate linking and sharing of data. Table 9.2 lists some of the well-established current QDAS choices. The individual QDAS websites listed in Table 9.2 are helpful for identifying the features available in the most recent release of a QDAS program. When comparing QDAS choices, the Computer-Assisted Qualitative Data Analysis (CAQDAS) networking website hosted by the University of Surrey offers informative reviews of many of the current versions of QDAS (see "Additional Reading"). The rest of this chapter is dedicated to helping you identify some of the other considerations to take into account when thinking about using QDAS.

Table 9.2 A Sampling of Common QDAS Programs

QDAS Name	Original Version Release Date	QDAS Website
ATLAS.ti	1993	www.atlasti.com
The Ethnograph	1984	www.qualisresearch.com
HyperRESEARCH	1991	www.researchware.com/products/hyperresearch.html
MAXQDA	1989	www.maxqda.com
NVivo	1981	www.qsrinternational.com/products_nvivo.aspx
QDA Miner	2004	www.provalisresearch.com/QDAMiner/QDAMinerDesc.html
Qualrus	2002	www.qualrus.com

GENERAL CONSIDERATIONS

From the outset, we should note that a basic understanding of qualitative analysis (as presented in the preceding chapters) is necessary to correctly and efficiently use qualitative data analysis software, just as a firm grasp of statistical tests and their underlying assumptions is required for optimal use of quantitative analysis software. However, where a researcher might rely on quantitative software to perform analyses and carry out statistical tests, qualitative analysis software does not *do* analysis for you. Because thematic analysis is by nature an iterative process, it is not possible to upload a data set and simply "run" an analysis. As detailed in Chapter 3, codebook creation and multiple rounds of coding are essential components of the analysis of qualitative data, with each subsequent round of data review adding to the overall understanding of the research question—and determining which queries or reports to perform. QDAS *facilitates* this process, enhancing the efficiency, consistency, and comprehensiveness of thematic analysis. These benefits apply equally to qualitative data management, coding, exploration, reduction, and reporting, as described below.

QDAS AS A DATA MANAGEMENT TOOL

Most QDAS packages serve, on a structural level, as large electronic filing cabinets, providing a centralized place for storing raw or processed data (audio files, transcripts and other documents, photos and images, and videos), information about the sources of the data (participant demographics, event descriptions, field notes), links to external data or sources (documents or websites), and in some cases, other data sets. This is the "textbase manager" capacity detailed in Table 9.1. Referred to by di Gregorio and Davidson (2008) as E-Projects, these electronic filing cabinets contain "all components of a project, meaning the descriptive, interpretive, and theoretical materials gathered or developed by the researcher . . . and [are], simultaneously, the vehicle by which these materials and the meaning assigned to them by the researcher can be communicated with others" (p. 11). In this capacity, QDAS enhances the efficiency of thematic analysis by enabling researchers to organize and work with all of their data in one program, and by providing a single repository that can be shared among team members, without sending tens or hundreds of individual data files. (The caveat being that a "master" file must be maintained and shared copies updated throughout the process.)

Another key data management feature of QDAS is the ability to group, link, or define subsets of the data within the software and assign labels or relationships to them. As these structures may be created and utilized at any point in the analysis—prior to importing data, at the outset of coding, after an initial round of analysis—QDAS packages "both reflect and significantly facilitate the 'cyclical' nature which is characteristic of many qualitative research and analysis processes" (Lewins & Silver, 2009, p. 5).

Data Management Tasks for Applied Thematic Analysis in QDAS

- Creation of a "project" or repository for all study related files
- Importation of data and related study files (guides, demographic information, descriptive source material)
- Organization of study files into folders, groups, and/or sets that will assist in filtering later searches
- (For team-based research) Designation of analysis team and lead analyst, along with protocols for file sharing and division of labor

QDAS AS A DATA TAGGING TOOL

The benefits of QDAS become more apparent as we move to reviewing and labeling data. It is still possible to highlight and annotate your source material as you would with pens and note cards, but whether you are interested in creating and applying structural codes to segment your transcripts by question/response, thematic codes to capture the content and context of the data, or memos and annotations to document thoughts about the data, QDAS makes the process easier. It also increases the chances that you and/or your research team will apply codes consistently and comprehensively (Weitzman, 1999). One reason for this is simply the centralized location of files and codes; when everything is in one place, it is easy to scan either the code or document list to see if there have been any omissions. Similarly, having a list of codes immediately adjacent to the material you are coding (as most programs make possible) provides an instant reminder of the codes available for application, organized alphabetically or hierarchically and linked to their definitions.

The ability to link things within QDAS additionally enhances the comprehensiveness of an analysis by creating searchable associations or connections between (1) codes and their definitions, (2) two pieces of data, (3) data and source information (e.g., demographics), (4) data and analysts' thoughts (e.g., memos or annotations), or (5) study material and external sources of information. Although some of these tasks may be accomplished without dedicated QDAS, the use of software exponentially increases the range and depth of coding, commentary, and retrieval options available to an analyst.

Data Coding Tasks for Applied Thematic Analysis in QDAS

- Creation of a codebook, with definitions and examples
- Association of data sources and supplemental information (demographics, descriptives)
- Application of codes, comments, and memos to study files
- Definition of linkages between and among data, data files, and analyst comments

---

QDAS AS A DATA EXPLORATION AND REDUCTION TOOL

The consistent and comprehensive application of codes or tags to your data in QDAS provides subsequent advantages in the exploration, reduction, and reporting of data. As mentioned, most of today's QDAS programs are, at their core, a hybrid of text- and code-retrieval and theory and conceptual network building programs, enabling analysts to quickly pull up all of the data coded with a particular code or combination of codes. Once coded data have been retrieved, QDAS facilitates additional coding or recoding of the previously coded material, enables hierarchical arrangement of codes, collapsing of similar items, and visual representations of code connections.

Boolean and proximity searches are typically supported, augmenting typical AND searches with OR, NOT, IF, NEAR, and so on. Additional, more quantitatively derived features, such as cross-tabs, frequencies, word searches, cluster analyses, tree maps, and models are also supported in many QDAS programs. These supplemental and data reduction features (see Chapters 5 and 6, respectively, for more on these techniques) assist both in reducing data or themes to recognizable patterns and in widening the analyst's lens on the data, offering views of both the forest *and* the trees. The ease with which QDAS layers filtering criteria (demographic or group qualities, for example) upon any of these search and explore techniques helps to further refine understandings of the data and is extremely useful for comparative analyses (see Chapter 7). Finally, use of QDAS to explore and reduce data this way is replicable, so that you and/or others might revisit a particular query or analysis to verify its accuracy in light of new information, providing a check on consistency and validity.

Data Exploration and Reduction Tasks for Applied Thematic Analysis in QDAS

- Review of structurally and thematically coded data
- Targeted searching and recoding of data
- In-depth examination of theme co-occurrences, by question, domain, or population
- Visualization of trends within the coded data via charts, maps, cluster analyses, or scatter plots
- Modeling of conceptual relationships within the data set

STUDY SIZE AND COMPLEXITY

QDAS is indeed a useful tool, but it may not always be necessary. Figure 9.1 illustrates several factors related to study size and complexity that you might consider. In general, small and simple analyses can often be accomplished in a standard word-processing program. Take, for example, a small study assessing a training program at a medical school. The education coordinator wants to learn residents' perceptions of the content and delivery of required educational modules. She conducts two focus groups and a few follow-up interviews to collect the

Figure 9.1 Assessing the Need for and Usefulness of QDAS

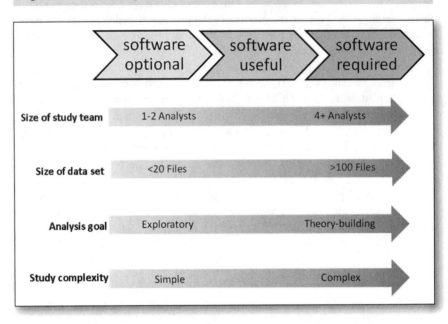

residents' opinions. The limited amount of data, paired with the limited scope of the analysis (i.e., a summary of what residents like and dislike, and their suggestions for improving educational sessions) obviate the need for QDAS in this case. The coordinator might simply use the audio transcripts to create summary tables addressing each of the research objectives.

"Obviously, the larger the sample and the more complex the analysis, the more essential a computer [and QDAS] will be" (Tashakkori & Teddlie, 2003, p. 371). Projects including more than 20 in-depth interviews or 10 focus groups, more than two analysts, or moving from descriptive to explanatory goals often not only benefit from but also may require QDAS (MacQueen, 2005). Qualitative studies of this type of moderate complexity are quite common, as stand-alone projects and integrated within larger research objectives. Lyerly and colleagues, for example, conducted 46 semistructured interviews with individuals and couples who had frozen some of the embryos created through in vitro fertilization procedures (Lyerly et al., 2006). The number of interviews alone might have made analysis "by hand" overwhelming, but the determining factor in this case for using QDAS was the research objective: To describe factors that affect infertility patients' decision making regarding their cryopreserved embryos, with the ultimate goal of constructing a national survey for infertility patients with frozen embryos. The researchers covered five major areas related to embryo disposition and sought to systematically document responses to better understand what topics and items should be included on the survey. They also incorporated information about the family—number of children, number of embryos, and number of years embryos were frozen—into the analysis, to sort and filter the data by these characteristics. QDAS made these analysis processes feasible and efficient.

For truly complex studies—those with mixed quantitative and qualitative data, more than 100 data files, a theoretical modeling goal, and/or a large analysis team (MacQueen, 2005)—QDAS is an essential tool to handle both the data organization and analysis tasks. Projects that fall into this category may involve data collected from different sites (perhaps by a geographically dispersed research team), various groups or stakeholders, or via several data collection methods (participant observation and survey, in addition to focus groups). These additional layers of complexity highlight the advantages of QDAS—efficiency, consistency, and comprehensiveness—whether in facilitating systematic cataloging and tagging of data files or in the ability to link between them. If the size and complexity of a project does warrant use of QDAS, the discussion below will help you evaluate the features of individual QDAS packages.

FEATURES AND FUNCTIONS TO CONSIDER

As mentioned, the array of QDAS features can be dizzying, not just for the "analysis" portion of the research, but for logistical and data management functions as well. Table 9.3 displays the range of features that enter into the consideration of different QDAS programs and the types of options available for each. The table is divided into five sections, each of which is explained in more detail below. Given the ever-changing nature of QDAS products and their features, we provide an overview of the standard features and issues to consider in selecting a QDAS program; links to current reviews of specific software packages are included in the "Additional Reading" section.

Logistics

Before exploring the features of a particular QDAS program, it can be helpful to take a step back and start with the fundamentals—the basic logistical issues that affect your software selection process. Price-point and required operating system are two of the more concrete, easily defined considerations. As noted in Table 9.3, some QDAS packages are available as freeware, hosted on or downloadable from the Internet. These programs may not provide everything you are looking for in a long-term QDAS solution but might serve your purposes for a specific project. Other programs offer student and educational licenses at a reduced price (often for a fixed period) while a Web-based application might charge a monthly fee. Your consideration of price will depend not only on the stated cost, but also on whether this is a short- or long-term investment—for you, a specific project, or an institution. There are also the "invisible" costs of time required for support and training, which are affected by whether your organization or institution supports a specific program (and can provide on-site training), and whether you have had previous experience (positive or negative) with QDAS.

Table 9.3 Features and Considerations in Selecting QDAS

Logistics

Feature	Questions to Consider	How the Software Options Vary
Price	How much of your budget are you able to allocate to QDAS? Will this be a one-time use of QDAS or a longer-term investment? Does your organization or institution have a site license or support a particular software package?	The cost of QDAS ranges from free shareware, to student pricing and educational site discounts, to full commercial price. $0 to >$2,000.
Platform/ Operating system	Is the software compatible with your computer and operating system? If you are working in teams, do all team members have access to appropriate computers?	Most QDAS programs are PC-based and run on MS Windows; several of these can be used on a Mac by running Parallels, BootCamp, or similar program.
Speed and stability	How much data (overall file size) will you have? How many (complex) searches will you want to perform of the complete data set? What are your computer's memory and processor specifications?	In general, QDAS can handle large volumes of data, but the larger your file size and the more complex the task, the slower the programs tend to run. (See Koenig for comparison of previous versions of QDAS.)
Languages supported	Will you need or prefer to have the software interface in a language other than English?	QDAS programs generally allow you to work with data in any language, though the software interface typically remains in English. Some programs now offer Spanish, French, Portuguese, Japanese, Simplified Chinese and German interfaces in addition to English.

Customer support	Does your organization or institution support the software? What is your preferred method of accessing formal software support?	Customer support services range from extremely accessible and helpful to difficult to access and understand. Institutions sometimes purchase site licenses and/or have an on-site expert in a particular QDAS program.
File location	*Data security issues* If you store files locally, is your computer encrypted? If storing on a network, is access limited? (And if so, can you access the network remotely?) If you use a QDAS program's Web-based storage system, what are the security measures in place? What level/frequency of internet connection is required? *File sharing issues* Are you going to be working alone or in a team? Will you need to share multiple versions of an analysis project among colleagues?	*QDAS file location* Some programs require specific data storage locations, while others are more flexible. The main options are to store data locally, on a shared network, or on the Web. Each has implications for data security and ease of file sharing. *Data file location* Many programs make a copy of the original data, which are then incorporated into the "project" as internal data; some require that data remain stored according to a specific file path that the program accesses as external data. The former is more conducive to file sharing than the latter.
User interface	Do you prefer to see several windows at once? How much are you willing to consult the manual? Do you prefer hotkeys to mouse clicks? Have you worked with a QDAS previously? [And if so, are there things about that program that you liked or disliked?]	Most QDAS programs are Windows-based in some regard, but the degree to which they are and the version of Windows they mimic are highly variable. Some are more intuitive than others, some provide multiple options for performing the same task, some allow a degree of customization of the main fields and toolbars.

(Continued)

Table 9.3 (Continued)

Team-Based Functions

Feature	What to Consider	How It Varies
Team access	How would you like to structure and distribute the team coding and analysis tasks?	Most QDAS programs allow analysts to work in separate copies of the same QDAS project and then merge versions; a few allow simultaneous work on the same project, with all changes saved automatically.
Merge capabilities	Will you require the capability to merge either different projects or different versions of the same project? Would you prefer to work simultaneously on the same project and have the program handle all merging?	Most QDAS packages provide some kind of merge feature; those that offer simultaneous access and instant merging may be less equipped to merge *different* projects together.
Intercoder agreement	Will you want the software to facilitate intercoder agreement assessments? How would you like to measure intercoder agreement?	The intercoder agreement functions in QDAS packages vary on method of assessing agreement: some measure percent agreement per code, some provide kappa scores per code, some allow export of data to separate programs for calculation of agreement.
Research log or journal	If sharing and merging files, how will you maintain version control? How will you document who has done what in the project? What kind of analysis activities would you be most interested in logging? How might that work in a particular software system?	A few QDAS programs contain a command log or archive function to keep track of operations and changes. It is usually possible to come up with a work-around to maintain a study log within other QDAS (through a combination of save techniques and memos or notes). In some cases, it is more effective to simply keep a separate activity log.

Data Types

Feature	What to Consider	How It Varies
Document types	What types of document files will you be working with?	A few QDAS programs restrict the types of document files you can import into the software, but most support the following: .txt, .rtf, .doc, .docx, .pdf.
Multimedia files	What types of multimedia files will you be working with? Do you want to be able to transcribe audio within the program? Do you want to be able to parse video? Is it important to you that audio/video is synced with text?	Programs vary; where multimedia files are supported, the following types are likely accepted: .mp3, .wma, .wav, .mpg, .mpeg, .mpe, .mp4, .avi, .wmv, .qt, .bmp, .gif, .jpeg, .tiff.
Quantitative data	Will you be incorporating quantitative data sets in your analyses?	Programs vary; where multimedia files are supported, the following types may be accepted: .xls, .xlsx, .txt, .mdb.
Qualitative data sets	Will you need to incorporate previously coded or analyzed qualitative data into your current analyses?	Some QDAS packages make it easy to import analysis projects from other software programs; with others it is possible but tricky; with some it is not possible.
Geospatial data	Would you like to link your data to spatial referents?	Several QDAS programs allow linkages to Google Earth maps; at least one imports Google Earth screen shots as visual data (though you could do this manually as well).
Codebook	Is there a particular way you like to organize your codebook? Do you prefer alphabetical to hierarchical arrangement of codes? Would you like to have code definitions linked to the codes or accessible from the codebook? Would you like the QDAS to scan your data and suggest codes? Would you like to be able to add codes to the codebook from within the coding function? Would you like to be able to import or export a codebook from/to another program?	QDAS programs vary on all of the issues identified at left. In terms of structure, most will allow hierarchical and/or alphabetical ordering of codes in the code list view; some will allow further customization. Some have an actual separate "codebook" with predefined fields, while many simply add codes to the list and allow you to define their properties. Importing/exporting functions for codebooks are of varying utility, when available.

(Continued)

Table 9.3 (Continued)

Data Tagging and Coding Functions

Feature	What to Consider	How It Varies
Code application	What's your preferred mode of coding? Will you do all coding on screen or some on paper to be entered later? Do you want to be able to automatically code structured text by speaker or question?	QDAS coding features include drag and drop coding, autocoding, quick code (by line number), menu-based code selection, right-click coding, and similar uncoding techniques. Most programs offer multiple choices for code application.
Code application display	Do you want visual confirmation each time you add a code to data? Would you like to see all codes applied to a data segment? Would you like to turn on/off coding displays? Would you like to be able to assign specific colors to specific codes?	All QDAS allows you to see what codes have been applied to a segment of data; in most cases display of this information is the default, but in some you must turn on the display or hover over the segment to see the codes applied.
Memos, comments, annotations	How would you like to make notes or comment on your thoughts as you move through coding and analysis? Would you like to append notes to specific files, groups of files, or the whole project (or all of these)? Would you like to link notes to other notes or other files? Would you like to see all attached notes when viewing coded data output? Would you like to be able to see all of your notes without data attached?	Almost all QDAS has some feature to facilitate capturing your commentary on the data, whether it is called a memo, comment, or annotation. Some programs include more than one feature, each defined by a specific commentary role.
Demographics	How do you plan to incorporate demographic information into your analysis? Would you like to link demographic characteristics to an entire file? Would you like to group files by defining demographic characteristics?	Given the range of files accepted by most QDAS, it is increasingly easy to link previously collected demographic information to the qualitative data in your project by importing it (in .xls for example). Many programs also allow you to add defining characteristics to a data file within the QDAS. In either case, links between the demographics and data allow for grouping and filtering.

Data Exploration and Reduction Features

Feature	What to Consider	How It Varies
Coded text retrieval	How would you like to view coded data (how much header or accompanying information would you like)? Would you like coded data reports to be interactive (where clicking on a particular data segment would take you back to that item)?	All QDAS excels at search and retrieval; the differences between programs consist of ease of use, interactivity, and options for additional information (other codes applied to the same segment, demographic or category information).
Code searching	What types of search techniques are most useful to you? (e.g., AND, NEAR, XOR, PART OF)	As above, QDAS programs generally excel at code searching as well, but differ on ease of use. Most include Boolean, proximity, and semantic operators that can be combined to define distinct search criteria.
Matrices	What kinds of data would you like to be able to include in a matrix display? Would you prefer numeric or textual output? How important is it to you that cells in the matrix output are active (i.e., can be clicked on to take you to source data)? In what format would you like to export your matrices?	QDAS programs typically provide a range of matrix functions to assist in finding and exploring relationships among data, sources, codes, etc., particularly code frequencies and co-occurrences. Some are directly linked to various data displays. Programs vary on whether/how queries are saved and/or exported.
Word search	Will you want to do word searches? Word counts? Key-word-in-context or regular expression pattern reports? Would you like to search one file or the whole data set? What type of output are you interested in?	Most QDAS offers some word search or word count function; the flexibility of defining the search (within and across files) varies.
Data displays	What kind of data displays will you find helpful? Would you like to construct your own theoretical model within the software? Would you like the software to build charts, cluster analysis dendrograms, or plots based on your sources, coding, or data?	QDAS programs are increasingly expanding ways to visually display your data. Various maps, charts, models, cluster analysis, and multidimensional scaling are available options.

The issue of computer platform is more straightforward: Do you typically work on a PC or a Mac? Most QDAS was developed for PC platforms, requiring Mac users to double-check compatibility and functionality of a specific software package. However, Windows emulation tools for Macs have closed this gap for many QDAS programs. The speed and stability of a given program will depend on the memory and processing specifications of your computer, and on the size and complexity of your data set (see Koenig [n.d.] for results of an experiment comparing the speed and stability of older versions of a few programs on common functions).

Though most QDAS runs well most of the time, there will undoubtedly be instances where you will seek support—either for the technical side of the software or for user-interface and training issues. QDAS developers place different emphasis on customer support; some are extremely responsive to online, email, or telephone inquiries while others are less so. Online user reviews often provide valuable information on how helpful a company's customer support services are. As mentioned above, having a local resource for software support is worth considering in the decision process.

One of the less intuitive logistical considerations in evaluating QDAS programs is determining where your data and software files can or must be stored. The first question relates to internal/integrated versus external/path-linked data files. Internal or integrated files are created when you upload data into QDAS and the program makes a copy of the data to store within the program. This increases the file size of your software-based project, but has the advantage of keeping all of your data and information together in one place. External or path-linked data files remain stored in a specific location—on your computer, a shared or network drive, or on the Web—while the QDAS stores only the information that you generate about the data. This substantially decreases the size of the software-based project but can also create problems if the original data sources are modified or moved.

Similarly, there are various locations on a computer to store a QDAS-generated project file. Some programs specify preferred local drive locations (e.g., My Documents or Program Files), so that automatic backup copies of your work can be made; most programs allow QDAS projects to be stored on network drives; and there is a movement toward storing data and project files on the Web. Added to these considerations are security and file-sharing issues associated with data location. Security concerns relate to loss of data if stored locally (in case of computer theft or crash), controlling access to data (both unauthorized access and version control) if stored on a shared or network drive, and Internet security risks if stored on the Web. File-sharing, at the level of data or QDAS project, can be accomplished with files stored at any of these locations, but with varying ease, efficiency, and control over access and changes.

A final, very important, logistical consideration is your subjective assessment of the ergonomics and aesthetics of a given QDAS user interface. Your initial impressions may be influenced by whether you are used to working in Windows or

Mac operating systems and whether you have previously worked with a particular QDAS. You will likely find yourself comparing what is similar and different from your normal computer use, identifying what you like and dislike, and finding things you do not understand. All QDAS programs will have a bit of a learning curve while you figure out what features are where and how to most efficiently accomplish coding and analysis tasks. With most QDAS, a little bit of time spent "playing" with the program can go a long way toward assessing how it fits your needs. To this end, almost all QDAS developers offer a free trial or demonstration period, during which you have access to the software to test it with your own data. Most also offer multimedia demonstrations and tutorials online, with supporting manuals and help functions. Taking some time to consider these various logistical issues can contribute to narrowing the field of potential QDAS packages, before coding and analysis features are compared. A few additional logistical issues relate to team-based research, as described below.

Team-Based Functions

As mentioned, your choice of QDAS can have implications for file sharing among members of a research team, with some programs designed to facilitate team-based work, others merely to accommodate it. One of the benefits of the movement of QDAS to the Web is the ability to have team members simultaneously access and work on a single project file, eliminating the need for file swaps and merges—but making an activity or research log even more essential. Most QDAS programs have been less rigorous than their quantitative counterparts when it comes to generating automatic logs of changes made to the codebook, coding, or queries, though there is movement in that direction. Some QDAS programs require creative thinking and work-arounds to generate a consistent and meaningful log of research activities to keep track of who is doing what within the project file. In the end, it depends on what you would like to capture and for what purpose; in many cases, a standing "research log" memo will perform better than an automatic log because it allows the analyst to incorporate comments or questions about what s/he was thinking at the time, better explaining research progress. This can be a helpful practice, even for the individual researcher.

QDAS does a bit better in the realm of supporting intercoder agreement or reliability checks, with most packages offering some way for two coders to compare coding of a single file, whether by calculation of percent agreement or a kappa score. For any QDAS package, it is important to understand how agreement is calculated by the software so that you can determine how to interpret software-generated assessments of intercoder reliability. In most cases, these reports serve as initial markers of disagreement that should be followed up with an element of qualitative comparison between coders. Different programs support qualitative comparison of intercoder agreement to different degrees, by facilitating (or not) printed versions of fully coded documents, for example.

Data Types

When it comes to specific file types supported by QDAS, the list is ever-growing. All of the major QDAS programs now accept some (usually wide) range of document and multimedia formats, as listed in more detail in Table 9.3. QDAS programs are also becoming increasingly robust mixed method analysis tools, allowing researchers to import quantitative data sets for inclusion alongside or integration into qualitative analyses. Linkages to geospatial referents such as Google Earth or other maps further enhance the depth and scope of the analyses possible in QDAS. And perhaps one of the more relevant features of several QDAS packages for this chapter is that QDAS increasingly recognizes and can work with qualitative data sets created in a different QDAS program. Researchers can now move old data sets into new software and continue work, reducing the pressure to find *the perfect* QDAS for current and future needs.

Coding

The issue of user-interface preference re-emerges when discussing QDAS coding features. All QDAS provides some (or many) mechanism(s) for creating a codebook, applying codes to files, viewing codes applied to a file, adding memos or comments to the coded material, and linking demographic or other categorical information to the data. The differences among programs boil down to user-perceived functionality, efficiency, and effectiveness to accomplish coding goals. For example, in some programs, coding is accomplished by dragging a code "onto" a segment of text; in others, you drag the text "into" the code. The process (function and effect) is essentially the same, but the ergonomics and efficiency may differ. Your past experience and familiarity with particular software programs, along with your preferred computer work style (mouse-, hot key-, or menu-driven) will likely be the biggest factor in choosing among QDAS coding features.

Figure 9.2 provides examples of text and image coding in three QDAS programs. The differences between the three are slight, despite the different source data being coded. In each, a code list is displayed in the toolbar margin. Data are selected by highlighting (or "framing" in the case of the image), and coding is accomplished through drag-and-drop. Applied codes are displayed in the margin of the data file. Coding screens in other QDAS programs are very similar.

Data Exploration and Reduction Features

One of the fundamental reasons for using QDAS is to facilitate review, exploration, and reduction of qualitative data to present a comprehensive response to a particular research objective. In this regard again, QDAS packages offer many of the same features, bundled slightly differently. All programs offer coded text retrieval, most by simply clicking on the desired code or item. Most also provide some form of word search and/or count function within or across files, adding an

Figure 9.2   Coding Screens for Text and Image Coding in Three QDAS Programs

Coding screen in NVivo 9

Coding screen in MAXQDA

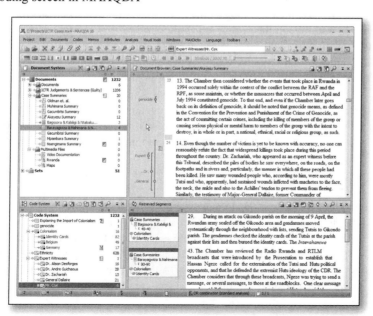

Image coding in QDA Miner

element of content analysis. Building on these two basic reporting functions, QDAS programs enable multiple searches for cross-cutting, co-occurring, or related codes (themes) using Boolean, proximity, and semantic commands, many of which can be combined further with noncoded data (for instance demographic or word search items). Data matrices provide a way to slice data by key study characteristics to compare coding frequency and code salience across groups (see Chapter 7), and though they often return numeric results, the cells of the matrix are "live" to the data and provide easy access back to the coded files. QDAS is also advancing quickly into the realm of more complex reductions and visualizations of qualitative (coded) information, providing cluster analyses, tree diagrams, charts, models, and multidimensional scaling of coded data as visual representations to assist in identifying larger, overarching themes (see Figure 9.3). The data management features of QDAS can be important in data exploration as well, providing easy ways to filter a search and quick accounts of who and what is included in the analysis.

Figure 9.3 provides some examples of data visualizations available in different software packages. Many current QDAS programs (ATLAS.ti, MAXQDA, NVivo 9, QDA Miner, and Dedoose) offer a few or several of these options; others stick to more text- and windows-based features (The Ethnograph, HyperRESEARCH, and Qualrus). If there is a certain type of data visualization or reduction function you are interested in, it is worth investigating a few QDAS websites. The line chart illustrated in QDA Miner below is a helpful tool for examining trends in data over time. The concept map taken from ATLAS.ti allows

Figure 9.3   Sample Data Visualizations From Three QDAS Programs

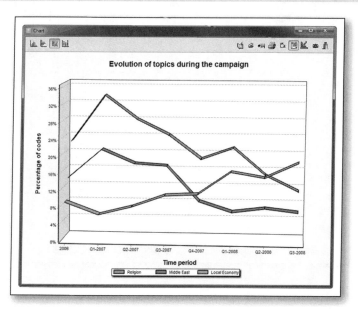

Line chart from QDA Miner comparing the evolution of three prominent topics over the course of a political campaign.

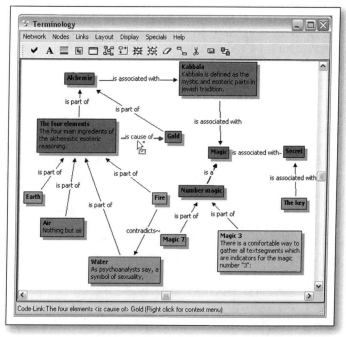

A network concept map from Atlas.ti linking the elements/topics within the analysis.

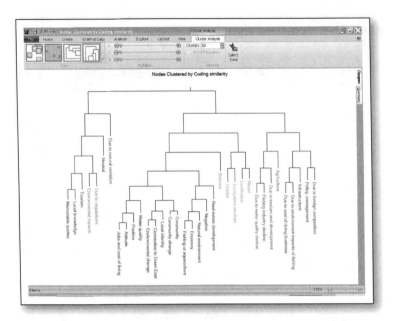

A cluster analysis dendrogram from NVivo 9 showing similarity of coding among nodes.

analysts to arrange elements from the QDAS project (codes, sources, data) in a flexible and evolving spatial representation of the connections among them, and to label and define these connections as they become apparent. The final cluster analysis dendrogram from NVivo 9 provides a quick visual review of how study codes (nodes) co-occur or cluster together. QDAS cluster analysis features offer different options, clustering on words per source rather than code application by transcript, for example. Note that both the concept map and cluster diagram could be helpful early in the analysis process, before coding is completed, or once several rounds of coding are finished.

QDAS packages that offer advanced data visualizations differ primarily on form rather than function for these types of tasks. Constructing certain searches or queries will be easier in some QDAS than others, but the output or results will be similar. As described in the section on size and complexity above, for a relatively small, straightforward analysis, nearly any QDAS program will do the basics of coded text retrieval, co-occurrence, and linkage with demographic or source data. As your analysis tasks (and data mix) become more complex, your QDAS selection process will focus more closely on the advanced organizational and analytic capabilities of the most-developed QDAS packages to determine which offers the best set of tools for a given objective.

SUMMING UP

The impressive proliferation of QDAS available to support researchers' applied thematic analyses has raised the standard of all of the QDAS packages in the last several years. No longer limited to search and retrieve functions (nor to textual— or qualitative—data for that matter), the range of QDAS programs addresses researchers' varied needs in similar, yet unique, ways. To choose among them, one might start with the more straightforward logistical considerations: What will be supported by the project budget, the study computer(s), and the base institution? Team-based work changes or adds to the desired QDAS specifications for a project, as does the nature of the research objective (exploratory or theory-building, for example), and the size and scope of the study. The more data and analysts involved, the greater the need for a sophisticated QDAS program that includes robust data management, intercoder agreement, and data exploration/reduction features. Among the most-developed QDAS packages, personal preference for ergonomics and aesthetics as determined through use of free trial or demo software will likely be a deciding factor. And since applied thematic analysis is a qualitative endeavor, reliant on an analyst's careful reading, labeling, and interpretation of the data, the program that best facilitates these qualities for *you*—through a combination of design, form, and function—will ultimately be your best choice. Below, we provide a matrix of features and functions to help readers with the decision process.

REFERENCES

di Gregorio, S., & Davidson, J. (2008). *Qualitative research design for software users.* New York: Open University Press.

Friese, S. (n.d.). CAQDAS (Computer-Aided Qualitative Data Analysis Software) [Computer software]. Retrieved from http://www.quarc.de/index.php?id=13

Koenig, T. (n.d.). *CAQDAS comparison.* Economic and Social Research Council. Retrieved from http://www.restore.ac.uk/lboro/research/software/caqdas_comparison.php#intangibles

Lewins, A., & Silver, C. (2009). *Choosing a CAQDAS package, a working paper* (6th ed.). Unpublished. NCRM Working Paper. Guildford, UK: University of Surrey. Retrieved from http://eprints.ncrm.ac.uk/791/1/2009ChoosingaCAQDASPackage.pdf

Lyerly, A. D., Steinhauser, K., Namey, E., Tulsky, J., Cook-Deegan, R., Sugarman, J., Walmer, D., & Wallach, E. (2006). Factors that affect decision making about frozen embryo disposition: Infertility patient perspectives. *Fertility and Sterility, 85*(6), 1623–1630.

MacQueen, K. (2005). What to look for in software for qualitative data analysis. In P. Ulin, E. Robinson, & E. Tolley, E., *Qualitative methods in public health: A field guide for applied research* (pp. 172–174). San Francisco, CA: Jossey-Bass.

Tashakkori, A., & Teddlie, C. (2003). *Handbook of mixed methods in social science and behavioral research.* Thousand Oaks, CA: Sage.

Weitzman, E. (1999). Analyzing qualitative data with computer software. *HSR: Health Services Research, 34*(5 Part II), 1241–1263.

Weitzman, E., & Miles, M. (1995) *Computer programs for qualitative data analysis.* Thousand Oaks, CA: Sage.

EXERCISES

1. Visit the CAQDAS site referenced in "Additional Reading" and read the reviews of two QDAS programs. Compare the two on the dimensions outlined in the review (structure, coding, retrieval, etc.). Based on the information presented, which would you choose for your project? Why?

2. Download a demo or free trial for each of the QDAS programs compared in Exercise 1 and explore each for 10 to 15 minutes. How intuitive are the interface and command structures? How easily can you navigate through the program without training or assistance? Would you alter your previous choice of software, based on the hands-on "feel" of the program? Why or why not?

3. Make a list of the five software-related issues covered in this chapter that you consider most important for the successful selection of QDAS for your project. Compare a few QDAS packages on these five characteristics.

ADDITIONAL READING

CAQDAS Networking Project. (n.d.). *Choosing an appropriate CAQDAS package.* Guildford, UK: University of Surrey. Retrieved from: http://www.surrey.ac.uk/sociology/research/researchcentres/caqdas/support/choosing/

Lewins, A., & Silver, C. (2007). *Using software for qualitative data analysis: A step-by-step guide.* London: Sage.

Mihas, P. (2010). *Qualitative software comparison.* Chapel Hill: University of North Carolina, Odum Institute. Retrieved from http://www.odum.unc.edu/odum/content/pdf/CompChart2010-11.pdf

Silver, C., & Fielding, N. (2008). Using computer packages in qualitative research. In C. Willig & W. Stainton-Rogers (Eds.), *The SAGE handbook of qualitative research in psychology* (pp. 334–351). Thousand Oaks, CA: Sage.

10

WRITING UP THEMATIC ANALYSES

LEARNING OBJECTIVES

Upon finishing this chapter, you should be able to:

- Appropriately customize a research report for different types of audiences
- List criteria that are important to include in a qualitative (thematic) research report and explain why each is important
- Effectively structure your presentation of findings from a thematic analysis, including within a mixed methods context

A cardinal rule of writing is to avoid annoying your audience. Although raising the blood pressure of your reader may be the goal of polemical rhetoric, for a research report (or proposal) it can be the fast-track to rejection. Yet we have often read manuscripts or published works that suffer from poor organization, lack of transparency, too much or too little information, unsupported assertions and conclusions, or a convoluted discussion. Any one of these shortcomings can seriously depreciate the readability of an otherwise good report and subsequently frustrate the reader. The purpose of this chapter is to help the reader effectively navigate through the process of preparing and presenting results from a qualitative study. We've extracted the practical guidance contained in the many existing publications on writing up qualitative research (e.g., Bochner, 1996; Denzin, 2000; Gibson & Brown, 2009; Golden-Biddle & Locke, 1999; Goodall, 2008; Green & Thorogood, 2009; Higgs, Horsfall, & Grace 2009; Meloy, 2002; Rubin & Rubin, 2005; Ulin, Robinson, & Tolley, 2005; Wolcott, 2008), and have combined it with our own experience publishing (and not publishing!) thematic data. Congruent with the underlying tenor of this book, we have attempted to present the information in a straightforward way and emphasize the pragmatic aspects of writing and publishing. The chapter covers four primary topics—tailoring writing to audiences, general guidelines for qualitative reports, and suggestions for writing the methods and results sections of qualitative reports. We have also included a brief section on presenting mixed methods research, as it is becoming increasingly common.

WRITING FOR YOUR AUDIENCE

Knowing and writing for your audience is one of the most basic rules of writing, and for good reason. It is probably the single most important principle when writing about research, or anything for that matter. Who the audience is for your research report should guide everything: the degree of specificity and length of certain sections of the report, the type of language used (technical versus lay), the overall length, framing of the argument, and tone of voice. Although each writing case is unique, some general rules of thumb can be applied for specific audiences.

Corporate and Lay Audiences

Private sector and lay audiences expect to get the bottom line up front, with little or no jargon. Unlike academics, and to a lesser degree funders, readers from the business and general public sector audiences typically do not spend a great deal of time reading long articles and analyzing every detail. As such, the message needs to be concise and written in clear colloquial language. Use bullets and graphics where appropriate. The report should also deemphasize methods and instead highlight findings. Along with the findings, the "so what?" factor needs to be made explicit. For corporate audiences, a good rule of thumb in this regard is to include at least one practical recommendation for each of the primary findings presented. For lay audiences, each finding might be followed by a possible implication or two for daily life. You can do this within the narrative itself or graphically. Opportunity maps are wonderful examples of the latter. Figure 10.1 shows a matrix-form opportunity map. The qualitative study aimed to better understand the experience of having a cold to inform product development for a large pharmaceutical company (Morris & Lund, 2001). Key findings from the research indicated that having a cold was not a one-dimensional experience. Rather, individuals tended to conceptually divide the experience into four stages—self-diagnosis (SD), getting a cold (GAC), having a cold (HAC), and getting over a cold (GOAC). Existing cold products on the market, however, tended to be limited to only a few dimensions of the entire experience. The map revealed the gaps between consumer need and experience and product availability, thus pointing to important market opportunities.

Opportunity maps assume many forms. Decision models, which explicitly designate key points in a decision process, are easily transformed into opportunity maps, whereby the researcher links a potential intervention to individual decision points.

Figure 10.1   Opportunity Map, The Cold Experience

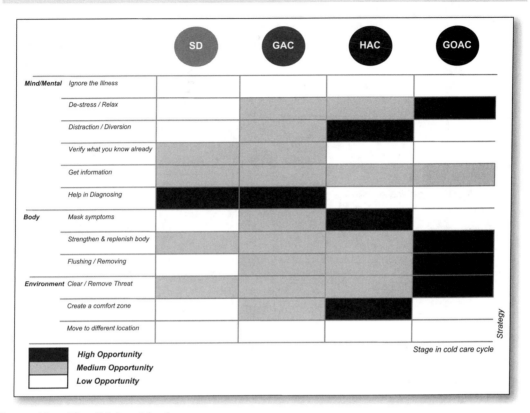

Source: Adapted from E-Lab model, n.d.

In Figure 10.2, we have annotated a decision model based on the work of Ryan and Martinez (1996) to illustrate this technique. The model depicts a part of the decision process that mothers in rural Mexico go through when they have to decide how to manage and treat their child's diarrhea (a leading cause of death among children worldwide). We have added hypothetical intervention points, assuming that the programmatic objective is to increase appropriate use of medication.

Academic/Scientific Audiences

Scientific audiences and journal readers vary with respect to their expectations of how a report should be written. Parameters are quite different across and within disciplines. For starters, many journals simply don't publish qualitative research (although you need to distinguish between those who don't and those who would but don't get many qualitative submissions). Other journals may not be interested in quantitative data, which would rule out mixed methods analyses. Standards

Figure 10.2 Annotated Ethnographic Decision Model of Medical Choice

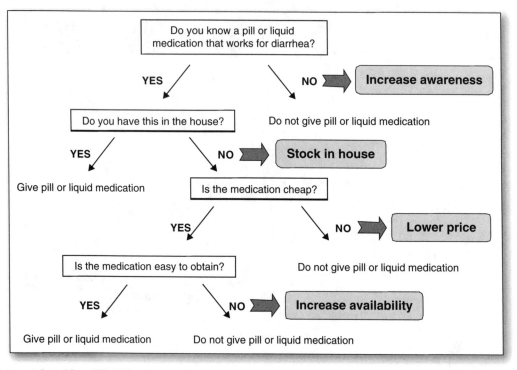

Source: Adapted from Hill, 1998.

also vary. Journals from some fields, for example, might be more likely than others to accept study reports that are based on smaller, nonprobabilistic samples (e.g., anthropology). Space limits also vary across journals and should be considered when planning a manuscript. For these reasons, and others, the first step in writing a manuscript for a peer-reviewed journal is to identify a specific journal for submission. Look through recent copies of the journal and see what has been published. Conversely, identify where key articles for your topic are being published. Try to locate impact scores for journals in your field. And if you are in doubt about whether or not your study/manuscript may or may not be appropriate for a certain journal, send an email to the editor with a brief summary of your idea; in many cases an editor can provide relatively clear direction.

Once you have identified a journal, outlining and writing begin. The high-level outline for most scientific research reports includes an abstract, introduction/ literature review, methods, findings or results, discussion, and/or conclusion. In some instances, the term "lessons learned" might replace the "results" header, thereby softening the audiences' expectations regarding more quantitative/statistically-oriented findings. Note, however, that the "lessons learned" approach is generally intended for reporting experience with program implementation rather than findings from research.

For academic audiences, jargon is also tolerated somewhat more than with other audiences. So too is a focus on the theoretical dimensions of the research problem. In fact, emphasizing the theoretical relevance of one's findings is often the prime objective in academically oriented manuscripts. How much theory is prudent to include, though, will vary from one publication to the next.

Another element that must be considered, especially with qualitative studies, is the amount of space allowed for a research report in any given journal. The range varies greatly, from less than 1,500 words to 5,000 or more. Qualitative studies typically require more space since the core findings are often presented in the form of a narrative (as opposed to tables), with supporting quotes. Often, you will be required to make strategic sacrifices if you are intent on publishing in a journal on the lower end of the word-limit continuum. One of the authors on one occasion, for example, had to make the choice to either cut the manuscript length in half or look elsewhere to publish. After deliberating, and concluding he could convey enough important information in half the amount of space, he chose the former option (see Guest, Bunce, Johnson, Akumatey, & Adeokum, 2005a).

In most cases, qualitative research reports are primarily in the form of a narrative with quotes, tables, and figures employed as supporting information. With posters prepared for large conferences or meetings, however, the balance of text to graphics is typically reversed. Space is limited to what can be legibly presented on the prescribed poster size, and to attract and maintain a reader's attention, greater emphasis should be placed on photos, figures, tables, and other graphic elements.

Funders

Some funders (e.g., USAID, private foundations) are another potential consumer of research and tend to fall somewhere in between lay and academic audiences. To a certain degree, the suggestions for corporate and lay audiences apply to funders as well—concision and nontechnical language are always a good idea, as is the practice of highlighting the implications of a study's findings. Below we've adapted material from an unpublished study report for a government agency as an illustration. The qualitative study documented community perceptions and decision making regarding malaria treatment and vaccinations in Africa, in anticipation of the roll out of a potential malaria vaccine (adapted from Hinson, Bocoum, & Kouanda, 2010, p. 56).

Community members seemed to be very concerned with the fact that the vaccine would not protect anyone over five years of age, or pregnant women. Many community members described how pregnant women suffer from miscarriages and should be protected. Caregivers frequently reminded the interviewers that, although children suffer, adults also suffer from malaria. Service providers confirmed that community members might be upset about this, and reported that for current vaccine campaigns, they are often asked why vaccines are only for children.

Recommendation: It will be extremely important to address why the vaccine is only available for children under five years of age. It will also be essential to address why pregnant women are not eligible for vaccination.

Unlike journals, there are usually no space constraints when writing a research report for a funding agency. A common practice, therefore, is to provide a relatively long and detailed report, but to preface it with an executive summary that synthesizes the key points and highlights recommendations. Two other general trends for these types of reports are including more detail than normal when describing the background of the project and devoting proportionately less space to the methods section. Note, however, that individuals within funding agencies differ greatly with respect to their scientific expertise and tolerance/desire for methodological detail. Again, invest time in learning about the expectations and preferences of your principal audience.

A Few Basic Writing Tips

Process

- Draft the title and abstract first. This forces you to organize your thoughts and think about what your key message (i.e., your hook) is.
- Before you start, draft an outline of what you want to write. Be as detailed as possible.
- Make sure that all of your sections are constructed around your main message.
- Look at your outline; make sure you know how you're going to conceptually connect sections. In some cases, they will flow naturally; in other cases, a transitional sentence or subheader will be needed.
- Use headers and subheaders as guideposts for both you and the reader.
- Set aside time each day or week to write. The more uninterrupted time you can devote the better. It's OK to work on parts of the manuscript out of order if that helps get the job done.
- Use active voice.
- Keep sentences concise.
- When finishing a writing session, try to stop in a place where you still have something to say. This makes it easier to start writing again in the next session.
- For each of your paragraphs, make sure your first sentence sets the stage for the rest of the paragraph (remember learning about "topic sentences" in English class?).
- Don't spend a lot of time editing your first draft. The goal is to get your ideas to paper. Focus on just writing; worry about word-smithing and proofreading later. Even the best writers may go through 5 to 10 drafts to get a finished product.
- Have colleagues review your draft(s) and give constructive feedback.

(Continued)

- Once the manuscript is completed, proofread several times and have a colleague proof again. Note that citation errors are the most common problem with submitted manuscripts (Onwuegbuzie, Combs, Slate, & Frels, 2009), so make sure the text and the reference list correspond exactly.

Content

- Make sure the body of the manuscript does what you say you're going to do in the abstract and introduction.
- In the "Results" section, use illustrative examples whenever possible, but keep them concise.
- Carefully consider any possible negative consequences your writing may have on the study participants or their community. As a researcher, your primary obligation is to protect your study participants.
- When referring to participants, specify the subgroup you're talking about (Is it everyone? Just subgroup a or b?).
- If presenting information from different data collection methods, always let the reader know which data type you are referring to (e.g., was finding X derived from a survey, in-depth interview, focus group?).

GUIDELINES FOR QUALITATIVE RESEARCH

The question of how to present qualitative research findings came to the foreground in the mid-1980s (Flick, 1998). Despite attention paid to data presentation in the subsequent decades, many researchers still perceive a lack of agreed-upon guidelines for reporting qualitative research (Caan, 2001; Roberts, Dixon-Woods, Fitzpatrick, Abrams, & Jones, 2002) and advocate increased standardization (Dingwall, Murphy, Watson, Greatbatch, & Parker, 1998; Hoddintott & Pill, 1997; Popay, Rogers, & Williams, 1998). Lists of criteria have been created to aid in this endeavor (Boulton, Fitzpatrick, & Swinburn, 1996; Seale & Silverman, 1997). Most of our examples in this chapter are derived from health sciences research, a field that has a history of (and literature) establishing standards and evidence-based practice. However, the issues we discuss are germane to all disciplines that engage in qualitative research. In this section, we present a summary of guidelines that was generated from a literature review on the subject. Note that we do not address the issue of whether or not guidelines should exist, and be adopted, for qualitative research. We present our arguments in favor of the affirmative elsewhere (Guest & MacQueen, 2008). Our suggestions in this chapter are primarily intended to help readers increase transparency of the data collection and analysis process and, subsequently, get their research published. Transparency is what makes evaluation of a research study possible and is the key to writing a good report.

Note that this section does not cover criteria that apply universally to all types of research—solid literature review, good research design and appropriate choice of methods, clear description of procedures, logic of argument, clear writing, and relevance to current theory or practice. These are important whether one is writing about an ethnographic study or a highly controlled laboratory experiment. We therefore limit the scope of this chapter to issues that are especially important for thematic analyses. We divide our suggestions into two fundamental components of research reports—the "Methods" and "Results" sections. At the end of the chapter (Table 10.3), we provide the reader with a checklist that summarizes what we believe to be key elements of a good qualitative research report.

WRITING THE "METHODS" SECTION

Basic Study Parameters

In our view, you can enhance the readability of the methods section of your report by beginning with a general overview of the study design and other basic parameters. Let the reader know up front whether the study is mixed methods, purely qualitative, or a qualitative component of a larger study. Specify when and where the study took place, what data collection methods were used, and among which population(s). It is also a good idea at this point to note the total sample size for the study, as well as details regarding consent procedures and ethics committee approval(s). Remember that the overall purpose of these few introductory paragraphs is to set the context for the methodological details that follow.

Sampling

Based on our review of the literature, we found that most authors agree that presentation of qualitative research should include a clear description of the sampling rationale and recruitment process (Anderson, 2010; Bluff, 1997; Fossey, Harvey, McDermott, & Davidson, 2002; Greenhalgh & Taylor, 1997; Hoddintott & Pill, 1997; Malterud, 2001; Russell & Gregory, 2003). Let the reader know how individuals were recruited. Was it through advertisements? If so, where were the ads placed? Perhaps recruitment was done by personally approaching individuals. If so, where and how was this done? Include some detail, but keep space limits in mind.

Likewise, a description of the sample itself is recommended (Miles & Huberman, 1994). At the very least, describe what eligibility criteria were used for your study, if any, and why, and then describe what types of individuals/ groups were selected. If the study involves more than one population/group, specify how many were sampled in each group. If more than one data collection method was used, clarify your sampling procedures further by indicating how many sampling units were selected for each method. Finally, describe the sampling approach used for each method/group. Note that for qualitative studies a nonprobabilistic sampling approach is the norm and a purposive sample is generally recommended (Giacomini & Cook, 2000; Popay, Rogers, & Williams, 1998) This does not mean that probabilistic sampling strategies cannot be, nor are not, used in qualitative research. When feasible and appropriate, they often are. It's usually the case, however, that for field-based qualitative research, obtaining a probabilistic sample is not feasible. For more discussion on this topic, see Guest and MacQueen, (2008). In their *Western Journal of Nursing Research* article, Bach, Ploeg, and Black (2009) provide an exceptionally thorough sampling and recruitment description, shown in the "Sampling and Recruitment Description Example" text box.

Sampling and Recruitment Description Example

<u>Sample and Setting</u>

Participants were recruited from an ICU [intensive care unit] and a cardiac respiratory care unit in a large teaching hospital in southwestern Ontario, Canada. These settings were chosen because, as previously indicated, approximately 42% of patients spend their last days in complex care settings (Heyland, Lavery, Tranmer, Shortt, & Taylor, 2000) and yet the role of nurses in end-of-life decision-making in such settings has not been extensively studied. Together, these two units have 17 beds and admit patients with a mean age of 60 years. Patients admitted to this particular ICU and CRCU experience complex medical, surgical, and cardiac issues and often require mechanical ventilation, dialysis, and fluid resuscitation related to drug overdose; the mortality rate is approximately 22% per year.

Participant recruitment involved the use of a variety of methods, including posters, informal meetings, and direct requests for participation. All clinical managers were given a poster, which briefly outlined the purpose of the research study and gave the researcher's name and contact information, to place in their units. A more personal approach was also used, where the researcher was present in the unit on several occasions to identify and gather groups of three to four nurses to speak with informally. It was hoped that this more personal approach, rather than a poster, would encourage some of the nurses to participate, would express the value of hearing their voices, and would emphasize the importance of understanding their nursing role at the end of life. Over the next several weeks, with little response to the above methods, nurses were effectively recruited through the researcher spending time on the units and identifying nurses who would be available for a spontaneous interview. The charge nurses also supported recruitment by posting a schedule and asking nurses to choose their interview times.

(Continued)

(Continued)

Potential participants were identified by purposive sample techniques. Participants had to be working in their unit for at least 2 years and therefore had to have reached a level of competence and had to have an awareness of the overall goals of their working environment (Benner, 1984). Consistent with Strauss and Corbin (1998), theoretical sampling was used to deliberately choose individuals who could contribute to the evolving conceptual framework. The participants would be able to provide rich descriptions of the phenomenon being explored and through their experience could further our understanding of the emergent themes. Sampling continued until saturation of categories and their properties was reached.

Source: Bach, Ploeg, & Black, 2009.

Most guidelines suggest that purposive sample sizes be determined on the basis of theoretical saturation—that is, the point in data analysis when new incoming data produce little or no change to the existing code network (Glaser & Strauss, 1967). The number of participants should be stated, as well as evidence that theoretical saturation or data redundancy was achieved (Bluff, 1997; Giacomini & Cook, 2000). We agree with these sampling guidelines, but further add that clearer explanations of, and empirical evidence for, theoretical saturation are needed. If saturation was not the criterion used to determine sample size, what was? In some cases, an author may cite one of the few evidenced-based articles for nonprobabilistic sample sizes (e.g., Guest, Bunce, & Johnson, 2006; Romney, Batchelder, & Weller, 1986) or state other determining factors, such as budget or logistical considerations. If a purposive sample cannot be obtained, and a convenience sample had to be used, it is a good idea to provide the specific reason(s) for employing the less-preferred sampling method.

For larger, more complex studies, explaining sampling parameters in a narrative form can get confusing for the reader, which is why we recommend using a table in such cases. A table can then be followed by, or include if space permits, a more in-depth written description of the targeted groups and rationale for selection. Below, we provide an example sampling table from one of the author's studies (without the in-depth description). This was a mixed methods study that included several data collection events conducted in two sites over the course of 18 months.

Data Collection and Processing Procedures

Bluff (1997) notes that authors of qualitative research should provide a description of when, where, and how data were collected. We agree with this basic suggestion but provide further guidance as to what specifically should be included in this description. At minimum, the year(s) data were collected should be reported. If temporal factors, such as seasonality, day of the week, or time of day, potentially impact the research process, these also need to be described. The region of the

Table 10.1   An Example of Sampling Parameters by Data Collection Method

Data Collection Method	Target Group/Area (age)	Sampling Approach	Sample Size
Participant Observation	High transmission areas/ venues	Census	**≤ 20 venues, 5 days per venue** (≤10 venues × 2 sites)
Focus Groups	Married men (18–49) Single men (18–49) Single women (18–49) Married women (18–49) Sex workers (18+)	Purposive	**20 groups** (2 focus groups × 5 groups × 2 sites)
Survey	Men (18–49)	Time/space	**1,600** (800 men × 2 sites)
In-depth Interviews	Men (18–49) Single women (18–49) Married women (18–49) Sex workers (18–49)	Time/space for men Purposive for all other groups	**150** (30 men; 15 per each of the other 3 groups) × 2 sites

country where research took place should be reported, unless there is reason to believe it will stigmatize a community or violate participant confidentiality. The specific context from which participants were recruited, as well as where data were collected (e.g., local bar, clinic), should be specified. The type of research instrument used to guide data collection should also be described. Was it a semistructured guide? If so, what part was structured? Were the questions asked verbatim, and in the same way of all participants? Or, was a less-structured approached used—for example, just domains of inquiry used to guide questioning?

In some cases, it can also be highly informative to include the precise questions asked of participants (if using a semistructured approach to questioning), to provide a richer sense of the responses' context. These can be included in the main body of text, a table, or an appendix. Guest and colleagues (2008), for example, presented the two questions from their in-depth interview guide, which formed the basis of their qualitative analysis. Note that the primary reason they included the verbatim questions is that their thematic analysis was part of a mixed methods study. The authors felt that the reader needed to see both the quantitative and qualitative questions used in the analyses to better understand how the two data sets related to each other. Below is an excerpt from their article (Guest et al. 2008, p. 1004):

For this analysis, theme frequencies were generated only for themes that emerged in response to two open-ended questions and corresponding subquestions:

1. Has participating in the TDF study affected your condom use? If so, please explain.

> *How do you feel about these changes?*
> *What do you think are the reasons for these changes?*

2. Has participating in the TDF study affected the number of sexual partners you have?

> *How do you feel about these changes?*
> *What do you think are the reasons for these changes?*

Recording and Transcription

Audio-recording qualitative data collection events is common practice, as it compensates for limitations of human memory and note-taking abilities (Fitzpatrick & Boulton, 1996). If data collection was recorded, this should be clearly specified. We recognize, along with others (e.g., Carey & Gelaude, 2008), that audiotaping is not always possible, or that there may be ethical considerations that mitigate against this level of documentation (see MacQueen, 2008). Exceptions can also be made for less verbose, more systematically collected qualitative data, such as freelists and pile sorts; notes can typically capture these data accurately. If audiorecording is not employed, for whatever reason, justification should be provided for its absence.

In our view, transcription of recordings is preferred but not always necessary (in fact, McLellan, MacQueen, & Niedig [2003] argue that transcription in and of itself does not guarantee rigor and in some cases can detract from it). Transcription is also expensive and time-consuming. However, when done properly, transcription makes analysis easier and provides more analytic opportunities: transcripts can be scrutinized more quickly than tapes and content analyzed using computers (note that you can code sound files as well, but you can't "scan" reports sorted by code in the same way you can with text). Transcripts are especially invaluable in team-based and multisite research, because both require a significant amount of data sharing and subsequent discussion of content (MacQueen et al., 2001). If transcripts are generated, the translation/transcript process should be made explicit (Pitchforth, Porter, van Teijlingen, & Forrest Keenan, 2005). Likewise, if transcription was not carried out, we suggest providing an explanation as to why not.

Reflexivity

Because qualitative data collection uses open-ended instruments that require a more informal type of interaction between researcher and participant, it is often argued that the potential for a researcher to bias responses is greater than for fixed-response surveys. Researchers have therefore advised authors of qualitative studies to be reflexive in their presentation (Dey, 1993; Mays & Pope, 2000; Pitchforth, et al., 2005), and describe how their presence may have affected the data collection process (Byrne, 2001; Horsburgh, 2003; Malterud, 2001). Although in some cases this practice might be justified, we argue that the researcher, research process, and research context can affect *all* types of data collection (see, for example, Macalino, Celentano, Latkin, Strathdee, & Vlahov, 2002; McCombie & Anarfi, 2002; Parsons, 1974; Paulhus, 1991; Rosenthal, 1966; Weeks & Moore, 1981). Given the pervasiveness of this methodological issue, it doesn't seem productive or fair to ask practitioners of qualitative research to discuss reflexivity or response bias to a greater degree than researchers in other disciplines (see also Chapter 4). In line with good overall scientific practice, we therefore recommend that qualitative researchers simply report the known potential for, and measures taken to minimize, relevant biases in their studies, as one would with any scientific study. The amount of detail needed will vary from one scientific publication to another, with social science–oriented journals generally requiring the most detail and biomedical journals the least.

Data Analysis Processes

One of the most common transgressions in presenting qualitative research is what we call the "black box" approach to data analysis. Some authors simply state that they "conducted a thematic analysis" in the belief that this is sufficient information (sadly, for some journals and audiences, this continues to be acceptable). We feel that inadequate description of analytic procedures and reasoning is one of the weakest areas in published qualitative research. In the paragraphs that follow, we provide some guidance as to what might be included in a comprehensive description.

We recognize that the appropriate method of data analysis depends on the research objectives and nature of the data collected, but certain fundamental steps can be taken to produce a better accounting of the analytic process. Describing decision rules for arriving at judgments during data analysis (Cesario, Morin, & Santa-Donato, 2002), or an "audit trail" of the analysis process (Hills, 2000; Miles & Huberman, 1994; Sharts-Hopko, 2002) enhances transparency; both are examples of good research practice. This includes describing how codes were developed and applied to the data, and the method used to address coding reliability (Carey & Gelaude, 2008; MacQueen, McLellan-Lemal, Bartholow, & Milstein, 2008). When multiple coders are engaged, the method for assessing intercoder agreement should be described (see Chapter 4). Finally, if qualitative data analysis software is used, the name and version of the program should be provided, along with the reporting functions used in the analysis (Anderson, 2010).

As a further indication of validity, some authors recommend that researchers seek and document feedback on their interpretation of data from the study population whenever possible (Bluff, 1997; Drisko, 1997; Giacomini & Cook, 2000; Mays & Pope, 2000). This process is sometimes referred to as "member checking" (Byrne, 2001), and can be a good gauge as to whether or not the research team's interpretation is valid. If space permits, authors can also provide code definitions (perhaps in an appendix) as an additional means for reviewers to assess validity. Access to code definitions allows other researchers to replicate the study (assuming interview questions are also available) and assess reliability. They could also serve as a foundation for codebooks in other studies.

WRITING THE "FINDINGS" OR "RESULTS" SECTION

Before delving into the primary findings of your study, we recommend first writing a description of the study population(s). This may be as straightforward as including a table with aggregate demographic summaries of study participants.

For richer, ethnographic types of studies, a thicker description of the study population may be warranted (and expected by readers), and include a description of the physical and/or cultural context in which participants are embedded, particularly if participant observation was used in the course of the study. Exactly what, and how many, data are presented in this initial section depends on the data collection and analysis methods used as well as the target audience for the report.

An introductory section of the "Findings" or "Results" may also include a paragraph or two that orients the reader to the main findings, and how they are organized. The excerpt below, from the work of Chur-Hansen, Russell Winefield, and Beckwith (2009), demonstrates nicely how an orienting paragraph sets up an ensuing presentation of findings. The authors begin the section by discussing the overarching uber-theme of "attachment" and then briefly describe its constituent concepts. The remainder of the "Results" section provides more detail—including illustrative quotes—for each constituent theme (not shown).

Results

All the themes identified can be related to a central theme of "Attachment." Attachment became apparent as a theme after the first interview and was discussed and described by all participants, although the word "attachment" was not used. Rather, participants discussed "love" for the animal, in the lay sense of the word "attachment."... Participants' talk which reflected attachment included discussion of their pets as a significant other, expressing a desire to maintain close physical proximity to the animal, due to a close bond with it, discussion of an avoidance of separation, and grief at possible or past loss of a pet. Illustrative quotes from the interviews are provided for each theme. (pp. 283–284)

In their article describing decision making about disposing of frozen embryos, Lyerly and colleagues (2006) follow a similar structure, but additionally include a description of the study sample:

Results

Subjects ranged in age from 30 to 48 years. Seventy-two percent of the participants were women; 15% were African American (Table 2). In 34 interviews, individuals currently had between 1 and 23 embryos in storage. Thirty-three individuals or couples expected to use some embryos for future attempts at pregnancy, 18 (39%) indicated willingness to donate unused embryos for research, 13 (28%) indicated willingness to donate unused embryos to another couple, 4 (8%) indicated willingness to thaw and discard unused embryos, and 16 (34%) were undecided about the best option for their unused embryos (Table 3). Seven broad themes emerged as important to

(Continued)

decision making about cryopreserved embryos: family and personal issues, trust, definition of the embryo, prospective responsibility to the embryo, responsibility to society, adequacy of information, and lack of acceptable options. (p. 3)

Finding Your Anchor

Now that you've written the introductory paragraph to your "Findings"/"Results" section, the real work begins. Visualize this: you've finished analyzing your 60 in-depth interviews and 20 focus groups (and maybe even 600 surveys if it is a mixed methods study!). Where do you begin to tell your story? This is probably one of the most difficult decisions to make when writing a research report. Data are complex, particularly thematic data that involve cross-cutting and hierarchical themes. Adding multiple sites and populations to the mix increases this complexity exponentially. Complexity can be represented in myriad ways, each potentially as valid and informative as the next. The first step in presenting results, therefore, is to find (or more accurately decide upon) your anchor. What will you lead your story with? What is the primary finding you want to spotlight in your results section (and subsequently refer to in your abstract and introduction)? Once this is established, the rest should follow logically.

For a strictly narrative presentation, you might start the story with what we call uber-themes. These are meta-themes, conceptually comprised of two or more data-driven themes that correspond to your content codes. Meta-themes do not have specific codes associated with them; they are at a higher level of abstraction and not directly observed in the data. If you have a coding tree, these would be your top level categories, or they might even be two or more of the higher level categories combined. What and how you choose to present, in terms of uber-themes, really depends on how your data are configured. Ask yourself, "What are the most interesting findings to my audience?", "What is the most robust data in my data set?" Make a decision and then begin your results section with a brief overview of your high level, uber-themes (as in the previous example on "attachment").

Tables are also excellent anchors. We've often started a "Findings" or "Results" section with a table of theme frequencies. This table can be annotated with comments, verbatim quotes, or virtually any information that conveys your message. Table 10.2 is from one of the author's studies that investigated the acceptability of a vaginal microbicide over a 6-month long study (Guest et al., 2007). The table, which is only a small section of what was actually published, is organized by questions asked of participants (e.g., What did you like about the gel?) and includes the most common themes identified in responses associated with a specific question. This was a longitudinal study in which the exact same questions were asked at various stages in the study, so the table includes data from all four time points at which data were collected. Such a presentation allows the reader to quickly see (and understand) the most common themes. It also reveals patterns over time.

Handwritten margin notes:
- Tell a story
- What do I lead the story with
  - primary finding
- Most interesting findings?
  - what is my most robust data

Table 10.2 Microbicide Acceptability Study: Frequency of Most Common Themes by Question, With Illustrative Quotes*

Theme	Month 1	Month 3	Month 5	Month 6
"Likes" About the Diaphragm and Gel				
Protection *I like it because I know that when I am using this method I am safe and nothing wrong will happen to me. (month 1)*	46	44	46	33
Ease of Use/Inconspicuous *I didn't feel it in the vagina. . . it was like before I wasn't using the diaphragm, it was just the same. (month 5)*	19	12	21	24
Positive Impact on Sex *Penetration is also very easy and is no longer rough and every time after sex I always feel like I could have more. (month 3)*	12	11	4	11
Lubrication (of gel) *[T]he gel lubricates you and it even lubricates when you get dry during the intercourse so it helps a lot. (month 5)*	7	9	9	8
"Dislikes" About the Diaphragm and Gel				
Physical Symptoms *What I don't like I am always wet in my vagina and I had a discharge, felt dizzy and nauseous. (month 1)*	13	5	3	2
Partner Disapproval *At first he said he couldn't penetrate me as he usually does and he doesn't feel comfortable with it. (month 1)*	7	0	0	3
Too Wet/Too Much Lubrication *[W]hen I am having sex with my partner, I become wet. I think this gel creates a lot of wetness. (month 1)*	4	4	3	0
Inconvenience *I have to insert the diaphragm whenever I want to have sex. (month 6)*	3	3	3	4
Smell of Gel *[T]he gel's smell was not good for me, it smelled bad. (month 6)*	1	0	1	3

* All frequencies in the cells refer to the number of unique interview participants expressing a theme.

Figures are another useful starting point for presenting data. For thematic data, graphical representations can take many forms, limited only by an author's imagination. One of the more common qualitatively oriented display methods is concept mapping (Kane & Trochim, 2006; Trochim, n.d.). A concept map is a diagram showing the relationships among concepts. Concepts are usually represented as boxes or circles and are connected to each other (or not) with arrows or other symbols. (Concept maps are used extensively in systems research. There are a plethora of symbols that have been developed and standardized but which vary by academic field.) The lines or arrows indicate some type of relationship between boxes/circles/ovals and so on. For a thematic analysis, boxes typically represent concepts such as themes identified in the data (i.e., codes) or higher level conceptual themes generated by the researcher. For an example with qualitative data, refer to Figure 7.1. In their simplest form, thematic concept maps may simply reflect the hierarchical structure of a coding tree, as depicted below in Figure 10.3.

Concept maps

Figure 10.3   Coding Tree Model Created in NVivo

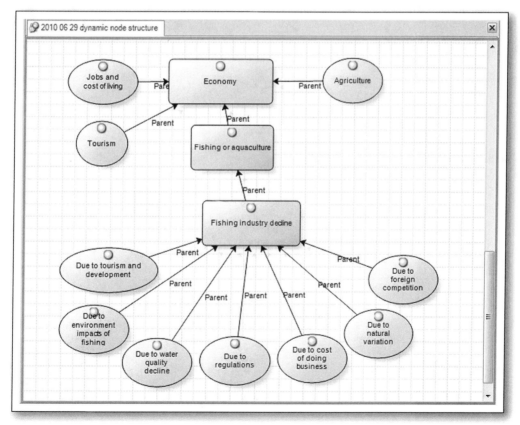

Source: QSR International, 2011.

Nowadays, however, QDA software packages are becoming increasingly sophisticated and some contain concept-mapping functions. Namey generated the concept map in Figure 10.4 with NVivo 9, which shows the interrelationships between themes that formed the larger uber-theme of "control" within the birthing experience. Note that although the model formed the basis for a resulting article (Namey & Lyerly, 2010), it was cut from the final iteration of the published article at the journal editor's suggestion: "We do not feel the addition of Figure One adds greatly to the presentation of findings and so we would suggest that the figure is removed from a re-submitted manuscript."

For more examples of concept maps, we suggest doing a simple Google image search for the term. This will generate more than enough examples to stimulate ideas for a study report.

Conceptual relationships can be amended further by adding symbols denoting valence or intensity. This quantified technique is illustrated in the Kawamura

Figure 10.4   Model of the Multifaceted Concept of "Control" in the Birth Experience

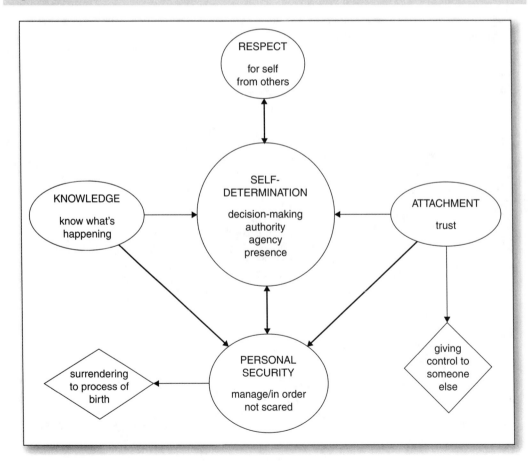

Ivankova, Kohler, & Perumean-Chaney (2009) model shown in Figure 7.5. In such cases, the narrative that follows would necessarily cover both the structure of the model, as well as the associated metrics. Depictions of more complicated conceptual relationships—for example, cluster analysis or multidimensional scaling, as described in Chapter 6—are also good anchor points for beginning the results discussion. Because graph-theoretic models present a relatively holistic picture of the data, the ensuing narrative can systematically delve into the subcomponents and details of the larger model. Note that visual output from any of the data reduction and comparative techniques described in Chapters 6 and 7 are well suited to serve as anchor points.

Structuring the "Findings"/"Results" Narrative

Once you've found your anchor, the next decision to be made is how the rest of the section will be structured. The simplest way to think about this is to ask yourself the basic question: What will the subheaders in this section be? Below, we offer some commonly used strategies, recognizing that the choice of structure is determined to a certain degree by how the introductory paragraph is framed and how one's anchor is presented.

High-Level Themes

Probably the most common method of presenting thematic results is by high-level themes—that is, a high-level theme constitutes a subheader. These leading themes can be of various types. They could be what we have called uber- or meta-themes, which are conceptual themes (i.e., there are no instances of them in the data themselves) comprised of two or more content-driven themes. They may be actual content-driven themes that the author has chosen to highlight from an analysis. Such a choice could include all of the themes—if the number is not too large so as to prohibit an account of each—or, more often, a subset of themes, determined by some benchmark (e.g., the most theoretically important or most frequently expressed). Each higher level theme is described, along with quotes and examples. Part of this description usually includes talking about the themes that comprise the broader theme (i.e., subthemes). If data and space permit, more subthemes and sub-subthemes can be discussed under each uber-theme. Remember to use appropriate headers to indicate the hierarchical nature of your data.

Subheader [handwritten annotation in margin]

There are copious examples of this type of presentation, since it is by far the most common; if you are looking for a specific citation, we offer one of the author's studies, which describes high-level themes associated with acceptability of vasectomy in Tanzania (Bunce et al., 2007). The study entailed both focus groups and in-depth interviews with several stakeholder groups across three districts. After coding the data, the authors conducted frequency reports and cross-tabulations to determine the relative importance of themes in the data and their linkages to one another, using the transcript or data collection event as the unit of analysis. Separate subanalyses were then conducted for each group and district. In their article, the authors sequentially describe six high-level, content-driven themes related to vasectomy acceptability—Economics, Spousal Influence, Religion, Provider Availability/Reputation, Future Uncertainty, and Vasectomy Knowledge. Within each section, they then compare and contrast responses by group and district.

A similar method of presentation, but using only focus group data, can be found in one of the author's studies among Thai military conscripts that investigated the relationship between alcohol consumption and inconsistent condom use with brothel-based sex workers (MacQueen et al., 1996). Data from 10 focus groups indicated that alcohol consumption was related to condom use in five primary ways.

1. Alcohol was consciously used by men to reduce inhibitions that constrained their interpersonal interaction with women and with each other.
2. It reduced inhibitions of individuals to sexual risk taking.
3. It provided a socially acceptable excuse for nonuse of condoms.
4. Alcohol was associated by conscripts with brothel attendance.
5. It was seen to enhance male sexual pleasure, in contrast to condoms, which were said to reduce pleasure.

Research Topic and/or Question

Another approach is to structure the results by your research topics or questions. A simple way to think of, and analyze, data in this way is to review all of the themes associated with a particular question or set of questions asked of the respondents (note: this is where structural codes are useful). You are telling your audience what you asked participants and summarizing how they responded. Each subheader is, therefore, a specific question or topic of inquiry. This method of presentation is particularly useful when your analysis is very targeted and precise and/or is part of a mixed methods analysis. A study conducted by Guest et al. (2005b) provides an example of this method. They conducted a thematic analysis of responses among HIV vaccine trial participants who were asked about their experiences with HIV risk reduction counseling during the trial. The authors structured the results by three domains of inquiry (each comprised of several questions): participants' overall experiences of risk reduction counseling, their perceptions of changes in their sexual behavior during the trial, and their suggestions on how to improve the counseling (note that these domains were the actual question sections on the study's in-depth interview guide). Under each domain, the narrative included descriptions of dominant themes that were expressed by study participants, along with quotes and examples.

In some cases, you may want to structure your findings with a little more granularity, by question. Beskow and colleagues (n.d.) used this approach to present findings from a study pertaining to recruitment for genetic research. Below we present an excerpt from their submitted manuscript (Table 10.3). Note that in addition to structuring their findings by question, they also include an introductory summative paragraph as well as a table with quotes and two levels of responses ("yes or no" and emergent themes). Combining various techniques like this can provide good bang-for-buck in terms of the information/space ratio.

Views About the Acceptability of Recontact for Genetic Research Recruitment

We asked a series of questions to ascertain interviewees' opinions about recontact—not necessarily genotype-driven—for the purposes of further research recruitment. Responses were consistently positive across all of the studies to our baseline question, "Generally speaking, if you're in one study do you think it's all right for researchers to contact you about being in another study?" Overall, a substantial majority (>85%) of interviewees said 'yes'. Many expressed a positive attitude toward research in general, including themes of altruism as well as supporting the goals of research. Several recognized recontact as an efficient way to facilitate research, particularly given that, when contacted, the person could decline further participation. Others suggested that willingness to participate in one study was a likely indicator of willingness to participate in additional research, particularly when the burden involved is low (Table 3).

The primary concern cited with regard to recontact was privacy. Only one person across all of the studies expressed a directly negative view, although several of those whose personal opinion was positive anticipated that other people might have issues with privacy or be distressed by recontact itself (Table 3).

Table 10.3 (Table 3 from example above)   Generally speaking, if you're in one study do you think it's all right for researchers to contact you about being in another study?

Response	Theme	Examples
Yes	Positive attitude toward research, altruism	• Because I think that it will help others, by getting more information as you go … you want to find out one answer, then you keep working to find more answers. (Epilepsy-D03) • I guess I figure anything that will help... figure out what gene it's on or figure out, you know, like what gives kids a predisposition to get it or whatever, I'm happy to do whatever I can to figure it out. (Autism, AGRE-S02)
	Efficient way to facilitate research	• Yeah, I think it's all right for them to contact you because … there's not a large pool of people with those characteristics… [T]hey already got the names and contact numbers … it's easier to do that than go out to the community and recruit new people and try to sift through those names and stuff. So just reasonable to assume that's how that would be done. (Autism, AGRE-S06) • If you don't contact people … that have the problem, and ask or at least offer to do studies, then you can't advance anywhere with it. So the worst they can do is say no. I don't see any problem with that. (Epilepsy-D14)

(Continued)

Table 10.3 (Continued)

Response	Theme	Examples
	Inclination to participate	• I think that if I was able to agree to do one, to be open to that … I don't see a reason why I should have a concern to do another one. (Epilepsy-D15)
	Minimal burden	• Well, I mean, it's just really not a whole lot to it, so I don't see where it's that big a deal … whether you're in two or three or one. I mean it's not that hard to do. (Epilepsy-D12)
No	Privacy	• Well, I mean, it's just really not a whole lot to it, so I don't see where it's that big a deal … whether you're in two or three or one. I mean it's not that hard to do. (Epilepsy-D12) • Well, I don't know. I mean, I just thought that was a one-time deal… So, that's really the only reason why I did it. I didn't think it was going to be a continuous string of them. (Epilepsy-D09) • I could see how maybe some people would feel like their privacy might have been violated… It wouldn't bother me, but it may bother others, I could see how other people might not be happy about that. (Diabetes-S08)
	Distress	• I could see how somebody could perceive it – you know be concerned or could raise alarms like "You know I was contacted because something was wrong." (Biobank-C07)

Related to structuring by topic or question is structuring by a study's research objectives, since most data collection instruments are structured according to these. Objectives can be theoretical, applied, or a combination of both. Objectives frame and drive the data collection and analysis and can, therefore, be a useful method of structuring the "Results" section.

Population or Subgroup

If a study involves more than one population, presenting results by population is an option, though less commonly employed than the two aforementioned strategies. This method is particularly useful when you are directly comparing groups to see if, for example, different stakeholders hold different views regarding a given subject, policy, or program. In this case, a data summary for each group is presented in the Results section. An article by Barden, Dowell, Schwartz, and Lackey (1998) provides a good example of this approach. Their study was aimed at understanding the reasons for the overprescription of antibiotics for children. They conducted focus groups among four different types of physicians and four different types of parents. In the "Results" section, they then successively summarized the findings from each group. The comparative analysis among the groups was intertwined in both the "Results" and "Discussion" sections. Below are two excerpts from the results portion of their article, showing the summarizing/comparing within the same paragraph.

Physicians in this [group 1] and the other three groups said that parental expectation to receive antibiotics was the principal factor that influenced them to prescribe antibiotics even when such treatment was not indicated.

A mother who had recently changed health care providers said, "Now my new physician fills me with so much information, I feel that my visits really empower me to care for my child." Many parents' comments in the other groups were similar. However, some parents in group 2 believed that broad-spectrum antibiotics rapidly cure an infection and prevent return visits to the physician.

Another example of this structuring can be seen in a study described by Torsch and Xueqin Ma (2000). Their article compares the health perceptions, concerns, and coping strategies among elders in two Asian and Pacific Islander American communities. Their qualitative comparison of health perceptions was conducted between elder Chamorros of Guam and elder Chinese of the United States, using a grounded theory approach. In the "Results," the authors present their findings from one group, followed by findings for the other group. They spend the next several subsections under "Results" comparing and contrasting data between the two groups across key themes (excerpt below).

Both healing traditions viewed the connectedness of mind, body, and spirit as central to healthy living. The cross-cultural comparison revealed that Chamorro and Chinese elders believed that health and illness were functions of behavior, lifestyle, and emotions, describing the importance of nutrition, physical activity, mental health, and social activity as components in health and illness. They each attempted to alter those situations and conditions in which they could actively make changes, such as cataracts and heart problems, and they accepted changes they considered beyond their control, such as normal aging. Both associated increased chronic health problems with later life, yet they perceived that a healthy life continued to be a possibility. This seemed to reflect a holistic perspective on health, which interactively connected body, spirit, and mind.

Although the Chamorro and Chinese Americans have common perceptions of health, the underlying philosophies leading to their beliefs about health are different. Chinese health perceptions reflected the influence of Confucianism, Taoism, and Buddhism. Ancestral and spiritual powers were worshipped and honored. The Chamorros' health perceptions reflected the influence of Spanish Catholicism blended with the ancient Chamorro belief that spirits affect health and illness. These perceptions have been changed in the 20th century to include an American/Western view of health and well-being; however, there continued to be a strong belief in the spiritual dimensions of life and health among both groups of elders. (Torsch & Xueqin Ma, 2000, pp. 477–478)

On a summary note, keep in mind that how one defines "subgroup" or "population" will vary. In some cases, for example, an author may want to structure findings at the most granular level—that is, unique individual cases—while for another analysis findings might be presented by large groups such as institutions, sites, or regions. The structuring methods we outline are primarily for didactic purposes and should be considered as examples to help an author organize their own studies and manuscripts. Like most other things in research, they are not immutable.

Additional Key Elements of the "Results" Section

We have reviewed structural elements of the "Results" section; however, good organization is not sufficient in and of itself. There are at least two other critical components related to results that should be incorporated into every qualitative research report—an indication of data range and prevalence/salience of themes and the inclusion of participant quotes.

Data Range and Salience

One potential problem in thematic analysis, particularly when dealing with large data sets, is the loss of perspective. Sometimes what appears to be salient in the mind of an analyst turns out to be less important than originally thought when the data are systematically summarized (or vice versa), so it is always good practice to double-check initial interpretations of data salience or prevalence. A commonly reported guideline, therefore, is to indicate how pervasive findings are within a study sample (Dey, 1993; Mays & Pope, 2000; Miles & Huberman, 1994; Patton, 2002; Pitchforth, et al., 2005; Seale & Silverman, 1997; Secker, Wimbush, Watson, & Milburn, 1995). Prevalence can be indicated with simple theme frequencies, percentages if the sample size is large enough, or general descriptors (e.g., a few, the majority, all). It is also good practice to report on data that contradict primary trends observed in the data set or the absence of such conflicting data (Dey, 1993; Elder & Miller, 1995; Mays & Pope, 2000; Seale & Silverman, 1997). Analysis of deviant cases can add value to an analysis (Fossey et al., 2002; Pope & Mays, 2000), particularly if re-examination of the data indicates that such cases might be indicative of important underlying social processes (see Chapter 5), but is typically not expected of most qualitative reports.

Quotes

In a qualitative research study, a lot happens between the point of data collection and the presentation of findings. Employing some of the suggestions above should help authors elucidate for the reader (and perhaps themselves) many of the key processes and events that occurred during the management, analysis, and interpretation of study data. But, undoubtedly, the most important practice in reporting on qualitative research is providing quotes. Quotes are the primary form of evidence to support an author's interpretation of the raw data. They show the reader that the findings presented are based on what participants have said (Cesario et al., 2002; Drisko, 1997; Fitzpatrick & Boulton, 1996; Patton, 2002). A reader can criticize an author's interpretation of the data, or components of the research design, but they cannot viably deny that a participant has said what has been quoted. This is the fundamental power that quotes embody and is why they are the foundation of a qualitative report. As Chenail (1995) stresses, quotes should be the "star" of a qualitative report.

Quotes are essential in defining key concepts, domains, or themes, which are often complex and multidimensional, and they help the reader assess face validity of the findings (that is, they give the reader the opportunity to assess an author's interpretation). Select quotes, therefore, based on their ability to exemplify an intended concept (Bluff, 1997; Secker, et al., 1995). Quotes containing concrete examples are particularly effective, as in the example below from Namey and Lyerly (2010). The authors talk about self-determination being an important dimension of "control" for women during childbirth. This is an abstract theme, yet a simple quote makes it easily tangible:

> *I got to say when I wanted pain meds and when I didn't. And I had a little button I could push to give myself more of the epidural and I pushed that sucker a lot during the pushing. That gave me a feeling of control. I didn't have nurses saying, "Here take these drugs and don't ask why". . I felt like [my husband] and I and [the midwife] and our nurse were all working together and that I was an active participant. I mean that's kind of obvious, I was the one pushing, but I just felt so incredibly involved and in control. (Lainey, European American, 27, hospital birth) (p. 771)*

Quotes also serve to help the author (and reader) distinguish between data themselves and interpretation of data. Although data always undergo some degree of interpretation, when making an assertion about your data, ask yourself, "What evidence (i.e., quote) do I have to support what I've just said?" Review your supporting quote in this context to assess how far removed from the raw data your statement is. If the connection is a distant one, be sure to acknowledge that you are interpreting, hypothesizing, or speculating.

The same guidelines apply to choosing quotes for focus groups and participant observation, though additional attributes should be considered. As we discussed in Chapter 5, it is good practice to convey the interactive aspects of focus groups to capitalize on the group dynamic embodied in the method. Quotes from focus group data that highlight interaction between participants are one way to do this. The following excerpt from a focus group with first-year pharmacy students about community placements clearly highlights disagreement among participants (from Anderson, 2010, p. 4).

Interviewer: *So you are saying that you would prefer health-related placements?*
Student 1: *Not exactly, so long as I could be developing my communication skill.*
Student 2: *Yes but I still think the more health-related the placement is, the more I'll gain from it.*
Student 3: *I disagree because other people-related skills are useful and you may learn those from taking part in a community project like building a garden.*

Likewise, participant observation is unique in that it captures conversation in a more natural setting, so when writing up participant observation data, try to find quotes that convey the contextual nature and candor associated with this data collection technique. Spitzer (2003) illustrates this technique in her article that describes the use of participant observation to study children with developmental disabilities:

> Sometimes, for the sake of safety, the situation morally may require the researcher to step back into the adult role to stop or redirect a child's behavior as the following excerpt from my field notes illustrates:

> *Mike walked over to where a wooden structure was leaning against a tree. It resembled a ladder, except the distance was twice as great between "rungs" and the "rungs" were only about a 1/2-inch wide. It looked just strong enough to support Mike's weight. Mike started to climb it like a ladder. "Mikey. Careful. Yea. I don't know how strong it is. Careful," I urged. As he climbed, I stood right behind him with my arms ready to catch him if I needed to. He reached for the top rung that was about a foot above my head. I did not think I could protect him if he went onto the next rung and slipped. I directed him, "Not that high, Mikey. Mikey. Come down. No. Not that high. Not that high. Stay. Thank you. Thank you. Thank you." (p. 69)*

Other best practices include labeling quotes with key demographics of the participant being quoted (Anderson, 2010; Pitchforth et al., 2005). If you have conducted a comparative analysis, at a minimum you should include the respondent's subgroup in quote attributions. Additional demographic information, such as gender, age or age group, race, and/or education level may also be helpful information to convey, both to provide evidence of the diversity of your sample and selected quotes and to allow the reader the same contextual information you had access to when you interpreted the meaning of a particular quote. In many cases, the meaning, significance, or import of a comment is related to or dependent upon the characteristics of its speaker. Your audience will know the general outlines of the types of participants you included, based on your description of the study sample, but there are individual level differences that can emphasize a point. For instance, consider the quote, "I think women should be able to have their babies at home." We may know that this quote was selected from among a sample of women who are mothers, and that the theme was highly salient among women who did choose to give birth outside of a hospital setting. Providing individual level information about the speaker helps to further contextualize whether these women were young, highly educated, very religious, and so on. Or maybe this quote came from an obstetrician, which would both change and strengthen its meaning. The specific type and level of detail that you include will vary by study and analysis, but at a minimum, give your reader the chance to imagine the speaker and how who she is relates to what she has said.

Another highly effective strategy is to select quotes that contain specific examples (which assumes that your interviewers probed for examples during the interview!). Concrete examples are exceptionally good for elucidating abstract themes and concepts, and can minimize the need for interpretation on the part of the analyst. Consider the following quote from a hypothetical participant, asked about how she feels when seeing her general practitioner: "I like my GP, but at the same time I feel that he's disrespectful towards me." As is, this quote is somewhat informative, but "disrespect" is an abstract concept and its behavioral expression can vary tremendously. Imagine that the interviewer had probed on the concept and asked, "What specifically does your GP do that you feel is disrespectful?", rendering the following quote: "He interrupts me while I'm talking, and often dismisses what I say." This latter response is much more concrete and less open to interpretation. Depending on the objective of the study you could probe even further and ask for specific instances of when the participant's doctor interrupted her or dismissed something she said.

The "Tips for Using Quotes" text box summarizes these and other tips for using quotes.

Tips for Using Quotes

- Begin looking for good quotes as soon as you start reviewing your data. Consider using a "Good Quote" code to tag them so you can easily find them when you are writing up results.
- Choose only the best quotes for a manuscript. A good quote illustrates clearly the concept being discussed.
- Quotes containing concrete examples of a theme are especially informative.
- A good rule of thumb is to use one quote for each main concept/theme being explained. Quotes are especially important if you are trying to provide evidence pertaining to a controversial issue.
- Don't overuse quotes. Doing so makes the manuscript read like one long transcript and gives the impression that not much thought has gone into the interpretation.
- Keep quotes to an appropriate length. Somewhere between two to four sentences is typically adequate.
- Make sure quotes are presented verbatim, no matter how bad the grammar. Taking out verbal fillers (e.g., ums, uhs, you knows) is okay, as long as they're not meaningful pauses or hesitations. Note that depending on your transcription protocol, your definition of "verbatim" might already exclude these fillers.
- Removing and adding (but not changing) words is OK as long as you indicate where and how you've done so, as in the following two tips:
  - If a chosen quote is too long, edit it by removing extra words/sentences and replacing with " . . . ".

(Continued)

(Continued)

  - If you feel adding an explanatory word/phrase will help the reader better understand the quote, use square brackets (e.g., "After I got home, [my husband] got very upset and began to yell at me."). The same applies for localized colloquial expressions with which the readers may not be familiar.
- It is okay to include the (verbatim) question in a quote, in addition to the response, if it is needed to provide the context for the response.
- Label each quote to indicate which type of participant is speaking (e.g., age, sex, occupation). At the very least, provide a participant ID number for each quote. Never use participants' real names.
- When selecting quotes to present, try to use responses from as many different participants as possible. Otherwise, it may appear that your findings are based on information from only a few sources.
- Although the standard form of presenting quotes is to weave them into the narrative, this is not the only form. Quotes can be part of tables (e.g., Table 10.2) or figures (e.g., Figure 7.1). Be creative. The goal is to convey your story in a credible, transparent, and engaging manner.

PRESENTING MIXED METHODS RESEARCH

Anchor and Structure

In Chapter 8, we discussed mixed method research and briefly touched upon presenting results from a mixed methods study. One of the topics covered was the relative priority a researcher gives to qualitative or quantitative data in a mixed methods design. In theory, this seems a simple task. In reality, though, the decision is not always so straightforward, for at least two reasons. First, unanticipated findings might emerge and change the importance and robustness of a given data set relative to the other; initial plans may need to be abandoned in light of the newly discovered relative strength of the data sets. In other words, one can't always know which data set will take priority in a report/manuscript *before* data collection begins. A second reason is that one study can often generate multiple manuscripts, each containing different data sets and QUAL/QUAN weightings. So, we agree with Teddlie and Tashakkori (2009) that specifying the relative priority of QUAL/QUAN when designing a study may not be as useful as others researchers might infer (e.g., Morse & Niehaus, 2009). Ultimately, the most important decision in this regard is with which data set, if any, does an author lead the "Results" section? If, for example, the quantitative findings appear to be most prominent after the analysis for a paper is complete, then lead with those. If the reverse is true, lead with the qualitative. That said, it is our experience that many journals and audiences have a preference (bias?) for quantitative data. Our advice is to gauge what bias a particular journal might have, and if you're still in doubt, lead with the quantitative findings.

After you decide upon an anchor point, you will still need to figure out how the rest of the results will be presented. Several options exist. One is to present all of the results from one approach and then follow with the findings from the other approach. This is a common technique, especially when leading with the QUAN data and the purpose of the QUAL data is to provide more insight into, and further explain, trends in the QUAN data. Some works of the authors are illustrative of this type of structuring (Guest et al., 2008, 2010).

Another option is to present a portion of one data set (e.g., from *one* domain, theme, or population) and then follow with the corresponding data from the other method. The result is a staggered presentation that looks something like: Topic 1, QUAN data>Topic 1, QUAL data>Topic 2, QUAN data>Topic 2, QUAL data> etc. (or vice versa). An example of this format can be seen in Guest and colleagues (2007). In their article, the authors describe changes in sexual risk behavior among participants enrolled in a clinical trial assessing the safety and feasibility of a microbicide/diaphragm combination for HIV prevention. The article is divided into two conceptual domains that reflect question categories in both the survey and in-depth interview instrument—frequency of sex over time (i.e., the 6 months of trial enrollment) and condom use over time. For each domain, the authors first present the results from quantitative analysis (see Figure 8.3), based on a repeated measures ANOVA to assess change over time. Following this they present theme frequencies over time, in the form of a table (see Table 10.2), and then a more in-depth discussion of each of the main themes.

As we mentioned in Chapter 8, some researchers, such as Bryman (personal communication), argue, rather convincingly, that choosing which method to prioritize for a *true* mixed methods study, as described above, should be a nonissue. They advocate instead that QUAL and QUAN results be fully integrated, and presented together, in the "Results" section. Table 8.5 illustrates a matrix technique that can be used for such a purpose, and that would serve as an excellent starting point for subsequent elaboration of a study's findings. How an author approaches the type and degree of integration in an analysis and subsequent manuscript largely depends on the author's and intended audience's view of mixed methods research. For most journals that are not specifically designated as mixed methods journals, a partially integrated approach is perfectly acceptable.

Guidelines for Mixed Methods Studies

The issue of guidelines for mixed methods research is a burgeoning field that is in constant flux. Many of the guidelines that have been developed are intended for explicitly mixed methods audiences and journals, and may not be applicable to more subject-oriented readers and media. In this section, therefore, we provide only a summary of some of the more commonly mentioned criteria for writing up and presenting mixed methods research ("Things to Consider When Writing Up a

Mixed Methods Study" text box), and ask the reader to keep in mind that adherence to these criteria may not be necessary to get published in journals that are substantively, as opposed to methodologically, focused. That said, it might only be a matter of time until mainstream journals (as well as funders) show interest in guidelines specific to integrated research, and our experience tells us that some funding reviewers may already want to see substantial detail as to how and when data and procedures are to be integrated. It never hurts to be prepared.

For more in-depth discussion of presenting mixed methods data, we refer the reader to additional sources on the subject (Bryman, 2006; Creswell & Plano Clark, 2010 [Ch. 8]; Dahlberg, Wittink, & Gallo, 2010; Leech & Onwuegbuzie, 2010; O'Cathain, Murphy, & Nicholl, 2008; Pluye, Gagnon, Griffiths, & Johnson-Lafleur, 2009; Sale & Brazil, 2004).

Things to Consider When Writing Up a Mixed Methods Study

- Provide a rationale for using a mixed methods approach. This can be done in the introduction and again in the introductory paragraph(s) of the "Methods" section.
- Make it clear how an integrated approach provides better understanding of your research problem/question than a mono-method approach does.
- Consider reflecting the mixed methods nature of the study in the title, especially if it will better inform the intended audience.
- If you suspect the audience is not very familiar with mixed methods studies or literature, you may want to cite examples of other studies in your field that have used a similar approach.
- Include a procedural diagram that effectively illustrates how each piece of the study was integrated (for some examples, see Creswell & Plano Clark, 2010; Plano Clark & Creswell, 2008).
- If using more than one sampling approach, make clear which approach was used for which data collection method(s) and study population(s) (Mertens, 2011).
- Specify what types of data were collected and how each type was analyzed (Mertens, 2011)
- Make sure that, at the very least, you satisfy the appropriate appraisal criteria for each type of data. Note, however, that some mixed methods authors, such as Bryman (2006), take the notion of quality assurance further and suggest that the optimal (though perhaps not so feasible) solution would be to develop criteria specifically for mixed methods research (i.e., "bespoke criteria").
- When discussing a particular finding, make it clear to which data set you're referring.

SUMMING UP

We conclude this chapter with a list of general best practices for research reporting ("Basic Requirements of Any Research Report" text box), and a checklist pertaining more specifically to qualitative research (Table 10.4). These tools are designed to get readers thinking about how they can increase methodological detail and transparency in their reports. But, a strong cautionary note accompanies these lists. A checklist can never replace sound research. A study that meets all of the criteria outlined below (or in the Appendix) but is poorly conceived, or not adequately described, should not be viewed as a high-quality study/ report. The criteria we outline are suggestions for enhancing rigor and transparency, but, in and of themselves, are not sufficient to guarantee excellence in qualitative research. Moreover, as mentioned in this chapter's introduction, qualitative research should exemplify general standards applicable to all forms of research—a well-thought-out research design, proper choice of methods, effective writing and logical presentation of data, and an explicit connection to current theory or practice.

Basic Requirements of Any Research Report

- The study's objectives and specific research questions are explicitly stated.
- The rationale for the study is made clear. The research questions are situated in the literature, and/or address some real-world problem.
- Sufficient data are provided to allow the reader to assess the author's interpretations and conclusions.
- Results are situated in the relevant literature.
- Practical implications of the findings, such as policy or current practice, are discussed (if an applied study).
- Limitations of the research are addressed.
- The conclusion synthesizes the report and reiterates the main findings and their relevance.

Table 10.4   Key Elements of a Qualitative (Thematic) Research Report

---

Methods Section

Number of participants/observational events stated

Rationale for sample selection discussed and commensurate with objectives

Evidence for theoretical saturation (for purposive samples only)

Year(s) data collected stated

(Continued)

Table 10.4   (Continued)

Methods Section

Temporal factors associated with data collection described (if time sensitive)

Region of country/city specified

Specific location of recruitment and data collection (e.g., bar, street) described

Type of research instruments specified

Sample questions provided where appropriate

Data recording described (audio, notes, etc.)

Translation and transcription procedures described (if applicable)

Code development/application process specified

Reliability of coding addressed and described

Name of software and reporting functions used provided (if used)

Ethics committee(s) approvals and consent procedures described

Results Section

Range of findings presented

Prevalence of findings presented

Conflicting data addressed (if applicable)

Verbatim quotes provided to support interpretation of data

Claims to generalizability of findings (if any) compatible with sampling strategy

Additional Rigor Enhancing Elements

Deviant case analysis presented (if applicable)

Participant feedback provided on researcher's interpretation of data

Code definitions provided in appendix

As Part of a Mixed Methods Study

Provide rationale for using a mixed methods design

Articulate how components of the research were integrated (if complex, use a diagram)

Ensure study satisfies appraisal criteria for both the quantitative and qualitative components

REFERENCES

Anderson, C. (2010). Presenting and evaluating qualitative research. *American Journal of Pharmaceutical Education, 74*, 1–7.

Bach, V., Ploeg, J., & Black, M. (2009). Nursing roles in end-of-life decision making in critical care settings. *Western Journal of Nursing Research, 31*(4), 496–512.

Barden, L., Dowell, S., Schwartz, B., & Lackey, C. (1998). Current attitudes regarding use of antimicrobial agents: Results from physicians' and parents' focus group discussions. *Clinical Pediatrics, 37*, 665–672.

Benner, P. (1984). *From novice to expert: Excellence and power in clinical nursing and practice.* Reading, MA: Addison-Wesley.

Beskow, L. M., Namey, E. E., Cadigan, R. J., Brazg, T., Crouch, J., Henderson, G. E., Michie, M., . . . Wilfond, B. S. (n.d.) (unpublished manuscript). *Research participants' perspectives on genotype-driven research recruitment.*

Bluff, R. (1997). Evaluating qualitative research. *British Journal of Midwifery, 5*(4), 232–235.

Bochner, A. (1996). *Composing ethnography: Alternative forms of qualitative writing.* Walnut Creek, CA: AltaMira Press.

Boulton, M., Fitzpatrick, R., & Swinburn, C. (1996). Qualitative research in health care: II. A structured review and evaluation of studies. *Journal of Evaluation in Clinical Practice, 2*(3), 171–179.

Bryman, A. (2006). Paradigm peace and the implications for quality. *International Journal of Social Research Methodology, 9,* 111–126.

Bunce, A., Guest, G., Searing, H., Riwa, P., Kanama, J., & Achwal, I. (2007). Factors affecting vasectomy acceptability in Tanzania. *International Family Planning Perspectives, 33*(1), 13–21.

Byrne, M. (2001). Evaluating the findings of qualitative research. *Association of Operating Room Nurses Journal, 73*(3), 703–706.

Caan, W. (2001). Call to action. *British Medical Journal, 322,* 7294.

Carey, J., & Gelaude, D. (2008). Systematic methods for collecting and analyzing multi-disciplinary team–based qualitative data. In G. Guest & K. M. MacQueen (Eds.), *Handbook for team-based qualitative research* (pp. 227–274). Lanham, MD: AltaMira Press.

Cesario, S., Morin, K., & Santa-Donato, A. (2002). Evaluating the level of evidence of qualitative research. *Journal of Obstetric, Gynecologic and Neonatal Nursing, 31*(6), 531–537.

Chenail, R. (1995). Presenting qualitative data. *The Qualitative Report, 2*(3).

Chur-Hansen, A., Russell Winefield, H., & Beckwith, B. (2009). Companion animals for elderly women: The importance of attachment. *Qualitative Research in Psychology, 6,* 281–293.

Creswell, J., & Plano Clark, V. (2010). Designing and conducting mixed methods research (2nd ed.). Thousand Oaks, CA. Sage.

Dahlberg, B., Wittink, M., & Gallo, J. (2010). Funding and publishing integrated studies: Writing effective mixed methods manuscripts and grant proposals. In A. Tashakkori & C. Teddlie (Eds.), *Handbook of mixed methods in social and behavioral research* (2nd ed.; pp. 775–802). Thousand Oaks, CA. Sage.

Denzin, N. (2000). The practice and politics of interpretation. In N. Denzin & Y. Lincoln (Eds.), *Handbook of qualitative research* (2nd ed.; pp. 897–922). Thousand Oaks, CA: Sage.

Dey, I. (1993). *Qualitative data analysis: A user-friendly guide for social scientists.* New York, NY: Routledge.

Dingwall, R., Murphy, E., Watson, P., Greatbatch, D., & Parker, S. (1998). Catching goldfish: Quality in qualitative research. *Journal of Health Service Research Policy, 3,* 167–172.

Drisko, J. W. (1997). Strengthening qualitative studies and reports: Standards to promote academic integrity. *Journal of Social Work Education, 33*(1), 12.

Elder, N. C., & Miller, W. L. (1995). Reading and evaluating qualitative research studies. *Journal of Family Practice, 41*(3), 279–285.

Fitzpatrick, R., & Boulton, M. (1996). Qualitative research in health care: I. The scope and validity of methods. *Journal of Evaluation in Clinical Practice, 2*(2), 123–130.

Flick, U. (1998). *An introduction to qualitative research.* Thousand Oaks, CA: Sage.

Fossey, E., Harvey, C., McDermott, F., & Davidson, L. (2002). Understanding and evaluating qualitative research. *Australian and New Zealand Journal of Psychiatry, 36,* 717–732.

Giacomini, M., & Cook, D. (2000). Users' guide to the medical literature XXII: Qualitative research in health care. Are the results of the study valid? *JAMA, 284,* 357–362.

Gibson, W., & Brown, A. (2009). *Working with qualitative data.* Thousand Oaks, CA: Sage.

Glaser, B., & Strauss, A. (1967). *The discovery of grounded theory: Strategies for qualitative research.* New York, NY: Aldine.

Golden-Biddle, K., & Locke, L. (1999). Appealing work: An investigation of how ethnographic texts convince. In A. Bryman & R. Burgess (Eds.), *Qualitative research: Analysis and interpretation of qualitative data* (Vol. 3; pp. 369–396). Thousand Oaks, CA: Sage.

Goodall, H. (2008). *Writing qualitative inquiry: Self, stories, and academic life.* Walnut Creek, CA. Left Coast Press.

Green, J., & Thorogood, N.. (2009). *Qualitative methods for health research* (2nd ed.). Thousand Oaks, CA: Sage.

Greenhalgh, T., & Taylor, R. (1997). How to read a paper: Papers that go beyond numbers (qualitative research). *British Medical Journal, 315,* 740–743.

Guest, G., Shattuck, D., Johnson, L., Akumatey, B., Clarke, E., Chen, P., & MacQueen, K. (2010). Acceptability of an oral prophylaxis for HIV-prevention. *Journal of Women's Health, 19,* 1–8.

Guest, G., Shattuck, D., Johnson, L., Akumatey, B., Clarke, E., Chen, P., & MacQueen, K.. (2008). Changes in sexual risk behavior among participants in a PrEP HIV prevention trial. *Sexually Transmitted Diseases, 35*(12), 1002–1008.

Guest, G., & MacQueen, K. (2008). Reevaluating guidelines for qualitative research. In G. Guest & K. MacQueen (Eds.), *Handbook for team-based qualitative research* (pp. 205–226). Lanham, MD: AltaMira Press.

Guest, G., Johnson, L., Burke, H., Rain-Taljaard, R., Severy, L., Von Mollendorf, C., & Van Damme, L. (2007). Changes in sexual behavior during a safety and feasibility trial of a microbicide/diaphragm combination: An integrated qualitative and quantitative analysis. *AIDS Education and Prevention, 19*(4), 310–320.

Guest, G., Bunce, A., & Johnson, L. (2006). How many interviews are enough? An experiment with data saturation and variability. *Field Methods, 18*(1), 59–82.

Guest, G., Bunce, A., Johnson, L., Akumatey, B., & Adeokun, L. (2005a). Fear, hope, and social desirability bias among women at high risk for HIV in West Africa. *Journal of Family Planning and Reproductive Health Care, 31*(4), 285–287.

Guest, G., McLellan-Lemal, E. Matia, D., Pickard, R., Fuchs, J., McKirnan, D., & Neidig, J. (2005b). HIV vaccine efficacy trial participation: Men-who-have-sex-with-men's experience of risk reduction counseling and perceptions of behavior change. *AIDS Care, 17*, 46–57.

Heyland, D., Lavery, J., Tranmer, J., Shortt, S., & Taylor, S. (2000). Dying in Canada: Is it an institutionalized, technologically supported experience? *Journal of Palliative Care, 16*(Suppl), S10–S16.

Higgs, J., Horsfall, D., & Grace, S. (2009). *Writing qualitative research on practice.* Boston, MA: Sense Publishers.

Hill, C. (1998). Decision modeling: Its use in medical anthropology. In V. de Munk & E. Sobo (Eds.), *Using methods in the field: A practical introduction and casebook* (pp. 139–164). Walnut Creek, CA: AltaMira Press.

Hills, M. (2000). Human science research in public health: The contribution and assessment of a qualitative approach. *Canadian Journal of Public Health, 91*(6), 4–7.

Hinson, L., Bocoum, F., & Kouanda, S. (2010). *Community perceptions of vaccines and malaria: Technical report of study findings from Burkina Faso.* Preliminary report for USAID. Durham, NC: PATH Malaria Vaccine Initiative and FHI 360.

Hoddintott, P., & Pill, R. (1997). A review of recently published qualitative research in general practice. More methodological questions than answers? *Family Practice, 14*, 313–319.

Horsburgh, D. (2003). Evaluation of qualitative research. *Journal of Clinical Nursing, 12*, 307–312.

Kane, M., & Trochim, W. (2006). *Concept mapping for planning and evaluation.* Thousand Oaks, CA: Sage.

Kawamura, Y., Ivankova, N., Kohler, C., & Perumean-Chaney, S. (2009). Utilizing mixed methods to assess parasocial interaction of an entertainment-education program audience. *International Journal of Multiple Research Approaches, 3*(1), 88–104.

Leech, N., & Onwuegbuzie, A. (2010). Guidelines for conducting and reporting mixed research in the field of counseling and beyond. *Journal of Counseling and Development, 68*, 61–70.

Lyerly, A. Steinhauser, K., Namey, E., Tulsky, J., Cook-Deegan, R., Sugarman, J., Walmer, D., & Wallach, E. (2006). Factors that affect infertility patients' decision about disposition of frozen embryos. *Fertility and Sterility, 85*(6), 1623–1630.

Macalino, G., Celentano, D., Latkin, C., Strathdee, S., & Vlahov, D. (2002). Risk behaviors by audio-computer-assisted self-interviews among HIV-seropositive and HIV-seronegative injection drug users. *AIDS Education and Prevention, 14*, 367–378.

MacQueen, K. (2008). Ethics and team-based research. In G. Guest & K. MacQueen (Eds.), *Handbook for team-based qualitative research* (pp. 21–38). Lanham, MD: AltaMira Press.

MacQueen, K., McLellan-Lemal, E., Bartholow, K., & Milstein, B. (2008). Team-based codebook development: Structure, process and agreement. In G. Guest & K. MacQueen (Eds.), *Handbook for team-based qualitative research* (pp. 119–135). Lanham, MD: AltaMira Press.

MacQueen, K. M., Nopkesorn, T., Sweat, M. D., Sawaengdee, Y., Mastro, T. D., & Weniger, B. G. (1996). Alcohol consumption, brothel attendance, and condom use: Normative expectations among Thai military conscripts. *Medical Anthropology Quarterly, 10*(3), 402–423.

Malterud, K. (2001). Qualitative research: Standards, challenges, and guidelines. *The Lancet, 358*, 483–488.

Mays, N., & Pope, C. (2000). Assessing quality in qualitative research. *British Medical Journal, 320*, 50–52.

McCombie, S., & Anarfi, J. (2002). The influence of sex of interviewer on the results of an AIDS survey in Ghana. *Human Organization*, 61, 51–57.

McLellan, E., MacQueen, K. M., & Niedig, J. (2003). Beyond the qualitative interview: Data preparation and transcription. *Field Methods, 15*(1), 63–84.

Meloy, J. (2002). *Writing the qualitative dissertation: Understanding by doing* (2nd ed.). Mahwah, NJ: Lawrence Erlbaum.

Mertens, D. (2011). Publishing mixed methods research. *Journal of Mixed Methods Research, 5*, 3–6.

Miles, M., & Huberman, A. (1994). *Qualitative data analysis* (2nd ed.). Thousand Oaks, CA: Sage.

Morris, M., & Lund, A. (2001). Experience modeling: How are they made and what do they offer? *AIGA Journal of Interaction Design Education, 3*, 1–4.

Morse, J., & Niehaus, L. (2009). *Mixed method design: Principles and procedures*. Walnut Creek, CA: Left Coast Press.

Namey, E., & Lyerly, A. (2010). The meaning of "control" for childbearing women in the US. *Social Science and Medicine, 71*, 769–776.

O'Cathain, A., Murphy, E., & Nicholl, J. (2008). The quality of mixed methods studies in health services research. *Journal of Health Services Research and Policy, 13*, 92–98.

Onwuegbuzie, A., Combs, J., Slate, J., & Frels, R. (2009). Editorial: Evidence-based guidelines for avoiding the most common APA errors in journal article submissions. *Research in the Schools, 16*, ix–xxxvi.

Parsons, H. (1974). What happened at Hawthorne? *Science, 183*, 922–932.

Patton, M. (2002). *Qualitative research and evaluation methods* (3rd ed.). Thousand Oaks, CA: Sage.

Paulhus, D. (1991). Measurement and control of response bias. J. Robinson et al. (Eds.), *Measures of personality and social psychological attitudes* (Vol. 1, pp. 17–59). New York, NY: Academic Press.

Pitchforth, E., Porter, M., van Teijlingen, E., & Forrest Keenan, K. (2005). Writing up and presenting qualitative research in family planning and reproductive health care. *Journal of Family Planning and Reproductive Health Care, 31*(2), 132–135.

Plano Clark, V., & Creswell, J. (2008). *The mixed methods reader*. Thousand Oaks, CA: Sage.

Pluye, P., Gagnon, M., Griffiths, F., & Johnson-Lafleur, J. (2009). A scoring system for appraising mixed methods research, and concomitantly appraising qualitative, quantitative and mixed methods primary studies in mixed studies reviews. *International Journal of Nursing Studies, 46*, 529–546.

Popay, J., Rogers, A., & Williams, G. (1998). Rationale and standards for the systematic review of qualitative literature in health services research. *Qualitative Health Research, 8*(3), 341–351.

Pope, C., & Mays, N. (2000). *Qualitative research in health care*. London: BMJ Books.

QSR International. (2011). 2010 06 29 dynamic note structure [JPEG image]: Retrieved from http://www.qsrinternational.com/FileResourceHandler.ashx/MediaResources/LowResImageFile/40/NVivo-9-model.jpg

Roberts, K. A., Dixon-Woods, M., Fitzpatrick, R., Abrams, K. R., & Jones, D. R. (2002). Factors affecting uptake of childhood immunisation: A Bayesian synthesis of qualitative and quantitative evidence. *The Lancet, 360*, 1596–1599.

Romney, A., Batchelder, W., & Weller, S. (1986). Culture as consensus: A theory of culture and informant accuracy. *American Anthropologist, 88*, 313–338.

Rosenthal, R. (1966). *Experimenter effects in behavioral research*. New York, NY: Appleton-Century-Crofts.

Rubin, H., & Rubin, I. (2005). *Qualitative interviewing: The art of hearing data* (2nd ed.). Thousand Oaks, CA: Sage.

Russell, C. K., & Gregory, D. M. (2003). Evaluation of qualitative research studies. *Evidence Based Nursing, 6,* 36–40.

Ryan, G. &, Martínez, H. (1996). Can we predict what mothers do?: Modeling childhood diarrhea in rural Mexico. *Human Organization, 55*(1), 47–57.

Sale, J., & Brazil, K. (2004). A strategy to identify critical appraisal criteria for primary mixed-method studies. *Quality and Quantity, 38,* 351–365.

Seale, C., & Silverman, D. (1997). Ensuring rigour in qualitative research. *European Journal of Public Health, 7,* 379–384.

Secker, J., Wimbush, E., Watson, J., & Milburn, K. (1995). Qualitative methods in health promotion research: Some criteria for quality. *Health Education Journal, 54,* 74–87.

Sharts-Hopko, N. C. (2002). Assessing rigor in qualitative research. *Journal of the Association of Nurses in AIDS Care, 13,* 84–86.

Spitzer, S. (2003). Using participant observation to study the meaning of occupations of young children with autism and other developmental disabilities. *American Journal of Occupational Therapy, 57,* 66–76.

Strauss, A., & Corbin, J. (1998). *Basics of qualitative research: Techniques and procedures for developing grounded theory* (2nd ed.). Thousand Oaks, CA: Sage.

Teddlie, C., & Tashakkori, A. (2009). *Foundations of mixed methods research: Integrating quantitative and qualitative approaches in the social and behavioral sciences.* Thousand Oaks, CA: Sage.

Torsch V., & Xueqin Ma, G. (2000). Cross-cultural comparison of health perceptions, concerns, and coping strategies among Asian and Pacific Islander American elders. *Qualitative Health Research, 10,* 471–489.

Trochim, W. (n.d.). *An introduction to concept mapping for planning and evaluation.* Retrieved from http://www.socialresearchmethods.net/research/epp1/epp1.htm

Ulin, P., Robinson, E., & Tolley, E. (2005). *Qualitative methods in public health: A guide for applied research.* San Francisco, CA: Jossey-Bass.

Weeks, M., & Moore, R. (1981). Ethnicity-of-interviewer effects on ethnic respondents. *Public Opinion Quarterly*, 45, 245–249.

Wolcott, H. (2008). *Writing up qualitative research.* Thousand Oaks, CA: Sage.

EXERCISES

Find two or three of your favorite qualitative articles (not written by you). Think about and list the qualities that make these articles enjoyable to read. If you don't have a favorite article, then find a couple from journals in your area of interest and note what you like and dislike about them.

Also, for each of the chosen articles:

- Identify the anchor point they use for the "Results" section.
- Check to see which of the criteria in Table 10.4 and the Appendix are satisfied. Which are not? How would you address any observed shortcomings?
- Note how these articles could be made more transparent and improved overall.

APPENDIX

BMJ Guidelines for Reviewers of Qualitative Research

These are the questions that BMJ editors should consider when appraising papers presenting original qualitative research (although we don't routinely use a checklist for this):

❑ Was the research question clearly defined?
❑ Overall, did the researcher make explicit in the account the theoretical framework and methods used at every stage of the research?
❑ Was the context clearly described?
❑ Was the sampling strategy clearly described and justified?
❑ Was the sampling strategy theoretically comprehensive to ensure the generalisability of the conceptual analysis (diverse range of individuals and settings, for example)?
❑ How was the fieldwork undertaken? Was it described in detail?
❑ Could the evidence (fieldwork notes, interview transcripts, recordings, documentary analysis, etc.) be inspected independently by others: if relevant, could the process of transcription be independently inspected?
❑ Were the procedures for data analysis clearly described and theoretically justified? Did they relate to the original research questions? How were themes and concepts identified from the data?
❑ Was the analysis repeated by more than one researcher to ensure reliability?
❑ Did the investigator make use of quantitative evidence to test qualitative conclusions where appropriate?
❑ Did the investigator give evidence of seeking out observations that might have contradicted or modified the analysis?
❑ Was a sufficient amount of the original evidence presented systematically in the written account to satisfy the skeptical reader of the relation between the interpretation and the evidence (for example, were quotations numbered and sources given)?

ADDITIONAL READING

Belcher, W. (2009). *Writing your journal article in twelve weeks: A guide to academic publishing success.* Thousand Oaks, CA: Sage.

Creswell, J., & Tashakkori, A. (2007). Developing publishable mixed methods manuscripts. *Journal of Mixed Methods Research, 1,* 107–111.

Guest, G., & MacQueen, K. (2007). Reevaluating guidelines for qualitative research. In G. Guest & K. MacQueen (Eds.), *Handbook for team-based qualitative research* (pp. 205–226). Lanham, MD: AltaMira Press.

Richardson, L. (1990). *Writing strategies: Reaching diverse audiences.* Thousand Oaks, CA: Sage.

Thody, A. (2006). *Writing and presenting research.* London: Sage.

Ulin, P., Robinson, E., & Tolley, E. (2005). Putting it into words: Reporting qualitative research results. *Qualitative methods in public health: A guide for applied research*

GLOSSARY

Applied research: Research that has the end purpose of solving practical, real-world problems. Often distinguished from theoretical research, in which the primary goal is to further existing knowledge or theory independent of any potential practical application.

Audit trail: Processes that keep track of and document the data analysis process. This includes documenting: individuals involved with specific data points and analytic activities, data included or not included in the analysis and rationale behind these decisions, methods used to find themes and apply codes to text, changes made to the codebook and reasons for changes, results of coding checks and actions taken, and any data reduction techniques employed.

Code: A textual description of the semantic boundaries of a theme or a component of a theme. A code is a formal rendering of a theme.

Code label: A short, descriptive mnemonic for a code that helps a coder quickly distinguish codes from each other.

Codebook: A structured compendium of codes that includes a description of how the codes are related to each other.

Coding tree: A visual display of the hierarchy or relationship of the codes (or selected codes) in a codebook.

Concept map: A diagram showing the relationships among concepts drawn from the data. Concepts are usually represented as boxes or circles and are connected to each other (or not) with lines, arrows, or other symbols. The lines or arrows indicate some type of relationship between the boxes, circles, ovals, and so on. For a thematic analysis, boxes typically represent concepts such as themes identified in the data (i.e., codes) or higher level conceptual themes generated by the researcher.

Concurrent (or parallel) design: A type of mixed method design in which the quantitative and qualitative elements of a study are implemented at the same time in a single study.

Content codes: Labels for themes, ideas, or concepts in the data that depend on the data themselves and the research objective and analysis goals. These codes cannot be determined a priori, since they are identified in and defined by the collected data.

Content-driven analysis: Any analysis that is guided by the content of study data. This approach is exploratory in nature and categories/codes are emergent, developed throughout the analytic process.

Co-occurrence: The presence of two (or more) codes or characteristics in a particular segment of qualitative data. For example, when two codes are applied to the same segment of text, they are said to co-occur in that segment.

Data range: The breadth of responses to a particular question or the variety of ideas related to a particular theme. Data range may be thought of as existing along a content-based continuum (negative views → positive views) or in terms of salience (commonly expressed ideas; outliers).

Data reduction: Any technique used to transform raw data into a more useful form of data, often by refining the amount, type, or characteristics of data included in an analysis.

Data reduction matrix: A special kind of table that facilitates a single view of multiple dimensions of qualitative data and their relationships. Data reduction matrices can be simple code summaries arranged by demographic characteristics, or more complex code co-occurrence tables for use alone or with graph theoretic techniques. Data matrices are helpful for identifying patterns in qualitative data.

Data salience: The importance or relevance of a particular theme or code within the data. Code frequency is often used as a proxy measure of data salience.

Deviant case analysis: An analysis strategy that aims to focus attention on deviant cases, in order to enhance validity, minimize data selection bias, and gain a more comprehensive understanding of the range and variation within a data sample on a particular theme. Deviant cases are those that diverge from the pattern, and may represent the extreme end of a dimension, but do not necessarily contradict a trend in the data.

Direct comparison: An analysis technique that compares responses across individuals rather than groups, commonly used when doing research with couples or other dyads. To do such a comparison, the data need to be collected so that data from individuals are linked to each other, using some sort of connecting identification numbers.

Ethnographic authority: A style and tone of writing ethnographic accounts from long-term field work in which the credibility of the findings presented is based on a researcher's intimate, in situ, knowledge of the study community. Less suitable for short-term, applied work, requiring that data collection and analysis procedures and the data themselves be made explicit, and tied to one's findings, to establish credibility.

Ethnographic decision model: A diagram or flow chart, typically in a branching tree or hierarchical structure, that depicts specific steps in a particular decision-making process, as identified through ethnographic research with experts who regularly make those decisions.

Exploratory qualitative analysis: A content-driven, inductive approach to data analysis. Analytic objectives are typically framed as research questions (as opposed to hypotheses).

External validity: The degree to which findings and inferences from a study can be generalized to other populations and contexts.

Face validity: The degree to which a concept, instrument, or finding intuitively makes sense (i.e., at face value). Generally determined by consensus among researchers, establishing face validity in qualitative research may also include consultation with research participants or community stakeholders (see member checking).

Graph-theoretic techniques: Mathematical processes of modeling pairwise relations among items in a particular group. In ATA, the pairwise relationships are often code co-occurrences, displayed in a matrix or matrices. Cluster analysis, multidimensional scaling, and network analyses are examples of graph-theoretic techniques.

Hypothesis-driven analysis: Any analysis that is guided by hypotheses. This approach is confirmatory in nature and entails searching data for instances of pre-defined categories/codes.

Intercoder agreement: The amount of similarity in code application between two (or more) coders. Used as a way to assess coding reliability, based on comparison of two independent coders' application of codes to the same data source or file.

Interpretivism: An approach to social science stemming from a hermeneutic tradition that emphasizes discovering deeper meaning in discourse, and understanding multiple realities (as opposed to one "objective" reality) that are represented in a collection of personal narratives or observed behaviors and activities. In contrast to positivism, an interpretive approach is less concerned with systematic and structured approaches to data collection and analysis.

Member checking: A measure of quality assurance in qualitative research in which study findings and interpretations are presented back to the study population for review and verification.

Memoing: The process of appending short narratives (i.e., a few sentences) to raw data, typically to document an analyst's thoughts about a certain section of data. Memos can also be other sources of data and in various forms of media.

Negative case analysis: A type of deviant case analysis that identifies and focuses attention on cases that contradict, as opposed to just deviate from, the general pattern or trend observed in the data.

Opportunity map: A graphical depiction of qualitative research findings: particularly those that point to areas that need improvement: that emphasizes areas for action or application (i.e., opportunities).

Phenomenology: An approach to qualitative research in which the participants' subjective perceptions, feelings, and lived experiences are the primary object of study. As an approach to data collection and analysis, its roots lie in humanistic psychology.

Positivism: An approach to research that is based on the fundamental ideas that (a) interpretations should be derived directly from data observed, and (b) data collection and analysis methods should, in some way, be systematic and transparent. Positivism is closely associated with the scientific method.

Qualitative research: Any research in which the data generated or used are not inherently numeric. Text is the primary form of qualitative data in social/behavioral research, but images and audio recordings are also used.

Reflexivity: A critical awareness, acknowledgement, and questioning of the ways in which the researcher's own attitudes or beliefs shape data collection, analysis, and interpretation.

Response interdependence: The effect, common in focus groups or group interviews, of individuals' responses influencing the responses of others in the group. In other words, individual responses are not independent of each other. This effect has implications for analysis and interpretation of group-level data.

Segmenting: A technique for bounding (chunking) text in order to (a) assess and document the overall quality of the data and (b) facilitate the exploration of thematic elements and their similarity, dissimilarity, and relationships. There are several approaches to segmenting, but to be effective, the boundaries of a given segment should allow the thematic features of the segment to be clearly discerned when it is lifted from the larger context.

Sequential design: A type of mixed method design in which the quantitative and qualitative elements of a study are implemented in two distinct phases, and in which one data set is dependent upon the other.

Spectrum display: A group-by-theme matrix in which the two vertical ends of the matrix have been bent around to form a circle or semicircle. Data fields are filled with solid circles that can represent either dichotomous data (circle/no circle) or degrees of thematic expression (shades of grey, with the darker indicating more frequent or salient expression). The center of the circle may contain information about the study sample, sample size for the overall study and each of the groups being compared.

Structural codes: Predetermined labels for sections of data that depend on a (semi-) structured interview or focus group guide as the basis for code development. A structural code definition generally includes both the main question and any probes intended to enrich the response to the question.

Structural coding: The application of structural codes to textual data in order to inclusively capture specific questions included in a (semi-)structured interview or focus group along with the responses to those questions.

Themes: Ideas, phrases, and/or concepts that identify or define what a statement is about or the core meaning of a response or expression. Themes exist at the interface between the analyst and the data being analyzed. Themes are the foundation upon which codes (formal renderings of themes) are based.

Triangulation: In social science research, triangulation refers to the combined use of two or more data sources, methods, or analytic frameworks in a single study.

Uber-themes: Meta-themes, conceptually comprised of two or more data-driven themes that correspond to content codes. Meta-themes do not have specific codes associated with them. They are at a higher level of abstraction and are not directly observed in the data.

AUTHOR INDEX

SUBJECT INDEX

SAGE Research Methods Online

The essential tool for researchers

**Sign up now at
www.sagepub.com/srmo
for more information.**

An expert research tool

- An **expertly designed taxonomy** with more than 1,400 unique terms for social and behavioral science research methods

- **Visual and hierarchical search tools** to help you discover material and link to related methods

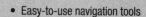

- Easy-to-use navigation tools
- Content organized by complexity
- Tools for citing, printing, and downloading content with ease
- Regularly updated content and features

A wealth of essential content

- The most comprehensive picture of quantitative, qualitative, and mixed methods available today

- More than **100,000 pages of SAGE book and reference material** on research methods as well as editorially selected material from SAGE journals

- More than **600 books** available in their entirety online

Launching 2011!

⑤SAGE research methods online